The Age of Youth in Argentina

The Age of Youth in Argentina

CULTURE, POLITICS, AND SEXUALITY FROM PERÓN TO VIDELA

Valeria Manzano

The University of North Carolina Press CHAPEL HILL

Designed and set in Calluna and Calluna Sans by Rebecca Evans
Manufactured in the United States of America

The paper in this book meets the guidelines for permanence and durability of
the Committee on Production Guidelines for Book Longevity of the Council on
Library Resources. The University of North Carolina Press has been a member
of the Green Press Initiative since 2003.

Library of Congress Cataloging-in-Publication Data
Manzano, Valeria.
The age of youth in Argentina : culture, politics, and sexuality from Perón to
Videla / Valeria Manzano.
    pages cm
Includes bibliographical references and index.
ISBN 978-1-4696-1161-7 (pbk.) — ISBN 978-1-4696-1163-1 (ebook)
1. Youth—Political activity—Argentina—History—20th century. 2. Youth—
Argentina—Social conditions—20th century. 3. Counterculture—Argentina—
History—20th century. 4. Social change—Argentina—History—20th century.
5. Politics and culture—Argentina—History—20th century. 6. Argentina—Politics
and government—1943-1955. 7. Argentina—Politics and government—1955-1983.
I. Title.
HQ799.A7M36 2014
320.40835—dc23   2013041152

Portions of this work appeared earlier, in somewhat different form, in "The Blue Jean
Generation: Youth, Gender and Sexuality in Buenos Aires, 1958–75," *Journal of Social
History* 42:3 (Spring 2009): 657–76, and "Rock nacional, Revolutionary Politics, and the
Making of a Youth Culture of Contestation in Argentina, 1966–76," *The Americas* 70:3
(January 2014), and are reprinted here with permission.

FOR MAURO AND LUCIO

Contents

Illustrations

Acknowledgments

This book was started during my time at Indiana University. My greatest debt is to Danny James. I will be always grateful for his intelligence, hospitality, and friendship. I would also like to thank Arlene Díaz, Jeff Gould, and Peter Guardino, who were friends *and* professors all along. They all nurtured my understanding of Latin American history and were living examples of how to conduct historical research. At the beginning of my graduate studies, I had also the fortune of working closely with Joanne Meyerowitz, who contributed to shape my understanding of the history of sexuality and gender in numerous ways.

Research for this book was completed with fellowships and grants from the Social Science Research Council, Indiana University College of Arts and Sciences, and especially the American Council of Learned Societies, which, with the support of the Andrew Mellon Foundation, awarded me one of its Early Career and New Faculty fellowships. While I was conducting research in Argentina, I found the guidance of many librarians, archivists, and private collectors. Among all of them, I would like to single out José Robles, in charge of the Archive of the Facultad of Filosofía y Letras at the University of Buenos Aires, and Daniel Ripoll, who preserved a magnificent collection of Argentine rock. Like most archivists in Argentina, their work is based more on personal sacrifice and commitment than on institutional support, and I truly appreciate their generosity in making their materials available to me. I am also greatly indebted to the many people who shared with me their memories of "being young" in the 1960s and 1970s in Argentina. Elaine Maisner at the University of North Carolina Press has been encouraging and constructive, even when this book was no more than a project. Readers will surely appreciate the editing that has been done by Ron Maner and John Wilson.

A great many other colleagues and friends provided support, encouragement, and ideas over the years. Besides being pioneers in the study of youth issues in the Latin American 1960s, Eric Zolov and Patrick Barr-Melej were superb and generous interlocutors. The same holds true for Ben Cowan and James Green. In the United States, many other people read or heard portions of this manuscript and made enriching and valuable comments. They include Paulina Alberto, Dain Borges, Christopher Dunn, Eduardo Elena, Paul Gootenberg, Donna Guy, Temma Kaplan, Rebekah Pite, Margaret Power, Karin Rosemblatt, and Mary Kay Vaughan. Matthew Karush and an anonymous reviewer, both assigned by the University of North Carolina Press, made wonderful suggestions for the manuscript, which helped substantively improve this book. I am particularly thankful to two people in Argentina: Juan Carlos Torre and Alejandro Cattaruzza. At times when I was doubtful of the significance of this project, Juan Carlos convinced me that it was important to study the "era of youth," as he calls it. Alejandro was close to this project from its inception: he made me think twice in order to circumvent truisms, and he was always willing to share ideas and memories. This project also benefited enormously from informal and formal conversations with, and the insights of, Omar Acha, Pablo Buchbinder, Lila Caimari, Adrián Gorelik, Mirta Lobato, Mariano Plotkin, María Ester Rapalo, Juan Suriano, and Hugo Vezzetti. I could not be more fortunate than having had two fellow travelers in studying the "sixties otherwise": my friends and colleagues Isabella Cosse and Karina Felitti.

Friends and family collaborated with this project in myriad ways, basically by making my life better. Many thanks to my friends and colleagues Cristian Aquino, Pablo Ben, Leandro Benmergui, Irene Depetris Chauvin, Ariel Eidelman, Laura Ehrlich, Katharine French-Fuller, Paula Halperin, Marlene Medrano, Mollie Nouwen, and Elena Scirica. Although for years we have been thousands of miles apart, my parents and my sister, Virginia, have succeeded in making the distance shorter. Because my parents themselves were young people in the 1960s, my conversations with them about this project were a constant reminder that it was worthwhile. Most crucially, their love and companionship were a bastion for me. As an example of a scholar, as a source of motivation, and as a loving elder sister, Virginia has always remained close.

Lastly, I thank Mauro Pasqualini who contributed to this book in countless ways. Mauro neither read every word I wrote nor tolerated all my obsessions when writing this book, and I thank him for that. I also thank Mauro for his unfailing confidence, for his intelligence and sense of humor, and for enriching my life. Our son Lucio arrived in this world when this book was close to an end. Life has been more rewarding ever since.

▶ The Age of Youth in Argentina

Introduction

THE AGE OF YOUTH

In September 1966, the weekly magazine *Confirmado* published a long "report on youth" to explore whether or not a "unified youth consciousness and experience" had spread in Argentina like, the reporter posited, it had in postwar Europe. The answer was not conclusive. On the one hand, the reporter claimed that "only by fantasizing could one view a link between Rubén, twenty-five, a construction worker who migrated from Santiago del Estero to the Greater Buenos Aires area, and Ricardo, twenty-one, an entrepreneur from downtown Buenos Aires." Moreover, he found even fewer connections between them and Ana, seventeen, a secondary school student from the lower middle class. On the other hand, the reporter did find commonalities. First, although their choices differed, the interviewees showed a particular engagement with "young music idols"—and were willing to "spend their money and time following them." Second, while the construction worker had stated his "fondness toward Peronism," and the entrepreneur his taste for "social democracy," the reporter thought that young people held a similar "moderate and rational" attitude toward politics. Third, if there was one realm about which young people agreed (and diverged from their elders), it was sexuality: "they accept premarital sex without prejudices," the reporter argued, "but they keep tying sex to love and marriage."[1] Only one among a myriad of reports the media ran throughout the 1960s, this one was unique in its interrogation of the category of youth (*la juventud*) by pointing out class and gender differences among young people (*los y las jóvenes*). As most reports did, however, this one also emphasized three key aspects that "youth" invoked and that young people helped transform in Argentina: culture, politics, and sexuality.

Youth as a category and young people as actors had at times a potent presence in Argentina's politics and culture in the first half of the twentieth century. Argentina was the cradle of the University Reform Movement,

1

launched in 1918 and largely coded as an antihierarchical youth revolt against what reformist students identified as the academic and political conservatism of most professors, their elders. Besides generating the conditions for a self-ruled university system, the reform movement paved the way for increasing student engagement with politics and helped fuel the creation of the youth branches of the Socialist and Communist Parties (in 1919 and 1921, respectively). Yet the language of youth revolt vanished as Reformism became a platform for the building of a cultural and political identity for the "progressive" middle class that cut across party and age lines.[2] On a different level, the expansion and diversification of mass culture ushered in the spread of specific youth fashions and leisure practices. The transnational "modern girl"—the slender, short-haired, independent young woman that Americans labeled the "flapper"—had its Argentine embodiment. At least magazines and tango lyrics produced that imagery and incited concerns about the sexual mores of youth in the modernizing Buenos Aires of the 1920s and 1930s.[3] Moreover, in the late 1940s, groups of middle-class boys, the *petiteros*, challenged patterns of neighborhood sociability in cafes, street corners, and social clubs where men of all ages interacted. Pouring into downtown Buenos Aires, Córdoba, and Rosario, the *petiteros* shaped a stylized fashion, listened to jazz instead of tango, and avoided intergenerational intermingling altogether.[4] By the mid-twentieth century, Argentines were familiar with the politicized university student, the "modern girl," and the iconoclastic boy among other youth figures that evoked challenges to the prevalent political, cultural, and sexual order. Yet it was only in the mid-1950s that an age of youth really began.

This book studies how youth became a crucial cultural and political category, and one of the most dynamic cultural and political actors in Argentina, from the 1950s to the 1970s. With an equal focus on the adults who spoke about and interpellated youth (from psychologists, educators, parents' leagues, and politicians to music producers and advertisers) and on young women's and men's experiences, the book investigates what the making of youth reveals about how Argentines imagined themselves during times of sweeping cultural transformation and political turmoil, which were suffused by a yearning for newness and change. It shows that youth, as a concept, embodied hopes and anxieties projected onto claims for change, and that young people inhabited, with varying degrees of intensity, that politically and culturally loaded category. Over those decades, the working- and middle-class women and men who occupied the category of youth, albeit in different ways, became the bearers of the most significant aspects of Argentina's dynamics of sociocultural modernization. By reconstructing the cultural, sexual, and political histories that shaped and were shaped by youth, this book unpacks those dynamics.

Youth was the carrier of sociocultural modernization *and* its discontents, as expressed in cultural rebellion and political radicalization. Beginning in the 1950s, young people benefited from a renewed social confidence in the virtues of accelerated change, which reverberated in the dramatic expansion of enrollment in secondary schools and universities. Young people's involvement with modernizing dynamics acquired more diffuse meanings as well: they created new spaces and styles of sociability; reshaped consumption practices; and challenged deep-seated ways of social and familial interaction. It was amid this transformative sociocultural process that youth helped to change gender relations, alter sexual mores and behaviors, and redefine the meanings of eroticism. Collectively and on their own, these experiences and practices incited contentious situations at the familial, cultural, and social levels—however different their degree and timing. Looking at both the drives for sociocultural and sexual change, and the oftentimes vocal reactions against them, gives us a means of grasping the embattled nature of modernization. Discontent was also nurtured by a transnational repertoire of images, sounds, and ideas that swept across the world. While one segment of the women and men who occupied the category of youth iconoclastically questioned the authoritarianism that set limits to sociocultural modernizing dynamics, others confronted the socially exclusionary traits of modernization and identified Argentina as a part of the rioting Third World. These discontents were embodied in a culture of contestation to which many actors forcefully tried to put an end. Propelling the converging movements in this age of youth, the unifying thread was how Argentines thought of, built up, and enforced authority in its political and cultural meanings.

This book highlights major junctures in the multilayered "age of youth." The first of these junctures occurred in 1956. In the wake of the coup d'état that overthrew Juan Perón's regime (1946–55), myriad actors projected onto youth their hopes for reconstructing a post-Peronist Argentina, imagined as rational, modern, and democratic. In that year, for example, the psychologist Eva Giberti started her successful "School for Parents," an experience created to teach parents new methods of socialization in the family milieu, including a reformulation of intergenerational relations and the erasure of the harsher forms of patriarchy. In 1956, also, the growing body of secondary school students became exposed to a controversial class of "democratic education," designed to expunge the effects the previous regime allegedly had on the moral and political values of youth. University students, meanwhile, embarked upon projects to make universities into showrooms for the country's sociocultural and economic "takeoff." Equally significant, 1956 marked the arrival of rock music in Argentina, around which youth organized new leisure and consumption activities.

Permeated by failed democratizing projects, the cultural substratum for the decade that began in 1956 was marked by longing for, and fears of, the new. The political projects that arose after the coup d'état that overthrew Perón were flush with democratic rhetoric but based upon the proscription of the most significant political force, namely, Peronism. The banning of Perón and his movement took place during the military government of the so-called *Revolución Libertadora* (1955–58). This military government also tried to reverse the social legacies of the previous regime, most notably the redistribution of wealth favoring the workers. When Arturo Frondizi assumed the presidency (1958–62), he promised to focus on national economic development in an effort to draw the Peronist constituency to his project. This meant in actuality the arrival of foreign investment to areas ranging from the automobile to the entertainment industry. Frondizi's "developmentalism," his attempts to court the workers, and his willingness to set the stage for a democratic process fell short. After the brief interlude of José María Guido's de facto presidency, Arturo Illia (1963–66) confronted similar dilemmas. Political instability only hastened the unfolding of deep sociocultural transformations, all of which pointed to the celebration of the "new." As the authority attached to the past was being symbolically and practically contested, the category of youth became a metaphor for change, echoing similar developments in Europe and elsewhere in the Americas.[5] As students, cultural consumers and producers, practitioners of a new sociability, and forgers of new sexual mores, young people became carriers and targets of modernization: as sociologist Juan Carlos Torre has aptly put it, they were modernization's "most significant symptom."[6]

By 1966, major shifts had occurred at various layers of the "age of youth," which together marked the beginning of a new juncture. In that year, for example, the trio Los Beatniks recorded "Rebelde" (Rebel), signaling the emergence of a vernacular rock culture. Most of the musicians, poets, and fans who built up this culture contested well-entrenched arrangements of masculinity while shaping a forceful antiauthoritarian ideology at odds with the moralistic ethos that the military regime led by

General Juan Carlos Onganía (1966–70) tried to enforce. Also in 1966 new fashion items spread among young women, notably miniskirts and tight pants, which were just as shocking as the male rockers' iconoclasm. These items sparked heated debates about sexual mores and, more broadly, were conduits for young women to redefine eroticism. Most famously, also in 1966, the Onganía regime intervened in autonomous public universities in an attempt to depoliticize the student movement. Rather than fulfilling its goal, the intervention helped radicalize a broader segment of students, who were captivated by the revolutionary wave that was sweeping across the world. The rocker, the revolutionary militant, and the "eroticized" young woman did not exist as separate figures when viewed from the vantage point of the "age of youth." Rather these figures interacted (at various times in one individual's trajectory, or in the various groups into which she or he was inserted) in the emergence of a manifold culture of contestation, which both built upon and called into question key aspects of the dynamics of sociocultural modernization that Argentines lived through, chiefly the persistence of political and cultural authoritarianism.[7]

This second juncture in the "age of youth," spanning the period 1966 to 1974, was characterized by diverging attempts to bring about radical social change. The Onganía regime had in fact tried to impose a sweeping makeover of Argentina society: "liberalize" its economy, deregulate social relations, and reconstitute hierarchies in all spheres of social life (including the universities). As evidence of its failure, in May of 1969 a series of concatenated revolts took place in Corrientes, Rosario, and Córdoba. There young people, mostly students, fought alongside workers and the lower and middle classes in protesting the Onganía regime and its social policies. May of 1969 represented the finale for that regime and the emergence of a new and expanding dynamics of societal politicization, whereby youth was a key protagonist. Young people engaged in unprecedented ways with student, political, and guerrilla groups (five of which had a national presence in 1970). In that context, the military began negotiations with the exiled Perón, which ended with a call to elections in 1973. Peronism now attracted a youth constituency, which envisioned that movement as a "national road" to Socialism. In the short "democratic spring" of 1973, first Héctor Cámpora and then Juan Perón presided over the dreams of national and social liberation, which for many seemed close at hand. Those dreams lasted but a short time, though.

As the 1970s continued, a broad array of cultural actors and political forces coalesced into a project whose purpose was to respond to that culture of contestation embodied by youth. From Catholic conservatives to right-wing Peronist groups, these actors and forces embarked on an "authority-reconstitution" project propelled by the ideas and concerns that had limited the scope of the modernizing dynamics unfolding since the mid-1950s. A new juncture, marked by this overtly reactionary project, started in 1974 and deeply transformed the conditions for the sociability, sexuality, and politics of youth. That year the Peronist government promoted legislative developments that restricted the distribution of the birth control pill; increased penalties for the trafficking and consumption of so-called illegal drugs (and authorized the monitoring of spaces where young people met up); and started shutting down schools and universities as legitimate sites for political activism. The last dictatorship (1976–83) amplified the "authority-reconstitution" project and promised to bring "order" to Argentina's society—fulfilling an apparent collective desire. Ideologically and culturally, that order would be based on upholding mottoes such as "family, fatherland, and God." More tragically but less overtly, the project for disciplining Argentina's society entailed the enforcement of state terrorism and the massive deployment of kidnapping, torturing, and "disappearing" the regime's "enemies." People aged sixteen to thirty at the time of being kidnapped accounted for 70 percent of the estimated 20,000 "disappeared." Most of them had participated in the multilayered culture of contestation that signaled the pinnacle of youth in Argentina's sociocultural and political life. With them, the age of youth had ended tragically.

Writing the History of Youth

As an investigation of the age in which both youth as a category and young people as actors came to occupy a prominent position in Argentina's public life, this study engages with the emergent scholarship on youth around the world. A relatively new field of inquiry, the study of this "age" has afforded historians with the chance to connect multiple analytical levels (social, cultural, political, sexual) and to start an interrogation of the mutually constitutive making of "youth" and "transnationality." As a sociocultural category, youth became prominent in the twentieth century. The psychological, educational, and social science discourse on youth circulated transnationally, embedding the category of youth with key traits of modernity. Youth represented an in-between age and signaled a passage, thus standing for transition and movement.[8] While the discourse on youth moved across borders, the sociocultural conditions that allowed women and men to occupy that category—like the expansion of the education system and the rise of mass culture, to name the obvious—also moved across the world, yet with different identities, modalities, and timing.[9]

As a cultural, political, and sexual history of youth, this book does not engage in the study of any particular generation—terms that have become so entwined that they are often conflated. In the humanities and social sciences, the term "generation" leads to the work of Karl Mannheim, who wrote that age groups, "like social classes," endow "the individuals sharing them with a common location in the social and historical process . . . limit them to a specific range of potential experience . . . and predispose them for a certain characteristic mode of thought."[10] The heuristic possibilities of this admittedly seductive concept are nonetheless limited for historical analysis. Membership in a common age group is hardly sufficient to ensure a unified perspective and experience. Even if large-scale events, like wars, provide an age group with a shared reference, its members would cut across so many cultural and social axes (such as class, gender, race, and religion) that the significance of their shared temporal coordinates would vary greatly. While surely aware of these problems, many historians continue tying youth to generation and at times they take generations for granted, failing to recognize the representational work they presuppose.[11] As cultural critic Leerom Medovoi has argued when analyzing the American "beat generation," it came into existence when it was named, that is, when the media and vocal members of an age group represented it.[12] In 1960s Argentina, for example, writer David Viñas claimed that he was part of a "frustrated generation," purportedly as a result of its common experience of intolerance toward the Peronist regime and of "betrayal" vis-à-vis the failed attempts to democratize and develop Argentina as embodied by President Frondizi.[13] That representation, and others that pop up in the 1960s, did not prosper beyond intellectual milieus. While I do not deploy a generational frame to study youth, I use at times the word "intergenerational" to refer to the relations among age groups, such as between adults and youth.

From midcentury to the late 1970s, the age groups that made up "youth" varied according to the institutions, regulations, or groups defining the parameters. Law 17771 reformed the Civil Code in 1968, for example, and established definitively twenty-one as the threshold of legal adulthood, but defined in a peculiar way the status of those between eighteen and twenty-one as "minors-adults," who could legally establish labor contracts, have full dominion over their earnings and possessions, and cast their vote. Meanwhile, in psychological practice and discourse, which was very influential in the public imagination, "youth" intermingled with "adolescence." In terms of age, in 1958 the Center for Developmental Psychology at the University of Buenos Aires declared that only individuals between fourteen and twenty-one would be eligible to undergo treatment. In 1972, the head of the Adolescent Psychology Department in a model public hospital said those between twelve and twenty-two could be treated. In that same year, when numerous competing groups merged into the Juventud Peronista (Peronist Youth), they engaged in a serious debate to figure out the appropriate age limits for their membership and finally established the age of thirty as the upper limit.

The malleability of who counted as "youth" serves to remind us that, far from a biological stage in life, youth is a historical construct intrinsically linked to modernization. In the wake of the global revolts of 1968, John Gillis and Paula Fass, historians who pioneered the study of youth, located the emergence of a discrete youth experience in the context of changing demographic, socioeconomic, and educational patterns. The development of capitalism and consumer culture in the nineteenth century in Western Europe and in the 1920s in the United States, Gillis and Fass respectively argued, set the conditions for the differentiation of one segment of the population who remained for a longer period in the educational system, postponed starting their own families, and eventually gained access to a disposable income.[14] As a globalizing force, neither capitalist development nor the consumer culture it generated were continuous in time and place. In the peripheral setting of Argentina, those modernizing dynamics acquired further social significance by becoming part of the "democratization of well-being" that Peronism delivered for broad sectors of Argentina's population.[15] It was in the midcentury, then, that a mass of young women and men began to occupy the category of youth.

The rise of youth as a visible category in Argentina was framed into debates touching upon democracy, authoritarianism, and modernization that transpired in local political and cultural venues. However, both the terms of the conversation and the rise of youth per se were part of a movement that, from the end of World War II and well into the 1960s, swept across the globe. As a burgeoning scholarship has begun to reveal, over these transformative decades the rise of youth paved the way for societies to reconfigure the concepts through which they imagined their futures. The work of historian Richard Jobs on postwar France, for example, offers a detailed analysis of how youth symbolized the promises of reconstruction and epitomized the thirst for newness.[16] Those metaphors, including the centrality of youth, reverberated in debates unfolding in post-Peronist Argentina, which shows how indebted domestic conversations were to European intellectual and cultural landscapes as well as how simultaneous the rise of youth was. Furthermore, in both countries the public conversation about youth brought irrevocably to the fore ideas of change in several so-called controversial terrains. As happened in British Canada and Tanzania, in France and Argentina, talking about youth implied talking about sex, and vice versa.[17]

The recent historical research focusing on youth and sexuality in the immediate postwar period and the 1960s has engaged in a revision of the ways of addressing "sexual revolutions." The works of Beth Bailey, Ann-Marie Sohn, and Dagmar Herzog on the United States, France, and West Germany shift the focus away from the exclusive attention to the most vocal groups (such as women's liberation and gay rights' movements) and from the calls to "free love" to emphasize an often unacknowledged yet crucial phenomena: in fact, they all identify the public acceptance of premarital sex as the cornerstone of the sexual revolutions.[18] Along with historian Isabella Cosse's work, which judges this occurrence as part of a "discreet sexual revolution," this book contends that the same held true for Argentina.[19] However, while premarital sex became publicly normalized in the intersection of the 1960s and 1970s, it had been a key subject of familial and cultural concern for over a decade, especially with regard to young women. The handling of premarital sex sheds light on the embattled dynamics of sociocultural modernization that Argentines experienced, as do the tensions between an eroticization of visual culture (based upon the rising display of the young female body) and the persistent and increasing mechanisms of censorship. In this last respect, therefore, the Argentine sixties sharply contrasted with the so-called "permissive moment" which marked the English, West German, or Italian sixties.[20]

The 1950s and 1960s in Argentina also ushered in the emergence of youth cultures associated with changes in consumption practices as with almost everywhere else in Western Europe and the Americas. Sociologist Talcott Parsons coined, in 1942, the term "youth culture" to refer to behavioral patterns among American adolescents, which he depicted as based on the "pursuit of 'having a good time,'" on consumerism.[21] In the same period the term "teenager" spread in business reports and the media alike, initially to denote a discrete market: that of the adolescents. A truism for those working on the United States and Europe, the demographics of the "baby boom" together with the mid-term cycle of economic affluence that began in the postwar were pivotal for the ubiquity of the teenager and for the expansion of goods targeting the young.[22] These conditions did not occur in Argentina. Although in the late 1940s there was a subtle recovery of the birth rates, it pales when compared with those in North American and West European contexts—as do the figures of the "youth market" in the decades to follow. However, these are not the main reasons why I depart from the most prevalent approaches to youth and consumption. By focusing on the creation of a "youth market" in which young people from all social strata interacted, historians have so far sidestepped a thorough evaluation of the ways in which consumption practices served to enact and shape distinctions among young people. Even the seemingly most homogenizing items, like the pair of jeans, could have been used for the shaping of distinctions: in early 1960s Argentina, for example, while working-class young men wore the locally produced *vaqueros*, middle-class young men sought out the imported American brands to signal their class-based, cultural distinction.

As an original case study, this book provides insight to what was foremost a transnational phenomenon. As a "unit" of analysis and experience, youth transcended national borders and, especially after the Second World War, became part of an increasingly interconnected network of ideas, images, and sounds.[23] Argentine young people participated in and localized that network. At the same time that they were becoming key political actors, for example, university student leaders rejected any comparison with their European counterparts and understood that "their 68" was insufficiently revolutionary. That happened as French and Italian students invoked Ernesto Che Guevara and Ho Chi Minh as their political heroes, vindicating the so-called Third World in the construction of their political identities. The interconnections did exist, but this book seeks to engage in a critical dialogue with the studies of youth in Europe and the United States. In particular, I hope this study will help destabilize the consensus related to explaining how youth developed as a significant cultural and political actor, from the midcentury to the 1970s, in terms of the interaction with postwar economic expansion and liberal democracy. These premises have been accepted as universal, yet they can hardly be sustained when incorporating comparisons with cases such as Argentina, where that "age" unfolded under economic instability and political authoritarianism. As for Latin America, I aim to contribute to the ongoing efforts in positioning youth at the forefront of scholarly attention. Historians have thus far largely focused on university students and countercultural formations in countries such as Brazil, Mexico, Chile, and Nicaragua.[24] I expect that this study will add to a better understanding of the dynamics of cultural renewal and political radicalization that made young people the most visible actors and youth the category upon which reverberated the pervading feeling of imminence, of "change about to happen" that characterized the central decades of the twentieth century in Latin America.

Politics, Culture, and Sexuality in Argentina

This book "uses" youth as a strategic device to explore political, cultural, and sexual histories of Argentina from the 1950s to the end of the last military dictatorship. It is my claim that those three "levels" scarcely had an independent development, and a multilayered history of youth can offer a privileged vantage point from which to analyze their interactions. The history of Argentina from midcentury to the 1970s has been overwhelmingly narrated through a political lens. This is hardly surprising: the dramatic effects imposed upon Argentine society by the last military dictatorship prompted scholars to investigate how *that* was possible. Scholars thus have studied the constant crisis of legitimacy once Peronism was politically proscribed between 1955 and 1973; the failed attempts to carry out developmentalist and democratizing projects—such as those tried by the administrations of Frondizi and Illia—and chiefly the role of the armed forces as arbiters of Argentine politics.[25] Similarly, political and intellectual historians have investigated the emergence of a "New Left" by paying particular attention to the reinterpretation of the Peronist experience undergone by intellectuals and militants as well as to the impact of the Cuban and other "Third World" revolutions in the 1960s.[26] Intimately linked with this study, scholars have researched the characteristics of the political radicalization unleashed after the imposition of military rule in 1966, which crystallized in the popular revolts that made the "Argentine May" of 1969 and expanded in the years to follow to include the emergence of multiple guerrilla groups.[27]

The involvement of young people in radical politics was perhaps the single most distinctive occurrence in the global political scenario of the 1960s and 1970s, and Argentina was not an exception. Young women and men, mostly but by no means exclusively from middle-class origins, engaged with the student, party, and guerrilla groups they helped create to shape paths toward social or national liberation (depending on their conception of revolution and Socialism). The engagement with the most extreme variants of militancy—armed struggle—has attracted the most scholarly attention. Recent essays have theorized the ways in which the logics of war may have superseded the logics of politics among groups embracing armed struggle and connected this with the shaping of revolutionary subjectivities permeated by "eschatological components" and a no less certain cult of political martyrdom.[28] Instead of insisting on these paths of analysis, I have opted to offer different elements in an effort to shift the focus away from the experiences of the "vanguard" guerrilla combatants. This study shows that the political coming of age of youth in the 1960s and early 1970s was both a part of and a reaction to the dynamics of cultural and social modernization. In their political socialization, young people came to conceive of Argentina as part of a rebellious political geography, that of the Third World. That belief did not only lead many to reject what a modernizing country would have to offer (an individually based path of social mobility, for example) but also to the conviction that, as a Third World country, Argentina had only one choice: speed up the political times to shape a revolutionary future. That belief in practice involved an increasing corporeal engagement with politics. Unlike previous leftist traditions, this one focused prominently on the body as a carrier of revolutionary practice, and especially of the pervading sense of imminence that, as cultural critic Diana Sorensen has argued, entailed "an anxious, sometimes optimistic sense of arrival about to take place, or to be voluntaristically ushered in."[29]

A similarly optimistic conception of "change" pervaded a series of cultural transformations unfolding since the mid-1950s, generally unified under the label of "cultural modernization." Scholars have paid attention to one of the most crucial avenues for that modernization: the remaking of the universities as autonomous research institutions, a process that reached its high point between 1958 and 1966 and was reflected in the expansion of student enrollments. Meanwhile, cultural historians, art and film historians, and literary critics have examined different aspects of cultural renewal, such as the crafting of successive aesthetic projects in the frame of the new centers of modern art; the transformation of cinematographic languages carried out by the "Generation of 1960"; and the gradual joining of aesthetic avant-gardes and political vanguards.[30] While most of these studies have focused on cultural production and, basically, cultural products that circulated among an expanded yet limited enlightened audience, other scholars have begun to address changes in popular culture, mass consumption, and everyday life, including the expansion of television, the transformations of advertising, and the appearance of new practices of sociability.[31]

Expanding on these themes, I complicate the narrative of sociocultural modernization that these studies construct. They tend to set clear-cut divisions between societal forces pushing for change and top-down "authoritarian traditionalist blockades," as Oscar Terán characterized, in cultural terms, the effects of the military regime imposed in 1966. Examining the experiences of young men and women who were both the carrier and target of most of the everyday aspects of social and cultural modernization sheds new light on their contested situation. One example will suffice at this point. Student enrollment at all levels of education greatly expanded in the 1960s and incorporated increasing numbers of middle-class young women into universities and working-class boys and girls into secondary schools. By reconstructing the experiences of secondary school students, I show how they lived in and complained about the enforcement of daily routines and hierarchical relations that permeated school life with authoritarianism, before and after the 1966 coup d'état.

The embattled nature of sociocultural modernization embodied in youth is perhaps most evident in the realm of gender and sexuality. While the literature addressing political dynamics or the ways in which cultural modernization unfolded in institutional development or the arts has been abundant, scholars have only just begun to turn their attention to women's history, gender, and sexuality in the 1960s. Scholars have unraveled the opening up of new educational and job possibilities for women, especially those belonging to the middle classes. They have also interrogated the traits of the emergent feminist movement of the 1960s and 1970s as well as its tense relations with the revolutionary left and the medical and cultural debates over the uneven availability of the birth control pill. Most of them suggest there was a prudent liberalization of sexual mores and behaviors, especially among young people.[32] Instead of focusing on midterm patterns of change, as most historians have done thus far, I have opted for looking closely at some junctures that I hope will illuminate the ways in which change, as it came especially to young women and men's sexual lives, was debated and shaped.

Telling a History of Youth

This book primarily narrates the experiences of and the discussions about urban youth, which by 1970 represented more than 80 percent of the age group between eighteen and twenty-four. Researching *how* youth became a central category and one of the most dynamic cultural and political actors in Argentina from midcentury to the 1970s required piecemeal work with disparate materials, from institutional archives to movies and from music records to police files. In addition, telling this story required familiarity not only with the literature on the history of youth in other geographical settings and temporal frames, but also with gender and sexuality studies, cultural studies on consumption, and popular music studies.

I based my reconstruction of how youth was discussed and understood—that is to say, categorized—on an examination of archival materials kept by the three most important state and private institutions dealing with youth and family issues (the National Council of Minors' Protection, the League of Mothers, and the Organization for Protecting Young Women); sociological and psychological reports; books of psychological, pedagogical, and sexological advice; pamphlets, party literature, and political presses; movies; newsmagazines and the popular press; and the three most widely read national newspapers. The national press and reports published in two business magazines, along with unpublished reports kept by a prominent agency, John Walter Thompson, gave me crucial insight into how advertisers and fashion designers imagined and appealed to youth, while published business reports and economic censuses and surveys did the same for the industrial aspects of rock music.

I began to gain access to the world that the secondary school students inhabited through the examination of daily memos by the Directorate of Secondary Education, official bulletins, and published memoirs. Student magazines, university publications, and academic programs, all from the University of Buenos Aires, allowed me to reconstruct the experiences of their university counterparts. Likewise, the archive kept by the School of Humanities and Social Sciences—which was a key institutional site for modernizing projects—was particularly useful to my understanding of student politics and everyday life. Besides the national press and newsmagazines, my investigation of young people's political involvement with revolutionary organizations and of their construction of a shared political culture was based on the examination of the political press, published and unpublished pamphlets, folk (protest) music, political documentaries, published memoirs, and unclassified police reports.

With the exception of the voices of revolutionary militants or countercultural organizers, it was particularly challenging to find ways to hear the voices of young women and men from the past. Doing so required me to deploy alternative methodologies. Highly mediated yet still audible, these voices can be heard in countless letters to the editor (from women's, lifestyle, and youth magazines) or in responses to the many reports and studies that not only the press but also psychologists, sociologists, and educators debated. They also are found in the form of song lyrics and music. Perhaps most fundamentally, I tried to listen to what young women and men did; or, to put it another way, to read the meanings of their practices. Those practices included bodily transformations (such as the male rockers' long hair) as well as the apparent epidemic tide of "runaway" young women and girls from the late 1950s and early 1960s. Reading those practices led me to work with other sources, like the Daily Reports issued by Federal Police listing runaways.

Besides making use of two oral history archives, I conducted twenty-five semi-structured interviews with former students at the School of Humanities and Social Sciences at the University of Buenos Aires and with former working-class young women and men from Valentín Alsina, a working-class neighborhood in the Greater Buenos Aires area. The School of Humanities was one of the "star players" of the dynamics of the university renovation in the 1960s, and the media took its students as the epitomes of "modern youth." While some histories of the Argentine 1960s used to take those students' experiences as a synecdoche for being young in that decade, I have opted for also incorporating the voices of 1960s working-class youth. Through these conversations, I intended to gain insight on how those formerly young women and men from different cultural and class locations narrated their lived experiences of being young in the 1960s and 1970s. While I did not expect to reconstruct factual data, neither did I engage in an in-depth evaluation of how my interviewees remembered their political, sexual, or cultural pasts. That evaluation would have demanded the framing of a different project centered, for example, on the building of social memories of youth, politics, and violence and on the entwinement of memory and generation. Aware of the porous lines between memory and history, in this book I have opted for relying more thoroughly on the methodologies of social and cultural history.

Telling histories of Argentina through the lens of youth, the eight chapters of this book focus on particular themes and problems while at the same time following a loose chronological order. Chapter 1 examines how youth was understood, debated, and regulated during the last years of Peronism and, chiefly, in the decade that followed its overthrow. In late 1953, Perón helped create the state-sponsored Unión de Estudiantes Secundarios (UES, Union of Secondary School Students). Besides affording secondary students with a chance of participating in sports, tourism, and other leisure activities, the UES incited a vociferous reaction among the regime's opponents, who understood that Perón was using it to manipulate and "pervert" youth. Many of those opponents would later on coalesce into an informal field of experts on youth composed of psychologists, state officers, educators, and Catholic institutions. These actors engaged in a contentious dialogue about family authority, the spread of the media, and the relaxation of sexual mores that young people purportedly embodied. In doing so, they connected their worries over youth with a reevaluation of the Peronist experience, and some of them projected onto youth the chance of eroding authoritarian practices from the family and the societal milieu, and of constructing a democratic and culturally modern Argentina. Although the allegedly progressive psychological discourse set the terms and dominated this public talk, conservative Catholic groups proved more influential in generating policies with regard to media regulation, policing of public entertainment, and education, policies that ultimately helped shape and condition young people's lived experiences and set definite limits to the modernizing sociocultural dynamics unfolding locally in the 1960s.

Chapter 2 focuses on the promises of and the discontent with those sociocultural dynamics through examining both secondary schools and universities, chiefly from 1956 to 1966. By reconstructing student experiences at both levels, I explore how secondary schools continued to be spaces wherein boys and girls interacted with and eventually reacted against authoritarian and hierarchical practices. By contrast, the admittedly expanding minority of young people who enrolled in the public universities, and chiefly at some particular schools (such as Humanities and Social Sciences, the test case I follow), represented themselves as the epitome of the modernizing 1960s. While the daily life of secondary school and university students took place in a continuum from their classrooms to the street corners, at times many of them went forcefully to a third space, the streets. I evaluate the novelties of student politicization in the early 1960s with regard to previous traditions of student politics in Argentina and show that the trope of the "revolutionary student" haunted the public imagination, helping to create consensus for the 1966 coup d'état, when the military intervened in the universities.

In Chapter 3 I move from duty to leisure to explain the spread of youth-led music and consumption. I contend that these realms became pivotal to the ways in which young people constructed a sense of generational belonging at the time that they irrupted, as youth, in the public arena. Secondary school and university students, working young women and men: they all created and participated in new leisure and consumption practices that were exclusively youthful and helped to juvenilize mass culture at large. However, in these realms young people also built up renewed, class-inflected senses of cultural distinction, thus complicating any understanding of youth and youth culture as homogeneous categories. A juvenilized mass culture was the social space where the groups that participated competed for the definition of taste, as it related to music idols, sites of entertainment, or fashion items.

The next two chapters explore the gendered dimensions of the dynamics of sociocultural modernization, including its reactions and discontents. Chapter 4 delves into the changes of gender ideals and sexual mores that young women came to embody. The increased incorporation of young women into the workforce and the educational system and their participation in sociability devoid of adult supervision (which served to transform dating and courtship practices) were culturally perceived as ways of "leaving home." Young women questioned on a practical basis deeply rooted notions of patriarchal authority and domesticity, generating familial dilemmas that sometimes led to girls' running away from their homes. Using the prism of what sociologists call moral panic, I focus on an apparent tide of runaway girls in 1963 to discuss the relations among cultural modernization, gender, and sexuality. In this latter respect, I show that young women indeed stood at the center of the most significant change in Argentina's sexual culture in the 1960s—the public acceptance of premarital sex—which further involved destabilizing domestic ideals based on a double sexual standard, yet that innovation was neither linear nor exempt from the embattledness that characterized cultural modernization.

Chapter 5 turns from young women to young men and explores the emergence of a rock culture as a window through which to analyze ideals and debates over masculinity. Beginning in 1966, an extremely active rock culture emerged in Argentina, one that attracted increasing numbers of working- and middle-class young men as poets, musicians, and fans, while young women remained largely excluded both on- and off-stage. Rock culture acted as a platform for young men to articulate a practical and poetical criticism of male "ordinary life." By upholding the symbolic potential of the *pibes* (boys) and forging what I dub a "fraternity of long-haired boys," rockers questioned the values attached to the hegemonic notions of masculinity, including sobriety and breadwinning capability. They also questioned the sites and practices through which they were supposed to be learned and internalized, such as the schools, the military service, and paid jobs. Drawing on a transnational repertoire of sounds and ideas, rockers shaped a cultural politics that on the one hand led toward "modernizing" masculinity (by endorsing values such as companionship and egalitarianism, for example) and, on the other, iconoclastically rejected the authoritarian and repressive components of the dynamics of sociocultural modernization.

Rockers and their cultural politics made only one subset of a broader culture of contestation that spread among young people. Chapter 6 explores the largest subset of that culture, namely, the involvement of young people in student, party, and guerrilla groups. I begin by reconstructing the juncture of 1968–69 to show that it was during the concatenated popular revolts in Corrientes, Rosario, and Córdoba in May of 1969 when young people, chiefly university and secondary school students, became visible political actors. In that process, they differentiated their politicization from what was unfolding among youth in Western Europe and North America. They also wanted to erase the markers of their youthfulness (for example, their student origins) in order construct bridges with "the People." In doing so, politicizing young people participated in the ideological and cultural transformations of the left, notably from the highly emotional assimilation of Argentina to the Third World. If there was a movement that informed and benefited the most from that assimilation and the politicization of young people, it was Peronism. It was within this political space that youth was most forcefully framed as a political actor and category and where a generational and familial language served to codify and enact ideological and political disputes. By 1973–74, these disputes were shaped as a dramatic family romance, whose resolution was overdetermined by the push to reconstitute relations of authority and hierarchies that had been symbolically "subverted" since so many young people had decided to *poner el cuerpo* (to put their body) at the service of a revolution.

Chapter 7 explores the embodiment of young people's political and sexual experiences as well as the making of the "youth body" as a political and cultural category. *Poner el cuerpo* acquired for young people manifold, sometimes competing meanings. It entailed, for example, positioning the youthful body as the center of renewed fashion trends that reformulated notions and practices of eroticism as well as making young people's bodies the carriers of transformations in prevalent sexual arrangements. *Poner el cuerpo* acquired a different meaning for the rising numbers of young women and men engaging in radical politics who worked on their own material bodies to make them resilient, and thus to comply with the untiring militancy required to forge a revolution that many envisioned as imminent. Many of these militants realized that *poner el cuerpo* could have still a more literal, dreadful meaning. As Chapter 8 explores, beginning in the civilian Peronist government yet amplified after the military coup d'état of 1976, a project for "reconstituting authority" was crucially played out in the territory of the youth body. While legislative developments restricted young women's access to the birth control pill and subjected to medical and judicial examination the bodies of "drug addicts"—a key device for that "authority-reconstitution" project—police, parapolice, and later, military squadrons engaged in more literal and tragic forms of battling an "enemy" that, in terms of age, was young. In the decade that started with the short democratic spring of 1973 and ended with a new spring in 1983, the "age" of youth in Argentina had ended.

1 ▸ Carving Out a Place for Youth

In 1962, in an article published by the journal of the University of Buenos Aires (UBA), psychiatrist Telma Reca noted the rising interest in youth developed within "the journalistic, scientific, and cinematographic milieus." While observing that mounting interest, she concluded that in Argentina "everybody is talking about youth; everybody has something to say."[1] Reca was a prominent speaker about youth, both as an expert in the media and as a professor at the UBA, where she trained the first cohorts of psychologists on adolescence and youth issues, terms that during that period, for the most part, were interchangeable. The psychological professionals and other "adult" actors (such as those from Catholic groups and state institutions as well as journalists and filmmakers) elevated youth as an object of analysis and concern. In its links with family life, authority and authoritarianism, and cultural and sexual mores, youth was as a venue for discussing the dynamics of sociocultural modernization. By discursively carving out a place for youth in modernizing times, those actors also shaped some conditions in which the experiences of flesh-and-blood youths—and, incidentally, adults—unfolded in the 1960s.

While part of a transnational phenomenon after the Second World War, the emergence of a broad discussion about youth in Argentina was framed by local preoccupations unfolding during Juan D. Perón's first two governments (1946–55). A prominent example of populist politics, Peronism promoted industrialization, the expansion of the domestic market, and wealth redistribution. It was largely supported by urban workers and represented a democratization of well-being epitomized by the ample increase of wages and the improvement of working conditions as well as in the expansion of education, housing, and health programs. That egalitarian component, coupled with a political style that endorsed antagonism, generated a wide oppositional bloc that united most of the upper

20

and middle classes and was represented in most political parties. As the
1950s wore on, that bloc came to include the Catholic Church and the
military. After anti-Peronists failed to win the popular vote in the mid-
term elections of 1954, a consensus began to build favoring a coup d'état,
which crystallized in the so-called *Revolución Libertadora* (1955–58). The
libertadores sent Perón into exile (he came back in 1972) and proscribed his
political movement in an unsuccessful effort to "de-Peronize" Argentine
society. That effort informed more "positive" projects as well, including
the one led by President Arturo Frondizi (1958–62) that focused on achieving the economic takeoff that the country allegedly needed to develop—a
crucial term for transnational debates over modernization. Yet Frondizi's
project also failed, partially because the integration of Perón's supporters
was unfeasible. The Peronist and anti-Peronist divide was one of the key
organizers of Argentine politics at least until the mid-1960s, when—as I
briefly discuss below—youth had seemingly left it aside.

It was in the last years of the Peronist governments that youth became
an object of contention, mainly since Perón politically and culturally mobilized secondary school students. For Perón's opponents, that mobilization
showed how the regime had corrupted the cultural fabric of the country by
subverting moral values, sexual mores, and social hierarchies alike. Hence,
one of the "legacies" of the Peronist experience was to situate youth at the
center stage of public discussions. To many cultural and political actors, a
main step in reconstructing a post-Perón Argentina involved the reeducation and scrutiny of youth. An emerging group of experts based their worries over youth in an alleged "crisis of our time," which for many entailed
a transition from a traditional to a modern society. This modern society
was ideally egalitarian, tolerant, and rational.

The dominant voices (psychological professionals) conceived of youth
as an agent in modernizing dynamics: youth helped to erode the residues
of authoritarianism in the family and ultimately in society and politics
through living their "normal rebellion" at a critical time. By contrast, some
particularly active Catholic groups who were influential also in the only
state-run institution devoted to youth emphasized the wearisome conduct
of youth. They focused on how confronting patriarchal authority at home
and in society made the spread of Communist ideas more likely. These
conservative Catholic groups intervened in education policy and cultural
censorship and thus set limits to the "progressiveness" of the local 1960s.
Theirs remained residual voices when it came to the representations and
understandings of youth, though. In the mid-1960s, psychological profes-

sionals, sociologists, journalists, and cultural producers seemed to have reached a consensus. They believed they saw the "Argentina of 1980" by unpacking the meanings of youth: a rational, democratic, and sexually prudent country.

Peronist Legacies

During Juan Perón's first two governments, a myriad of political and cultural actors promoted an understanding of children as the only privileged individuals in the new, egalitarian Argentina. It was not until 1953 that the government mobilized youth as both a cultural category and as political actors. This mobilization took place at a paradoxical political time. In 1951, Perón had won the favor of two thirds of the voting population, which for the first time included women, and after the election his government attempted to control the entire political space. This effort was marked by an increasing repression of political opponents. In that context, Perón proposed the creation of the Unión de Estudiantes Secundarios (UES), an institution designed to organize students' leisure activities and to engage them in the cultural renewal that his "new Argentina" claimed to enact. The UES epitomized Peronism's moral corruption to the anti-Peronist field, whose effects touched primarily on youth.

The location of youth at the center of public attention was one of the legacies of Peronism, as important as the emergence of new educational opportunities. As a sign of and a means to achieve the democratization of well-being that Peronism promoted, secondary education expanded dramatically between 1946 and 1955, when the total enrollment went from 217,000 to 467,000 students.[2] The transition rates from the primary school to the secondary school are particularly telling: while 23 percent of the children who finished the seventh year of primary school went to the first year of secondary school in 1940–41, the percentage rose to 48 percent in 1950–51 and to 63 percent in 1955–56.[3] Although almost one half of the students dropped out before completing their secondary degrees (usually when they got an intermediate certificate that qualified them for the job market) the percentage is nevertheless significant, since it shows that a majority of Argentine families now had both the financial means and the cultural expectations to support upward mobility for their children through education.[4] It was during Peronism, therefore, that adolescents from the middle classes and from the upper strata of the working classes began to gain access to the secondary schools.

The proliferation of secondary schools indicates that rising numbers of young people maintained a relationship with the state through the school system, but it does not explain why and how Perón attempted organizing them. Some scholars have claimed that the UES was the means through which youth became included in the "organized community" that Peronism attempted to create, a means that also served to indoctrinate a new generation.[5] Across the same lines, other scholars interpret the creation of the UES as another step within the increasing authoritarianism Peronism displayed in the early 1950s, signaled by the project of enlisting the population in state-controlled organizations akin to the Fascist project.[6] It is possible that the framing set forth by the Italian minister of education, Giuseppe Bottai, in the 1930s, in particular, had served as an example for the organizational structure delineated for the UES. As with groups of youths aged thirteen to eighteen in the Gioventù Italiana del Littorio, the UES was a school-based, voluntary association, divided by gender, and geared to politicize the students' "after-school" time.[7] Unlike its Fascist counterpart, though, the UES was hardly doctrinarian and militaristic. It did, however, provide occasions for the intermingling of boys and girls, and it served to address discussions about authority. Equally important, the UES represented a test case for how Perón imagined and tried to define the future of "his" Argentina.

Within the Peronist discursive framework, the interpellation of youth worked as a response to the possibility of the generational stability of the "new Argentina," a task that required both continuity and change and that became all the more important as political confrontation mounted. Perón frequently argued that the youths of the mid-1950s had been the "privileged children" of 1945. "Now" was their time to collaborate, given that they had benefited from the expansion of the health and education systems, the opportunities for leisure, and the "good food" Argentines had enjoyed over the past years.[8] Perón significantly dedicated to youth what was his last annual address to Congress, stressing that the young people of 1955 were the "first product of the Revolution" and that they would carry the burden of perpetuating it on their shoulders.[9] The reasoning attributed a historical responsibility to a particular age group envisioned as molded by the social well-being that Peronism had impressed upon the country. Perhaps responding to the belief in the existence of a generation gap in postwar Europe and the United States, Perón also stressed that, in Argentina, "bonds of love" tied the generations, which helped maintain the "project of grandeur" that Peronism represented.[10] Amid that apparent continuity, however, the new generation had particular tasks. Youths might learn how to "act independently and autonomously" and to become "modern men and women."[11]

The Peronist discourse on youth entwined political and cultural requirements and, unlike the one that the Italian fascists deployed in the 1930s—with its focus on respecting hierarchies and obedience to authority—it emphasized the ideas of autonomy, independence, and modernity. However, it became apparent that not all youths were willing to face these challenges. At the time that the UES was created, the state-sponsored Confederación General Universitaria (University General Confederation) could not compete with the reformist student centers at most public universities, which were pillars of anti-Peronism.[12] As the 1950s pressed onward, in addition, the state tightened its repressive tactics toward university students, ranging from the prerequisite of police "certificates of good conduct" in order to register for classes to the imprisonment of student leaders.[13] The university students were targets of mockery as well. The pro-government press, for example, depicted them as always "wasting their time in senseless discussions."[14] The press also used derogatory terms to refer to another segment of youths, whom they called the *patoteros* (gangsters). The *patoteros* were working-class adolescents, portrayed as hanging around cities and towns without anything else to do but organize petty scandals. While the university students signaled a political menace, the *patoteros* represented a threat to the sociosexual order.[15] They were young people, but they were not the youths that Perón envisaged as the venue for the continuity of the "new Argentina." The secondary school students, instead, were devoid of the political traditions that university students had, and seemed more disciplined than the *patoteros*. Since 1953, youth meant secondary students and UES in Peronist discourse.

In the official accounts, the UES was the organization whereby secondary school students would learn "to govern themselves" and practice a new sociability. All students at public schools could affiliate with the UES. In Buenos Aires, where the organization rapidly crystallized, the headquarters of the feminine branch were located in the presidential residence in Olivos and the masculine ones at an elegant resort in Recoleta.[16] In late 1953, the feminine president claimed her branch had 60,000 members nationally, while the masculine president claimed 42,000 members.[17] If we attribute credibility to these figures, 52 percent of the secondary students in public schools were affiliated with the UES. Affiliation, though, did not mean participation. In 1954 the presidents repeatedly called on students to "make use" of their membership.[18] What could students do in the UES? First, they could attend the movies for free. UES members had access to coveted seats in movie premieres because of the close relationship Peronism cultivated with local celebrities.[19] Second, and most notably, youths were called to practice sports. The UES favored the practice of basketball for girls and boys, and soccer for boys. Furthermore, youths could make use of swimming pools and fitness facilities.[20] In a widely publicized opportunity, boys and girls were encouraged to practice motorcycling, and Perón himself used to offer them practical lessons when riding his own motor scooter.[21] Finally, in the summers of 1954 and 1955, the UES offered free vacations to its members in Bariloche, Córdoba, and Chapadmalal (on the Atlantic coast), at the same time that it organized groups of boys and girls from provinces such as San Juan, Tucumán, and Santiago del Estero to visit Buenos Aires.[22]

The UES was probably less successful than expected but still attracted large numbers of youths. It is likely that the cultural and gendered aspects of this state-controlled group were more significant than the doctrinarian ones. At the UES, youths had a chance to partake in mixed groups devoid of adult supervision. In the early 1950s, the secondary schools of Buenos Aires and Córdoba were not coeducational, and the prospects for interacting in dance halls were restricted since they hosted youths and adults alike.[23] Besides the daily interactions, the UES offered boys and girls a space to organize parties, like the ones held for the Carnival of 1954, where they dressed as "existentialists" (wearing black apparel) or as "Americans," wearing jeans and drinking Coke. This was a luxury that the working classes could hardly afford at the time.[24] These chances had different meanings for girls, who regularly outnumbered boys in the UES. To many girls, the UES entailed the possibility of thwarting the school-home continuum and performing activities that they had previously been prohibited from engaging in, including motorcycling. This development allowed them to assume defiant attitudes to conventions and mores with regard to the "correct" place for women. Those attitudes and sociability, moreover, had the blessing of the country's highest authority. Perón increasingly, and defiantly, sought to empower the youths involved in the UES by claiming that they might "learn only through their own experiences, delineate their own sense of morals, and leave all hypocrisy behind."[25]

The very existence of the UES awoke anxieties among the Catholic groups, which became strongholds of the Peronist opposition in the critical biennium of 1954–55. Both the hierarchy and the many groups formed by the lay people—such as the League of Mothers and the League of Fathers—conceived of any state attempt to mobilize youth as a threat to the authority of the family and the Church over moral issues. In late 1954, the Argentine Catholic Action sent a communiqué to its members that called for their boycott of the UES. In the same period, Congress passed "anti-clerical" laws granting equal rights to so-called illegitimate children and also granting the right to divorce in a mounting battle between Peronism and the Church.[26] In that context, the UES was catapulted into the spotlight. In a pamphleteering campaign geared to gain civilian and military consensus to support a coup d'état, Catholics focused on the evilness of the UES. First, several pamphlets pointed out that Perón sought to attain the complete loyalty of youth. Pamphlets insisted on the fact that Perón had bought "youths' dignity," and many had already "sold their consciousness for a motor scooter."[27] Second, the pamphlets accused the UES members of spying on opponents at school and of exerting pressure on principals to expel teachers, a task that showed how the "next Peronist political generation" was being formed.[28]

Nonetheless, Catholic and non-Catholic opponents alike signaled a more explosive evil the UES represented in their view: sexual promiscuity. Pamphlets and communiqués illustrated this alleged promiscuity by stating that the girls of the UES were encouraged to wear tight short pants and nylon blouses, "to satisfy the desires of Perón and his aides."[29] Just like the motor scooters, those dressing items embodied the fantasies that opponents projected onto the UES: a voyeuristic Perón "corrupted" the girls, who accepted being corrupted in exchange for material advantages. The promiscuity that the opposition attributed to the UES was further embodied into a place: the feminine headquarters at the presidential residence. A memoir by a former attendant reveals the organizing ideas surrounding the "aphrodisiac paradise," as the author terms it. With plenty of food, beautiful gardens, and goods to be enjoyed, the residence promoted and pleased the "consumerism, the frivolity" of the UES goers. In that climate of plenty, he pointed out, youth "liberated their sexual instincts."[30] Political opponents imagined the UES as their contemporary Sodom and Gomorrah: the references to sexuality, especially when combined with youth, allowed them to articulate other terms (like "tyranny" and "corruption") and construct a coherent narrative of decadence. The vicious relationship they saw as taking place between Perón and the youths corroded the basis of Argentina's future: it was crucial to expel Peronism from power.

In September 1955, a military coup d'état overthrew Perón and began

The girls of the UES. *Esto es* No. 11, February 9, 1954, cover.

a "de-Peronization" of Argentina, which included investigation of the effect of the "legacies" that the former regime allegedly had passed on to different social and political actors, including youth. The military that led the so-called *Revolución Libertadora* had the support of the Socialist, Communist, and Radical parties, as well as of the Catholic Church and most unaffiliated intellectuals. As they came into office, the *libertadores* sought to examine the supposed irregularities that had taken place during the Peronist regime within different state realms, including the UES. To that end, they appointed an investigative subcommittee composed of four women, who represented either the intellectual segments that were excluded from academia and public service in the previous ten years, or the oppositional political parties.[31] Its report identified two lasting "legacies" that Peronism would have left to youth. First, they asserted that the experience of the UES showed that youths were willing to engage in a "deviated conception of life," marked by the chance of "getting anything without any effort." Second, they highlighted that Perón "used the youth impetus of renewal" to promote the "questioning of authority" at the school and family levels, which resulted in "uncontrolled liberties."[32] To the subcommittee, the "uncontrolled liberties," coupled with the subversion of the established hierarchies, constituted the bequest that Peronism left to youth and, by extension, to Argentina's future. In his attempt to configure a youth organization adapted to his needs, Perón would have forged an undisciplined, hedonistic, and sensual youth, whose values and attitudes challenged the ones of previous generations. To these investigators, even after Perón had been expelled from power and the UES dismantled, these legacies remained and constituted one grave dilemma that adults (parents, educators, teachers, psychological professionals) would have to face to reconstruct a post-Peronist Argentina.

Youth was crucial in the project of reconstructing a "de-Peronized" Argentina. As part of this attempt, the *libertadores* issued a decree—the infamous 4161—that prohibited even mentioning the name of Perón publicly. One of its first violators was Marta Curone, the last president of the feminine branch of the UES, who spent months in prison.[33] Along with that vengeful repression, the executive power issued a youth-oriented decree, this time to create a program of Democratic Education geared "to safeguard, with efficacy and haste, the civic spirit of the new generations." Conceptually centered on the assumed dichotomy between totalitarianism and democracy, the program mandated that first-year students discuss the value of individual rights and then learn about the "annihilation of the individual personality in totalitarian regimes" by drawing on examples from Nazi Germany, Fascist Italy, Soviet Russia, and Peronist Argentina. Second-year students would focus on how totalitarianisms manipulated the education system and propaganda. Finally, third-year students would learn how Peronism "exalted the masses," "discontinued liberties and rights," "persecuted opponents," and "subverted hierarchies." Specifically, they would discuss how Peronism "mobilized and deceived youth in state-sponsored organizations," an obvious reference to the UES.[34]

At the same time that the emergent and market-oriented youth culture bourgeoned with the kind of leisure activities and sociability that the UES had offered to its members, that "youth state-sponsored" organization became a dirty word in Argentina's public culture. Between 1956 and 1973, adolescents in all secondary schools were required to study the Democratic Education program. It is hard to imagine how youths who came from Peronist families handled the obsessively anti-Peronist tone of the Democratic Education program, especially those who in the second half of the 1950s had created multiple "Peronist Youth" groups in contexts of semi-legality and repression; and those who engaged with and tried to "revolutionize" Peronism in the early 1970s.[35] More generally, the youths exposed to that program could contrast the abyss between a formal democratic rhetoric at school, and the absence of democratic practice in their ordinary lives, since Argentina was ruled by the military for eleven out of the seventeen years the program was taught. The program of Democratic Education was out of place from its inception, yet it responded to the anxieties and fears that broad segments of the cultural and political elites manifested in the immediate aftermath of Peronism.

The program of Democratic Education constituted still another layer within the larger debates over youth initiated with the creation of the UES. The debates that surrounded the experience of the UES, before and after the overthrow of Perón, helped to place youth at center stage. In this respect, besides the expansion of educational possibilities, another legacy of Peronism involved rising concerns over youth and its connections with politics, culture, and sexuality. On the eve of the 1960s, many of the organizations and intellectuals that had consistently opposed Peronism actively participated as experts in the emergent professional study of youth. Catholic groups for the "defense of the family," as well as psychologists, psychiatrists, and educators that helped build an anti-Peronist bloc, then attempted to understand and regulate youth.

misunderstood progression   *highly conservative*

Youth, "Crisis," and the Shaping of the Sixties

Between 1958 and 1961, *La Razón*, the most widely read daily in the country, informed its readers of 170 public lectures, conferences, and roundtables that revolved around the topic of youth. Taking place in schools, theaters, churches, and union headquarters spread throughout Buenos Aires, Córdoba, and Rosario, the events brought together thousands of participants. Educators, psychologists, and priests were the most frequent speakers.[36] Most of those "experts" connected their worries over youth to the perception that Argentina had come to a critical juncture marked by rapid political and sociocultural change, a time of sweeping instability of institutions, values, and norms. Youth served to address the anxieties generated by the awareness of change and became a segment of society upon which state officers, Catholic groups, and psychological professionals tried to act. All these actors were crucial in generating representations, images, and policies that spoke to the dynamics of sociocultural modernization at the dawn of the 1960s.

The crisis-of-our-time motif spread through journalistic and expert commentary alike. It was nevertheless systematized in the work of sociologist Gino Germani, who in 1956 framed what would become one of his most famous pieces of interpretation of Peronism against the backdrop of "an era of vast transformations not only of the circumstances surrounding us but also of us, of the ways we think and feel." The crisis affected

?

the economy and the structuration of society, morals, culture, and politics; however, these layers did not align. When analyzing the way the crisis worked at the level of morals and culture, Germani specified that "people do not believe in traditional norms anymore, and are not willing to consciously and rationally choose what they before accepted without hesitation." The crisis thus implied a transition from so-called traditional to modern norms, values, and social forms, a process that Germani evaluated positively because it entailed "the elevation of the power of reason vis-à-vis the nonreflexive approval of what tradition and the past dictate." Yet the transition itself generated dilemmas sometimes expressed in politics: the masses, he argued—by following Erich Fromm—feared freedom, and that was the terrain from which "totalitarian experiences," like Peronism (from his perspective) emerged.[37]

How to guarantee that this transitional crisis unfolded into modern—rational, secular—social forms and values? One of the venues was to democratically socialize individuals at the most basic level: the family. This was a general goal shared by Germani and his collaborators, as well as by most of the psychological professionals that discussed youth and family issues in the public arena. Germani carried out research on the traits of the family in a "changing society" and found that, within the urbanized middle and working classes, families tended to be nuclear and smaller than the families of the recent migrants to Buenos Aires from rural areas. Equally important, the "modern families," he observed, showed "a more egalitarian climate, the decrease of paternal authoritarianism, and the greater importance of the wife and the children."[38] Those families were at the same time the product of a positive, ongoing transition and the means for rearing the coming generations into nonauthoritarian socialization, or the building blocks of a modern, rational, and democratic society. The model of a nonauthoritarian family, which left behind harsher forms of patriarchy, was further constructed and diffused through the work of the most prominent psychological professionals. These professionals, chiefly the psychoanalytically oriented, acquired prominent visibility by the late 1950s. As historian Mariano Plotkin has noted, psychoanalysis had become an "interpretative key" through which many middle-class Argentines tried to unlock the meaning of the rapid political and cultural changes they experienced.[39] Psychoanalysts, psychiatrists, and psychologists contributed influential discourses on, and practices for, youth and its relation to the familial and cultural spheres.

Two psychological professionals acquired a major role: Telma Reca and

Eva Giberti. Reca was one of the most renowned childhood and adolescence psychiatrists. She was pivotal to the training of the first cohorts of psychologists at the UBA where she taught a required course on adolescence that provided students with valuable practical orientation.[40] From 1959 to 1966, Reca was head of the Center of Developmental Psychology and Psychopathology, an organization that provided practical outreach for students, offering free treatment to children and adolescents.[41] Reca also organized public discussion of youth, holding conferences and giving lectures to explain the traits of the "new youth." Along the same lines, psychologist Giberti initiated her project of the *Escuela para padres* (School for Parents), a program she developed through the media and public workshops. Along with her husband, Florencio Escardó (a Socialist pediatrician who served from 1958 to 1961 as the vice-rector of the UBA), she promoted ideas for renovating, or modernizing, the family.[42] She wrote advice columns in women's and childrearing magazines and also in *La Razón*. As Giberti recalls, her success among parents and teachers was perhaps not only related to the fact that she was capable of writing and talking in a jargonless yet "scientific" language, but also to the fact that there was an existing audience anxious to learn how to "parent" who were worried by the changes they noted in their families.[43]

These psychological professionals connected their understanding of the "adolescent crisis" to the sociocultural "crisis of our time," and they believed that one would ideally help solve the other. Reca reminded parents that the adolescent crisis had hormonal and endocrinological as well as psychic roots. Along with sexual awakening, the adolescent crisis created a "normal state of rebelliousness" that generated conflict with parents who still relied upon the idea of "obedience based upon tradition." These clashes, however, were to be welcomed: through living their normal rebellion in a deeply critical time, youth helped push against "the authoritarianism that we, adults, still display," paving the way for a more "rational" society.[44] Giberti, for her part, stated that the adult generation embodied "the last echelon that separates the patriarchal from our modern times," represented in youth. While youths' role was to question the established norms, adults might cooperate through building up a democratic sense of authority at home, which would be the basis for a "democratic culture."[45] In tying youth to adolescence, and adolescence to hormones and rebellious conduct, these professionals made youth an involuntary agent for familial and cultural change.

The psychological experts projected onto youth the promise to mod-

a promise toward a the 60's → immence but also dread

ernize Argentina's society. Their project resembled what cultural critic Leerom Medovoi notes in his analysis of the figure of the "rebel" in the United States of the 1950s. While many voices panicked, Medovoi shows that psychoanalysts and sociologists such as Erick Erikson and David Riesman vindicated youth rebellion, which they thought of as both a key moment of identity-building and a means to keep the principles of questioning alive in an otherwise conformist society.[46] The psychological experts in Argentina also celebrated a normally rebellious youth. In their view, youth would become agents to a cultural modernization that Argentines needed to pass through in their own transition to a modern society, like the one that Germani foresaw. In contrast to contemporaneous developments in the United States and Western Europe, though, the Argentine sociologists were silent in almost all discourse concerning youth. They neither found nor constructed the "deviant subcultures" that their English or Italian counterparts did, nor were they interested in analyzing the patterns of consumption and sociability that their American peers were.[47] As if a division of labor were taking place, the Argentine sociologists did not challenge psychologists as experts in youth issues. Yet psychological professionals were not alone in the discussions about youth.

The League of Mothers accounted for one of the most active Catholic groups in favor of the defense of the patriarchal family and especially of its youngest members, purportedly threatened by the attendant forces of "liberalism" and Communism. Created in 1951, the League of Mothers aimed at protecting the family from the supposed pernicious effects of dynamics such as the incorporation of women into the extradomestic labor force, the pervasiveness of the new media, and the concurrent decrease in authority of the father over his wife and children.[48] As with other Catholic groups formed by lay people, the league gained influence after the 1955 coup d'état, when it became one of the leading moral watchdog organizations. In 1957, the League of Mothers fueled the creation of a Family Front to coordinate efforts to pass pro-family legislation, including increased penalties for adultery and abortion.[49] Meanwhile, the league's counselor, Father Manuel Moledo, gave as many lectures as the psychological professionals, but he focused on how youth lived in troubled homes and launched themselves ill-equipped to interact with "sensualist music, literature, and movies."[50] For those conservative groups, that environment was cause and consequence of the hedonism and materialism linked with the "atheistic liberalism," the first step in the weakening of morals that made the terrain ripe for "Communist infiltration."[51] The conservative

generally extremely conservatly

the role of consumerism

Catholic groups waged a Janus-headed war on "liberalism" and what they viewed as its logical continuation, Communism, just as Vatican-oriented family groups in postwar Italy (whose structure and agenda the Argentines tried to emulate) did. The war was one in which youth's "moral well-being" came to occupy a dominant rhetorical and political role.[52]

The conservative Catholic groups amassed a substantial constituency and gained remarkable political influence in response to their perceived "crisis." In contrast with Reca and Giberti, these groups posited that only the reconstitution of patriarchal authority could fix the ongoing crisis. Thus, when the League of Mothers began its own "school"—aimed at emulating Giberti's—the first workshop was entitled "Authority and Liberty." While it called for learning how to combine both, the coordinators did not harbor doubts: authority should prevail.[53] Parents could hear the school's advice on prime-time radio, since the League of Mothers was given free radio space, and it also gained access to popular television programs.[54] A sizable number of women attracted by the prospect of defending their families and children from the propagandized cultural and political perils flocked to conservative Catholic groups (as also happened in Mexico and Brazil at the same time).[55] In 1962, the League of Mothers claimed an affiliation of eighty thousand women who were organized by parish in middle- and working-class neighborhoods in the largest cities.[56] The league also developed a notable ability to exert pressure on successive governments, whether they were civilian or military. Either by participating directly in state institutions or by lobbying the executive power or Congress, the League of Mothers and other conservative Catholic groups helped shape public policy, especially in cultural and educational arenas.

Conservative Catholic groups had the majority of seats in the only state-run institution devoted to youth created during Frondizi's administration. In the eyes of many political actors, Frondizi synthesized the aims of democratizing politics, developing the economic structure, and modernizing the sociocultural spheres, which were thought of as crucial for the "takeoff" that would put the country on the road to development.[57] In the refoundational rhetoric he used in his electoral campaign, Frondizi referred to youth as the "oil that will fuel the takeoff."[58] Yet the series of policies that touched upon youth carried out during his administration illustrates the limits of that modernizing project. Besides his administration's controversial educational policy (which I discuss in the next chapter), the government's only guidelines consisted of reorganizing the Consejo Nacional de Protección de Menores (CNPM, National Council for the Protection of Minors) to patrol the "moral well-being" of youths, conceived of as minors. Created to manage the thus-far chaotic system of institutions for reeducating children and adolescents deemed abandoned or "delinquent," the CNPM would also perform so-called preventive tasks, including the policing of the media and cultural "environment" surrounding all under-age youth.[59]

The CNPM and the conservative Catholic groups contributed to the enforcement and institutionalization of censorship in the name of the "moral well-being of minors," thus making the Argentine 1960s different from the "permissiveness" experienced in some European countries.[60] While legislative developments in England and Germany decriminalized homosexuality and discontinued the legal category of obscenity, in Argentina the opposite happened.[61] Old edicts regarding "public order" and new anti-Communist legislation paving the way for "detentions for checking penal antecedents" (passed in 1958 and 1965) informed the persistent persecution to which homosexuals were subjected. Likewise censorship was mounted to block "politically subversive" and "morally harmful" materials alike.[62] The CNPM and the Catholic groups exerted pressure on district attorneys and judges to prosecute those who violated Article 128 of the Penal Code, which prohibited the diffusion of obscene printed materials. The list of prohibitions included Vladimir Nabokov's *Lolita* and Henry Miller's *Nexus* along with pornographic and popular magazines that incorporated semi-nude photographs. As the 1960s progressed, in addition, two-dozen Argentine writers and publishers were prosecuted.[63]

While conservative Catholic groups and the CNPM worked within already existing legal frameworks when censoring print materials, they helped create new ones concerning the censorship of other forms of visual media. The Leagues of Mothers met with television producers to discuss the shaping of "moral codes" and repeatedly convened in workshops with parents to train them in "appropriate ways of watching" television.[64] Their lobbying efforts crystallized in 1965, when a presidential decree mandated that television programs that showed "the dissolution of the family, sexual deviancy, and eroticism" would be automatically discontinued.[65] These groups replicated similar censorship programs with television that had worked so well in film. In 1959, they had lobbied the executive power to create a Committee of Film Qualification that was in charge of rating movies according to their content for minors. The representatives of the CNPM and the Catholic groups comprised ten of the nineteen voting members, and they mandated harsh decisions throughout.[66] In late September of

1963, moreover, the de facto government of Dr. José M. Guido (1962–63) issued a decree that broadened the scope of a new Board of Film Qualification, which was allowed to cut movies that affected "our national security, threatened by the ideological infiltration that weakens the internal front through the corruption of morals, the scorn of tradition, the dislocation of the family, and the relenting of spiritual values."[67] The vagueness of the decree eventually made all movies subject to censorship. For instance, the board approved the discontinuation of Frédéric Rossif's *Morir en Madrid*—which contained footage of the Spanish Civil War—because it gave "a good impression of the Communists" and then mandated scenes of Lars Lindgren's film *Dear John* be cut because they showed "a hand between one woman's legs." Argentine distributors, producers, and filmmakers knew that it was not safe to import or produce movies anymore.[68] Mobilizing a rhetoric centered on the "defense of minors," in fact, these conservative groups set some of the most restrictive conditions of the 1960s in Argentina and affected adults as much as they affected youths.

It was in the educational milieu, significantly, where the imposition of restrictive conditions produced overt clashes between the psychological professionals and the Catholic groups, as these two examples illustrate. In 1958, the UBA decided to make the two secondary schools they ran coeducational. Representing the beliefs of Reca and Giberti, among others, pediatrician and UBA vice-rector Escardó defended coeducation as a way of building up a more "natural interaction between the sexes."[69] The League of Fathers was afraid that the establishment of coeducation at the UBA schools would pave the way for its generalization in all public schools. So they sent a press communiqué where they drew upon an encyclical Pious XI issued in 1929 to condemn coeducation because "its naturalism" did not acknowledge "original sin" and the "fact that the sexes are different."[70] The Leagues of Fathers and Mothers interviewed the minister of education, who assured them that he would not "innovate": the secondary schools in the "modernized" Buenos Aires of the 1960s continued separating the sexes.[71] The success of the conservative voices did not stop there. In 1959, the League of Mothers denounced the hiring of psychologists by the principals of several secondary schools, who planned to discuss with female students their school and family problems. These initiatives, the League of Mothers claimed, represented the tip of the iceberg for the erosion of family authority and were "Communist by nature."[72] A secret report sent to Frondizi reproduced the same ideas. "The girls engaging with this initiative end up questioning their role as students, daughters, and mothers:

these are seeds for Communist infiltration."[73] The ideas of "dislocation of family authority" and "Communist infiltration" reinforced one another to signal how serious the situation was. In that case also, the minister left no doubt and did not authorize the psychologists' participation.

As if a symbolic exchange were taking place, however, while the conservative voices successfully participated in policymaking that set some of the cultural conditions for youth sociability in the 1960s, the psychological professionals became *the* experts on youth and family and were regarded as the most legitimate voices. Psychological professionals instilled the idea that adolescence and youth were a convoluted period within the life cycle, a crisis that individuals might normally overcome in their transition to adulthood. That discursive normalization of the youth crisis, along with the guidance to avoid authoritarian practices within the family, reached broad segments of the population, especially among the middle classes. Parents who were willing to "modernize" parenting strategies read advice columns and participated in workshops. Youths meanwhile not only had appointments with psychologists, but also took advice from them on negotiating with their parents on issues related to authority at home, as Giberti proudly noted.[74] Most basically, when emerging in public discourse, youth became a conduit for larger anxieties vis-à-vis the modernization of society, the meaning of change, and the visualization and imagination of the future.

Toward the Argentina of 1980

As the 1960s unfolded, the public interest in youth did not lessen, but the ways and intensity of addressing it changed. In contrast with the 170 lectures that *La Razón* reported in the preceding triennium, it only reported 39 during the period between 1962 and 1965. Giberti likewise was given gradually less space within the daily, and her column was discontinued in 1966.[75] The psychological professionals kept working to provide clinical treatment, yet their presence in the public arena decreased along with the anxieties that youth had awoken in the past years. By the mid-1960s, psychological professionals and sociologists also showed a degree of satisfaction: they observed that the harsher forms of patriarchal authority seemed to have vanished among urban families, in which children enjoyed greater respect and more liberties. The picture was promising and reflected well upon youth, or "the Argentina of 1980," as a journalist deemed it. In fact, a new journalism and a new cinematography further shaped the images and

Shot from *Los jóvenes viejos*.
Museo del Cine Pablo Ducrós
Hicken Archive.

data that showed a "modern youth" that in turn became the cipher that displayed their own modernization.

As the 1960s went on, perhaps the last powerful representations encoded in the "crisis-of-our-time" motif were provoked by the movies of the movement called the "Generation of 1960", which made youth one of its thematic cornerstones. Although they did not share a common filmic language and did not make the same choices in generic and formal patterns, many of the filmmakers who gained access to the domestic film industry around 1960 did effectively cultivate similar attitudes against the previous "commercial" model of production and engaged in a serious commitment to renovating the local scene.[76] Admirers of directors such as Michelangelo Antonioni and Jean-Luc Godard, these filmmakers were under thirty years old and represented, or self-represented, what they depicted as a "new youth." That was the case with one of the most prolific members of the "Generation of 1960," director and producer Rodolfo Kuhn. He devoted his three first movies, *Los jóvenes viejos* (1962), *Los inconstantes* (1962), and *Pajarito Gómez* (1965) to representing youth.[77] *Los jóvenes viejos* (*The Old Youth*) tells the story of three young middle-class male friends: one of them works as a television producer; another is a law student, and another attempts to make a movie "on guys just like us." Always dissatisfied, their worries revolve around finding any meaning whatsoever in their existence, which is marked by the habits of hanging around Buenos Aires and listening to jazz. They travel to Mar del Plata, where they meet three girls whose attachments to the social and affective worlds appear as elusive as theirs. They conceive of love and sex as possible ways to escape from their senseless lives, but they can barely communicate. In one of the many self-reflective dialogues that permeate the movie, the friends only find a response to their feelings: "What are we?" one friend asks. "We did not have two wars," another responds: "No, but we had Perón." The comparison to European and North American youth is obvious, and the dialogue suggests that Peronism had had the same effects on Argentina's youth as war had had on the major powers.[78]

Los jóvenes viejos helped instill the image of a weary, unsatisfied, but "authentic new youth" on the center stage and attempted to portray a generation marked by Peronism and the frustrated projects geared toward overcoming its legacies. Like many movies of the "Generation of 1960," Los jóvenes viejos made use of several formal traits to produce a sense of authenticity, like the avoidance of studio settings and the use of unknown actors. The movie strove to create naturalistic ambiance to document the existence of a youth characterized by its purposeless, its tiredness, its self-absorption, and its inability to contribute to a better future. Movie critics for the most part welcomed and praised the authenticity. While some pointed out that the movie reflected certain groups of youth, others directly argued that it depicted the common life and feelings of a "generation that was born in the years of collective anguish we experienced." This was precisely the movie's argument.[79] In that vein, Kuhn's Los jóvenes viejos shared a common theme with the beliefs of some intellectuals, most notably writer David Viñas: that is, seeing young people as members of a shared generation that came to life in the controversial political and cultural Peronist years and that was frustrated, if not betrayed, by the failure of Frondizi to democratize and develop Argentina. To Viñas, it was a "frustrated generation" that could not reinvigorate Argentina, and its goal was to "save its dignity, its face."[80]

The movies of the "Generation of 1960" and Los jóvenes viejos in particular stirred up public discussion over the authenticity of that "frustrated generation" they sought to document, and over the ways of overcoming it in political and cultural terms. Catholic and Leftist critics shared a negative reception of Los jóvenes viejos. A renowned Catholic critic deemed the movie pretentious and accused Kuhn of "falsely showing an anguished youth only interested in sex."[81] Leftist essayist Juan José Sebreli, for his part, dismissed the movie because of its "mystifying" attempts at portraying a "false alienation" among the petit-bourgeoisie, and denounced the "blame-it-on-Perón" attitude that it endorsed.[82] Leftist militants, mainly youth leaders, reacted as well. Socialist Elías Semán, for example, stated that "our youth is not what our 'colonized' filmmakers show: the problems of our youth are the problems of our people."[83] The Communist youth press, for its part, offered a different twist: it kept the term *jóvenes viejos* as shorthand to refer to the youths they envisioned as already "lost." The *jóvenes viejos* were identified as those emulating fashionable trends from abroad, and they were thought to represent a moral crisis that impinged on certain segments of Argentina, against which Communists might ideologically fight.[84] The reactions to *Los jóvenes viejos* resembled what historian Richard Jobs has hypothesized about Marcel Carné's *The Cheaters* (1958) in France. In both cases, the debates over the movies involved anxieties about the chances of "reinvigorating" the culture. If the depictions in those movies of new youth were "authentic"—and that was a major point of the arguments—then the collective future looked as uncertain as the youths on the screens.[85]

Intense as they were, the appeal to a "frustrated generation" as well as the cultural and political debate it awoke lasted only a short time. That appeal had been at the center of a renovated intellectual scene—with David Viñas as its star—and of a new cinematography; the "frustrated generation," though, vanished with the "Generation of 1960" and its *jóvenes viejos*.[86] As the decade went on, other cultural materials made of youth a critical subject of attention, but imbued with more optimistic characteristics. Certainly, one of the features of the dynamics of cultural modernization of the 1960s involved the emergence of newsmagazines like *Primera Plana*, *Confirmado*, and *Panorama*, which helped to configure a new and enlightened readership. Addressed to a middle-class audience, these magazines, which followed patterns similar to *Time* and *L'Express*, forged a distinctive journalistic writing, became beacons of taste and cultural legitimacy, and incorporated other areas of social and cultural life into the realm of "news."[87] They promised, for instance, to unravel the behaviors, feelings, and expectations of youth. Since youths were allegedly difficult to communicate with, the "experts" writing in the new magazines used sociologically informed techniques that would allow them to overcome the obstacles and then portray how youths "actually" were. Echoing the psychological professionals, the magazines represented youth as the silent agents who would modernize Argentina's culture. They therefore depicted a youth far from any idea of rebellion or feeling of dissatisfaction.

The new magazines represented youth as a homogeneous category, which they associated with a prudent relaxation in sexual mores and also, as a whole, with a prudent attitude toward politics. After conducting an in-depth interview with six adolescents from different social strata, an "expert" from *Primera Plana* pointed out that they spoke of sexual issues in a rather natural way, and most approved of premarital sexual relations, yet not all of them were willing to agree that they had engaged in sex.[88] Another survey, conducted by *Panorama*, reached similar conclusions: while "90 percent of the surveyed adolescents" approved of premarital sex, boys were still reluctant to accept that girls lost their virginity before marriage, and girls emphasized that they could dare to have premarital sex only in a frame of "seriousness, responsibility, and proven fidelity."[89] The "expert" of *Confirmado* completed the picture by concluding that "without class distinctions," youths approved of premarital sex, yet sexual relations "almost always" took place "in contexts that lead to marriage."[90] The surveys thus built up a representation of a sexualized but prudent youth: they talked about sex, broke some prejudices, but kept associating sex with marriage. The magazines brought tranquility to their readerships. Unlike the "liberality" of the European youth, the local variety promised a discreet transformation of the sexual mores, far from any revolution.

If the "new youth" of the first half of the 1960s was not revolutionary in sexual terms, it was even less revolutionary in its political interests. The reporter of *Confirmado* argued that "their profound disinterest in politics" was the only discernible generational marker. The local youth, he concluded, "Tends toward a conformist position, accepting the world as it is."[91] Other journalists preferred to equate that seemingly apathetic attitude to a rational mindset. In a youth roundtable organized to commemorate the 150th anniversary of Argentine independence, an observer noted that the mid-1960s youths had forgotten "past animosities," which was a clear reference to the divide between Peronism and anti-Peronism. The attendees, he noted, had a "pragmatic approach" to that issue, which promised to dissolve the divide altogether.[92] Another survey concurred with that finding. While interviewing youths from different social strata who were born on October 17, 1945—the birth date of Peronism—the journalist found that just a few totally discarded or wholly praised the Peronist experience. Many valued, for example, its politics toward childhood and criticized its "lack of civil liberties." To the journalist, youths were able to reevaluate Peronism and rationally differentiate "what was best from what was worst."[93]

The construction of a representation of a politically inactive youth went hand in hand with the creation of an imagery of the "revolutionary minority." In early 1964, after the gendarmerie dismantled the guerrilla group Ejército Guerrillero del Pueblo (Guerrilla Army of the People), some analysts pointed to the relation between the guerrillas' age and the spread of "terrorism." By drawing on pseudo-psycho-sociological jargon, for instance, a journalist constructed a hypothetical, generalized interpretation of youth involvement in radical politics. He stated that while the majority remained apathetic, a minority was driven to the "armies of terror" by a mix of "resentment, non-conformism, and youth rebellion."[94] Likewise, the magazines represented a segment of the university students as the counter-image of the mainstream "new youth." In the context of a mounting campaign to get the state to intervene in the universities, the students were viewed as the loci of political radicalism.[95] An editorial writer from *Primera Plana* clearly established the split: a minority of university students looked for a "refuge in Marxism or in the far-right," but the majority remained apathetic.[96] The "new youth," to the editorial writer, could potentially become a stabilizing force in politics as well.

By the mid-1960s, the optimism that pervaded the representation of a "new youth" went hand in hand with a generalized confidence in the possibilities of bridging the gap between the "adult" and the "young" generations in the realm of prudently modern families, and it found an echo in sociological and expert commentary. In 1965, one sociologist published the findings of a survey she conducted among middle- and working-class mothers on childrearing practices. She asserted that urban mothers tended to be sincere, open-minded, and affectionate, did not demand blind obedience from their children, respected their desires, and promoted family dialogue on issues like sex and vocations.[97] Another sociologist, for her part, after conducting a survey with male industrial workers, noted that they were willing to collaborate with their wives in performing domestic chores and childrearing, and that they highly valued family dialogue and respected their children's personalities and decisions.[98] The celebratory visions of the familial changes were apparent. In a roundtable that joined Germani and psychoanalyst Armando Bauleo with the priest Moledo—the League of Mothers' counselor—the participants concurred that the "turning point" in the "youth crisis" had already passed. Likewise they all agreed that "modern families" were preferable because they allowed for honesty and companionship between the generations. They could not agree, though, on the issue of premarital sex.[99]

Youth sexuality was perhaps the single issue that awoke the most serious concerns from the "adult" world, and that was the reason why the new magazines insisted on prudence toward ongoing changes. The "new youth" of the mid-1960s did not generate such a wave of anxieties and debate as its predecessor of the mid-to-late 1950s did. Rather, psychological professionals, sociologists, and journalists of the new magazines could demonstrate a degree of satisfaction through the representation of a politically inactive and sexually prudent "new youth." This "new youth," sociologists confirmed through their findings, had been raised in a realm of modernizing families. These families supported and promoted dialogue and tolerance and avoided the harsher forms of patriarchy. In turn, the "new youth" promised to gradually change sexual mores and eventually become a stabilizing force in politics. The Argentina of 1980, as imagined through the attributes endowed to the "new youth," would be rational, perhaps democratic, and prudent: it would have overcome the "transition" to a modern nation.

▶ As cultural critic Lawrence Grossberg has noted, the term "youth" does not have its own center: it is a "signifier of transition and change."[100] All the voices that attempted to mobilize, categorize, and discuss youth in the 1950s and the early 1960s also attempted to signify transition and change. They projected onto the cultural category they were constructing their hopes and anxieties regarding broader sociocultural and political issues in a country that, for the most part, was also thought of as undergoing its own "critical transition." Carving out a place for youth meant also defining the parameters for young people to "act" their age. Through their enduring conversation, an array of cultural and political "adult" actors helped set many of the conditions in which the experiences of flesh-and-blood young people unfolded: to a degree, they decided where and how youths could interact, down to even what movies they could watch; they expanded the notion of "normalcy" with regard to youth's behaviors, habits, and attitudes, within the family and sexual realms; and, chiefly, they decided that youth had become of critical importance. They imbued young people with a renewed sense of importance.

In terms of the historical emergence of youth as a cultural category, there were three key moments. The eruption of a public discussion took place when Perón mobilized and insisted on projecting onto youth the possibilities of generational continuity of his project. His political opponents constructed a narrative that centered on the ways in which Perón, through his alleged manipulation of youth for political purposes, generated the conditions for "perverting" sexual mores, producing hedonistic values, and subverting social and cultural hierarchies. From the outset, the talk about youth combined political, cultural, and sexual discussions.

These were crucial in the second moment, which was marked by the emergence of experts and their association of youth with the "crisis-of-our-time" motif. Among those experts, conservative Catholic groups and psychological professionals represented broader positions trying to influence modernizing dynamics that, for better or worse, both viewed as ongoing. The Catholic groups attained a remarkable organizational success. Embedded in Cold War rhetoric, these groups promoted a connection between "liberalism" and Communism that had youth as its main target. Perhaps the mobilization of those connections explains their political influence: in the name of "youth's moral well-being," these groups participated in the apparatus of censorship (as well as other decision-making processes) that affected youths and adults alike. While prominent in the shaping of some conditions that made the local 1960s, these groups resembled a reactionary force. The psychological professionals, on the contrary, contributed to the normalization of the "youth" and of the "social" crisis, tying the resolution of both to the erasure of the more entrenched forms of patriarchal authority at the family and cultural levels. These professionals perceived youths to be in the privileged position of involuntary agents of modernization: youth promised to remove authoritarianism at home and in society while living their "normal" crisis at a particular time.

By the mid-1960s, youth came to be celebrated in the public arena. The critical momentum of the eruption of the public talk had already been left behind, along with the notion of crisis and the belief in the existence of a "frustrated generation." The representations of youth in this third moment emphasized some attributes such as prudence and rationality. The new magazines, for instance, depicted the "new youth" as the carrier of slow, careful steps toward a "modernization" of sexual and cultural mores. Most fundamentally, youth appeared as politically inactive. For many cultural actors, the youth of the mid-1960s represented the rise of rationality in all spheres of life, and some even dreamed that this type of dispassionate attitude would entail the crossing out of the Peronist/anti-Peronist divide. That was the youth landscape drawn by the mid-1960s. In the years that immediately followed, youth came to the spotlight again to signal that the serene landscape represented nothing more than desires and hopes. Talking about youth, however, always meant talking about desires, hopes, and fears.

2 ▸ The World of the Students

Increasing numbers of youths between thirteen and twenty-four years of age gained access to secondary schools and universities in the 1950s and 1960s. The vast matriculation of newcomers in the education system signaled the most basic dimension of the sociocultural modernization Argentines lived through: a porous and accelerated dynamic that held the schools and colleges as privileged sites. Yet looking at this dynamic from the vantage point of the student experience at both levels shows deep ambivalences. While secondary schools were sites for the developing of new peer-based sociability, they continued enforcing authoritarian practices and pedagogies. The experience of the secondary school students was as constitutive in shaping the 1960s as was the college experience. Hindsight presents a rather acquiescent view of the decade as one pervaded by notions of progressive change. Yet authoritarianism and change marked the dual sociocultural modernization that was embodied in youth.

As the world of the students enlarged, more youths organized their daily lives around the schools and their attendant spaces. Intermittently, they participated in political activism that crystallized within a third space: the streets. The political socialization of students in Latin America has attracted attention since the 1950s, when local and international scholars tried to visualize and formulate the traits of the "democratic" and modernizing elites that those countries needed for their "takeoff" toward development.[1] That interest was also related to the role that the student movement had in politics at the university and national levels. In Argentina, since 1918, the student movement had been overwhelmingly aligned with the ideas and projects shaped within the University Reform Movement. The basic principles set by the Reformists for the universities—autonomy, student participation in the university government, freedom of cathedras, and the social function of knowledge—served also as cornerstones

44

for projects of social transformation that emphasized democratic values and modernizing ideals, including laicism. In practical terms, though, those tenets were applied on a limited basis. During Juan Perón's governments (1946–55), moreover, the state suppressed university autonomy and banned student organizations such as the Federación Universitaria Argentina (FUA) and the Federación Universitaria de Buenos Aires (FUBA). Reformist students along with some Catholic students became strongholds of anti-Peronism, and they actively supported the coup d'état that overthrew Perón in 1955.[2]

From 1955 to 1966, an ideologically changing but always significant student movement did participate in university and national politics, contributing to the makeover of the universities into showrooms for "modernization" and, afterward, forecasting their critique from a radical perspective. The Reformist-oriented groups and projects provide a window through which to access those changes. Between 1955 and 1958, students of both Reformist and Catholic orientations contributed to the "de-Peronization" of the universities; but their alliance ended when Arturo Frondizi's government (1958–62) decided to pass new legislation allowing the private sector to create title-granting universities, previously a state monopoly. In September and October 1958, *laicos* (laity)—the largely Reformist defenders of the state monopoly over higher education—and *libres* (free)—the Catholic defenders of the new arrangement—clashed in the streets on a daily basis. The unfolding of the *laica o libre* conflict brought important realignments within the Reformist bloc, which had been an eager participant in the intrauniversity politics. Although a majority of the secondary school and college students refrained from participating in politics as the 1960s continued, a minority affiliated with Reformist groups joined ranks with groups from divergent political and ideological backgrounds to pave the way toward increasing radicalization. In that process, the old divides between Reformist and non-Reformist, *laicos* and *libres*, and even Peronist and anti-Peronist began to blur, giving birth to a new student movement where the term "Reform" was gradually replaced by "Revolution." The military that led the 1966 coup d'état tried to put an end to that process by intervening in the public universities. Yet, in their effort to depoliticize university life, the military merely exacerbated the expansion of the radical tide far beyond the "active few."

Schools, Corners, Streets

Beginning in the 1950s, a growing segment of adolescents organized their daily lives around school. Girls and boys from lower-middle- and working-class backgrounds for the first time gained access to secondary schools, which endowed them with a sense of entitlement. For most students the experience became the keystone for creating new sociability beyond the school doors and, in some cases, for beginning their political involvement. A source of potentially stirring experiences, the secondary schools nonetheless provoked mounting criticisms. For the most part, the schools preserved the attributes they had had in the first half of the twentieth century, chiefly their emphasis on discipline and encyclopedism, which became the traits students found to be unbearable. As crucial venues for modernizing sociocultural dynamics—such as social mobility, homogenization, improved literacy rates, and egalitarian forms of interaction—the secondary schools enforced also authoritarianism.

The dramatic expansion of enrollments at the secondary level of education began during the Peronist governments, but in the decades that followed it became more diversified in terms of gender and class. From 1945 to 1970, the total enrollment more than quadrupled, from 201,000 to 985,000 students.[3] Although the dropout rates remained high, so did the percentage of the age group thirteen to eighteen that attended the secondary schools. At the national level, in 1960, 23 percent of that age group was enrolled, and the figure jumped to 52 percent in Buenos Aires.[4] In 1970, the national percentage had almost doubled to 45 percent, and Argentina followed Uruguay and Chile as the Latin American countries with the highest rates of enrollment.[5] There are three remarkable characteristics in that expansion. First, the student body became feminized: in 1950 girls accounted for 47 percent of the student population, and in 1970, 53 percent.[6] During the 1950s, girls enrolled overwhelmingly in a traditionally feminine branch: the "normal," or teaching-training schools. In the 1960s growth in the normal branch stagnated, and girls flocked to the commercial branch.[7] This latter trend signals another characteristic of the secondary level: the class diversification of the student body. The commercial and technical branches trained students in tasks related to office and industrial jobs, respectively. Those branches attracted an increasing number of boys and girls from the lower middle class and from the upper stratum of the working class.[8] Finally, the secondary level became gradually privatized and, basically, Catholicized. This process began when the authorities of the *Revolución Libertadora* restored official subsidies to the private schools that Peronism had discontinued. Between 1956 and 1958, for example, 110 Catholic secondary schools were founded. In 1970, 30 percent of the students were enrolled in private, largely Catholic, schools.[9]

The expanded secondary level of education was a battlefield of diverging cultural and political projects. Consolidating their share in the secondary level through their own schools, the Catholic hierarchies and "defense of the family" groups went a step further in an attempt to shape the public system as well. Conservative Catholic groups exerted pressure on educational authorities to introduce religion and moral education in secondary schools—something they achieved in Córdoba in 1963, for example—and to reorient their curriculum toward the forging of "Christian humanistic personae."[10] Yet their most significant achievements were related less to the changes they promoted than to their ability to block changes they opposed. After the Catholic triumphs in the battles for (not) establishing coeducation and for (not) extending psychological orientation in schools, educators and psycho-pedagogues raised their voices. In August of 1958, for instance, representatives of public schools gathered en masse in Buenos Aires to discuss how the schools could help youths "undergo the emotional changes of their age" and "adjust to a shifting society."[11] Neither in this nor in subsequent conferences, though, could they articulate actual proposals for reforming the secondary level. In 1962, the chair of the School of Education at UBA concluded that the secondary school stood as an "obstacle" to change: "from the daily schedules to how the students are asked to walk," she concluded, "everything is rigid at the secondary schools."[12]

Nor did the secondary schools lose their "rigidity" over the course of the 1960s. Since their founding in the late nineteenth century, the secondary schools' overarching goal was to offer youths a general cultural background. The baccalaureate programs epitomized the aims of the humanistic school: as reservoirs of encyclopedic culture organized around subjects such as language and literature, history, and civic education, they did not train students to practice any professional activity but endowed them with general knowledge. In the 1950s and 1960s, although educational planners discussed better ways to train the "human resources" the country needed for development, and although the baccalaureate branch lost ground to the job-oriented commercial and technical branches, the humanistic matrix pervaded the entire secondary level.[13] Students from the first to the third years at all branches were exposed to a so-called common cycle, where sixteen out of thirty-two weekly hours of classes centered on the humanities.[14] Yet not only were the study plans rigid, so too was the focus on obedience and discipline as the organizing principles of school life. Ratified in 1957, the official *Reglamento* (bylaws) prescribed that the first duty of the students was to "obey their superiors inside and outside the school," the second related to punctuality, and the third dictated standards on hygiene and clothing. Academic performance, meanwhile, was the last item addressed.[15] Progressive educators in scholarly pieces and public lectures quoted the *Reglamento* to exemplify that "the school took from the barracks a cold authoritarianism," which contradicted any hope of forging "democratic citizens." That authoritarianism, one educator concluded, was met with rising opposition, since "today's students reject the school as it is."[16]

interesting *contradiction*

Students and some educators alike centered their criticisms on the pedagogical encyclopedic styles. Encyclopedism, for example, captured the attention of the American sociologist Robert Havighurst, who visited ten public schools in Buenos Aires and Mendoza in 1961. He depicted the prevailing classroom routines of teachers delivering lectures and the students taking notes as well as memorizing. When he visited a female-only school, for example, Havrighurst was "impressed more than ever with the common feature of the Argentine secondary school—namely, the earnestness of the pupils to recite." He wrote that the girls "flourished their hands in the air and sometimes got completely out of their seats in an effort to attract the attention of the teacher when she asked a question." Instead of lecturing, that teacher "organized a recitation that was a rehash of the textbook," without even trying to "encourage the students to apply what they read."[17] While Havighurst showed that some students had internalized the rule—and were willing to recite—other students voiced their disgust. In 1956, a student group complained that at school they were viewed as "empty receptacles in which to pour as much insignificant content as possible." This had not changed ten years later, when 78 percent of the eight hundred students surveyed by a team from the University of La Plata pointed out that the "magisterial classes" were the major obstacle to a good school experience.[18] With the "magisterial classes" at its core, encyclopedism meant boredom and fear. While being interviewed for a report, Jorge, a fourth-year student at a commercial school, stated that "school just makes me drowsy until I am called to the front."[19] To be called to the front meant to be evaluated. Gerardo still recalls the fear he felt at the prospect of being called. "It was arbitrary in the worst possible way,"

he recalled. "I can see my fellow classmates' faces when called 'to the front.' ✓
We all panicked."[20]   *Late 50's Authoritarian Rule*

The school experience was marked by authoritarian practices embodied in pedagogical styles and also in daily prescriptions and discipline. Exposed to, and participating in, the emerging consumption and leisure practices of youth, the boys and girls that flooded the secondary schools found those routines and prescriptions all the more outdated and authoritarian when compared with their "outside" lives. That was the case, for example, with the enforcement of the series of rules regarding the *Reglamento*'s dress codes. In the late 1950s, for instance, the students of two schools in an industrial neighborhood in Greater Buenos Aires were asked to write essays that focused on their school life. Some of the girls picked the issue of discipline as related to clothing. A third-year student complained that the *celadores* (caretakers) "zealously" looked over "the shine of our shoes, the length of the girls' *guardapolvos* [white cloth worn at the official schools], and the remote possibility of makeup." Other girls found it "ridiculous" that the school principals did not allow them to attend classes in pants, "now that all youths are wearing pants."[21] As for boys, when they began to wear their hair longer, principals in many schools added a twist to the *Reglamento*. In late 1968, they mandated that boys' hair should be eight centimeters above their shoulders. Speaking of this and other decisions, a schoolboy stated, "we form a line, stand up when the teacher enters the classroom, and keep our hair as short as a soldier. This is simply absurd."[22] As the 1960s went on, students were outspoken in finding those authoritarian practices "absurd" and "ridiculous."

Students found at least three ways of questioning school authoritarianism. One of the most widespread "tactics of resistance" was called being *en la luna* (on the moon, i.e., distracted) throughout the school day, chiefly when the teachers lectured. While some educators related that lack of attention to psychological aspects of adolescence such as the "tendency to daydream," others realized that it was a collective rather than individual issue. In a widely read pedagogical textbook, for example, an educator called on her colleagues to redefine their teaching methods because "the students 'on the moon' are shouting to us without words."[23] On the other hand, educators and state officers also grew preoccupied with indiscipline, which they—quite rightly, perhaps—attributed to the students' dissatisfaction with school. A report showed that, in 1963, the school principals had applied 55 percent more disciplinary sanctions to students than in 1957. Although those percentages are questionable—since they did not take into account increased enrollments—they offer insight into how state officers and educators perceived the "state of rebellion."[24] Finally, a highly visible segment of students questioned the school and, in some cases, the society that created it through political activism. Although a decree passed in 1936 made any political activity at the secondary schools illegal, on different occasions and with variable intensity, students could circumvent and challenge the legislation.

In September and October 1958, the participation of secondary school students marked the distinctiveness of one of the largest student-based mobilizations in twentieth-century Argentina: the *laica-o-libre* battles. In that context, two of the more long-lasting student groups came to the surface: the Unión Nacionalista de Estudiantes Secundarios (UNES, Nationalist Union of Secondary School Students) and the Federación Metropolitana de Estudiantes Secundarios (FEMES, Metropolitan Federation of Secondary School Students). The UNES joined right-wing nationalist students enrolled in private Catholic schools and in public baccalaureate institutions. Closely linked to university groups at the UBA and at the University of Córdoba, some members of the UNES founded the ultra-rightist and anti-Semitic group Tacuara, where they stood as vanguards of the *libres*.[25] On the other hand, the FEMES (created in May of 1958) was linked to the Federación Juvenil Comunista (FJC, Communist Youth Federation) and to the Reformist university students.[26] The boys belonging to the UNES and the FEMES, in fact, were among the bravest combatants in the daily struggles. For example, on September 5, 1958, students of the Colegio del Salvador organized a meeting indoors to defend the *libre* cause. Backed by members of the UNES, they left the school and engaged in a violent confrontation with the *laicos* affiliated with the FEMES. The police expelled the *laicos*, who fled to the nearby Plaza Congreso, where 119 underage boys were detained.[27]

Besides street fighting, secondary school students, mainly those identified as *laicos*, showed remarkable organizational skills, eagerness to engage in radical action, and ability to articulate their overarching demands (such as keeping the state monopoly over the university system and preventing the spread of religious education) with other, more quotidian and localized ones. As the conflict mounted, the students created "leagues" in Córdoba, Rosario, Tucumán, and Buenos Aires. The "League of the South," for example, joined students from two-dozen schools in the southern industrial neighborhoods of the Greater Buenos Aires area, who rejected "any chance of having the Church deciding our curriculums," as they wrote in a pamphlet. This league was also on the front line of the most drastic actions that the students could undertake: the "taking" of student buildings.[28] Over several weeks, a dynamic ensued in which the students occupied buildings, and the police moved them out. In some cases, parents became involved, such as at a female-only school in Buenos Aires, where parents accompanied the "sixty occupying ladies" when the police went to evict them and did not offer any resistance. In contrast, boys in seven technical schools and baccalaureate colleges, also in Buenos Aires, refused to abandon their schools, so police used tear gas to eject them and sent them to juvenile delinquency courts.[29] Further, some students connected their defense of laicism to their condemnation of school authoritarianism. A group of girls enrolled in a commercial school took control of the school building and also visited the newspapers to complain that the school's principal was "authoritarian like a Nazi."[30] The politicized context emboldened these students to denounce how authoritarianism unfolded at their particular school. In turn, the vast student involvement in the *laica-o-libre* battles indicated a desire to momentarily abandon school routines.

That episode of mobilization, though, was extraordinary. As soon as Congress passed the law authorizing the creation of title-granting private universities—which gave a victory to the *libres*—the Ministry of Education intensified its campaign to deter student activism in the schools. After the demise of the *laica-o-libre* battles, in fact, only the most active members of the FEMES and the UNES continued doing political work at particular schools, which included some incidents of street fighting. In August of 1960, in a male-only baccalaureate college in Buenos Aires, several members of the UNES attacked a student while they cried out, "Communist! Jew!" The FEMES coordinated a campaign against anti-Semitism and led a successful student strike to condemn the episode. Yet the Ministry of Education also took advantage of the episode: after conducting an exemplary trial against the principals of that school, the minister fired them for not enforcing the decree prohibiting student activism.[31] Right after these episodes, the FJC underscored how difficult it was to carry out activism at the schools. A report for 1962, for example, stated that the FJC had 679 members at schools in the City of Buenos Aires and 288 in the Greater Buenos Aires area. The report recognized that this was a tiny minority that also included "sympathizers." Instead of focusing only on the effects of the repressive legislation, the report also explained the FJC's weakness in cultural terms: "Most students," the report concluded, "are influenced by the *yanqui* way of life; they like the 'twist' and are not interested in politics."[32]

The FJC conceived of that situation as still another battle, this time not against the *libres* but against *yanqui* imperialism.

State officers and some educators were also concerned about the ways in which secondary school students engaged with the "new rhythms"—like rock 'n' roll and the twist—and tried to regulate student sociability at the end of the school day. At the same time that the Ministry of Education made efforts to prevent political activism from happening at the schools, it promoted the creation of school clubs. From a rather paternalistic perspective, the Ministry of Education believed that these clubs could be sites where youth after-school life could be kept under strict adult supervision. The ministry suggested that the clubs might organize activities like vocational theater lessons, chess championships, or visits to museums.[33] Not surprisingly, the clubs were a fiasco: students did not engage in creating them and did not participate in other extracurricular activities either. Given the unexpected success of folkloric music—which in the early 1960s competed with rock 'n' roll for youths' attention—the Directorate of Secondary Education promoted a folkloric dancing contest, but the insistence of the invitation to students suggests that they did not engage. Instead, many students requested permission to attend similar contests organized by a television show.[34] The problem was not the activity per se, but the organizer and venue. For the students, enjoyment and leisure were exactly the opposite of school life.

While most students made it clear that they did not want to stay in the schools, they did create new, peer-based social life around the experience of attending school. Quite literally, the corners of schools became a frontier zone, where both students and state officers claimed "sovereignty." Novelist Bernardo Verbitsky, for example, vividly narrated how the school corners became the "students' kingdom" and described how in the City of Buenos Aires, where schools were not coeducational, corners turned into "boxing rings" for boys and girls, who made "eye contact" and began to talk.[35] The daily practice of spending time on the corners expanded as much as the enrollment rates. For boys and girls, gathering on the corners entailed removing themselves from the adult gaze, at least for a brief time period, every day. As the practice became more popular, however, the Directorate of Secondary Education insistently asked the school principals to inspect what students did on the schools' surrounding areas but—again— this very insistence speaks of the principals' inability to do so.[36] For the most part, students kept the corners as their territory. They also had one day as their own: September 21, the beginning of spring, was "Students'

Day." From the mid-1950s onwards, students from public and private schools occupied plazas, forests, and central streets and also organized picnics and dance contests.

For a rising segment of youths the school experience entailed a chance to shape new forms of sociability, within and outside the classrooms. Furthermore, a majority of these adolescents were first-generation students, and their experience qualified them to discuss issues of authority in the familial realm and to revise entrenched ideals of upward social mobility. A former working-class boy, Carlos, for example, recalls that his parents seemed to respect him for his education, and he learned to "manipulate the situation to have more liberties." When I asked him how that worked, he told me: "I had decent grades, and then I could do whatever I pleased."[37] Being a first-generation student—and being male—provided Carlos with a chance to negotiate liberties at home. In exchange, though, Carlos and other first-generation students carried heavy burdens. Eduardo, for example, recalls that he felt "the pressure of the entire family in each exam" that he took at school. He knew the economic sacrifice that his parents made putting him through school—instead of his having to go to work at a factory, as his older brother did—and he "did not want to fail."[38] In fact, both families projected onto their sons the desire for intergenerational social betterment.

Beginning in the Peronist years and continuing well into the 1960s, many Argentines resumed the century-long project of upward social mobility through climbing the educational ladder. They shared an ideal that children could and should be better educated than their parents, primarily so they could be wealthier afterward. This was a crucial component of how successive generations of Argentines imagined the entwinement of their individual advancement with the collective "progress" of the nation. Education, and chiefly that in the secondary schools, was seen as the key to gaining "respectable" jobs. This ideally would allow children of blue-collar workers to move to white-collar positions and thus become a part of the labile "middle classes."[39] In the 1950s and 1960s, lower-middle- and working-class families could afford to have their children in secondary schools, something made apparent by the fact that the participation of boys aged fourteen to nineteen in the labor market dropped from 73 percent in 1947 to 57 percent in 1970.[40] A segment of social scientists over the 1960s cast no doubts: the expansion of enrollments in the secondary schools paved the way to social homogenization and cultural modernization.

Secondary schools, though, did not only represent "affordable" access to the dynamics of sociocultural modernization; they were also venues for institutionalized authoritarianism—which accompanied and conditioned those dynamics. As the students complained, "encyclopedic authoritarianism" prevailed at the schools, which continued focusing on discipline, order, and the enforcement of routines. The schools remained immutable, dissatisfying the students as the 1960s bore on. The students who moved to college, mainly to certain schools, found a different world. From 1956 to 1966, some schools promoted academic experimentation in which students participated in myriad ways. Moving from the secondary school to one of these more innovative schools meant stepping into a world that, in comparison, seemed livelier and more "modern."

College Times

After the ousting of Peronism, a political consensus began to emerge about the need to renovate higher education, a project that entailed creating new national universities and intensifying the research component of the university system to produce knowledge for a "changing society." Although allegedly all-encompassing, that project was limited to specific schools at particular universities, such as La Plata and the UBA. At the UBA, mainly between 1957 and 1962, professors, alumni, and students agreed upon a series of transformations that resulted in creating a research-focused institution, including rules for establishing an academic career, hiring full-time professors, and opening new programs and careers, chiefly in the natural and social sciences.[41] At specific schools, furthermore, students played a leading role in the renovation of university dynamics and in the orientation of their careers. Less formally, they also created new forms of sociability and cultural consumption, becoming the epitome of "modern youths."

As it was the case with the secondary level, the growth of university enrollment began during the Peronist years and continued throughout the decades that followed. Total enrollment increased sevenfold between 1945 and 1972, ballooning from 48,000 to 330,000 students.[42] The increase in university enrollments was a transnational phenomenon, which spread through other Latin American countries as well. In Brazil, for example, total enrollment almost doubled in only four years, going from 142,000 students in 1964 to 258,000 in 1968, while in Mexico it jumped from 70,000 in 1959 to 440,000 in 1974.[43] There was nevertheless a crucial difference between Argentina and its Latin American neighbors. In the early 1960s, the country ranked third in the world with regard to the percentage of university students in the population: there were 756 university students for each 100,000 inhabitants, while in Mexico there were 207, and in Brazil, 117.[44] Although a minority, the percentage of university students among the twenty to twenty-four age group steadily grew: 5 percent of that age group was enrolled in 1950; the figure jumped to 11 percent in 1960; and that number rose to 20 percent in 1972.[45] In Argentina, the university "penetrated" into larger middle-class segments and gradually incorporated children of small traders, clerks, teachers, and highly qualified manual workers. In the mid-1960s, 70 percent of the college students were first-generation. Further, as happened at the secondary level, the student body became increasingly feminine: at the UBA, young women comprised 26 percent of the students in 1958 and rapidly increased to 41 percent in 1972.[46]

In terms of student enrollment, feminization, and cultural visibility, no other site changed as intensely as the "star" of university renewal: the School of Humanities and Social Sciences at the UBA. This school exemplified the scope and limits of the Reformist-oriented, modernizing projects. The creation of new majors in the biennium 1957–58—such as psychology, sociology, anthropology, and education sciences—renewed the school's impetus, which was reflected in the expansion of enrollments. While between 1958 and 1968 the overall enrollment at the UBA grew 29 percent, the School of Humanities and Social Sciences grew 248 percent. The student body, of which 75 percent were women, went from 2,200 students in 1958 to 8,900 in 1968. In 1968, half of the students were enrolled either in psychology or sociology.[47] The school also became a beacon of cultural modernization in the public realm. Some of its professors, such as sociologist Gino Germani or psychoanalyst José Bleger, dominated the intellectual milieu. The areas of study they transformed were endowed with a halo of modernity that helps explain why youths wanted to pursue them, even when they were not certain about their future professional lives. A close look at this unique example, a virtual enclave, helps grasp how "cultural modernization" was perceived and shaped in the early 1960s and how some college students were linked with the desired, and feared, cultural, sexual, and political change.

Like most of their colleagues in other schools and universities, the students enrolled in the post-Peronist School of Humanities and Social Sciences participated in its overhaul. Initially, the centrality that the students acquired was based upon their role as opponents to Peronism. During Perón's governments, a handful of Reformist students had kept their student center alive. Sometimes they invited professors who had been expelled or resigned from their positions in an effort to create a "parallel" university.[48] The student center launched strikes opposing the imposition of a class on political formation, and many students were imprisoned.[49] When the 1955 coup d'état unfolded, activists occupied the building and then engaged in a controversial initiative: they helped select new professors by evaluating mainly their political pasts, vetoing candidates whose vitae showed "Peronist" signs.[50] As it happened in all national universities, a tripartite government of professors, students, and alumni ruled the UBA. From 1957 to 1964, the Movimiento Universitario Reformista (University Reformist Movement) held the student center and the bulk of representatives in the school's governing council.[51] The tripartite government enabled students to participate in the decision-making processes.

Many students helped shape the curricula and the theoretical developments of their careers. One success story took place in the recently created Psychology Department, whose foundation had entailed compromises among different theoretical approaches, out of which initially the so-called academic psychology prevailed. However, most of the students who flooded into the Psychology Department—which went from 13 in 1958 to 1,450 in 1960—were attracted by the prospects of getting psychoanalytically oriented training.[52] Joining some professors, the students made use of their department council, or *junta*, to request curricular changes. For example, student support was crucial for having one professor, a sympathizer of psychoanalysis, teach the most important class of the department.[53] Likewise a group of anthropology students pushed their professors to organize fieldwork regularly, but they did not succeed when requesting social anthropology classes. They thus turned to sociologists, such as Germani, who agreed to invite American anthropologist Ralph Beals to teach seminars.[54] Students acted collectively to reorient their careers according to what they thought would be the best theoretical choices. This was in contrast to what happened in Córdoba. There a "traditionalist bloc" of professors prevented the creation of social science majors, which explicitly contradicted students' wishes. At the School of Humanities and Social Sciences at the UBA, students generally had their voices heard, which implied recognition of their role in building a "modernized" intellectual realm.

The memories of former students of the School of Humanities and Social Sciences echo a feeling of optimism and the perception that they were active participants, even protagonists, of a changing cultural milieu.

A former history student recalls his college life by contrasting it to both his secondary school experience and his job as an office clerk. While he uses terms like "monotony" and "boredom" to describe his tenure in the office and the secondary school, he recalls college life as "something exhilarating." A former sociology student also described "the school and its nearby areas" as places "full of life," where she and her fellows "felt better than at home."[55] What did that life mean for many of these youths? Probably the prospects of getting professional training in their chosen fields and engaging in theoretical and academic discussions accounted for their perception that school was an exhilarating space. Moreover, the revived sense of life at the School of Humanities and Social Sciences was not exhausted there: a new sociability and cultural consumption produced the representation, and self-representation, of that specific school and its student body as both locus and vanguard of cultural modernization.

In spatial terms, until the mid-1960s, much of the school's activity took place at the heart of downtown Buenos Aires, which was becoming an ever more cosmopolitan and iconoclastic enclave. Until 1965 the school consisted of a series of buildings spread throughout Viamonte and Florida streets. Especially at night—since a vast majority of the students held part- or full-time jobs during the day—the bars and cafés concentrated on those streets became the privileged sites of the students' sociability.[56] A former anthropology student, for instance, recalled that he arrived at the Coto Bar in the evening, where he read, met his friends, "discussed politics, [and] a bit of the news." He then went to class, returning to the bar as soon as the class ended so they could continue talking until late at night.[57] The bars could act as alternative classrooms as well: some intellectuals organized study groups on authors that were not studied in the formal curriculum, like one devoted to Jean-Paul Sartre.[58] Besides a variety of bars and bookstores, the neighborhood featured movie theaters that screened European films and cine clubs, one of which was organized by the student center.[59] Moreover, beginning in 1963, the School of Humanities and Social Sciences shared its neighborhood with a modern art center par excellence, the Instituto Di Tella (IDT), which aimed to make Buenos Aires a global capital of contemporary art through encouraging the production and circulation of avant-garde works, mainly in the visual arts, music, and theater.[60] A former student stated that her education consisted of classroom experience, a diversified reading program, and visiting the IDT. That "privileged triangle," she argued, was the basis for the "cultural frame of the early 1960s."[61] The students of the school helped shape and display the modernization of Argentina's culture as members of a renovated college life, as readers, and as art consumers.

Yet modernization had limits even in that enclave, as illustrated by a major sex affair. In 1959, the student center's periodical, *Centro*, published a short story titled "La narración de la historia," by philosophy student Carlos Correas, which narrates the homosexual encounters of a middle-class university student and a working-class boy.[62] Right after the publication of that issue, the school's governing council complained "that the pages of a publication connected with this school are used against its good name and prestige." In addition, Catholic students requested the banning of *Centro*.[63] Aware of that request, the district attorney Guillermo de la Riestra—infamous because of his censorship undertakings—initiated a prosecution of Correas and of *Centro*'s editorial committee. His actions included spectacular raids of the student center's offices, authorized by the rector who also gave a judge the home addresses of the committee members.[64] Finally only Correas and *Centro*'s main editor, Jorge Lafforgue, were prosecuted for "disseminating obscene materials." Lafforgue recalls that most "liberal professors just kept their mouths shut." Although he personally asked professors and students for their solidarity, "they simply didn't care."[65] The outcome of the affair shows the enclave's limits. On the one hand, it is likely that no other student periodical, much less a commercial press, would have dared to publish Correas's story. It was a bold decision that ultimately led to the end of the project of *Centro* because its financial and political support had been undercut. On the other hand, then, besides the legal prosecution, the students faced the active opposition of Catholic students, the rector, and the school's governing council, all of whom were theoretically committed to a democratizing rhetoric (including the right to free speech). Correas's story tested the limits of the acceptable at the School of Humanities and Social Sciences: representing homoerotic desire was unacceptable.

As the 1960s continued, though, the School of Humanities and Social Sciences embodied a vanguard of the sexual and political revolutions alike. When magazines conducted surveys to unravel Argentina's sexual mores, for example, they regularly interviewed "a student at the School of Humanities," seemingly because they would discover more radicalized statements. A twenty-year-old psychology student, for instance, showed her "liberality" when she responded to a question about premarital sex by arguing that "virginity doesn't have any value: if women did not possess a hymen, someone would have invented another taboo."[66] The "girls-of-Humanities" stood for the liberalization of heterosexual mores. Basically, the school epitomized student and professorial political radicalization. The official bulletin of the Episcopal Committee, representing the Catholic Church's hierarchy, for example, singled out sociologist Germani and psychologist Telma Reca as the "Marxist harbingers" at that school—ironically, neither of them was a Marxist. That representation permeated the commercial weeklies as well. In 1962, a magazine published a report that dubbed particularly sociology students as the tip of the iceberg of the "Communist infiltration" at the UBA.[67] With its high profile, the school occupied a prominent place within an intensifying anti-Communist campaign.

In 1964, an episode "confirmed" the suspicions regarding the School of Humanities and Social Sciences' radicalization. The Ejército Guerrillero del Pueblo (EGP, Guerrilla Army of the People), a group led by journalist Jorge Masetti and supported by Che Guevara, developed a rural *foco* in Salta province. The experience proved a disaster: some of the thirty guerrillas died of hunger, while other soldiers killed comrades who tried to leave the project. Still others were killed or imprisoned by the gendarmerie. Two of them were students at the school.[68] In a broadly publicized announcement, the school's governing council (whose members had shifted toward the Left from the time of the Correas affair) deplored "the tragic death of the students in Salta." The dean, social historian José Luis Romero, stated, "They were not common delinquents, but youths who, wrong or right, have adopted a dramatic solution in response to well-known situations of our country."[69] The press amplified the meaning of those episodes, and a journalist went as far as to conclude that bars near the school hosted a "plethora of real or imagined bearded guerrillas."[70] That perception reached the academic realm outside Argentina as well. In what was perhaps one of the most influential pieces of research on student politics, Seymour Lipset singled out the School of Humanities and Social Sciences as "by far the most radicalized" in Latin America.[71] However, neither academics nor journalists mentioned that the EGP had amassed support from other groups as well, notably from students and intellectuals who had recently split with the Communist Party in Córdoba.[72] Far from the raucous claims of the press, which the Church hierarchy, politicians, and even academics posited at the time, this episode also signaled profound changes within the student movement.

The "Radicalized Students" and the Demise of Reformism

The most active groups within the student movement participated in the changes that took place across the political spectrum, but particularly on the Left. In this process, left-wing Reformist groups joined others—including Catholic and Peronist groups—to criticize what they viewed as faults of Reformist-oriented, university-focused projects linked to notions of development. Former divides between Reformist and non-Reformist, *laicos* and Catholic, and even Peronist and anti-Peronist began to blur in practice within a student activism gradually becoming more tethered to anti-imperialist and eventually anticapitalist ideas. The activists comprised, for sure, a minority of the student body. And they showed evidence of a deep makeover, epitomized in the figure of the "radicalized student." To some scholars, journalists, politicians, and professors, the "radicalized students" jeopardized the smooth operation of the university and the fate of the nation as such. Those students and the institution of the university itself became the target of increasing anti-Communist attacks that ended only with the military intervention after the 1966 coup d'état.

Between the *laica-o-libre* conflict in 1958 and the military intervention in 1966, Reformism underwent both a university-based political success and also continuous splintering. On the one hand, for the first time in a relatively long period, most national universities were ruled in a Reformist-oriented fashion, as student and faculty groups agreed on defending the principles of co-government and autonomy, among others. On the other hand, Reformism split permanently because of disagreements about extrauniversity or even extranational issues, as exemplified in the discussions triggered by the Cuban Revolution. As in other Latin American countries, the Cuban process first awoke expectations far beyond the Left. In March of 1959, for example, the UBA's rector Risieri Frondizi praised the Cuban students "who accompanied the last movement for the dignity of America."[73] He focused on how the Cuban students had helped oust dictator Fulgencio Batista and reminded his audience of the need to enforce "Reformist ideals" such as the defense of the peoples' right to self-determination and the possibility of forging a "Latin American unity."[74] As the Cuban revolutionary process unfolded, initial supporters such as Frondizi began to turn away. In contrast, some on the Left interpreted the Cuban process as the final step of the Reformist movement: "only the old Reformist student Fidel Castro," David Viñas wrote, "is fulfilling the old Reformist project."[75] For left-wing Reformists, attaining "old" ideals meant updating anti-imperialist and radicalized components.

The support of the Cuban Revolution, though, served to forge practical alliances between Reformist and non-Reformist activists. The "Cuban Party," as sociologist Silvia Sigal has dubbed it, was an imaginary identity that cut across Marxist and nationalist students and intellectuals.[76] In April 1961, the "Cuban Party" was the vanguard of the rallies against the U.S. invasion of the Bay of Pigs. Writing about those days, an American sociologist teaching at the School of Humanities narrated how the members of one "pro-Cuban committee" entered the classroom to invite the students to join a march: out of forty-five students, only three remained in their seats.[77] In fact, in Buenos Aires, Rosario, and Córdoba, thousands of students protested, and three dozen spent nights in prison. In addition to repudiating an overt imperialist intrusion like the Bay of Pigs invasion, these activists also conveyed an apparent fascination with the Cuban guerrillas' epic, something they shared with their peers in Mexico and even the United States.[78] In Argentina, fueled by groups that had just split from the "old" Socialist Party, students created organizations of solidarity with Cuba—which served to both discuss the "Cuban revolutionary road" and the unfulfilled goal of preparing brigades to help in situ. In some settings, such as Córdoba, the Cuban "turn" created a clear-cut divide between moderate and left-wing Reformism, with the former refusing to join solidarity organizations.[79] More generally, in consolidating the "Cuban Party," these organizations reframed the prevalent political identities in the student movement, making irrelevant or secondary the divide between non-Reformists and Reformists.

A renewed, more radicalized anti-imperialism became the touchstone for criticizing how university "modernization" was implemented, which generated more fissures among Reformists. In the early 1960s, the initial enthusiasm around university modernization had begun to vanish at its epicenters, like the UBA. The university's financial problems limited its renewal, which for the left-wing students paved the way for "imperialist penetration" into academia. An ex-president of the FUBA explained: "it all begins by financially strangling our university with the approval of our disciplined government, to then look for the 'support' of the 'philanthropic foundations.'" The foundations would set conditions to the research agenda by imposing topics and creating obstacles to producing "knowledge to liberate our country."[80] Students criticized not only the government for cutting the university budgets but also the professors who received grants from the Rockefeller and Ford foundations. These professors embodied what the students dubbed "scientificism," or, as one activist put it, "the ideology of those who modernized the university to produce scientists for imperialism."[81] The censure of scientificism introduced tensions among former allies: "old Reformist" professors could hardly agree with students that harshly criticized them.[82] Some of these students likewise opted to dispose of Reformism. The Tendencia Anti-Imperialista Universitaria (TAU, Anti-Imperialist University Trend), a tiny yet typical group at the UBA, for example, claimed that the results of the laica-o-libre conflict and scientificism had killed Reformism.[83] TAU and other groups linked to what came to be known as "national Left" advocated overcoming Reformism by a working-class based, anti-imperialist bloc.

The renewed anti-imperialist drive and the will to "connect" with the workers became the ideological priorities for the student movement. Although it was not until the late 1960s that the approach of student and labor activism reached broader significance, there were localized encounters before then. In 1963–64, the Confederación General del Trabajo (CGT, General Labor Confederation), led by orthodox sectors of Peronism, organized planes de lucha (action plans) to protest against rising costs of living and unemployment rates. They basically wanted to demonstrate to the new president, Arturo Illia (1963–66) how powerful their movement was, even with its leader in exile. That context showed two novelties. First, the CGT, which in the laica-o-libre conflict had refused to support the Reformists, now invited them and all the student groups to participate in the protests, which included building occupations. Second, Reformist and non-Reformist groups did support the planes de lucha. A meeting at the CGT headquarters, for example, joined the Reformist FUA, the Humanist League, and the Social Christians.[84] This illustrated that the labels "lay" and "Catholic" were losing their ability to map student alliances. In many respects, though, Catholics were just starting to make inroads in some universities, such as the Littoral, the Northeast, and Córdoba. There, the Integralistas, a "social humanist" group independent from the Church's hierarchies, gained power after displacing the Reformists from the student preferences in 1960. The Integralistas followed the debates set in motion during the Second Vatican Council (1962–65) and endorsed the ideal of a Christian commitment to social change.[85] In fact, in the university milieu they and some groups of the "national Left" were the first to think of Peronism as a way of shaping a "national revolutionary road."

Representing a visible minority, the figure of the "radicalized student" nevertheless awoke notorious reactions. Attuned to Cold War rhetoric, many groups voiced their desire to curb university politics altogether. In conservative quarters, "tripartite government" was a synecdoche for Reformism, which in turn was viewed as only the first step in the passage from "liberalism" to "Communism." Writing for a forum of the armed forces, for example, an army ideologue assured his readers that the mere existence of a university government shared by professors, alumni, and students entailed a "total subversion of hierarchies and authority," which, he thought, paved the way for the "disorder that made Communist infiltration possible."[86] For the ideologues of the armed forces and conservative nationalist intellectuals, the solution was to quash the Reformist-oriented process. The Catholic hierarchies concurred and repeatedly requested the government to intervene in the "houses of higher education" that were, in their view, "Communist hotbeds."[87] For these voices, the involvement of students in the EGP came as a self-fulfilling prophecy, which they believed to be confirmed once again in 1965. In May, student and labor groups rallied to prevent the government from sending troops to back the United States in the invasion in Santo Domingo, which ended up violently. This context caused rightists to double their critics. The most influential business association asked Illia to "suppress the tripartite government."[88] Some representatives likewise asked the Ministry of the Interior to scrutinize the "Communist penetration" at the Schools of Law and Humanities at the UBA and at its university press.[89]

In the mid-1960s, the "radicalized students" and the universities at large had become the prime candidates for the creation of a political movement to support a military coup d'état. The "indiscipline" and "Communist infiltration," political commentators argued, were signs of the impossibility of maintaining formal democratic procedures both within and outside the universities. Journalists and politicians deployed a discourse focusing on order: besides what they hyperbolically conceived of as an excess of politicization that had "radicalized students" as protagonists, the critics argued that the universities had not fulfilled their academic goals.[90] From their perspective, the same held true for the country, where Illia's government was marked by an "excess" of party politics accompanied by inattention and a lack of initiative in facing issues related to economic growth and stability. Most of the press used the same arguments in attacking the university and the government and backed a military coup d'état, which was finally led by General Juan Carlos Onganía on June 28, 1966.[91] The press, most political parties, the CGT, and Perón himself welcomed the coup, which had the blessing of the Catholic hierarchies. The UBA was the only institution that opposed it.

The so-called *Revolución Argentina* (1966–70) represented what political scientist Guillermo O'Donnell termed an authoritarian-bureaucratic regime. Committed to a project of socioeconomic planning and strong anti-Communism, the regime announced it had goals, but not definite time frames to accomplish them. The first objective was to economically modernize the country, which involved stopping inflation and setting the conditions for increasing foreign investment. To that end, the regime also argued for stifling politics, beginning by suppressing Congress and outlawing political parties.[92] Once the parties were neutralized—of whom none complained, except for the Communist Party—the next target was the university. On July 29 the government passed Law 16912, which mandated that the national universities would depend on the Executive Power and thus lose their autonomy. At the same time, the government sent the police to occupy the schools of architecture, sciences, and humanities at the UBA. Police repression reached a crescendo at the School of Sciences, where the dean and a visiting American professor were beaten and taken to police stations, along with 120 professors and students. This became known as the *noche de los bastones largos* (the night of the long sticks).[93]

The intervention and the violence exerted during the *noche de los bastones largos* confirmed that Onganía regime would not make any concession in its goal of "depoliticizing" the universities, even though it did so at the cost of losing its initial legitimacy at home and abroad. The fact that an American professor was among the beaten led the U.S. State Department to express its "deep concern" to the Argentine authorities.[94] The *New York Times*, for its part, equated the police attacks to "the tactics used by Hitler's storm troopers in the 1930s."[95] Public opinion did not find other news promising either, particularly the resignation of 1,200 professors at the UBA. Research teams in the most innovative scientific programs went into academic exile, while the psychology and sociology departments were almost totally dismantled.[96] To depoliticize university life, the Onganía regime cut short the project undertaken since the end of Peronism. Professors and students who participated in that project recall the decade between the 1955 and the 1966 coups d'état as a "golden era," a time marked by dynamism and creativity that the universities had not witnessed before or after.[97] Contemporaries, mainly those engaged directly with the university or those who had children attending, perceived this loss as it unfolded. Their reactions toward the intervention may help explain why the Onganía regime rapidly lost popularity: an opinion survey showed that the support of the regime among the middle classes had decreased from 60 percent in July of 1966 to 42 percent in March of 1967.[98]

The opposition to the Onganía regime grew rapidly among the "radical-ized students." The major opposition movement arose in Córdoba, where the third-largest university was located: its student body swelled to 22,000 students in 1966, one quarter that of the UBA's. Córdoba, the birthplace of the University Reform Movement in 1918, had begun to forsake Reformism as the force propelling student activism.[99] That was plain in August 1966, when the Integralistas fueled the student movement that opposed the in-tervention and also the way in which Córdoba's most prominent or "sacred family," the Nores Martínez family, had achieved major positions in the province and national governments.[100] While the students did not attend classes—an old action within the Reformist repertoire—a group of seventy Integralistas began a hunger strike at a parish, whose priest was commit-ted to the Second Vatican Council's ideals. Meanwhile, students challeng-ing the official ban distributed pamphlets to explain their demands to the neighbors. On August 21, the police repressed one demonstration by first shooting the students and then beating and detaining the nurses and doc-tors who were aiding the students.[101] Rather than discouraging protest, police repression propelled new forms of student organization, like the Coordinating Committee, which joined Integralistas and Reformists and had a leading role in the tragic days of September.[102]

On September 7, 1966, Santiago Pampillón was participating in a dem-onstration when he was shot in the head. Neither the students nor the thirty witnesses who saw the event had any doubt about what happened: the police had shot him. During the five days he lay agonizing in a hospital bed, the Coordinating Committee occupied the Barrio Clínicas, a student neighborhood. The barrio became a "Soviet," defended from the police with Molotov cocktails, stones, and some guns.[103] Although this was not its first occupation, this one showed an ideologically and politically diverse student movement united. The occupation also served as a display of soli-darity that the students had received from the local chapter of the CGT.[104] The alliance between students and workers was embodied in Pampillón. He was a twenty-four-year-old second-year student of aeronautical en-gineering who worked at the automobile factory Kaiser, where he acted as a delegate to the mechanics union. Without being an activist at the university, Pampillón went to the streets in the context of the military intervention. He sympathized with a Reformist group, but he was nonetheless a fervent Catholic. As he fought for his life, priests and Integralistas prayed, Integralistas and Reformists barricaded an entire neighborhood, and neighbors helped with food.[105] Students in Buenos Aires, La Plata, Tucumán, and Rosario mobilized when news of his death spread.[106]

Amid the extensive displays of grief after Pampillón's death, Córdoba's governor stated that he was "sorry for this one, and for the deaths that will come," thus showing how the Onganía regime at large was planning on coping with dissent. Yet Pampillón's death and especially the mobilization in which it had taken place also marked other crucial changes. First, the epicenter of student and labor organization was transferred from Buenos Aires to other major cities, where further political articulations crystallized, some of them around radicalizing Catholics. Second, for the first time in decades, the student groups shared the same situation with others "outlawed" in the political spectrum. For many students, it became apparent that there was not a solution for the "university problem" outside a "solution" for the "country's problem." That solution did not cut across Reformist ideals anymore. Student political radicalization, which had been an "issue of the few," actually began when Onganía sought to eradicate politics from the university.

▶ In 1965, student activists within the TAU produced a reflection on their "status." They claimed that, as students, they constituted a "marginal sector within the capitalist society" inasmuch as they were not "subservient to the system" to make their living. Moreover, they could be unattached to the social class to which they belonged by birth and had "more autonomy than the intellectuals to act politically." In a would-be generalized interpretation, the TAU activists conceived of their status as both marginal and empowered. From the vantage point of marginality vis-à-vis the class structure of Argentina, they thought it possible to cooperate with different segments of society—the working class and, to a lesser extent, the middle class—to become the vanguard of a bloc they envisioned as necessary to liberate the country from its "economic, social, and cultural dependency on the imperialist forces."[107] Out of the "transitory irresponsibility" that, according to Pierre Bourdieu, characterized the condition of youth and students, TAU activists cultivated a major responsibility: nothing less than becoming a vanguard for liberating the country.[108] They were, of course, a few activists who embodied the "radicalized student," a pervasive trope among the observers of the student world as the 1960s went on.

That world encompassed more than student politics, though. The student world connected broad sociocultural and political dynamics that at the same time expressed and contributed to the modernization Argentines underwent in the 1960s.

I have tried to grasp some aspects of that modernization by looking at the world of the secondary school and university students. To begin with, in the 1950s and 1960s, enrollment and matriculation at the secondary and university levels increased dramatically. The student world quantitatively expanded, and that expansion acted as an avenue for cultural modernization Argentines experienced in different realms. It was reflected, for example, in how power relations and authority were negotiated in many families. Drawing again on Bourdieu, most secondary and university students were "first generation" rather than "inheritors."[109] In a society that valued education as a privileged means of climbing the social ladder as well as showing sociocultural betterment, the "first generation" of secondary school and university students acquired a sense of empowerment vis-à-vis their parents and possibly a greater sense of mission and responsibility. These first-generation students embodied the resumption of longstanding projects of sociocultural advancement, now coded in terms of modernization.

The experience of school and college attendance, though, offers a unique glimpse at the ways the educational field reflected the ambivalence of sociocultural modernization. By looking at the example of the School of Humanities and Social Sciences at the UBA, an "extreme" modernizing case, I showed that the students who gained access actually participated in the process of academic renovation, theoretical discussions, and political activity. Equally important, they became the cornerstone of a broader cosmopolitan atmosphere that encompassed other spaces of sociability. In many accounts, the 1960s thrived in those areas and had that school's students as main protagonists. That "modern spirit" nonetheless had its limits, as the Correas affair shows. In the larger educational context, which includes the secondary level, those limits were even more prominent. The secondary schools had nothing in common with the School of Humanities and Social Sciences that epitomized the 1960s. Rather, the secondary schools remained largely tied to old pedagogical styles and goals, marked by what was known as "encyclopedic authoritarianism." The rigidity of the school system sharply contrasted with the emergence of a burgeoning youth culture. In fact, as many protested, the secondary school students underwent a "double life," as youths and as students. It is not surprising that ever-increasing numbers of secondary school students criticized the school and the routines it entailed. It is not surprising either that, when they saw a loophole, they actively participated in student politics.

The secondary school and the university students, however intermittently, loudly occupied the streets. In 1958, during the *laica-o-libre* episodes, students became crucial political actors. The governmental and congressional support to the *libres* came as a shocking surprise to the Reformist-oriented groups. In fact, the story that began in 1958 and ended in 1966, in this respect, was the story of the demise of Reformism as the organizing principle of most student political activity. At the universities, Reformism continuously split between rightwing—or moderate—and left-wing factions. As the 1960s continued, the left-wing student activists participated—and ultimately were protagonists of—debates that cut across the Left regarding the reevaluation of Peronism; the desirability of a cross-class, anti-imperialist bloc; and the viability of the "Cuban road" toward revolutionary change. Gradually less willing to cooperate with a university modernizing project that the student activists regarded as "pro-imperialistic" in its alleged scientificism and more committed to building new alliances, the new student movement left the Reformist and non-Reformist, lay and Catholic, and Peronist and anti-Peronist divides behind. Composed of the "active few" in most national universities, the new student movement was publicly encapsulated in the figure of the "radicalized student." Catholic and military ideologues, the media, and politicians from divergent political parties: they all increasingly projected onto that figure the fears of a "Communist infiltration" that jeopardized the university and the country alike. Endowing itself with the task of "dismantling the state of subversion and the factors that sought to transform the universities into foci of public perturbation," the military that led the 1966 coup d'état put an end to the Reformist project within the universities.[110] The military paved the way for a much broader and more radical turn among the students of the era by discontinuing university autonomy and the tripartite government, exerting physical violence over professors and students, and attempting to make the university—and more broadly, the educational spaces—centers for fostering a "Christian and Occidental personality."[111]

3 ▶ Surfing the New Wave

MUSIC, LEISURE, AND CONSUMPTION

In February of 1963, Argentina's oldest women's magazine, *Para Ti*, published a test for its readers to determine whether they belonged to the *nueva ola*, or "new wave." The test asked the readers, among other questions, whether they preferred dancing to the twist and listening to rock more than other musical styles, going out in peer groups rather than with just a couple of friends, and wearing blue jeans and sweaters instead of skirts and blouses. If the responses were positive, the reader belonged to the "new wave," which was "healthy and normal" for those under twenty-two years old.[1] Doubtless, most young women and men under that age would have responded positively to that test: they had become "new wavers." The term "new wave," in fact, began to spread to the journalistic and popular vocabulary by the early 1960s. Perhaps as a translation of the French expression *nouvelle vague*, the "new wave" label was applied to the new musical styles, which were venues for the transformation of youth cultural consumption, leisure activities, and fashion. The term "new wave" signaled renewal and served as shorthand for the changes within an increasingly juvenilized mass culture that were crucial markers of the sociocultural modernization Argentines underwent in the 1960s.

This chapter reconstructs the emergence of that "new wave" by focusing on the spread of youth-led music, leisure practices, and consumption. These realms became pivotal to the ways in which young people constructed a sense of generational belonging at the time they erupted, as youth, into the public arena. Secondary school and university students, working young women and men: they all participated in leisure and consumption practices that were exclusively youthful, and that helped juvenilize mass culture—a phenomenon that echoed similar developments worldwide and that signaled the transnational character of youth consumption.[2] However, in their consumption and leisure practices young people also built up a renewed, class-inflected sense of cultural distinction. The territory of a juvenilized mass culture was the social space where—drawing on Pierre Bourdieu—the groups that engaged competed for the definition of taste, as it related to music idols, sites of entertainment, or fashion items, such as blue jeans.[3] While looking at this competition in a juvenilized mass culture, we will discuss some of the prevailing accounts of the history of youth in its connection to consumption. By focusing on the creation of a "youth-led market" in Europe and the Americas in which youths from all social strata engaged, scholars have tended to sidestep a thorough evaluation of the ways in which consumption practices served to enact and reshape distinctions among young people.[4] Those dynamics complicate any understanding of "youth culture" as a homogeneous category.

Let's Dance

In February of 1957, *La Razón* informed its readers that rock had already achieved "Argentine citizenship." The reporter portrayed the first dance contest at the Luna Park stadium; depicted the winning couple as composed of two "*criollo*-type youths"; and acidly asked what "the people in their *pagos* [the interior provinces] would say if they knew their children were abandoning traditions."[5] The report touched on several traits of the arrival of rock in Argentina: it came as a dancing practice, it was embraced by young people, and it incited anxieties related to the lost of "tradition." Rock, as a cultural form, initially cut across class and gender lines to help youths construct a sense of generational belonging and connect their cultural consumption to youths worldwide. As in other settings, in Argentina rock sparked vociferous reactions related to the dangers it allegedly posed to the sexuality of youth and to the national cultural fabric alike. This opposition emerged from different cultural and political sites—state officers, Catholic groups, and left-wing parties—and routinely surfaced in the public arena, but could not diminish the pervasiveness of rock among youths, favored by the tolerance of parents and fueled by the culture industry.

Like in the United States, rock gained full access to the Argentine cultural milieu through movies.[6] Historians of rock have singled out *Blackboard Jungle* (dir. Richard Brooks, 1955) as pivotal to inciting the rock furor, since Bill Haley's "Rock around the Clock" played over its opening credits. The movie helped introduce rock music while connecting it to the worrisome behavior of the working-class schoolboys, whose relationship with the "heroic" white teacher is the crux of the movie. It was followed by a series of cheaply produced, teenage-led movies known as teenpics, which depicted a much more candid world of rock where boys and girls—mostly middle-class and white—claimed their right to enjoy themselves through dancing or singing.[7] Rock teenpics flooded into the Argentine theaters at a time of change in the movie business. In January of 1957, state officers discontinued regulations that, passed during the Peronist governments, had restricted the release of foreign movies in order to promote the local industry. In that year, 701 foreign movies were screened, 397 of which were American-made—including *Rebel without a Cause* (dir. Nicholas Ray, 1955).[8] Perhaps because of the expansion of the offerings, 1957 marked a record in attendance: at the 206 movie theaters in Buenos Aires alone, 75 million tickets were sold.[9] Youths were the most assiduous moviegoers. While Argentines went to the movies seven times a year on average, youths went fifty times.[10]

The screening of rock teenpics initiated the rock furor and also the first reactions against it. During the summer of 1957, youths were known to dance in the aisles and on the seats in movie theaters. Just a month after the first releases, moviegoers found that their "frenetic dances" would not be allowed. In Buenos Aires, the owner of the Ambassador Theater called in the police to stop the dancing. A group of youths opposed to the decision were expelled from the theater but kept dancing on the streets and chanting against the police. As a result, three were detained and charged with police edicts of vagrancy and resistance to authority. At the entrance of the Normandie Theater, some blocks away, twenty-five couples danced after the screening of Will Price's *Rock, Rock, Rock*. There the police accused them of interrupting traffic and took them to the police station. Similar scenes occurred in Córdoba, Mendoza, and Bahía Blanca.[11] In this last city, too, an "anti-rock" group (supposedly composed of tango fans) provoked the wrath of dancers by interrupting a contest at a social club while shouting that "rock is a degenerate form of music" and calling rockers "a degeneration of humanity."[12]

The ideas of degeneration and moral disorder shaped the criticism rock received in its early days, culminating in the prohibition of public dancing in Buenos Aires. In late February of 1957, presumably pressured by the Catholic Leagues of Mothers and Fathers, the mayor issued a decree that prohibited dancing "through exaggerated contortions that affect the normal development of dance meetings, or in ways that could affect morals, or when it generates collective hysteria."[13] The mayor's decision reenacted a long-standing approach to music in general, and dancing in particular. As musicologist Susan McClary has noted, Western thought has long maintained a hierarchical dichotomy of mind and body, and music was usually associated with the "lowest" side. From Plato onwards, she asserts, music and its promise of opening up new bodily practices were conceived of as a locus of sexual and cultural disorders.[14] In late 1950s Buenos Aires, that tradition manifested itself in the fears of collective "hysteria" and contortions that "affected morals." Yet it bears noting that these feelings pointed to what was becoming a youth practice par excellence. Argentines had long performed "sensual dances" (tango, of course, and Caribbean rhythms such as mambo and cha-cha-cha were very popular also in the 1950s), but even when it took time for them to gain respectability, no decree had been issued to prohibit them. In contrast to the United States or Germany, where rock awoke fears of "sexual miscegenation" and social disorder that might be incited by black, African, working-class rhythms, in Argentina race and class worries went unmentioned.[15] Rock stirred concerns about the perils of overt sexuality and the defiant attitudes it generated among youth.

Youths indeed challenged the enforcement of the municipal decree by claiming what they perceived as their right to enjoy themselves. At least one hundred youths launched themselves into the streets after viewing Fred Sears's *Don't Knock the Rock*, a teenpic that, besides showing Little Richard perform "Long Tall Sally" and "Tutti Frutti," tells the story of rock's triumph over conservatives in a small American town who tried to prohibit live rock acts but were bested by youths, helped by rock promoter Allan Freed. Possibly identifying with their peers on screen, the young moviegoers symbolically took over the plaza surrounding the Obelisk, the central landmark of the City of Buenos Aires, and just danced.[16] Interviewed by a daily, three "rioters" that had spent the night in a police station stated that they liked dancing and doing what "youths do everywhere." When asked what they found so persuasive in rock, they responded that they enjoyed "the feeling, the movement: it is rapid, it is new." They did not think of abandoning other dancing practices; instead, they wanted to take advantage of a rhythm that was their own.[17] The "rioters" avoided any politicized criticism of the mayor's decree. Instead, they focused on their claim to take pleasure from music and dance that they conceived of as uniting them with their peers abroad. They implied that, like the conservatives in the movie they had just seen, the mayor was outdated. In fact, popular and women's magazines concurred. As one magazine asserted, rock was a "harmless fashion for today's youth." Endorsing the idea that certain childrearing practices led toward greater familial understanding, these magazines suggested parents tolerate their children's leisure options and, in doing so, helped to "familiarize" rock.[18]

A growing segment of the culture and entertainment industries attained a prominent role in making rock "familial" and respectable. Multinational and local companies collaborated to create a circuit of distribution, promotion, and production of rock in the second half of the 1950s. The subsidiary of Radio Corporation of America (RCA)—which had operated in the country since 1931—imported or locally pressed rock records in its catalogue, including Elvis Presley's, and Coral, the distributor Decca Records, imported Bill Haley's singles. Meanwhile Escala Musical—a local firm created in 1954—promoted rock music on its television and radio programs as well as within the network of dances it organized in social clubs. In its programming, Escala Musical integrated rock and other dancing styles—from rumba to tango—and addressed the novelty to the young *in* the family.[19] This strategy resulted from two challenges the entrepreneurs faced. First, they strove to remove any linkage of rock to disorder by making of it a "familial" musical style. Second, although the offering of recorded rock was guaranteed, the entrepreneurs did not find enough local talent to make all-rock dances at a time when syndicated musicians exerted pressure to have live acts in every dance hall.[20] The solution was to find local rockers.

Between 1957 and 1960, a first wave of rockers emerged in Argentina: they poured into the dance halls and the radio stations, sometimes selling more than the American artists they covered in English or Spanish versions. This was a common occurrence in other countries as well, from Mexico to France.[21] In Argentina, Eddie Pequenino and Billy Cafaro (whose Spanish cover of Paul Anka's "Pity, Pity" sold 300,000 copies in 1960) acquired celebrity status. Pequenino's story is worth telling because it resembles others and illustrates how multinational firms changed their business strategies to adapt to and shape the local markets. Pequenino, son of a lower-middle-class Italian family, developed a passion for jazz: he was a trombonist and, by the mid-1950s, had achieved some recognition while playing with the orchestra of Lalo Schiffrin. As a way of making a living, Pequenino switched to rock.[22] To this end, he created his own band, Mr. Roller y sus Rockers, and signed a contract with a subsidiary of Columbia Broadcasting System (CBS) to produce a record with covers of Bill Haley, like "See You Later Alligator," whose titles were translated into Spanish while the lyrics were not. Ironically, while in the late 1950s CBS did not produce rock 'n' roll records in the United States, in a peripheral setting like Argentina it was the first company to produce local rock talent.[23]

Cultural and entertainment entrepreneurs attempted to endow the local and international artists they promoted with a halo of youthfulness and a sense of sexual and cultural containment, of change within tradition. In that frame, Bill Haley fit better than Elvis Presley. In May of 1958, Haley went to perform in Buenos Aires, an event for which Pequenino's combo served as supporting band. Hundreds of youths escorted Haley and his Comets throughout his visit. The tickets to his performances sold out quickly, and youths crowded the surrounding areas of the theater as well.[24] He was received as an idol for the entire family and chiefly for its youngest members. Haley's personal characteristics—he was thirty-two years old, married, and "straight" in terms of clothing and on-stage attitudes—had made him an unsuitable candidate to occupy the throne of rock in the United States, but the same traits opened the door to success in Argentina. A women's magazine interviewed Haley, who was quoted as saying that his only defect was "not to be able to be away from my family." Fanzines likewise portrayed Haley as a celebrator of other traditions: a cover of *Antena* showed him drinking mate and wearing a poncho.[25] With Haley there was nothing to be afraid of: he would help integrate Argentine youths into a transnational culture without jeopardizing family values or even breaking with national traditions.

Youths developed new leisure practices around rock while the media and entertainment made it an acceptable musical style for the young, *within* the family. Psychologists and educators expressed concern about the lack of leisure options available to youths and noted the declining attendance figures at sport clubs, church groups, or extracurricular activities at school. In a rather paternalistic way, some experts proposed that the government devote funding to create youth recreation programs.[26] They failed to recognize that when adult supervised leisure programs did exist— like the school clubs promoted by the Ministry of Education—youths avoided them, choosing instead to stay among peers in, for example, *barritas*—groups of boys and girls. In a roundtable, a boy explained that his barrita (composed of a dozen youths from nearby schools) did not accept "adult norms" and had "its own values and tastes."[27] The barritas were a visible novelty, mainly among the middle classes, becoming a major institution in the organization of youth sociability. Besides going together to the movies and bars, Mabel G. recalls that her barrita organized parties at private homes. The boys provided the beverages for those big house parties (called *asaltos*) and the girls handled the food. They all brought records, and Mabel pointed out that, almost invariably, these were rock records.[28] The *asaltos* were a frontier zone: they took place in family settings yet were controlled by youths, and the "lousy" rock served to keep adults away from the party.

While the private parties served to shape the leisure practices of middle-class boys and girls, other, older youths helped reconfigure public nightlife in the major cities. Beginning in the early 1950s, a series of nightclubs appeared on the northern banks of the Rio de la Plata, in upper-class neighborhoods relatively far away from downtown Buenos Aires. Those nightclubs attracted a youth audience endowed with enough spending power to purchase cars. Rather than rock, young women and men listened and danced to "authentic" jazz and Brazilian bossa nova. The press used to link these nightclubs to the "caves" in Paris or, with reference to Federico Fellini's 1960 movie, to a hedonistic and sensualistic lifestyle termed "Dolce Vita."[29] While only a small fraction of youths gathered in these nightclubs, they became highly visible. Besides the press, movies of the "Generation of 1960"—like David Kohon's *Tres veces Ana* (1961), or Rodolfo Kuhn's *Los jóvenes viejos* (1962)—used them as filming locations and helped make them the epitome of the revamping of sexual mores, since they suggested pre-marital sex and therefore the end of the "taboo" of female virginity until marriage. More immediately, though, these nightclubs expanded the sites available for youth leisure. By 1963, a report stated that adults had abandoned nightlife, which had become a youth territory.[30]

Just as stylish nightclubs and *asaltos* served to organize the weekend leisure of middle- and upper-middle-class youths and adolescents, social clubs acted as the sites of leisure for many working-class youths. Early in the twentieth century, the sports clubs and social clubs had become crucial components of social life in the neighborhoods of the largest cities. For a low fee, members had access to sports facilities, informal educational practices, and libraries. The social clubs also cemented local sociability by organizing kermises and family-oriented parties.[31] Although the 1930s and 1940s might have been the golden years of many clubs, the City of Buenos Aires still registered 560 clubs in 1964.[32] Since these clubs attracted working-class youths—mainly as sports practitioners—the FJC (Communist Youth Federation) insisted that its members affiliate with them and claimed, in 1964, to have active members at 250 clubs in Buenos Aires. The FJC's leaders conceived of the clubs as an arena where Communists could help offset the "decadent cultures of rock 'n' roll," which they identified as a way through which "*yanqui* imperialism" acted to "colonize youth's minds."[33] Ironically, the social clubs had redefined themselves as the primary locus of youths' rock-based leisure, becoming fully integrated into a circuit dominated by Escala Musical and the music business.

In the triennium 1960–62, the combination of changing economic policies and expansion of multinational firms resulted in an unparalleled growth of the record industry. During Arturo Frondizi's government (1958–62), the development of basic industries—iron, steel, and oil—in order to avoid dependence on foreign supply became an urgent task. Frondizi and his aides thought it vital to attract foreign investment to finance the industrial takeoff and, to that end, in 1959 Congress passed a new law that benefited foreign companies by cutting their taxes and allowing them to remit more of their revenue to their home countries. Coupled with that regulation, the country faced a sharp trade-balance crisis in 1959 and again in 1962. To combat the imbalance they limited all imports not essential to industrial production.[34] Records were part of the nonessential imports. In this context, the U.S.-based firms already established in Argentina— RCA and CBS—began a sustained expansion. The welcoming conditions for foreign investment might have been key to CBS, which in 1959 chose Argentina as the location for record production for other South American markets (while Mexico served Central America and the Caribbean).[35] In 1961, moreover, CBS opened its new recording studios in Buenos Aires, which was the "most modern in Latin America."[36] The growth of RCA, by contrast, seemed modest, although it resulted in a major landmark for youth music: in mid-1960, RCA relocated its artist-and-repertoire man, Ricardo Mejía, from Mexico to Buenos Aires with the aim of launching a "new wave."[37]

The shaping of that "new wave" fueled the expansion of the record business. Although complete data do not exist for this time period in Argentina, the available information suggests that 1961 marked the takeoff: while in 1960 record sales reached $6.7 million, in 1961 they rose to $9 million.[38] That rise might be attributed in part to the substantial introduction of simple (i.e., two-sided vinyl) records and, largely, to business strategies of the companies that shaped that "new wave." When he arrived in Buenos Aires, Mejía began his search for "talent"—an endeavor that bore fruit some years later—targeted at young people because they were the niche market for increased record sales.[39] The growth of record sales went hand in hand with the increase of sales of record players. In 1961 there were fourteen firms producing record players using foreign licenses. Yet it was a local firm, Winco, that dominated the local market and exported to South America as well. Its success came when it launched its automatic record player, Wincofón. While its ads at first targeted a family audience, they soon began to address youth: a Christmas ad in 1961 showed a boy and a girl claiming their Wincofón. In 1962, an ad read simply: "Wincofón is twist-tested."[40]

The twist was not the only newcomer to the musical landscape in 1962, nor was it the most successful: folkloric music seemed to win the battle against the twist. The engagement of young people with folklore helps explain the heyday that music enjoyed in the early 1960s. Folkloric music— a label that covered several rhythms—made solid in-roads among urban audiences. Its progress was helped by mass migrations from the interior provinces to the cities. Beginning in the 1930s and accelerating during the Peronist years, the entertainment sites that attracted the recent migrants to Buenos Aires were conduits for the expansion of folkloric music and dances, while radio and movies publicized folkloric artists and the government amplified a perceived relation between folklore and nationhood through its diffusion at schools. Folkloric music was well suited for collective singing, and educational authorities promoted the creation of school choruses.[41] In 1961, though, while secondary school students avoided engaging in the chorus contests organized by the Directorate of Secondary Education, they participated en masse in singing contests on a television show.[42] In that year, also, RCA signed a contract with Los Chalchaleros, a prominent band that, by February of 1962, shared top chart rankings with Chubby Checker, the "king of twist."[43] Folklore's preeminence can be seen beyond record sales. In 1962, *La Razón* informed its readers that the local supply of guitars was insufficient to meet the increasing demand fueled by youths. To the reporter, the conclusion was simple: folklore had won the war against twist by winning the favor of the new generation of Argentines.[44]

It is possible that a twist-versus-folklore war never existed, yet the way in which both musical styles resonated with young people elucidates some traits of the relationship between youth and music. First, as three girls interviewed in 1962 pointed out, they could sing folklore and dance the twist: there was no incompatibility between the two.[45] Many youths negotiated their use of popular music in a situational fashion: depending on where they were or when it was, they could switch among different musical styles. While many made use of rock 'n' roll and the twist to build up purely youthful leisure practices, other youths enjoyed folkloric singing. Second, while a significant segment of youths navigated the choices among rock/twist and folklore, others rejected what they perceived to be "foreign rhythms" out of anti-*yanqui* sentiments. The FJC, for example, insistently endorsed folklore as the most suitable music for youths' leisure time.[46] Extreme as they were, the FJC's stances surely reverberated among unaffiliated youths as well. Finally, in contrast to other Latin American settings, the record industry soon attempted to "localize" rock/twist as it shaped the youth market. While in Mexico, as historian Eric Zolov has shown, rock was contained by producing songs in Spanish after some initial years of "cultural disruption," in Argentina that containment was carried out by integrating rock into a series of other dancing or singing rhythms.[47] Rock/twist not only was geared to the young members of the family, it also did not conflict with "tradition." That double integration enabled the immense success of *El Club del Clan*.

El Club del Clan and the Struggles over Cultural Taste

In the second week of March of 1964, Ramón "Palito" Ortega, age twenty-three, performed on six television shows and at eighteen social clubs, news on him occupied more than seven thousand column inches in newspapers and fanzines (including six covers), his songs were broadcast nine hundred times on the radio, and he received a thousand letters from fans.[48] Observers were shocked by the success that Ortega and other singers on the television program *El Club del Clan* had achieved: they had completely flooded the mass media with their images. Mass culture had become juvenilized as the 1960s went on, and the sounds, images, and styles deployed in the enlarged media landscape conveyed youthfulness and sweetened optimism. By no means was it a local phenomenon; rather, it was part of an increasingly transnational repertoire of youth-based cultural consumption. In Argentina, the juvenilization of mass culture and *El Club del Clan* as the incarnation of a "new wave" of idols and fans served as the main reference points for the first systematic criticisms of the culture industry and its supposedly alienating effects. Journalists, filmmakers, and a plethora of other observers likewise projected onto the young idols and fans anxieties related to the "masses." Equally important, criticism of the "new wave" was the territory on which struggles over cultural taste occurred.

Promoted by RCA, the youth ensemble performing on the television program *El Club del Clan* was instrumental to the juvenilization process. The story of that ensemble dates back to 1960, when RCA's executive Mejía arrived in Argentina to search for "young talent." In 1962, Mejía had already chosen a dozen youths, changed their names, and shaped their personas to mold them into a clan of "happy youth."[49] The clan aimed to represent a microcosm of the Argentine youth and their musical tastes. For example, "Tanguito" Cobian sang tangos; Chico Novarro and Raul Lavié sang tropical rhythms and boleros; and Jolly Land, the "Americanized young woman," sang pop songs. Violeta Rivas, for her part, performed translations of Italian pop songs, while Johny Tedesco sang rock and did the twist, and Palito Ortega, the representative of "the interior provinces," sang boleros, folkloric music, and performed the twist. *El Club del Clan*, broadcast from late 1962 to late 1963, achieved unprecedented ratings. It bears noting that, while in countries like France the diffusion of youth music had radio programs and magazines (like *Salut les copains*) at its epicenter, in Argentina it was television that paved the way for the youth explosion.[50] The difference might be partly explained by the pervasiveness of television in Argentina. In 1964 Argentina there were 68 sets per 1,000 inhabitants, while in France there were 53, in Mexico, 33, and in Brazil, 29.[51] Most fundamentally, as media historian Mirta Varela has shown, local television had begun to produce a "modernizing façade" that went hand in hand with the representation of the "modern family" as a site where the generational gap, as a marker of renewal, was represented as a low-intensity conflict.[52] *El Club del Clan* fit within and contributed to that framework: it conveyed a sense of cultural renewal around the young "idols," represented intergenerational conflict in terms of musical styles, and solved the quandary by integrating—as entrepreneurs did—rock/twist, the music for the young *within* the family, into a continuum of local and international rhythms.

El Club del Clan became the center of a network of records, radio programs, fanzines, and movies. In 1963, RCA launched three LPs that compiled the songs performed on the television show. As a marketing strategy, the retail price of the LPs was reduced to one-fourth that of the average album, which resulted in one million copies being sold.[53] The firm also launched the most successful soloists in the local and regional markets: Ortega's records, for example, were on the top of the Mexican, Peruvian, and Chilean charts in 1964 when his albums constituted 50 percent of the record sales of RCA in Latin America.[54] In Argentina, as a result of the television show and its soloists' success, the records of "domestic origin" jumped from 60 percent of the total sold in 1962 to 75 percent in 1963.[55] These records permeated the radio airwaves as well. At least six radio programs, broadcasting fifteen hours per day in Buenos Aires, concentrated on youth music in 1964.[56] Those sounds were reinforced by the omnipresent images of El Club del Clan's singers: fanzines like *Antena*—the most widely read—carried interviews and pictures, while its publisher launched *Nuevaolandia* to target the fans of the "new wave." Fans also had the chance to watch two films, *El Club del Clan* (1964) and *Fiebre de primavera* (1965), both directed by Enrique Carreras.

What were the traits of *El Club del Clan* as a text that navigated through and juvenilized mass culture? It was a music-based, youth-led text that celebrated contained fun, youth as a value per se, and family life. Whether twists or boleros, the songs were meant for dancing rather than listening. In contrast to what was perceived about rock in its early days, the performers on stage danced in an orderly fashion that suggested a controlled enjoyment. Other elements of their body language reinforced the conveyance of fun: with the exception of Palito Ortega, they *always* smiled. Why did they smile? The song "Qué suerte" (How Lucky) gives some clues,

Qué suerte que tengo	Luckily I have
Una madre tan buena	Such a good mother
Que siempre vigila	That always looks after
Mi ropa y mi cena.	My clothing and dinner.
Qué suerte mi padre	How lucky, my father
Callado y sereno,	So quiet and serene
Qué suerte saberlo	How lucky, I know he is
Tan justo y tan bueno.	So just and so kind.
Qué suerte el amor.	How lucky, love.
Qué suerte la escuela.	How lucky, the school.
Qué suerte que esta noche voy a verte.	How lucky, tonight I'll see you.[57]

"Qué suerte" could have been the anthem of El Club del Clan: it condenses sweetened optimism, reinforces traditional imagery surrounding gender roles (a caretaker mother, a quiet father who makes "just" decisions), celebrates romantic love (while concealing any reference to sexuality), erases perceptions of "rebellion," and does not challenge even the most questioned institution, the school. Written and composed by Palito Ortega and Chico Novarro, "Qué suerte" was performed by Violeta Rivas. She played the "girl next door" character who told everyone how lucky she was to be a girl in love. El Club del Clan promoted cultural conservatism, barely hidden by a patina of youth renewal. Unlike the sexualized imaginary that permeated the lyrics to the songs and the self-presentation of the youths of the Brazilian ensemble La jovem guarda, and unlike the practical ques-

Shot from *El Club del Clan*, Palito Ortega. Museo del Cine Pablo Ducrós Hicken Archive.

tioning of conventional ideals of womanhood epitomized in the Italian Rita Pavone's notoriously androgyne figure, El Club del Clan delivered explicit mandates: conform to established gender roles and family values and "have fun"—in an orderly way.[58]

El Club del Clan also produced the framework for the emergence of particular young local celebrities: Ramón "Palito" Ortega occupied the center stage, perhaps because he projected the romance of hard work, upward mobility, and national integration. Initially, Ortega competed for popularity with Johny Tedesco, whose youth image reverberated in his clothing and his performed musical styles, the twist and rock.[59] Ortega prevailed in the popular preference despite the predictions of RCA. Music producers explained afterward that Ortega sang better and composed his own songs: he was, in their view, a popular creator.[60] Plausible as it might be, this explanation circumvents the fact that Ortega's larger appeal consisted of the ways in which the interweaving of his artistic persona and life story resonated in the public milieu. As repeated in countless interviews, the Ortegas lived in a sugar mill in Tucumán province, where the father worked as an electrician and the kids labored as newspaper sellers or cane cutters. Ortega migrated to Buenos Aires at the age of fifteen, where he worked in badly paid jobs and used his sparse free time to learn the drums and guitar. The tale of humble origins and hard work intersects with an extra element: RCA "discovered" Ramón, baptized him Palito, and allowed him to display his artistic virtues.[61] The tale re-created ingrained ideas of success through popular music. In contrast to the old tango idols' stories, however, Ortega's narrative began by emphasizing that he represented the "unprivileged interior provinces" rather than Buenos Aires.[62] While *El Club del Clan* integrated the young within the *family*, Ortega promised to unite the *nation* under the banner of popular (i.e., youth) music.

At the same time that Ortega consolidated his popularity, other "young talent" emerged and produced controversy. For example, Roberto Sánchez—aka Sandro—shaped his public persona along sexualized rather than romantic lines and so tested the limits of what was permissible in the juvenilized mass culture of the early 1960s. Sandro was the son of a working-class family in Greater Buenos Aires who soon developed a fascination for rock music, and particularly for Elvis Presley. In 1963, when he was only eighteen years old, Sandro gained access to a record studio with "Los de Fuego"—a band from his neighborhood. Sandro invoked ideas of passion and "disorder" both in musical and sexual terms. Sandro's style heavily borrowed from Marlon Brando's, including the use of leather jackets, cigarettes, and motorbikes. Fanzines used to depict Sandro as part of an "irascible youth [*juventud iracunda*]" and contrasted his persona to Palito Ortega's.[63] While Sandro also gained access to social clubs and television programs, his style sometimes clashed with customary understandings of "manners and morals." In 1964, when performing in one of the most widely viewed television programs of the decade, Sandro danced, making contortions that the producers dubbed "obscene." Sandro was dismissed from the program and soon thereafter relaunched his career as an admittedly sexy ballad singer, becoming famous throughout Latin America in the early 1970s. One decade before, though, his was an uncomfortable presence in the juvenilized mass culture dominated by *El Club del Clan*.

The idols of *El Club del Clan*, and mainly Palito Ortega, instigated an unprecedented growth of fans. As media scholar Cornel Sandvoss put it, "fandom" refers to the "regular, emotionally involved consumption of a given popular text."[64] Who were the fans of the "new wavers" and how was the consumption of the text, or idols, shaped? In sociodemographic terms, journalists pointed out that "Palito's kingdom" reached working-class and lower-middle-class neighborhoods across the country.[65] However, not all fans engaged in the same level of involvement. Ricardo, a former working-class boy from Lanús, recalls that he purchased records, watched television shows, and went to live shows as much as he could because he "liked dancing."[66] Ricardo "liked the new wave," invested money and time in following his idols, but was mostly interested in the opportunity to have fun. Others related to the idols in a more committed fashion, as in the case of the participants of fan clubs. While some boys took part, the clubs chiefly appealed to girls, who exchanged pictures and records. The girls of Johny Tedesco's club, in addition, went so far as to hold knitting sessions to provide their idol with the sweaters he wore.[67] While they shaped a community—something that perhaps allowed many to outwit the continuum of home and school, or home and job—these girls built their fandom practices by drawing on deep-rooted notions of femininity. As the mother of the song "Qué suerte," the girls "took care of the clothes" of Johny, who many fantasized about as their boyfriend. All in all, the girls and boys (like Ricardo) did not subvert the messages of having fun and conformed to traditional gender roles and family values that *El Club del Clan* forcefully endorsed.

Perceived as an unparalleled occurrence, the sweeping visibility of the singers of *El Club del Clan* and their fans awoke reactions across the political and cultural fields. Left-wing militants and cultural critics underscored the perils the "new wave" presented to any revolutionary project. As had happened since rock's early days, Communist youths worried about the imperialist menace over the younger generation of workers, whom they conceived of as the ultimate target of their activism. The "U.S.-dominated" music industry, television, and advertising agencies, an observer pointed out, had created a "poison termed *new wave*" that threatened to make youth drowsy.[68] A young letter writer further asserted that the "new wavers" represented "the screen that the oligarchy needs to dominate the country," although he remained confident about the youths: "They will resist: boys and girls will keep their pants on [*se pondrán los pantalones*] and no new wavers will prevent them from doing so."[69] Left-wing cultural critics, for their part, were not so convinced of the possibilities of resisting the "new wave." In one of the most widely read essays of the 1960s, Juan José Sebreli mapped out the daily habits of different social classes. When discussing the middle class, Sebreli reckoned that the "new wave" had positive effects: the vigorous celebration of youth it promoted, he asserted, served to split ingrained patriarchal norms. When his analysis centered on the working class, the positive effects vanished. Working-class youths, he asserted, seemed to be only interested in "twist dancing," and he feared the "alienating effects" of such texts as *El Club del Clan* might have on them.[70]

Rodolfo Kuhn's third movie, *Pajarito Gómez, una vida feliz* (1965), brought the relation between the "new wave" and cultural alienation to center stage.[71] *Pajarito Gómez* tells the story of the creation of a popular idol. The story begins with an interview where the idol's biography is invented to fit a tale of humble origins and hard work, which is meant to mimic Ortega's story. When a journalist—paid by the record company—asks him about his childhood, the idol recalls his house in a slum and the mistreatment he received at home, yet those memories are just the visual binding of the sequence: the overlapping aural binding is the journalist's voice, who notes, "So, he grew up in a poor, cheerful home; his mother and teacher were his first loves; he liked singing as a *pajarito* [little bird]. Pajarito Gómez, a happy life." The idol loses his name, his biography, and his agency: he becomes an "industry" puppet. The "industry" invents a romance with a female "new wave" singer and organizes a contest among fans whose prize is to spend twelve hours with the idol. The chosen fan—a girl from a provincial town—finds that talking with the idol is impracticable beyond clichés. In his only display of "agency," he attempts to rape her, which acts as a reinforcement of her disillusion. That Pajarito cannot transcend the "machinery" is confirmed when he dies in a train crash. His death is still another chance for the "industry" to make profits. Equally important, the movie's final sequence shows how fans react to Pajarito's death. At his funeral, hundreds of youths cry, until one decides that the best way of paying homage to him is dancing, and they all end up dancing the twist around the corpse.

The movie built on and amplified broader discussions over the so-called machinery that produced, manipulated, and alienated idols and fans alike. Most reports on *El Club del Clan*, certainly, centered on the production of popular idols and on the profits that producers and agents made in that process.[72] *Pajarito Gómez* nonetheless went beyond unraveling the idol-side of the story. Director Kuhn and scriptwriter Francisco Urondo argued that they tried to show how "pseudo-artistic forms" were deployed to "alienate people."[73] An entire tradition of thought on modern culture reverberated in Kuhn and Urondo's authorial intentions, notably the theses set forth in Theodor Adorno and Max Horkheimer's *Dialectic of Enlightenment* (1944), which pointed out the alienating and totalitarian effects of what they termed the "culture industry" under monopoly capitalism. The book, though, had not been translated into Spanish, and the concept of culture industry was not in use in the early 1960s, before most sociologists and cultural critics became interested in analyzing mass culture.[74] Yet it is probable that, like other intellectuals, Kuhn and Urondo were familiar with the work of other thinkers associated with the Frankfurt School—

such as Herbert Marcuse—who engaged with the problematic of alien-ation as well, and whose work was known in the country. In any case, as film critics pointed out, *Pajarito Gómez* was one of the first systematic critiques of mass culture in Argentina.[75] Throughout the course of its de-velopment, mass culture had become juvenilized. Talking about it thus meant talking about youth.

Pajarito Gómez and the commentary on the "new wave" employed gen-dered metaphors to represent idols and fans as "masses." The interpreta-tions of the "new wave" that focused on the machinery largely worked with the dichotomies between activity (the "industry") and passivity (malleable idols/fans), and between high ("true artistic," liberating forms) and low ("pseudo artistic," alienating forms). As cultural critic Andreas Huyssen has noted, beginning in the mid-nineteenth-century, mass culture had been conceptualized in terms of passivity and inferiority, thus endowing it with the attributes associated with the feminine.[76] In the Argentina of the early 1960s, the uses of that gendered language in referring to the "youth mass culture" intersected with other images. In the popular humor magazine *Tía Vicenta*, for example, the "new wave boy" was depicted as effeminate: he was devoid of the initiative to begin dating, was afraid of inviting girls to dance, and seemed to be interested only in clothes and haircuts.[77] Un-like other, more "virile" forms of popular music—such as tango—singers and fans of the youth-led music were described as feminine. That imag-ery was reinforced through the deployment of terms like "hysteria," a per-ceived feminine pathology. Thus, the disk jockeys that programmed "new wave" music on the radio were baptized "the fathers of hysteria," and the depictions of live shows were full of references to "scenes of sudden hys-teria."[78] As sociologist Joli Jensen has suggested, the portrayals of fandom are haunted by images of deviance, like the one of the hysterical crowd.[79] These portrayals related to the anxiety that the "masses" incited upon their eruption into the political and cultural arena, an anxiety now projected onto the "young masses."

The juvenilized mass culture became the terrain for the unfolding of battles over cultural taste, reverberating in a keyword: *mersa*. The term mersa entered the popular vocabulary in the mid-1950s to designate "people of the lowest condition," and was connected with marginal groups related to gambling or theft.[80] In the early 1960s, its usages shifted from these connections to become an adjective that qualified people and con-sumption practices considered in "bad taste." The magazine *Tía Vicenta*

(Aunt Vicenta) played a vital role in shaping the new meanings. As the editor Landrú recalled, he placed the word *mersa* in the context of upper-class youth characters, or *caqueros*, who used it to designate the "taste" of the lowest classes, and he aimed to make fun of both.[81] In 1964, Landrú included a column where two young upper-class sisters—María Belén and Alejandra—dictated what was "in" in fashion, nightclubs, cars, or music by providing details of brands or singers, along with an array of expressions that marked their class and cultural standing. More important, they also stipulated who or what was "out," or *mersa*. Violeta Rivas, her haircuts, and her clothes; Palito Ortega, his songs, and his gestures; the clubs where they performed; the girls that made up the fan clubs: they were all labeled *mersa*.[82] The term achieved such success that Landrú launched contests to choose the "ideal *mersa*," encouraging people to cast their vote: Ortega and Rivas were at top of the lists.[83] As a journalist noted, *Tía Vicenta*—which sold 400,000 issues weekly—had encouraged a scavenger hunt where "all want to find *mersa* clothes, words, and attitudes among their friends, but no one admits that they belong to that category."[84]

The ways in which the term *mersa* was used and disseminated signaled two concurrent dynamics. On the one hand, as in other contexts of rapid sociocultural change, humorists made this cultural fluidity visible by exaggerating it; they also attempted to grasp cultural novelties through the invention of new labels. The term *mersa* was loaded with derogatory meanings, indicating the ways in which the upper and middle classes elaborated their distinction vis-à-vis what they envisioned as "plebeian" cultural practices in a fast-changing mass culture. On the other hand, since mass culture had become juvenilized, the struggles over cultural taste were played out largely in the territory of youth cultural consumption. It was not accident that María Belén and Alejandra, in their early twenties, deemed *mersa* the practices of their generational peers. In *Tía Vicenta*, the example was "Mirna Delma," Maria Belén and Alejandra's sibling. She represented a "neighborhood girl" from the lower middle class, who tried to be sophisticated by using the language of romance novels and wore "inappropriate" clothing and colors. Further, she idolized Ortega, and when the "twist mood" had passed, she kept dancing it.[85] In its most common usage, then, the term *mersa* pointed to the attempts to set hierarchies within the class-inflected heterogeneity of youth cultural consumption.

By the mid-1960s, in musical terms, the heterogeneity of youth consumption was apparent and shifts were on their way. By 1965, record sales of the "new wavers" decreased and the successful soloists—Ortega and

Violeta Rivas—spent most of their time touring Latin America, renovating their repertoires to better fit into what was then called "melodic song."[86] At the same time, as almost everywhere else in the world, Beatlemania hit Argentina. This contributed to the making of a new aesthetics that sharply differed from the one previous pop idols endorsed. In fact, in some neighborhoods in Buenos Aires, Rosario, and Córdoba, passers-by could easily detect droves of young men who grew their hair longer and began to construct in bodily terms a more contesting attitude toward "manners and morals." Some of these long-haired young men had participated in the "new wave," though. Born to a family of musicians in Rosario, Félix Nebbia Corbacho—aka Litto Nebbia—came down to Buenos Aires with a neighborhood band in late 1963 to perform for the television program *Escala Musical*. In the same year Alberto Iglesias, aka Tanguito (1945–72), son to a working-class family from Caseros in the Greater Buenos Aires area, had recorded an LP of covers with a band called The Dukes. Neither of them had succeeded in the framework of the "new wave." Protagonists of a bohemia of long-haired young men hanging around downtown Buenos Aires, in 1967 they famously met and composed "La Balsa" (The Raft), which would be first anthem of the emergent rock culture. As I discuss in Chapter 5, that culture affirmed itself in opposition to the "new wave" (which does not preclude the fact that Nebbia and Tanguito participated in both of them).

The "new wave" had been at the center of deep changes of mass culture, of its criticisms, and of the struggles over cultural taste. *El Club del Clan*, as the epitome of the "new wave," became the face of a whole media ensemble that acquired a juvenilized façade and gave young idols and fans unprecedented visibility for the first time. The conformist "sweetened optimism" that *El Club del Clan* advocated also became a target for criticism fueled by left-wing militants and cultural critics who denounced the "imperialist menace" behind the movement and the perils of "cultural alienation" it represented. In fact, *El Club del Clan*—the "machinery" behind idols and fans—incited the first systematic criticism of mass culture at the time of its sweeping expansion and change. It was on the terrain of a juvenilized mass culture that new cultural struggles took place. The term *mersa* organized the struggle over cultural taste and served to address broader anxieties among the upper and middle classes regarding the shaping of their own cultural distinctions. The realm of "youth" fashion amplified these struggles.

Fashioning the "New Wave": *Vaqueros* or Blue Jeans?

Beginning in the mid-1950s, blue jeans—like rock music—came to epito-mize youth in Argentina (and in most places in the West). As sociologist Fred Davis has asserted, dress acts as a visual metaphor for identity and for noting the culturally anchored ambivalences that resonate among and within identities.[87] In Argentina, jeans were the first dress item worn ex-clusively by youths, who increasingly dressed differently from the older generation. The jeans, though, served also to signal and reinforce distinc-tions among youth. Jean styles, brands, and "nationalities" were subtle venues for elaborating and displaying intragenerational differences, some-thing that was codified in the opposition between (local) *vaqueros* and (imported) jeans and that added one more layer to the disputes between *mersas* and *caqueros*. One crucial difference, however, was that until the late 1960s young women were not important consumers of jeans, but they nonetheless found other ways of fashioning their "new wave-ness."

On September 1, 1958, *Clarín* carried a full-page ad. In capitalized let-ters and boldface the ad announced: "Far West has arrived." The ad stated that the "authentic *vaquero*" was a "joyful, durable" item and informed its readers that it could be worn "at home, to go to the club, and even to go to work." A drawing of jumping, doubtlessly masculine legs with rolled-up *vaqueros* dominated the ad, conveying a sense of dynamism and youthful-ness. It targeted the pants to working- and middle-class young men inas-much as it emphasized still another trait of the new item: it was cheap.[88] Although promoted as an American good and endowed with an American label, the Fábrica Argentina de Alpargatas locally produced the Far West *vaqueros*. The company was one of the largest textile factories in Argentina and produced the slipper-like, rustic shoes—*alpargatas*—worn by rural workers.[89] In the early 1950s, perhaps to emulate the original use of blue jeans in the United States, the company began to produce denim fabric in a failed attempt to provide rural workers with pants. A chance to use the denim appeared in 1957, when the rock teenpics began to make their way into Argentina and showed the potential of creating and exploiting a market other than rural workers. In relaunching denim pants, the com-pany had the support of the local representatives of the oldest advertising agency in the United States, J. Walter Thompson.[90] In 1957, Thompson helped Alpargatas's executives choose a label with American resonances and target a new market: young men.[91]

Until working-class young men dared to wear the jeans—in fact, *vaque-*

ros—their clothing and that of their middle-class counterparts largely replicated their parents' dress code. As in many other Western countries at that time, boys experienced a rite of passage to adulthood when they achieved the right to wear long pants, preferably suits. Although psychologists such as Eva Giberti began to advise parents that the rite needed to be rethought in an era when boys wanted to be adolescents before becoming adults, the tradition persisted.[92] The jeans came to break with that tradition as well as with intergenerational dressing codes: it made visible an age that was neither that of a child nor an adult but a young person. Working-class boys were the vanguard of *vaquero* consumers. Carlos, a former working-class youth from the Greater Buenos Aires area, for example, still remembers when and how he purchased his first pair. "I was fifteen or sixteen," Carlos said, "and I was paid 250 pesos per week as an apprentice in Campomar [a local textile factory], so I gave 150 pesos to my family, kept 70 as pocket money, and could only save 30 per week. A vaquero cost almost 350 pesos. I didn't go to the movies or to soccer matches for a while, but I had my vaqueros at the end." His detailed memoirs reveal that Carlos is still proud of having purchased his first Far West as he did, by saving from his meager salary as an apprentice. When I asked why he put so much effort into getting those *vaqueros*, Carlos simply said, "To think I only had those old grey pants; with the *vaqueros* you felt like a new person."[93] For working-class young men, like Carlos, the new pants conveyed a sense of renewal. As it happened with rock music, wearing them was a venue for connecting the consumption of Argentine youths with their peers abroad. At the same time, however, that consumption awoke stigmatizing reactions.

Representations of *vaquero* consumers blended sociocultural and sexual anxieties. In one of the few studies of a "gang" in the Greater Buenos Aires area, for example, one sociologist focused on its members' self-presentation, which included "an exhibition of their virility on the street corners, wearing their ever-tighter *vaqueros*." In this study, as in others around the world, the sociologist linked jeans consumption to ideas of social and sexual disorder.[94] This was also apparent in other representations of young men in jeans. In the popular film *La patota* (dir. Daniel Tinayre, 1960), a group of men, all of whom wear jeans, rape a young female teacher when she arrives at the working-class neighborhood where they live. While, in this representation, *vaquero* consumers were depicted as committing sexual violence, in others they were linked to homosexuality. One of the first surveys of the gay scene in Buenos Aires, for example, stated that "homosexuals assume the same styles of present-day irascible youths [*jóvenes iracundos*]: blue jeans and white shirts, to the point that it is extremely hard to distinguish them from each other."[95] Leftist writer David Viñas, for his part, coined the expression "Marlon Brando category" to refer to working-class boys who hung around "tightening their *bluyíns* [blue jeans], waiting to sell their ass to the best payer."[96] The "Brando boys" who exhibited their bodies to conquer other men constituted, in Viñas's view, plebeian sexual deviants who contributed to bringing the moral hypocrisy of a bourgeois society to the surface. In any case, *vaqueros* metonymically evoked working-class boys, depicted as socially and sexually threatening.

By 1963–64, however, American jeans had begun to make in-roads into Argentina, and the local market expanded by incorporating new consumers. Jeans made by Lee and Levi Strauss became particular luxuries: they were imported in small lots, sold on the most exclusive shopping streets, and priced four times higher than local brands.[97] The consumption of Levis or Lee jeans required a certain shopping expertise: first, to find them, and second, to determine their authenticity. Middle-class young people were developing such expertise and could afford imported brands. As the media reported, middle-class youths were increasing their consumption of consumer goods. Aside from records and record players, other products such as soft drinks were consistently targeted to young people. When Pepsi arrived in Argentina in 1961, it triggered an advertising "war" with the already established Coca-Cola. Pepsi created an advertising campaign with the slogan "To Live with the Pepsi Generation." Advertising agencies recognized the potential of the young consumer and began to conduct surveys to determine their tastes and choices.[98] In terms of clothing, though, their choices were already obvious: middle-class young men were expert "hunters" of Lee and Levis. A fifteen-year-old boy, for instance, reported that he regularly checked for the arrival of new "models" in a store whose name he refused to reveal to "keep the exclusivity." When asked how to distinguish imported jeans from locally made ones, he just answered, "You have to look at the rivets, and at the pockets."[99]

Alpargatas's executives reacted negatively to the suggestion that a "national" brand could not hope to reach a large segment of blue jean consumers. Although proud of having sold 902,405 pairs of Far West jeans in early 1966, Alpargatas asked its marketing and advertising agency, J. Walter Thompson, to conduct a survey to determine how to appeal to the blue-jean consumers who had never purchased a pair of *vaqueros*. Thompson's representatives conducted interviews with five hundred middle- and upper-middle-class young men to examine their consumption choices. When asked about their blue jean preferences, most judged the local *vaqueros* as "excessively blue, rustic, and tight" when compared with the "faded-blue, finely finished, and loose-fitted" Lee and Levis.[100] Targeting that segment, depicted as composed of "young men eager to succeed in life," the firm launched a second brand called Super Far West. Alpargatas paid for an unusually intense and original advertising campaign, but Super Far West was a fiasco: middle- and upper-middle-class young men did not even go to the retail stores to try the new brand.[101]

Wearing American brands of blue jeans was one of the ways middle- and upper-class young men signaled their distinctiveness (and is another example of the uses of "Americanness" within youth cultures). Through well-informed insight into fabrics, colors, and fittings, middle- and upper-class young men went far beyond technicalities: they appealed to aesthetic ideas of elegance and "good taste." When they did not even try *vaqueros*, they made apparent that, as noted by Pierre Bourdieu, "Tastes are perhaps first and foremost distastes, disgust provoked by the horror or the visceral intolerance (sick-making) of the taste of others."[102] They projected onto the *vaqueros* their intolerance of working-class boys' taste and elaborated a way of emphasizing distinctions. As many Latin Americans before and after them, middle- and upper-class youths in 1960s Argentina invested imports with attributes related to authenticity and cultural renewal.[103] Wearing an "authentic" pair of American jeans involved being indisputably included into an international youth culture, while neglecting that belonging to their generational peers that "only" wore national *vaqueros*. Hence, the experience of a peripheral setting, like Argentina, helps rethink an enduring consensus among scholars of 1960s youth. By studying European youth, scholars have suggested that what was new and seen as "typically American" in the 1950s—rock and jeans—became the repertoire of an internationalized youth culture in the 1960s.[104] When looking at the story of the blue jeans in Argentina, that statement could be only partially endorsed. When young men adopted and adapted jeans, the links to "America" had not blurred. The authenticity of American jeans became a sign by which to elaborate distinctions among young men.

Unlike young men, young women did have chances of differentiating their dressing practices from the ones of previous generations of women. On the eve of the 1960s, women's magazines suggested renovating the predominantly opaque colors of tailleurs, tricots, skirts, and dresses and incorporating instead pink, light-blue, and white for "girls age eighteen."

As the 1960s wore on, skirts became increasingly shorter and tighter, and their colors began to include orange and red, which some magazines depicted as the ideal for "dancing the twist and rock," first, and "the shake," afterward. Likewise, fashion advisers called for switching to natural fabrics, meaning basically wool and cotton.[105] The concept of "natural" became crucial to the advice related to haircuts and makeup as well. Whether short or long, advisers insisted that "eighteen-year-old women" should under no circumstances dye their hair, just brush it everyday; and similarly in relation to make up: just a fine line to underline the eyes, and pink, rather than red, lipstick.[106] By 1963 most magazines carried textile designs—taken from French or Italian catalogues—along with instructions on how to make them at home, a widespread practice among working-class and lower-middle-class families.

In the early 1960s, pants began to make their way among young women, yet formal and informal dress codes prevented many from wearing them regularly. In 1961, *Claudia* magazine interviewed men to gain their insights on "women in pants." They agreed that pants were "convenient" sometimes and that they were to be worn *solely* by young women. Women concurred: they argued that pants did not threaten the "feminine grace" of young women, if they were worn on the appropriate occasions.[107] The mayor of Rosario, José R. Araya, was harsher: he passed a decree prohibiting women from wearing pants on the streets, since it affected "morals and customs."[108] This was an extreme case (whose enforcement is difficult to assess), but other strict, national-level formal dress codes also prohibited girls from wearing pants in secondary schools. They also affected teachers at the primary school level, a profession chosen by many university students.[109] Working women in other occupations were not supposed to wear pants either. Manuals for female job seekers advised them not to attend a job interview wearing pants because "not even the humblest workshop would hire you."[110] Young women could only wear pants to perform leisure activities.

To a lesser degree, the dichotomy between *vaqueros* and blue jeans also served to signal distinctions between young women. In the late 1950s, Alpargatas launched its Lady Far West brand. It targeted girls, for example, in ads that appeared in September, when secondary school students organized picnics to celebrate Students' Day.[111] The images of girls in *vaqueros*, as had happened with the boys, conveyed a sense of Americanness. An ad for Far West jeans appeared in 1959 showed a drawing of a couple composed of a young man with a ducktail and a blonde, short-haired young woman drinking Coca Cola: they both encapsulated the Americanness represented in the rock teenpics that flooded into the Argentine movie theatres.[112] As the 1960s wore on, however, the "authentic" Americanness of the jeans came to the spotlight for some young women as well, who would not accept the local *vaqueros*. María Ester recalls that, as a middle-class young woman, though she did not wear jeans regularly, she used to spend hours trying to fade the "excessive blue of the Lady Far West" with a stone. Although she knew that it would be the subject of quarrels, she also took her brother's Lee jeans and wore them. When I asked why she worked so hard on her *vaqueros* and dared to clash with her brother over wearing his jeans, she said, "The *vaqueros* were vulgar: as people said, they were *mersa*."[113]

It was not until the second half of the 1960s that young women fully embraced jeans, in the process of total renovation of feminine fashion that was also signaled through the spread of the miniskirt. In its first years in Argentina, thus, jeans served to carve out a specifically masculine youth fashion, which instilled itself between a childhood fashion dominated by the short pants and an "adult" fashion marked by suits and grey clothes. Certainly, as with rock and the twist—and in connection to the spread of that youth music through movies—jeans were the first dress item to be targeted to and appropriated by young people, especially boys. Just as it happened with youth-led music, jeans also served to shape a sense of generational belonging at the same time that they functioned as a means through which young people built up class and cultural distinctions. Ironically, it was perhaps more evident with regard to jeans than with regard to music that Americanness acted as an avenue to display cultural, class-based distinctions among youths. In terms of clothing, many youths appropriated the American item par excellence, yet its "authenticity" became the center of controversies that helped make clear that "youth" was far from being a homogeneous category in early 1960s Argentina.

▶ In June of 1964, President Arturo Illia officially greeted seventeen-year-old Italian pop singer Rita Pavone: he invited her to visit the government house and congratulated her for her far-reaching success among the Argentine youth audiences. In Illia's words, Rita Pavone represented the "healthy values of what we have come to know as 'new wave.'"[114] By no means was Illia the first president to receive "stars": Juan Perón, for example, had done the same in the early 1950s when he welcomed actresses like Gina Lollobrigida in the government house. Yet the difference is worth noting: Illia did not receive "stars" that appealed to an intergenerational audience but rather those who embodied "new wave" values. The anecdote signals the symbolic importance that youth had acquired in the public milieu by the mid-1960s. In fact, "youth" largely created itself and became publicly recognized through musical styles, leisure practices, and consumption. These realms were key to the creation of a sense of generational belonging among young people, and constituted the arenas in which youths from different social strata could act their age. In the same movement, though, these arenas acted as sites whereby young people elaborated distinctions. As had happened before, the building of cultural distinctions was played out in mass culture: in the early 1960s, however, mass culture had become juvenilized.

The juvenilization of mass culture was triggered by the arrival of rock to the Argentine media and cultural landscape. In contrast to other Latin American countries such as Mexico, where rock first appealed to middle-class young people, in Argentina it came as a musical and dancing form that cut across class and gender lines to become the baseline for a new, specifically youthful, sociability. Rock served to organize the leisure practices of young women and men, at the same time that it incited reactions related to the dangers it posed to youth "morals" and the "national traditions." Geared to limit the spread of rock, the opposition fell substantially short: it could only set temporary limits on the advance of a musical form that young people embraced as their own, with the frequent consent of their parents, and the "contribution" of a considerable segment of the cultural industries. Culture and entertainment entrepreneurs—perhaps to thwart the opponents—soon targeted rock to young people *within* the family. As the promotion of Bill Haley demonstrated, rock would serve to connect the Argentine youths with their peers abroad without any danger of losing local "traditions" or challenging sexual mores and family values. Haley and other visitors, however, could not satisfy the seemingly voracious demand for "rockers," and in that context the first local talents emerged. Local and transnational companies took advantage of developmentalist policies enacted in the late 1950s to expand their facilities and activities in the country. In that expansion, youth-led music acquired a prominent role: young people were the ideal music consumers. As the 1960s continued, however, it was apparent that young people integrated their consumption of rock and the twist with other musical forms, such as "folkloric projection." Appropriating and expanding that hybrid consumption, El Club del Clan would gravitate to the center between 1963 and 1965.

The experience of *El Club del Clan*, crucial to the juvenilization of mass culture, incited heated debates about the culture industry, the "masses," and cultural taste. *El Club del Clan* emerged from and contributed to the expansion of a media network. As a youth-led, musical-based text integrating local and international sounds filtered through a patina of "youthfulness," *El Club del Clan* endorsed family values, the consecration of deeply rooted gender roles, sexual containment, and restrained fun: it promoted cultural conservatism. In many ways, fans seemed to have "consumed" it within these parameters. The unprecedented irruption of youth idols and fans, which permeated the media, incited the first systematic reflections on the changes in mass culture. Cultural critics, left-wing militants, filmmakers, and journalists focused on what they thought of as a process of "manipulation" and "cultural alienation." In doing so, they conflated the images of idols and fans, conceived of as "masses," and deployed gendered language that spoke of passivity and inferiority, unleashing also struggles over cultural taste. In the mid-1960s, those struggles took place on the cultural terrain of youth consumption, where the term *mersa* served as an organizing principle. A term that rapidly spread through popular vocabulary, it was allegedly used among youths from the upper and middle classes to designate the cultural, purportedly "bad" taste of youths from the lowest social strata. In the mid-1960s, it metonymically invoked the "new wave" idols and fans alike.

The battles over cultural taste were reinforced in the realm of youth fashion, an arena for the daily elaboration of class-inflected, cultural distinctions. The jeans interpellated broad segments of young men and—more limitedly—women, thus becoming a marker of a generational identity. Among youth, the main controversy over jeans revolved around the dichotomy between the local *vaqueros* and the American imported brands. In the case of young men, jeans helped to open up a loophole between childhood and adult dress codes, thus paving the way for a youth fashion. They helped signal the emergence of youth as a visible category. Working-class young men were the vanguard of *vaquero* wearers and were represented as embodying cultural and sexual disorders, expressed in their "tightened" and "rustic" pants. Middle-class youths—whether men or women—dubbed the *vaquero* wearers as *mersa* and sought out Lee or Levi jeans, which they could afford and recognize. Through wearing "authentic" jeans, they elaborated class-based distinctions, thus replicating, upon the terrain of fashion, similar developments that took place in the realm of youth-led music. Most youths did create and participate in new, and properly youthful, cultural consumption and leisure activities in early-1960s Argentina. As it happened in the realm of fashion, however, youths neither wore the same jeans nor endowed them with the same meanings.

4 ▶ She's Leaving Home

YOUNG WOMEN, GENDER, AND SEXUALITY

On May 29, 1962, Norma Penjerek, age seventeen, left her apartment in a traditional lower-middle-class neighborhood in Buenos Aires to attend a private English class. Her class ended at 7:30 P.M., yet she never came home. On June 1, her parents filed a missing-persons report. In mid-July, forensic tests confirmed their worst fears: a body found in the outskirts of Buenos Aires was identified as hers. What had happened to Norma Penjerek? After a year had passed with no significant news, in July of 1963 a sex worker declared to a judge that Norma had fallen into the "trap" of one of the groups devoted to drugs and pornography—or, as contemporaries would say, invoking the title of Federico Fellini's movie, into the "Dolce Vita"—and that the leader of the group later decided to kill her. The declaration was false, and the police never found Norma's murderers. Perhaps because it went unresolved, the "Penjerek case" caused the most intense moral panic in 1960s Argentina. As the sociologist Stanley Cohen put it, moral panics emerge at times of social uncertainty, becoming events for "drawing the line" between those mores and behaviors that will be tolerated and those that won't. Moral panics, he argues, are at the same time transparent—that is, anyone can know what is happening—and opaque, since their broader meanings are usually mediated.[1] The moral panic constructed around the Penjerek case served to address anxieties regarding the perceived vanishing of patriarchal authority and domesticity. More precisely, it constituted a response to the awareness that young women were metaphorically—and sometimes literally—leaving home.

Young women experienced, carried out, and suffered from the consequences of the changes that the dynamics of sociocultural modernization entailed earlier and more dramatically than their male counterparts. The scholars who have studied the history of gender and sexuality in 1960s Argentina have thus far accounted for the opening up of new horizons for young women, chiefly among the middle classes, as well as for the prudent liberalization of sexual mores.[2] While most of these studies have focused on mid-term patterns of change, they have overlooked a more situational analysis of how change—as it related to young women's lives—was shaped, understood, and debated. This chapter shows that *las jóvenes* (young women) or *chicas* (girls)—exchangeable terms in public vocabulary—practically contested prevalent ideas of "home" by remaining longer in the education system, fully participating in the labor market, helping shape youthful leisure activities, daring to experiment with new courtship conventions and to acknowledge publicly that they engaged in premarital sex, and marrying later in life. In doing so, young women in the 1960s challenged dominant ideals of domesticity premised on separated spheres for men and women and on equating womanhood with wifehood and motherhood. That ideal became normative for the middle classes in the first half of the twentieth century and, as scholars noted, for the working classes as well, chiefly during the Peronist regime (1946–55).[3]

In the late 1950s and early 1960s, young women occupied a problematic space: while their pursuit of renewed educational, labor, and cultural expectations signified a collective yearning for change, the resistance they faced revealed how entrenched the status quo was and how difficult change would be. In particular, young women's changing experiences destabilized deep-seated notions of patriarchal authority; in the process women created countless dilemmas within their familial and cultural milieus. When young women's expectations and experiences began to expand and shift, their choices of vocations, their leisure preferences, or their courtship practices became arenas of confrontation in many families. Although advisers in popular and feminine magazines and psychologists tried to help parents navigate this new reality, the dilemmas persisted and sometimes led to young women running away, perhaps as a rejection of what they perceived as parental authoritarianism. In a sensationalist fashion, the media and conservative Catholic sectors embedded the "tide-of-runaways phenomenon" with sexual, cultural, and political meanings: the Penjerek case confirmed their fears, becoming an avenue for many unaffiliated parents to try to curtail their daughter's growing autonomy and thus recuperate their perceived lost authority. In an extreme, heightened way, the Penjerek case also served to catapult discussions about young women and sexuality into the spotlight, and to respond to ongoing "liberalizing" attitudes and practices. Young women indeed stood at the center of the most significant change in Argentina's sexual culture in the 1960s—the public acceptance of premarital sex—further destabilizing domestic ideals based on a double standard of sex requiring men to have their first sexual experience before marriage and women to preserve their virginity. The cohorts of women who came of age in the 1960s were the first ones to voice their approval of premarital sex in the public arena, and did so in the frame of a discourse connecting sex with love and responsibility. This helped represent the novelty as "modern" and prudent at the same time.

Leaving Home

In the late 1950s and early 1960s, young women's life experiences and expectations began to differ remarkably from those of previous generations of women, like their mothers'. Young women comprised the majority of the thousands who left their provinces to migrate to large urban areas, beginning in the 1930s and increasing in the decades that followed. Young women likewise swelled the enrollment in secondary schools and universities, and they made new career and vocational choices, thereby gaining better and more diversified access to the labor market. They also helped shape youth leisure activities, which were vital to the development of a sense of generational belonging and to forging new modes of interaction between the sexes. As had happened in the 1920s with the "modern girl," the growing autonomy that young women were gaining conflicted with the persistent and restrictive norms enforced at the family level.[4] "Leaving home" was a metaphor for young women's life experiences and for public perceptions about them: it was an index of change in family and cultural terrains.

Young women in rural areas and provincial towns had begun to leave their homes in the 1930s as a part of the process of mass migration to industrializing cities. That movement continued in the decades that followed, and young women, whose average age when migrating was twenty, were the majority of the newcomers in Rosario, Mendoza, and Buenos Aires.[5] In the late 1950s and early 1960s, many young women wrote to President Arturo Frondizi's young daughter, Elenita, stating their migration desires. This was the case for Marta, a nineteen-year-old letter writer from northern Santa Fe, who tried to convey to Elenita her despair. She had a primary school education and a "talent for accounting," but could find neither a job nor "any incentive to live" in her hometown. Adelaida, age twenty, concurred: in her "miserable town," she wrote, she was "wasting her life." Both letter writers asked Elenita's help for getting any job, assuming it was in Buenos Aires.[6] One of the few ethnographic studies focusing on migrant populations in the early 1960s depicted similar feelings among young women in a northwestern province. The anthropologist concluded: "they could not work because they didn't have jobs, were isolated in a depressing family life, poorly dressed, and bombarded with the images of another way of life through the radio." Most of the interviewed young women wanted to migrate to large cities to find jobs, enjoy themselves in leisure activities, and continue their education.[7]

While by the 1950s most migrants had become integrated into networks of family and friends already established in major cities, representations of the lonely, dreamingly innocent, and "at-risk" provincial girl haunted the public imagination. Released in 1958, Lucas Demare's movie *Detrás de un largo muro* (Behind a Long Wall) narrates the story of Rosa and her widowed father, who, after losing their farm, are left with no choice but to migrate to Buenos Aires. They soon discover that their lives would be far from the fantasy that the city lights in movies had promised. Like their relatives, they go to live in a slum, or *villa miseria*. Rosa finds a job in a factory and spends time in the company of a young man who ultimately rapes her. One of the most popular melodramas of the 1950s, the movie examines some of the key motives regarding young migrant women who were "at risk" of losing their innocence, namely their virginity, by coming to the city. These notions were also crucial to the Obra de Protección de la Joven (OPJ, Organization for Protecting Young Women), an international Catholic organization. Founded in 1951, OPJ's most pressing goal was to place social workers at train stations in Buenos Aires to prevent migrants from "falling into vice-related organizations."[8] Convinced that the arrival in large cities was tantamount to a dangerous rite of passage, these social workers sought to identify girls arriving alone, foster them for weeks in an elegant house the government gave to the institution in 1957, and (if the young woman's moral sense was adequate enough in the eyes of the Catholic social worker) place them as domestic workers in the homes of upper-class families.[9] At the same time that it helped enforce relations of social subordination, OPJ also attempted to build "homelike" environments for the young women.

Without moving away from home, thousands of girls in the 1950s and 1960s also began to "leave home" on a daily basis to attend secondary schools. The increase in school enrollment at the secondary level was largely due to matriculation by young women: whereas in 1950 they accounted for 50 percent of the student body, in 1960 they already outnumbered boys and were 54 percent of the student body in 1970. Although most educators and surely many parents viewed the girls' arrival in the secondary schools as a sign of (and a path to) the country's cultural modernization, it nevertheless constituted rocky terrain for some families.[10] That was the case with Alicia and Mabel, two sisters from a working-class family in the Greater Buenos Aires area. Alicia graduated from primary school in 1956 and expected to go on at the secondary level, but her parents did not grant her permission. Even though Alicia would not have to commute because her neighborhood, unlike others, had both public and private secondary schools available, her parents probably feared her daily interactions with boys and preferred her to stay at home and carry out domestic chores, gaining training in a "female" trade later.[11] Mabel, for her part, graduated in 1964, and she recalls that she worked "on a strategy" to convince her parents to grant her permission. "The key," she says, "was my insistence on that I never liked doing stuff in the home." In addition, when Mabel's time to enroll arrived, she indirectly benefited from the fact that many of her female neighbors had begun to attend secondary schools as well. "Times were changing," Mabel notes.[12] Indeed they were. While taken for granted by middle-class girls, matriculation at secondary school was still a sticking point for some working-class families.

Likewise, choosing a school orientation was another arena of confrontation where many parents tried to assert their authority against the will of their daughters. This was exemplified by the changing popularity of the teacher training schools. As had happened throughout the century, in the 1950s girls enrolled en masse in the teacher training schools. In the 1960s, partially as a result of the changing preferences of young women, enrollment in these schools stagnated and then declined, while attendance in the commercial branch, which was aimed at training students to find office jobs, grew at an average of 11 percent annually.[13] The changing percentages mask embattled situations. Psychologists persistently advised parents not to overlook their children's desires, and noted that vocational decisions created frequent clashes since oftentimes "impositions prevailed over negotiations."[14] Many girls started to perceive teacher training as an imposition. Teaching had for decades been accepted as the most respectable career for women, who represented 90 percent of all teachers in 1962.[15] At that time, however, many girls expressed their discontent. Interviewed about their experience at a teacher training school, girls agreed that their parents forced them to choose it, and letters written to women's magazines reiterated that sentiment.[16] Moreover, the supply of teachers began to outpace its demand. Illustrating that imbalance, two-dozen young women from Entre Rios, Buenos Aires, and Santa Fe wrote to Elenita Frondizi asking for her help to find a teaching position. Two letter writers from Córdoba appropriated the common lexicon used to speak about teachers and wrote that without teaching, their "sense of mission vanished" and consequently they would "fail the fatherland" and their families alike.[17] The widespread difficulty to secure a position upon graduation added one more layer to the declining prestige of the teacher training school and augmented the interest in other possible jobs.

Throughout the 1960s, young women helped expand and diversify the female extradomestic labor force. While in 1947 women comprised 18 percent of the economically active population, in 1970 the figure had jumped to 28 percent. In terms of age, the fact that young women stayed in the educational system longer than before was reflected in the fact that the fourteen-to-nineteen-year-old age group slightly decreased its participation in the labor market, but better-educated young women in the twenty-to-twenty-four age group increased theirs from 39 percent in 1960 to 44 percent in 1970.[18] These were, likewise, the first cohorts that did not withdraw massively upon reaching the threshold of twenty-five years old, associated with marriage and motherhood. Equally important, they carried out a diversified variety of jobs, mainly within the service sector of the economy. While most had jobs as employees in retail stores or in household services (likely as domestic workers), a large percentage worked in public administration or held office clerk positions.[19] In fact, unlike the declining allure of the schoolteacher, the *secretaria ejecutiva* (executive secretary) epitomized the modern young woman and surely propelled many girls to pursue their studies in the commercial branch. As a distinct category from the *secretaria*, the *secretaria ejecutiva* signaled a new professional and cultural profile. Interviewed in 1966, a *secretaria ejecutiva*, age twenty-one, who worked for Ford Motor Company, said that she had received training in a private academy. There she had learned "commercial and international law as well as public relations." She and other interviewees felt confident that they were not "dull dolls" anymore, but active professionals who, after spending eight hours in offices in downtown Buenos Aires, went to watch experimental movies or visited centers of modern art.[20] Those who worked for multinational companies, received a decent salary, dressed well, and engaged with the latest avant-garde developments were numerically a minority among the large contingent of working young women, but they embodied some of the collective meaning of and aspiration to modernity and independence.

The *secretaria ejecutiva* was not the only image of the modern young woman: the college student occupied an analogous position. The college student body gradually became proportionally more female like high schools already had. For instance, while in 1958 young women accounted for 25 percent of college students, by 1972 they represented 38 percent.[21] In terms of careers, young college women in the 1960s also made new choices. As we have seen, they comprised the majority of students in the humanities and social sciences departments, but they also increased their numbers in the economics and law schools. Unlike with the secondary schools, though, young women coming from working-class families had limited access to college education. This began to change somewhat toward the early 1970s. In the 1960s, mostly middle-class young women had the opportunity to attend college. For example, in 1968, at the largest university in the country, 86 percent were "first generation," showing how expectations and experiences differed from those had by previous generations of women.[22] Projecting an image of autonomy and carving out their own futures, college women nevertheless encountered barriers in a male-dominated environment. In 1972 men constituted 87 percent of faculty, an index that demonstrates how limited the possibilities were for female graduates seeking academic appointments.[23] Moreover, although young women were actively involved in the student movement, only a handful achieved leadership positions (for the most part, as student representatives to the school, rather than university-level governing councils), and this was also true for the schools where women made up a majority of the student body. Yet at the same time that they reproduced structural, long-standing gender inequalities, colleges became sites for mixed sociability in unprecedented ways.

Albeit with different intensities and modalities, college and secondary school students, working and unemployed girls and young women, all strove to participate in a new sociability that was youth-based rather than intergenerational. That sociability took place in schools and at jobs and fundamentally in the realm of leisure, where young women and men began to interact without adult supervision. Among middle-class adolescents, the *barritas*—mixed groups—were formed as a socializing institution and proved an alluring novelty, chiefly when it came to the organization of parties at homes on the weekend. Advisers recommended that parents encourage these parties: they saw them as the best way to meet their daughters' friends and to monitor their social lives.[24] Yet for many lower-middle- or working-class families, this was not a viable option: as one letter writer noted, her house was too small to host people.[25] These young women did nonetheless participate in new forms of youth sociability. The spread of rock music and dance in the late 1950s was crucial for re-signifying leisure spaces, such as neighborhood-based social clubs, which had long served as places for young people and adults to dance to popular rhythms.[26] By becoming "rock clubs," those spaces turned into youth-only territories; at the same time they preserved—as the home parties did for middle-class adolescents—a certain halo of security provided by being located in their neighborhoods.

Young women's extended leisure activities at any venue, however, incited frequent clashes in the family milieu. Progressive family advisers told parents to be tolerant of their daughters' choices to go out at night, dance, and flirt. These activities, a psychologist reminded her readers, were "signs of a secular process of women's emancipation, and can not be stopped."[27] While the experts suggested parents reevaluate their attitudes, young women complained insistently of their parents' refusal to grant them permission to go out at night and of their strict curfews. A young woman age twenty, for example, wrote that she worked as a teacher and earned her own money, yet her parents would not let her go out at night, "even with female friends." Another girl, age seventeen, commented on her strategies to contest her parents' "obsessions" with her "morals." She complained that she was "getting tired of lying" to her parents: since they did not want her to go anywhere, she just made up excuses.[28] In fact, many parents feared that allowing their daughters to go out at night, alone or with their mixed *barritas*, posed potential dangers to their sexuality and risked "promiscuity," as some termed flirting and dating.[29]

On the eve of the 1960, courtship conventions began to slowly change, and this constituted one of the most contested arenas at the family level. The interaction of young women and men in new leisure activities and sites for sociability—including college—was crucial to forging fluid and relaxed relationships, where flirting, for example, became normalized. Likewise, throughout the 1960s an array of practices between the poles of flirting and formal "premarital" dating emerged. All in all, courtship became connected with experimentation and choice for boys and girls.[30] However, when these practices began to emerge, they inspired growing parental anxiety. Letter writers regularly addressed difficulties in coping with their parents when flirting or dating. While grateful that her mother let her go out with her boyfriend, for example, a young woman age nineteen complained that she was "obsessed with the kissing issue!" Another girl, age seventeen, wrote to convey her "desperation." When her parents realized that she was dating a young man, age nineteen, they threatened to send her "to a reformatory."[31] Albeit with varying degrees of drama, these dilemmas cut across cultural and class lines. María Rosa, daughter of an upper-middle-class Jewish family, recalls that while she was an anthropology student, she began to date a young man her age. Her parents approved of him, but "were so reluctant" to grant her consent to go out that the couple decided to marry very young. "We wanted to be together and I wanted to leave my home," she concludes.[32]

While some youths like María Rosa could make the decision to leave behind wearisome parental oversight to start a "home" of their own, many young couples could not afford marriage. Housing, in particular, constituted a widespread problem, a phenomenon that sharply contrasted with the recent Peronist past. Under Peronism, the state had programs that subsidized the purchase or building of family homes.[33] Housing was one key issue for *Los de la mesa diez* (The Ones of Table Number 10), Osvaldo Dragún's play first staged in 1958 and then adapted as a movie, directed by Simón Feldman and released in 1960. The play and movie tell the story of Maria and José, the rich girl and the poor boy, which begins and ends at "table 10" of a café in Buenos Aires (the metaphor for the impossibility of their starting a "home"). After the movie's premiere, its actors, director, playwright, and producers engaged in a debate with an audience composed of young people. The audience reaffirmed that the problems that the movie depicted were "not fiction[al]."[34] Marriage was financially challenging. Some reports stipulated that getting married and starting a new "home" in 1965 was six times more expensive than it was in 1930: a couple of office clerks had to save for more than forty-eight months in 1965, in comparison with eight months in 1930, for the down payment and the purchasing of the basic furniture for a two-bedroom apartment.[35] This riddle partially explains the increase in median age for marriage, which went from twenty-two for women in 1930 to twenty-six in 1965.[36]

While certainly disturbing for middle- and working-class couples, the hardships of finding the means to secure a new "home" do not fully capture the intricacies of the sociocultural dimensions of "leaving home." Financial problems overlapped with the gendered dimensions of sociocultural modernization: young women delayed starting their own "homes" at the same time that many of them began to "leave" their family homes. By staying longer in the educational system, participating in the labor market, experimenting with new leisure activities, and shaping new courtship practices, young women questioned the ideals of domesticity and equating womanhood with motherhood and wifehood. Amid these practical contestations and the expanding horizons that young women pursued, parents tried to reassert their authority. The maladjustments between young women's experiences and expectations and patriarchal authority created daily dilemmas. In some cases young women could solve the quandary by marrying early to start a new "home." And in other cases young women set in motion a desire to literally "leave home."

The Making of a Moral Panic

An often-invoked desire expressed by young women, "leaving home," or rather, "running away from home," also represented a concern for educators, the media, and psychological advisers. In fact, a tiny but increasingly visible minority of young women set in motion the desire to leave their homes, and their fate came under the spotlight in the early 1960s. Many moral watchdogs and segments of the media believed that young women left home to pursue a hedonistic and sexualized lifestyle, known as the "Dolce Vita." This was the general framework to encode the moral panic around the Penjerek case, a panic in which the Catholic conservative groups were at the vanguard of a broad spectrum of voices that included state officers, politicians, and unaffiliated parents. An informal yet vast alliance supported practices aimed at restricting young men's and, chiefly, young women's increasing autonomy, which they saw as a means of reconstructing patriarchal authority and of reinforcing domestic ideals that many thought were vanishing. An analysis of the making of that panic shows that well into the 1960s cultural conservatism permeated Argentina's culture. It also offers a window to observe how discussions of politics, sexuality, and youth intersected.

The practice of running away has always been a way to melodramatically represent a response to family conflict. It reappeared forcefully by the late 1950s, both in film and in the lives of some young women. Two popular melodramas released in 1958, *Demasiado jóvenes* (Too Young, dir. Leopoldo Torres Ríos) and *Una cita con la vida* (A Date with Life, dir. Hugo del Carril), for example, focused, respectively, on the story of a working-class girl and a middle-class girl who begin dating boys their age against the wishes of their cold and unaffectionate parents. In the midst of tense intrafamilial relations, the young heroines run away from their homes. Both episodes are short-lived and serve as shocking events, attempts to re-craft the young women's relations with their parents, who turn into models of affection and tolerance. The movies echoed the concerns of Edward Cahn's *Runaway Daughters* (1956), released in Argentina—to box office success—in 1957 as *Adolescencia*. In contrast to the American movie, though, the Argentines focused on lone girls rather than on a "teenager group," and represented running away as a desperate attempt to repair familial lives depicted as wearisome. However, when actual young women voiced their desire to run away they focused less on the possible results of their actions than on the causes. For example, in letters written to a teacher, one secondary school girl emphasized her feelings: "I just want to leave: they [her parents] give me no peace." A second girl further dramatized: "My parents are my jailers: I want to leave this prison." By drawing on the same metaphor, a third girl confessed: "I have the growing desire to run away, to leave the prison behind."[37] Letter writers to women's magazines repeated that desire, which they connected with parental rejection of their boyfriends and "over-control over everything I do," as one girl put it.[38] "Leaving home" represented, to these girls, a means to circumvent what they depicted as suffocating parental authoritarianism.

Psychologists and psychoanalysts, like the movies and educators, also helped publicize the issue of runaway girls and their troublesome familial relations. Consulted by the media, some psychologists argued that young women ran away—or threatened to—so as to blackmail their parents who, "afraid of losing them, conceded everything." They suggested parents not "fall into this trap," yet also reminded them that "presumed or real runaway girls" were a symptom of "things that had gone awry," and that they needed psychological help.[39] For their part, the heads of one of the first adolescent psychology programs at a public hospital reported that, in 1961, 38 out of 120 patients had begun treatment because of permanent clashes at homes. While the doctors believed that these adolescents' behaviors were healthy and helped them "affirm their identity," they were alarmed at the "high rate of runaway girls" they had seen.[40] Another psychoanalyst reported on the clinical case of a girl who went into analysis right after running away. Because her parents became exceedingly strict after discovering that she was flirting with an older boy, the girl pretended to be sick and asked to be hospitalized. She took to the streets after being momentarily overlooked by the nurses. When the psychoanalyst asked her the reason, she answered, "to get away from my parents."[41]

The examples show a rising societal concern with the handling of intergenerational relations, chiefly as it came to young women and their desire to leave home. But how extensive was the practice of running away for young women? At least in the City of Buenos Aires—as in some North American cities at the same time—police data show that in the late 1950s it was on the rise.[42] Federal police issued a daily report listing runaways (*fugas*) and disappearances (*desapariciones*). In their terms, someone was defined as *fugado* when the person filing the report had clues about intentionality, like a quarrel. On the other hand, someone was defined as *desaparecido* when there was no clue as to why they left. Young women between fourteen and twenty-five made up 85 percent of all the reported cases between 1953 and 1965. In 1953, 491 young women were reported as *fugadas* or *desaparecidas*; 629 were reported missing in 1955; 648 in 1957; 724 in 1960; 683 in 1963; and 679 in 1965.[43] Although the cases comprised a tiny minority of the fourteen-to-twenty-five age group, the statistics indicate an ascendant curve that reached its height in 1960 and then decreased. Existing data also provide insight into the class standing of the girls, since they include the police stations and thus the neighborhoods where the cases were reported. While most neighborhoods were represented every year, working- and lower-middle-class neighborhoods had the highest numbers in 1953 and 1955.[44] These findings concur with others for the first half of the twentieth century, which showed the predominance of working-class girls who ran away and, at that time, were sent to prisons.[45] However, the data show that beginning in 1957 the majority of cases were reported in middle-class neighborhoods.[46] Thus the increase of *desapariciones* and *fugas* on the eve of the 1960s was due to this practice spreading to middle-class girls.

Police data also offer a glimpse into the age of *fugadas* and *desaparecidas* as well as some of their patterns of "leaving home," but provided no clue as to where young women went or how long they stayed away from their homes. Police data show that the median age of young women who ran away fell from eighteen in 1953 to sixteen by 1963. Although cases were reported throughout the year, in 1960 a large percentage—around 30 percent—was reported between January and March. This coincided with school vacations, possibly when young women would have spent more time at home. Finally, the reports contained scant evidence to support the most common representation of runaways and surely the most common fear among parents: that young women left their homes in the company of boyfriends. In fact, looking at police data for eight years, I only found six cases in which the persons who filed the report—possibly the parents—indicated that girls had "definitely" run away with boyfriends.[47] What happened to these girls? Most young women likely would have spent relatively short periods away from home, perhaps as a sign of their unhappiness with what they conceived of as parental authoritarianism or to show their discontent with particular decisions. For example, María Emilia recalls that she ran away for just one day in 1961, when she was sixteen. "We always fought at home," she recalls. "My parents made a fuss about everything: my friends, my clothing, what I read . . . everything." Tensions escalated, especially when her mother decided to transfer her to a private Catholic school that she did not like: "I just left and spent the night at a friend's. My mother came to look for me." In contrast to what the movies showed, nothing at her home changed after she ran away: "My parents were even stricter, and I ended up at that school," she concluded.[48]

While most cases were short-lived attempts at resolving family dilemmas, the media soon created connections between runaway girls and what was dubbed, after the release of Federico Fellini's movie, "Dolce Vita." In March 1961, for example, *La Razón* informed its readers of the case of a girl, age eighteen, who after graduating from secondary school and having a quarrel with her parents about a "petty issue" decided to run away and go to a seaside resort on the Atlantic coast. Once there, the newspaper story described how the girl "looked for work in a nightclub" and how she met an "elegant" woman who promised her a job. The girl visited the woman's house ("a true den of iniquity worthy of the Dolce Vita") where she interacted with youths "lost to the worst vices," including cocaine. Fortunately, the chronicle concluded, the girl managed to "get out of that life" and "let people know its secrets."[49] Several components of that exemplary story would often be repeated: running away as a result of "petty quarrels" at home, the "elegant woman" as a nexus, and the move to leisure resorts.[50] The archetypal narrative drew on previous tales about women's "fall" into prostitution, yet the story line was not only updated to reflect contextual references to youth culture; it also focused on middle-, rather than only on working-class, young women—as was the case with prior narratives of "women's falls" in tango and popular melodrama since the 1920s and 1930s.[51] In the media representation, then, the Dolce Vita amounted to a hedonistic lifestyle (sexual activities and drug or alcohol abuse) and represented the destination for young women who ran away from their homes, either because they chose to join that life or because they "fell" into criminal networks. The Penjerek case was made to fit into the prevalent narratives of the Dolce Vita.

Returning to the case described at the opening of this chapter, the unsolved murder of Norma Penjerek—a "girl next door," to draw on media language—was the basis of what amounted to the most famous moral panic of the 1960s. The only child of a lower-middle-class Jewish family from Flores, a typical neighborhood in the City of Buenos Aires, Norma was a senior at a female-only secondary school. Norma's mother, a housewife with primary schooling, proudly told the reporters that her daughter was deciding whether she would pursue a university career—likely dentistry—or continue her training to become an English teacher. Just as many other youths used to go to the movies to watch American films and listen to songs with English lyrics, Norma was "really into her English classes." Her mother regretted allowing her to attend her English class starting at 7:00 P.M. on May 29, 1962. It was a rainy and rather unusual evening: the Confederación General del Trabajo (CGT, General Labor Confederation) had called for a general strike, and the streets were empty.[52] On that evening Norma Penjerek disappeared. Her body was found in mid-July. What had happened to Norma? The lack of answers favored the spread of rumors. Initially, some saw Norma's murder as a possible vengeful act against her father or as part of the wave of anti-Semitism that swept Argentina in 1962. The police examined the never-proven connections between Norma's father and the Mossad, the Israeli secret police, which had worked in Argentina to extradite Nazi war criminal Adolf Eichmann, who was executed in Jerusalem the same week that Norma disappeared. Similarly, some read the Penjerek case as another example of anti-Semitic activities carried out by Tacuara, an extreme right-wing nationalist group that had attacked several Jewish students.[53] Yet most people soon believed that the Penjerek case simply represented one of the many *fugas* and *desapariciones* of young women.

Although it bears recalling that the actual number of reported cases of *fugas* and *desapariciones* in the City of Buenos Aires had began to drop since its peak of 1960, and although Norma's mother vehemently refused the notion that her daughter had run away, neither the media nor the groups involved in family and youth issues cast doubt as to whether the Penjerek case fit into the already-established pattern. Moreover, that certainty reached "confirmation" in July 1963, when the sex worker Mabel

Sisti offered a judge her declaration. According to Sisti, Norma Penjerek had met an "elegant woman" named Laura Villano who acted as a link between her and a house in the Greater Buenos Aires area. There Penjerek and other girls would have consumed drugs and taken part in nude photo sessions. Sisti went on to assert that the head of that house was Pedro Vecchio, who had a troublesome relationship with Norma. One day when she wanted to leave, Vecchio murdered her and hid the body.[54] Sisti shaped her declaration to the judge in the style used by the press when reporting on young women's *fugas* and *desapariciones*. Sisti's declaration provided a curious public with names and places that would acquire celebrity status, and stories went so far as to indicate that, at the supposed crime scene, pornography and vampirism were involved.[55] Although afterwards Sisti contended that she had made her declaration under police threats, and that none of her testimony was accurate—as the judges later proved—her story was critical in promoting the moral panic stretching from August to October 1963.

The multiple anxieties that young women's changing life experiences as well as the so-called Dolce Vita had incited since the early 1960s soon became outright panic. One of the signs of that panic, perhaps the most widespread, was the reinforcement of parental supervision. Some parents took their daughters to school and, in many cases, forbid them to go out after sundown.[56] Other parents asked the minister of the interior to establish a "state of siege" so the police could more easily imprison the suspects, Vecchio and Villano.[57] Although the police in fact took several weeks to imprison the suspects, they soon began to carry out raids. On September 28, the police raided 2,800 nightclubs in the Greater Buenos Aires area: a thousand people were taken into police stations to have their penal records checked. Among the detainees were one hundred boys and girls under eighteen years old.[58] Meanwhile, federal police patrolled the Palermo area, known for its parks, in search of *raboneros* (truants) from secondary schools who should have been in class. The minister of education asked school principals to telephone the parents of children who did not attend classes and to publicize the names of the thirty-nine boys and twenty-six girls identified by the police in Palermo on October 8, posting the roster of truants at the entrance of every school.[59] Meanwhile, conservative Catholic groups supported the most extreme policies while at the same time attempting to frame them more broadly. A communiqué from Catholic Action claimed that it was by favoring "the most absolute liberty for adolescents and youths" that "all moral deviations were made possible in Argentina."[60] An editorial writer concurred and asked parents to curtail the "liberties that young people enjoy," given that "many adolescents cannot elude the dangers they face."[61]

The most vehement voices wanted to narrow the "excess of liberties" for young men and, chiefly, young women. In doing so, they openly voiced the fears that lay behind many parents' attitudes vis-à-vis the autonomy that their daughters demanded and carved out. The Penjerek case served as an excuse to discipline young women by reinforcing patriarchal authority and by drawing them back to the safety of "home." It is not surprising, then, that not only conservative Catholic groups but also many unaffiliated parents supported policies promising to restrain young women's gradual autonomy, which also meant a chance to reconstruct their perceived loss of authority. It is also unsurprising that the voices of some advisers, like Dr. Eva Giberti, went mostly unheard. An aim of her "School for Parents" was to help democratize family relations that she saw as hierarchical and authoritarian. Besides advocating for increased family dialogue, she suggested that parents gradually grant more autonomy to their adolescents.[62] During the Penjerek case, she assured parents that their "fear was logical," yet advised them to limit their control over their daughters. Young women, she went on, needed to learn to take care of themselves.[63] Hers, however, was a lonely voice at the time: one that called for preserving a certain faith and tolerance within the family and, in doing so, dismantling the panic.

Rather than receding, though, the panic escalated and became gradually more politicized, thus showing the mobilizing potential of the connection between youth "deviance" and what began to be known as the "enemy within." In fact, no political actor could afford to remain silent. From the minuscule, left-wing Movimiento Nacional de Liberación (Movement for National Liberation) to the powerful CGT, going through all the variants of the Unión Cívica Radical (UCR, Radical Civic Party), the entire political spectrum signaled the "grave moral crisis" that the Penjerek case represented and created connections between morals, corruption, and politics.[64] No politician, though, became more identified with the issue than former representative Ernesto Sanmartino of the UCR, who acted as the Penjereks' lawyer and was a "moral entrepreneur" in his own right. Making use of his privileged position as the family's lawyer, Sanmartino repeatedly called press conferences to argue that by following the path of runaway or abducted girls, it was possible to discover that the "Dolce Vita's main players" were "linked to Communist cells that used drugs and sex as components of a broader plan to infiltrate our country."[65] Sanmartino's conspiracy-oriented reasoning achieved broad legitimacy since his was *the* authorized voice in a case that shocked almost everyone. His rationale was indebted to and part of a transnational anti-Communist discourse. As scholars have shown for the United States in the McCarthy era, fears of "deviant sexuality" melded with fears of the "Red scare," leading to a politics of containment of both.[66] Cold War rhetoric centered on the figure of the "enemy within" made its way into Argentina in the early 1960s, gaining societal approval by blending with gendered and sexual fears.

The moral panic around the Penjerek case was, in Stanley Cohen's formulation, "a line-drawing reaction" that served to delineate the figures of political and sexual deviants alike.[67] It served to articulate an informal alliance that joined those who believed that revamping patriarchal authority was the only guarantee not only for caring for young women's lives but also for preventing the "Communist threat" from spreading. That alliance had a public ceremony in a demonstration to support Sanmartino and the Penjereks attended by ten thousand people: "worried mothers and fathers from both the most humble and richest neighborhoods," a journalist wrote. Besides cheering the lawyer, the crowd applauded Secretary of Information Nélida Baigorria, who argued that "the greater the liberties for today's girls," the greater their servitude to "drugs and uncontrolled sexuality" and to the "activities of Communists."[68] In this view, the Communist "folk devil" corrupted girls' morals and ruined their futures. Rising to the surface in countless public contexts—most notably in the months preceding the imposition of the last military dictatorship in 1976—the connection between "deviant" youth, sexuality, and politics could incite intense mobilization but, concretely, could not help to solve a legal case. We will never know who killed Norma Penjerek. The only suspects were freed in late 1963: the judges did not find enough evidence to keep them in jail. As the 1960s went on, moreover, concerns about young women *fugadas* and *desaparecidas* diminished and the term "Dolce Vita" vanished.

A gender-centered analysis of the processes of sociocultural modernization reveals how the moral panic around the Penjerek case came at a time that young women were symbolically and sometimes literally "leaving home" in greater numbers. This brought about an attempt to set limits to that movement. And it was not the only such attempt in the 1960s. For example, in August of 1966, a month after General Juan Carlos Onganía imposed a military regime (1966–70), state officers within the municipality of Buenos Aires as well as federal police conducted a morality campaign aimed at regulating youth's leisure activities and presumed "uncontrolled sexuality." This campaign involved raids in nightclubs and hotels and harassment of young men with long hair and young women who wore miniskirts. Although it also relied on blatantly anti-Communist rhetoric, the campaign failed to achieve the broad societal involvement incited by the Penjerek case. The press and most of Buenos Aires' citizens envisaged the 1966 campaign as a politically driven endeavor that came "from above," interpreting it as an authoritarian backlash against the "liberalizing" trends that Argentines had gone through.[69] The moral panic around the Penjerek case, by contrast, had allowed for the public voicing of tensions that affected many families, which revolved around the "crisis" of patriarchal authority and domesticity.

The moral panic around the Penjerek case also served to catapult an interrogation of young women's sex lives to center stage before a hyperbolic, moralistic audience. In this respect, both the Penjerek case and the ensuing morality campaign were extreme, conservative responses to emergent cultural trends and practices that shaped and expressed a more "liberal" understanding, especially with regard to youth sexuality. Far from the distorted and exaggerated imagery of the Dolce Vita and from the notions of "uncontrolled sexuality" permeating the journalistic commentary, young women certainly stood at the heart of the changing sexual culture in 1960s Argentina. In this sense, too, they were "leaving home." Many young women contested the cultural and sexual mandates prescribing female virginity until marriage as a condition for respectable femininity as the 1960s went on.

Sexualizing Young Women

In a study of what he dubbed the "Argentine sexual revolution," essayist Julio Mafud underscored that the changing sexual mores he depicted were taking place among "*young* women and *young* men."[70] In the 1960s, talking about sex meant talking about youth, and vice versa. Sex was increasingly discussed in the public arena, where experts—sexologists, psychologists, and psychoanalysts—journalists, and youths themselves carved out a new understanding connecting sex to love and responsibility. The implicit debate revolved around whether or not marriage was the only legitimate site for its practice. In this respect, young women were also at the forefront, embodying the most significant change in Argentina's sexual culture in the 1960s: the public acceptance of premarital sex. Needless to say, this was a global trend, one of the cornerstones for the sexual revolutions that swept across the world.[71] In Argentina, while opposition mounted from different quarters, the new attitude made solid inroads and was read as evidence of the modernization of sexual mores and as a sign of the "irreversible" path to equal rights for men and women. However crucial this development was for recognizing women's right to enjoy their sexuality, the changes that accepting premarital sex brought to gender order were ambivalent: they implied a redefinition, rather than the disappearance, of a double sexual standard.

At the start of the 1960s, however, young women and men expressed remarkably different concerns about sex when they had the chance of speaking publicly. For example, 520 youths age seventeen to twenty-three who were students at the University of Buenos Aires—who would later be identified as the "vanguard" in terms of sexual attitudes—took part in workshops on "youth psycho-sexual problems" during the winter break of 1959.[72] The students discussed premarital sex, masturbation, homosexuality, frigidity, and contraception. The psychologist and the educator who coordinated the workshops reported that students showed a mix of "anguish and interest." Moreover, they stated that students lacked sexual information and could "barely relate sex with love." They attested that only 5 percent of the students enrolled had "incorporated sexual intercourse to their affective relations" and underscored that most young women refused to do so "because of cultural tradition and fears of pregnancy." The experts concluded that the students displayed a "traumatic" relationship to their own sexuality and were pushing "for change and sex education."[73] Secondary school students also cried out for discussion of sexuality and accurate information. In 1960, for example, boys and girls taking part in roundtables and conferences concurred that they were not receiving "sex education at home," and one girl argued that she did not think her mother was "a suitable candidate to talk to."[74]

Sexologists, doctors, and psychologists intended to meet and carve out the youth demand for sex education by combining scientific discourse and morality tales, exemplified in the initiatives carried out by the Catholic progressive monthly *Nuestros Hijos* and by the pediatrician Florencio Escardó and his wife, the psychologist Eva Giberti. The experts for *Nuestros Hijos* tried to explain to parents how to convey sexual knowledge to their children. The doctors explained, for instance, the glandular changes taking place during puberty, suggesting that they were distressful but unavoidable and normal. Parents were called to distinguish between pathology—like homosexuality, an "illness based on infantile crises" that merited treatment—and "normalcy," like masturbation.[75] *Nuestros Hijos* endorsed a single standard of continence for both women and men. While doctors believed that keeping this standard was harder for men, they acknowledged that young women also needed to be educated to choose continence; otherwise they would see continence as "repression," while "organizing orgies in their heads."[76] Escardó and Giberti, for their part, also emphasized the "glandular changes of puberty" and worked to normalize youth sexuality.[77] Furthermore, although both praised the importance of "healthy" sexuality within marriage (meaning that both partners should reach orgasm), they saw premarital sex as undesirable. Escardó even discouraged the practices that were known as petting in the United States, because they incited psychic imbalances. "It is a family responsibility," he wrote, "to teach girls the difference between a superficial touch on the face and insistent touch of the pubis or the breasts."[78] Thus Escardó and Giberti made young women responsible for setting limits on premarital sex, and mothers responsible for keeping tabs on their sexual behavior.

Despite the experts' efforts to make parents the transmitters of "enlightened" sexual information, by the mid-1960s there had been limited results. In 1964, Dr. Mauricio Knobel—a psychoanalyst who later became the most authoritative voice in adolescent analysis—conducted a survey of boys and girls ages eleven to thirteen, in public and private schools, to find out their level of knowledge about menstruation. Most girls responded with references to pain and suffering to the question "What do you know about menstruation?" and only a few focused on biological processes. The same was true when asked, "What is the purpose of menstruation?" While just a few girls related it to "development," boys were the only ones who connected menstruation to "reproduction." Likewise, he noted that boys got information from friends, whereas girls only listed their mothers as sources. Knobel concluded that parents—and chiefly mothers—"keep transmitting distorted values and taboos."[79] Giberti reached similar findings after a survey conducted of 420 adolescents receiving psychological treatment at a public hospital. She found that mothers said "the truth" about pregnancy, but provided idiosyncratic information on menstruation, mostly revolving around taboos such as "not taking showers." Meanwhile, the majority of the girls surveyed did not relate menstruation to the possibility of getting pregnant.[80] The picture Knobel and Giberti painted about girls' lack of accurate sexual information was worrying, mainly as they both recognized the spread of a new sexual attitude.

The new attitude toward premarital sex emerged gradually among youth throughout the 1960s. The erosion of the "taboo of female virginity" was at the core of the revamp of sexual mores, and it touched upon the sexual perceptions and ideals of young women and men alike. The rising public acceptance of premarital sex destabilized the double standard prescribing female virginity before marriage at the same time it tolerated—and expected—male sexual experience before marriage. Perhaps in an attempt to preserve their assumed sexual prerogatives, many young men showed anxieties vis-à-vis potential promiscuity. Interviewed about their attitudes regarding premarital sex, eight out of ten university students approved of having sex with their girlfriends, yet many wanted to ensure that they were the "first" and to be certain that the girls were not "having sex for fun," as a secondary school student put it.[81] Even counterculture organizers Miguel Grinberg and Juan Carlos Kreimer, while celebrating the association of sex with love, feared the "sport-like attitude towards sex" that they said was generalized among girls.[82] Few would concur with Ezequiel, age twenty-three, who in a roundtable stated, "sexual relations do not necessarily need to be related to love." His assertion proved, perhaps, ahead of its time. Meanwhile his peers at the roundtable agreed that virginity was "overvalued" and that premarital sex could take place within a loving relationship, which would be "doubled if the partners showed sexual compatibility," as one woman put it.[83]

A discourse centered on love, affection, and responsibility allowed many young women and men to create a new outlook on sex and, in doing so, begin to erode the "taboo of virginity." This new attitude crystallized in the late 1960s. In 1969, for example, a survey conducted by *Análisis* to determine "how youths love each other" noted that 57 percent of those from twenty to twenty-five years old did not think that "virginity" was important. Likewise, 67 percent of the men and 57 percent of the women approved of premarital sex; while 19 percent and 13 percent, respectively, thought that it was dependent "on the relation." The survey noted also that the rate of approval of premarital sex was higher among middle- and working-class youths, particularly those who held secondary or university diplomas.[84] In fact, the approval rating among the Argentine youths resembled those registered in other countries. Similar surveys showed that in France 70 percent of young men and 65 percent of women approved of premarital sex in 1970, while 55 percent of both sexes approved in Spain.[85] The awareness of a global transformation of attitudes toward premarital sex figured prominently in the ways some young women articulated their opinions. Interviewed by *La Bella Gente*—one of the first youth magazines—six girls who approved of premarital sex related their acceptance to an "international trend" toward "liberalized attitudes," as one office clerk, age seventeen, put it. These girls, like most young people in the 1960s, emphasized that sex should not be disengaged from love, and that love should end in "a marriage devoid of sexual taboos." While the girls identified themselves as Catholic, all agreed that sex was no longer a "sin."[86]

The Catholic family groups and Catholic spokespeople in the media responded to this new attitude by cautioning young women against it and by sexualizing marriage. The endorsement of the notion of marriage as a site where partners might achieve true sexual satisfaction was not new to Catholic groups: already in the 1950s, *Nuestros Hijos* advised young readers to read sexology books to prepare "for a perfect body communion" once married.[87] In 1967 the Christian Family Movement went a step further: after lobbying the church's hierarchy to make prenuptial courses mandatory for couples pursuing religious marriages, it passed a syllabus that required discussion of "the delights of sex."[88] Yet these Catholic groups and spokespeople publicly condemned premarital intercourse. Beginning in the mid-1960s, the women's magazine *Para Ti* and lifestyle magazine *Siete Días* hired priests to answer letters. They chose to answer letters written by girls who had premarital sex and subsequently experienced "troubles," such as being left by their boyfriends. The priests replied that these young women were "used" by men, who then chose virgins for marriage.[89] Other "troubles" were pregnancy and abortion, and the priests warned those who "went to doctors" of the moral and legal consequences of their actions.[90] By responding to these selected letters, priests focused on the fears that surely concerned many young women.

In the 1960s, many young women continued to fear unwanted pregnancies because they did not have access to contraception despite the active public debate over contraceptives. Secondary school and college students voiced their concerns about sex in a series of workshops in 1967: out-of-wedlock pregnancies ranked first, often in association with abortion. Some girls like Laura, age sixteen, asked about "How the Pill works."[91] In fact, largely triggered by global concerns over the birth control pill and, later, by Pope Paul VI's encyclical *Humanae Vitae* (1968)—endorsing periodic abstinence as the only approved method of family planning—the press took on contraception, including descriptions of how devices and techniques worked.[92] Information about contraceptives was available, but their use was limited and uneven. Access to contraceptives was, and is, class-based. Among married couples, reliance on condoms and co-itus interruptus (withdrawal) prevailed throughout the 1960s. The birth control pill, meanwhile, was restricted to upper-middle-class women.[93] Most women probably worried about possible side-effects and the cost. The use of the Pill, according to surveys in pharmacies, was restricted to adult women and only "a few students came to get it," as one pharmacist noted.[94] Thus, although young women surely had the chance to learn how the pill worked and knew that it was reliable, they—like their peers in the United States, Italy, or Chile—had limited access to it.[95] If they wanted to have sex, they depended on their partners to avoid pregnancy.

How extensive was the practice of premarital sexual intercourse in the 1960s? Although data on sexual behavior are inconsistent, there are threads of evidence that suggest it probably increased with a growing pub-lic tolerance toward premarital sex. It bears noting that, as scholars have shown, the incidence of premarital and extramarital sex, chiefly among the working classes, was high throughout the twentieth century. This was shown by the high rate of out-of-wedlock births, which was 26 percent of the total in 1960.[96] As surveys with middle-class young women showed, more and more of them dared to have intercourse before getting married. One survey conducted of 207 recently married couples in 1967 found that 14 percent had had premarital sex. In addition, in a survey she conducted from 1965 to 1968 of 420 unmarried youth, Dr. Giberti found that 18 per-cent of girls had had sexual intercourse.[97] As one doctor noted in 1970, the practice was not generalized: within "not intellectualized" sectors, he argued, it was more limited than within the "intellectualized" ones. In 1969, one survey carried out among female college students showed that 80 percent had "lost their virginity."[98]

In addition to the inconsistent survey data, one other piece of evidence points to the spread of extramarital and premarital sexual intercourse: the boom of room-by-the-hour hotels. Unlike the United States and countries where a campus culture existed, both middle- and working-class youths in Argentina usually lived with their parents until they married or began to "cohabitate."[99] Most young people lacked private places or even cars, and the room-by-the-hour hotels, or *albergues transitorios*, were the only places where many young people could go to have uninterrupted sexual liaisons. In 1960 the City Council of Buenos Aires passed a new regulation allow-ing hotel owners to offer "rooms per hour" to couples "of both sexes."[100] This and subsequent regulations specified that the *albergues transitorios* must be located at least one hundred meters from schools and churches and could not publicize their services on billboards or in pamphlets, in response to complaints of conservative groups.[101] The transitory hotels proved a success: in 1960, 169 hotels turned into "per-hour" hotels; the figure jumped to 420 in 1965 and 769 in 1967. When asked about the demand for their flourishing business, hotel owners and employees indicated that their clientele was composed of two strands: adults who went "after office hours, around 6:00 to 8:00 P.M." and "scores of young, dating couples," who went mostly late at night.[102]

Finally, other evidence suggests that women engaged more frequently in premarital sex and helped "legalize" its practice: in 1965, Congress and the Senate passed Law 16688, which made a prenuptial medical certificate mandatory for women. Legislators presented the plan as an extension of the antivenereal prophylaxis law 12331 passed in 1936. Framed in a eugenic paradigm that conceived of venereal diseases as hereditary and damaging to the future of the "race," in 1936 legislators approved the creation of a medical system for the prevention and treatment of venereal diseases. They also abolished legalized prostitution and prescribed a prenuptial medical certificate for men. The law focused on the male body as the potential carrier of venereal infections that the state would try to control. Only doctors at public hospitals and health centers could administer the blood test proving that men were healthy and thus authorizing them to marry.[103] In 1936, legislators could not accept that women planning to marry could transmit venereal diseases: they were supposed to be virgins. In 1965, legislators used the same arguments centered on antivenereal prophylaxis that their peers had deployed thirty years before. UCR Senator César Abdala, for example, claimed, "Between 1953 and 1963, the rate of infections like syphilis and gonorrhea increased notably."[104] With no need for debate, legislators agreed that women would also be required to obtain a prenuptial medical certificate.

Law 16688 implicitly recognized that women could have sex before marriage. In contrast to what happened with Law 12331 in 1936, this one did not incite debate among legal or medical experts. Newspapers barely even reported the news while some only noted that similar laws existed in other countries like the United States, Mexico, and Dominican Republic. Yet none editorialized on the subject.[105] Only *Confirmado* conducted a survey of doctors and women regarding the prenuptial certificate. Commenting on the survey, the journalist pointed out that even those who opposed the law thought that "it legalized an obvious reality: women's sexual liberation." The journalist concluded ironically, "today, the image of the maiden awaiting the wedding night to offer her treasure to her chosen one is contradicted by the experience of doctors and sociologists."[106] Albeit exaggerated, the statement sheds light on the incipient normalization of premarital sex in Argentina's public life, and young women were fueling this change.

▶ Young Women in early 1960s Argentina were literal and figurative protagonists in a series of major changes regarding sexuality, domestic ideals, and the ways in which patriarchal authority was understood and practiced. Rather than a linear path toward the expansion of horizons and opportunities for young women and the liberalization of sex mores, the changes in their life experiences followed a more sinuous route. The signs indicating that these life experiences would be markedly different from those of previous generations were subject to contention, expressing themselves in familial and broader cultural realms. The persistence of this contentiousness well into the 1960s showed how embattled the changes were and also made visible ongoing cultural dynamics that encouraged "modernizing" attitudes toward sexuality that had young women's experiences at their core.

Young women in the early 1960s questioned the premises of domesticity and patriarchal authority and, in doing so, "left home" as it was then known. Rather than self-aware, this questioning was eminently practical: by remaining longer in education, fully participating in the labor market, and shaping mixed leisure activities, for example, young women helped extend the "legitimate" spheres for women's actions. They created a span of time to experiment with jobs and careers as well as with new modes of courtship and sexuality. The gradual acceptance of premarital sex, in fact, further undermined the ideal of "domestic" femininity vis-à-vis sexual issues as well. Yet many young women faced daily battles when they dared to make decisions about careers, dating, or even weekend plans. Alongside increased educational, leisure, and sexual opportunities they found and carved out for themselves, many also confronted the persistence, and perhaps the reinforcement, of patriarchal authority at home. In practical ways, young women helped place patriarchal authority in the spotlight—chiefly in the discourse of advisers and psychologists—and began to erode its presumed naturalness.

The perceived contention of patriarchal authority formed the crux of many familial and cultural dilemmas, which both preceded and informed the construction of a moral panic around the Penjerek case. This panic addressed an attempt to set limits on the movement "away from home." While trying to reattract literal or imaginary runaway young women to the presumed safety of "home," many of these actors further tried to turn "home" into a safeguard against the supposed Communist menace. In doing so, they linked young women's changing life experiences to a broader disruption of societal order. The Penjerek case, though, was a doubly unsolved crime. First, on a literal level: we may never know who murdered Norma Penjerek and what happened to her. Second, the responses to her case constituted an effort to deal with ongoing cultural dynamics that set the conditions for the emergence of a new sexual attitude that complemented the symbolic movement "away from home" many young women experienced. In this vein, the Penjerek case acted as a watershed: it allowed us to see how deeply "conservative" discourses permeated Argentina's culture, while simultaneously underscoring its shortcomings.

The modernizing discourse that gained favor in the 1960s served to further destabilize those notions of "home" premised on domestic femininity and on the imagery of women as virgins until marriage, while men were free to sexually experiment. By drawing on a discourse centered on love and responsibility, 1960s youth helped redefine sex and the contexts in which it could be practiced. It bears noting that this attitude was seen as a sign of the cultural modernization Argentines underwent collectively, yet also as not totally disruptive to domestic ideals. What became publicly accepted was *premarital* sex: sexual intercourse in a heterosexual relationship that ideally led to marriage. In the increasingly tolerant landscape, young women—especially in the middle class—dared to experiment further with premarital sex, although they continued to fear unwanted pregnancies and relied on their partners for contraception. It is worth noting that many young men expressed anxieties vis-à-vis the potential "promiscuity" of young women once the so-called "taboo of virginity" began to fade. Toward the late 1960s, it became apparent that the sexual double standard had not vanished but had been redefined within a profound eroticization of Argentina's culture that also put young women at center stage. Yet these were other cohorts of young women who perhaps did not suffer from the same familial and cultural dilemmas that their predecessors did in the early 1960s. Both cohorts, though, may have had the chance to listen, in 1967, to Lennon and McCartney's "She's leaving home"—off the memorable *Sergeant Pepper's Lonely Hearts Club Band*. Young women in Argentina had already begun to do so: The Beatles just offered the most suitable soundtrack.

5 ▶ A Fraternity of Long-Haired Boys

ROCK AND A YOUTH CULTURE OF CONTESTATION

Some days after the coup d'état led by General Juan Carlos Onganía in 1966, the rock trio Los Beatniks recorded a simple album with Columbia Broadcasting System (CBS). The leading voice, Moris, composed the lyrics, including those to the song "Rebelde." "People call me the rebel," he wrote, "because rebel is my heart / I am free / and they want to make / a slave of tradition / out of me." As CBS was not interested in promoting their work, Los Beatniks moved ahead and organized a promotional party that ended with all of its members semi-naked at a public fountain in downtown Buenos Aires. The press reported on the event, though not in the culture section but rather in the police section: the trio went on to spend three days jailed in a police station.[1] This foundational episode outlines the contours of the first decade of Argentina's rock culture (1966–75). First, it introduces the main actors, who were rockers—poets, musicians, fans—the culture industry, and the state. Second, this episode shows rockers' most common attitude: an iconoclastic reaction against the rules and perceived authoritarianism of everyday life. Finally, it shows how rock culture was viewed in the public arena, which was as an epitome of cultural, gender, and sexual disorder.

Argentina's rock culture was among the liveliest in Latin America and offers a vantage point for analyzing the dynamics of sociocultural modernization and its discontents. The scholars who have studied Argentina's rock culture have thus far tried to understand its specifics and have shown that it is hardly definable in solely audible and linguistic terms—even though it is not irrelevant that the local rockers (like their Chilean and Colombian but unlike their Mexican counterparts) produced songs written and performed in Spanish.[2] As cultural critic Lawrence Grossberg notes for the United States, rock was the basis for a cultural politics that attempted to transcend the limits of everyday life and "articulate a sense of anger, dissatisfaction, occasionally protest."[3] The Argentine rockers appropriated practices and styles from a transnational repertoire and used them to cope with their everyday lives, which they often viewed as meaningless and dehumanizing. As it happened in other Latin American countries, the Argentine rockers' rebellion against their everyday life was over-determined by their practical opposition to authoritarianism.[4] Rock culture sensitized young people, especially young men, to cultural and political authoritarianism, hence crucially contributing to the shaping of a heterogeneous, multilayered, and radicalized youth culture of contestation that was full-fledged in the 1970s.

That youth culture of contestation became one of the markers of Argentina's history in the late 1960s and early 1970s. Onganía and the military that imposed the so-called *Revolución Argentina* did so under the premises that the political system could not guarantee the "order" that Argentines needed to develop and, in turn, to prevent the spread of Communism. As a result, they restricted all political activity—from party politics to student activism—at the same time that they tried to infuse a traditionalist moralistic ethos into the citizenry in an effort to forge individuals respectful for social and cultural hierarchies. Although the military tried hard, they could neither pacify the country nor stop the cultural rebellion associated with youth. Young people, in fact, were key protagonists of the concatenated popular revolts that, in May of 1969, marked the political finale of the Onganía regime. Moreover, between 1969 and 1973—when elections were held and Peronism could for the first time in seventeen years freely compete—Argentines lived an intense cycle of political participation pervaded by increasingly radicalized projects. Guerrilla groups represented the most extreme examples of that radicalization, and at least five of them staged actions at a national level promising to move the country toward national and social "liberation." Those promises seemed closed to fulfillment in 1973 when Héctor Cámpora, with the Peronist ticket, won the elections and set the stage for a short democratic spring, a powerful juncture of political and cultural openness that many young people experienced with passion. That spring lasted a short time, though. Juan Perón led the turn toward the right during his third and final presidency (from October 1973 to his death on July 1, 1974). His government ended with the launching of a political project meant to reconstruct authority at all levels of social life. A broad youth culture of contestation spread from Onganía to Perón, from authoritarianism to revolutionary projects. It finally suffered from state repression and social scorn. Rock culture made up one strand of that culture of contestation.

Throughout its first decade, rock culture was almost exclusively male. It was nurtured by the discontent of rising contingents of young men with the new and old institutions that punctuated their passage to adulthood—secondary schools, conscription, and paid jobs—as well as with the values of respectability, discipline, and respect for hierarchies. Rock culture was one of the venues through which middle- and working-class youth delineated a practical, rather than self-conscious, opposition to the ways in which hegemonic versions of masculinity were shaped.[5] In the "pioneering years" of Argentina's rock—coincident with the Onganía regime—they built up an iconoclastic, cross-class fraternity of long-haired boys, which incited not only police repression but also a wide-ranging homophobic reaction to uphold a defense of patriarchal authority and so-called correct "manners and morals." The study of rock culture thus offers a lens for viewing how young men confronted the values that premised the hegemonic constructions of masculinity as part of a cultural politics that privileged the pursuit of hedonism and companionship.

It became apparent that rockers' fraternity had expanded both onstage and offstage as the 1970s went on. The fads and body styles that originated among rockers and filtered through the market now transformed the aesthetics of masculinity and paved the way for redefining how it could be performed. Those changes, however superficial, were one avenue for modernizing masculinity. Most fundamentally, young men attracted to rock encouraged that modernization by focusing on values such as equality and authenticity, which allowed for imagining and eventually enacting new projects of love and family—values more evident in the hardcore countercultural projects linked, also, with rock culture. In a context of rising politicization and radicalization in which youth occupied the center stage, rockers' alternative masculinity and their reaction to the cultural authoritarianism pervading everyday life were seen as insufficient. Rock culture's interaction with the overtly political subset of the youth culture of protest during the 1970s was porous yet tense. In the symbolic confrontations between these subsets, there was a competition over the interpellation to working- and middle-class young men.

Boys Will Not Be Men

In the late 1960s and early 1970s, popular singer Palito Ortega, who reached the top of the charts with each single he recorded, was the protagonist of a long series of movies chronicling the allegedly common pattern of coming of age for young men in Argentina. Ortega, thus, fulfills his military service and learns to love his country and his fellow soldiers, encounters his first girlfriend, exchanges blue jeans for grey-flannel suits, gets married and joyfully copes with his in-laws, and still remains faithful to his old friends. For the young men attracted to rock culture at the time, Ortega as a popular idol as well as a role model for coming of age personified exactly what they did not want to be. Rock culture sprang from and expressed young men's discontent with the cultural sites that organized the dynamics of boys becoming men and the ways in which these sites enforced the values of respectability, discipline, and consumerism. Rockers instead called for individual authenticity, which they believed was embodied by the *pibes* (boys).

Throughout the 1960s, the process of growing up for young men—as for young women—incorporated their rising enrollment in the secondary schools, critical spaces for the organization of their daily life and venues for experimenting with new and old forms of authoritarianism. While 23 percent of boys in the fifteen-to-nineteen age group were enrolled in a secondary school in 1960, the figure doubled in 1970. In Buenos Aires, though, the figure jumped to 65 percent.[6] Young men were evenly distributed into baccalaureate colleges and technical schools, which were the "stars" for policy makers interested in promoting socioeconomic development.[7] Yet during the 1960s the authorities viewed young men less as contributors to development and more as potential defenders of the nation from so-called internal and external enemies. Since the imposition of military rule in 1966, educational authorities asked school principals to have male students above sixteen years old practice shooting guns.[8] For many boys, shooting guns was merely the most evident example of how the school enforced a militaristic order, which transpired also in the daily school routines. In 1968, a survey of five hundred students showed that a majority complained about "senseless routines." In subsequent years, boys expressed similar feelings: "at the school you are subject to what others want to make of you," one boy argued. In what was a common belief worldwide, many youths in Argentina also believed that "Everything I am is out of the school."[9]

Young men frequently noted a bifurcation of their school and their out-of-school life, which was expressed, for example, in body styles. The schools acted as a major arena for the battles over the length of boys' hair. The *Reglamento* (bylaws) prescribed that students "should always attend in a hygienic condition and wear pertinent clothing." As the authorities clarified, boys were required to wear grey pants, a jacket, and tie.[10] Moreover, in 1969 the principals of twenty-five schools in Buenos Aires, Rosario, La Plata, and Córdoba addressed the new fashions by sending notes to parents detailing that their boys' hair should be no less than eight centimeters above their shoulders. Otherwise they would be unable to enroll.[11] Because many boys aspired to wear their hair long, this prohibition represented the schools' arbitrariness and elicited countless battles. For example, in 1971 the authorities of a school in Buenos Aires expelled an eighteen-year-old boy because, in their view, he did not wear appropriate clothing and had his "hair too long." The boy's classmates protested in solidarity, and twenty-five of them were expelled as well. A similar episode took place at the start of the 1972 school year, when four hundred students of another school in Buenos Aires refused to comply with the clothing and hair requirements and called for a student strike until they were allowed to wear their hair longer. The long hair battles then intersected with other struggles over the disciplinary system. While some students at the Colegio Nacional planted a bomb at a sentry box from which the caretakers controlled them, others entered the schools en masse to avoid being expelled for wearing their hair long.[12]

Often overlooked in the accounts of youth politicization of the early 1970s, those battles nevertheless showed that many young men were willing to confront new and old forms of authoritarianism, which in this case was geared toward creating bodily signs of respectability. The secondary schools were privileged sites for generating discontent among young men. Not coincidentally, the band that made of rock a mass phenomenon in the 1970s, Sui Géneris—namely, Charly García and Nito Mestre—formed while they studied at a military school. Sui Géneris appealed to a school-based audience by interpreting adolescents' concerns (like their first sexual encounters) and by deploying school metaphors and language. For example, in "*Aprendizaje*" (Learning), García wrote, "1 learnt to be / formal and polite / 1 had my hair cut / once a month"; the boy "failed in formality" because "[he] never liked society."[13] The school provided the rules that governed boys' daily life, perceived as senseless and authoritarian. While in times of rising politicization García never identified his poetical work as political, he acknowledged that it had an ideological dimension: "writing about the school," he said "is writing about repressive ideology."[14] In the vanguard of the anti-institutional and antiauthoritarian cultural politics that rock represented, García also wrote "*Botas locas*" (Crazy Boots), a denunciation of what he viewed as the most absurd of the institutions punctuating the boys-will-be-men dynamics: conscription.[15]

Conscription had long represented a rite of passage to adulthood and had long elicited criticism. Established in 1902, conscription was first widely implemented in 1911 when the immigration process was at its height and a radicalized labor movement had emerged as well. From the elites' perspective, it was supposed to forge patriotic sentiments and mold citizens to be respectful of the principles of order and hierarchy. It was met with opposition during the first half of the twentieth century, both from individuals and collectively: for example, anarchist militants rejected the repressive and militaristic ethos it endorsed.[16] Conscription, however, was naturalized in the public milieu until at least 1968, when Law 17,531 slightly changed the terms for its fulfillment. Until that point, all young men age twenty participated in a lottery; then half of them were excluded while the other half underwent physical examinations and, if acceptable, joined the military. It didn't matter if they held jobs or studied. Law 17,531 stipulated that young men could finish their degrees before complying with the conscription. But delay did not imply exemption, the only one of which was being the head of a household. Argentina's terms for conscription were comparable to those of Brazil and Colombia, while Mexico and Chile had more flexible legislation.[17]

Moreover, amid rising political radicalization in which young men played a vital role, the military and at least one guerrilla group, the Marxist Ejército Revolucionario del Pueblo (ERP, People's Revolutionary Army), endowed conscription with new significance. Beginning in 1970, the army updated its lectures on ideological training given to its low-ranking cadres and conscripts. Five out of the fifteen lectures revolved around the alleged dangers that "Communism" posited to the nation and to the family. The lectures showed an enemy, depicted as monstrous, already acting within the geographical borders of the nation, infiltrating schools, colleges, parishes, and also the military.[18] In September of 1973, or four months after the resumption of civilian rule and weeks before Juan Perón became president, an ERP unit tried to take out an army commando unit. In that misadventure, which ended with all the guerrillas imprisoned, the ERP had the logistical support of one conscript within the commando unit. Interestingly, though, it was another conscript who stopped the guerrillas' success.[19] Both the army and the ERP claimed this episode for propagandistic ends. Thus, the army depicted its loyal conscript as a patriotic and bold young man who saved the nation and his group of "future men of the fatherland." For its part, the ERP described its conscript as "the people's soldier" and celebrated his courage.[20] In 1974 and 1975, as the military was

128 A Fraternity of Long-Haired Boys

called to stifle popular protest and guerrilla activities, the ERP addressed the conscripts to avoid their involvement with repressive actions. The ERP developed a tactics of recruitment and recommended that the conscripts take advantage of military training for the "popular war"—suggestions that did not actually work.[21] 7 wait what

For many young men, though, conscription was an arena ripe for shaping discontent with authority. Interviewed after the passing of the Law 17531, sixty-five conscripts from every corner of the country stationed in Buenos Aires complained about the daily routines, the bad food, and the unhealthy conditions of the barracks. Finding nothing like the imagery of conscription as the egalitarian space for the mingling of young men from different regions and social backgrounds where they learned to become patriotic and courageous citizens—ideals posited by the movies featuring Palito Ortega and the military alike—the conscripts expressed anger for the humiliation they suffered from their superiors.[22] Subsumed into the "subordination and courage" required (as the military slogan mandated it) to forge men out of boys, those humiliations were seen as outrageous for the youth attracted to rock culture. In one of the few memoirs by a rock fan, then poet and musician, Miguel Cantilo commented that, for him and his friends—who had already chosen "a life opposed to conventions [that] collided with the military model"—conscription represented a "death trap." Yet Cantilo also points to their families who, "hypocritical accomplices with the military," thought that conscription would be useful to "make a man out of you."[23] In his view, there was a continuum between the "death trap" set by the military and the expectations that parents projected onto it to instill discipline and obedience among their boys.

The values of discipline, respectability, and respect for hierarchies were supposedly learned and internalized in conscription and, for an increasing number of boys, in the secondary school. These were also the keystones for the ideal responsible worker. The labor market showed two novelties related to young men's changing experiences and expectations. First, census data show that boys remained longer in the education system and that reduced their participation in the labor market: 73 percent of the young men ages fifteen to nineteen held jobs in 1947, but by 1970 the figure had dropped to 55 percent. An increasing segment of young men in the 1960s, thus, were better educated than their fathers, and began working for pay later in their life cycle as well.[24] Second, young men in urban areas had an increasing opportunity of finding jobs in what became the most dynamic sector of the economy: the tertiary, or service, sector. With the important exception of Córdoba, which attracted a vast young male population to its industrial belt, the jobs created in the industrial sector paled in comparison with the tertiary sector. The service sector accounted for 47 percent of the employed population in 1947 and 52 percent in 1970.[25] Even though the bulk of those positions was in commerce-related jobs, the second largest area was in administration, that is, office clerks in public and private areas. The quintessential representation of the white-collar employee, the *oficinista* (office clerk) came to occupy a prominent position in the imagination of the young men attracted to rock.

Rockers created dystopian ideas vis-à-vis their potential futures, and the *oficinista* embodied their most feared prospects for life. For rock poets, the office clerk incarnated the monotony and conservatism that the large cities required of their workers. In their first single, for example, the folk rock duo Pedro y Pablo (Miguel Cantilo and Jorge Durietz) sang:

Yo vivo en una ciudad	I live in a city
donde la gente aun usa gomina	where people still use hair wax
donde la gente se va a la oficina	where people go to the office
sin un minuto de más . . .	without a minute to lose . . .
Y sin embargo yo quiero a ese pueblo	And, yet, I love these people,
porque me incita a la rebelión.	because they lead me to rebel.[26]

In the lyrics, the city's people are all male and they are the *oficinistas*, always in a hurry, still using "*gomina*," the hair gel that the older generations used to slick back their hair as a sign of respectability. City people elicit ambivalent reactions: The singers love them, but only because they lead them to "rebel." The beloved and despised *oficinista* was rockers' counterfigure: he illustrated, in a pathetic way, the "system's success." As some rock fans pointed out, the orderly behavior and respect for authority required in the schools and the barracks resulted not in a "warriorlike man" but in the office clerk who "has included these values into his life: poor little thing!"[27] The *oficinista*, then, came to represent the end point of a process that many young men confronted and that resonated worldwide. In the 1950s, in North America, for instance, the "organization man"—in David Riesman's formulation—who purportedly aimed to conform to prevalent cultural norms was met with oppositional figures such as the "young rebel" and the bohemian young poets.[28] In the Argentina of the 1960s also the "square" *oficinista* and the "hip" rocker, as public figures, took shape in a concurrent fashion.

Through their vilification of the *oficinista*, rockers also engaged in a

broader criticism of the middle classes. In the 1960s, essayists popularized the image of an individualistic, conservative, and moralistic middle
class. Juan José Sebreli, thus, focused on the *oficinista* as the embodiment
of "petit bourgeois alienation." Manipulating paperwork instead of producing, Sebreli claimed, he "navigated the surface of things." His structural position explained his obsession with order and appearances, applied
also to other spheres of his life, from the family to sex. The nationalist
essayist Arturo Jauretche also touched upon how the *medio pelo* (parvenu)
struggled with his or her appearance and with living an inauthentic lifestyle pervaded by superficiality and emulation—which Jauretche found
problematic since it created a divide between the middle classes and "the
people."[29] As other scholars have noted, the criticism produced by nationalist and leftist middle-class writers worked as a literature of mortification,
as self-revenge for the political role that class played during the Peronist
regime and its aftermath.[30] Although they were less politicized, rockers
also framed their criticism using mortifying rhetoric. However, their criticism pointed to a cultural and generational rebellion against becoming an
oficinista, like the fathers of many of them. → *cyclical?*

The questioning of the *oficinista* intersected with the perception of a
link between working and consuming: for youth attracted to rock, the
oficinista seemed imprisoned in an oppressive routine meant to satisfy a *long hours?*
never-ending consumerist drive. Arguments about consumerism swept
across rock cultures worldwide. Although scholars differ in their assessment of the extent of rockers' confrontation, most agree that rock culture
itself stemmed from and reacted against the rising of affluent societies and
of consumption as a key arena for the building of identities.[31] In not-so-
affluent Argentina, sarcastic reflections on the efforts to achieve "status"
through consumption prevailed, and the *oficinista* evoked both the desire
and the failure of these efforts. That was the crux of *La fiaca* (Laziness),
Ricardo Talesnik's play first staged in 1968 and then adapted as movie,
directed by Fernando Ayala, and released in 1969. The focus is on the story
of Néstor, a middle-aged office clerk, who surprises his wife and his co-
workers when he decides not to go to work anymore because he *tiene fiaca*
(became lazy). In a telling sequence, the movie mixes images of Néstor's leisured life with the disappearance of the appliances from his home: as he is
unable to pay the monthly installments, he loses the washing machine and
the television set. Such an offense to the family's status is unbearable to
his wife, who pushes Néstor to go back to work. In 1971, journalist Tomás
Eloy Martínez also wrote ironically that the *oficinista* held three jobs at the

same time and, in order "show others that he is doing great," was willing to "sell his house to buy a car."[32] The localization of the relationship between working and consuming reverberated in the rockers' milieu. One of trio Manal's blues touched on these cultural mandates imposed onto men: "It is not necessary to have a car / or four well-paid jobs / no, no, no *pibe* / for having someone to love you."[33] Appealing to the child, the songwriter cautions him about the risk of becoming a man who overworks in order to overconsume, the result of the boys-will-be-men process.

The young men attracted to rock culture in Argentina contested the sites and practices whereby the values of discipline, respectability, and consumerism were supposed to be learned. Their contestation was premised on the symbolic potential of the *pibe* as a source of authenticity. As in Manal's song, the *pibe* should not become *that* man or, for that matter, not become a man at all. In fact, rockers seemed to call for being *pibes* forever and thus keeping the spontaneity and freedom associated with boyhood. This link resembled what the anthropologist Eduardo Archetti found among football fans, who singularized an "Argentine style of play" by drawing on ideas of boyhood, creativity, and authenticity.[34] Stemming from and reacting against the process in which hegemonic masculinities were shaped, rockers proposed to remain *pibes* and, moreover, they practically created an imagined fraternity of boys.

A Fraternity of Long-Haired Boys

In June of 1967, Los Gatos recorded the simple "La Balsa" (The Raft) with the local subsidiary of Radio Corporation of America (RCA). Composed by José Alberto Iglesias, aka Tanguito, and Litto Nebbia, it called on young men to drop out, to build an imaginary raft, and *naufragar* (be shipwrecked). "La Balsa" achieved immediate success, selling 250,000 copies in six months. Moreover, it indicated that Spanish would be the language for Argentina's rock, in contrast to Latin American countries with active rock cultures, such as Mexico, where mostly English was used. Most important, it became the first anthem for a group of young men it helped identify as *náufragos*: like shipwrecked sailors, they would live adrift or, rather, against the current with their imaginary raft. As their counterparts abroad did, these early rockers were also recognizable because of their long hair. In late 1960s Argentina, wearing long hair and engaging in rock sociability entailed the risk of police detention. The homophobic reaction that informed the police raids cut across other social spheres as well. Rockers did create homosocial spaces and fraternal bonds, which excluded women and served to carve out ideals of masculinity centered on companionship, pleasure, and hedonism. In doing so, they reelaborated previous projects of cultural revolt.

Beginning in the early 1960s, young poets and artists pointed to the need to build a space for a rebellious youth, halfway between the commercialized and the politicized. Poet Miguel Grinberg had a pioneering role. He was one of the first translators of the Beatnik poets in Argentina and a regular pen pal with Allen Ginsberg and Lawrence Ferlinghetti. Through his literary magazine *Eco Contemporáneo*, Grinberg tried to mobilize a generation of *mufados* (exasperated). They would be youth who, unlike those engaged in politics, "psychically revolutionize their own territory." Likewise, the *mufados* would differ from the youth linked to commercialized cultures, epitomized by Palito Ortega and his celebration of "squareness."[35] Grinberg was hardly alone in his interest in cultural experimentation. By the mid-1960s, a series of new spaces and practices emerged in relation to the Instituto Di Tella (IDT), an art center that praised novelty and youth as key values. In the public arena, most of the experimentation in the IDT and nearby was viewed as scandalous. Often compared with the Swinging London, although more similar to the Zona Rosa in Mexico, the streets adjacent to the IDT—the *manzana loca* (crazy block)—comprised a cosmopolitan enclave, where the "unconventional" prevailed: there, the first miniskirts were sold and worn, and stores imported the records by Jefferson Airplane and Jimi Hendrix.[36] As portrayed in the movie *Tiro de Gracia* (dir. Ricardo Becher, 1969), that area exerted a pull on artists such as Sergio Mulet, the director of the literary magazine *Opium*, who proclaimed that he and his fellows were "apolitical revolutionaries."[37]

The rhetoric centered on the "unconventional," the iconoclastic mood in some enclaves, and the will to build a cultural space between the commercialized and politicized youth— all of these reverberated in the nascent rock culture in Argentina. As narrated countless times in stories, everything began at La Cueva, a pub in Barrio Norte, where young men gathered to listen to jazz and then to informally play rock music. La Cueva was a site for the would-be "pioneers" of Argentina's rock to interact, and they included Moris—trio Los Beatniks' leader—Litto Nebbia and other members of the quartet Los Gatos, Tanguito, Javier Martínez, and poet Pipo Lernoud. Around twenty years old, most of those young men had detached themselves from their family settings. Los Gatos, for example, migrated to Buenos Aires from Rosario with a contract to play music at social clubs organized by an entertainment company. As Nebbia recalls, they barely made a living and could only afford to rent rooms in humble hotels, where they mingled with Moris, Martínez, and Lernoud. These were middle-class boys from Buenos Aires: moving to the hotels entailed, for them, forging lifestyles other than those connected with the family, schools, and paid jobs. Familiar with the Beatles and Rolling Stones, they had scarce expert musical training but learned in an autodidactic fashion, within the continuum of the hotels, La Cueva, and La Perla, where Nebbia and Tanguito allegedly composed "La Balsa."[38]

While "La Balsa" was climbing to the top of the charts, some *náufragos* organized an event that positioned them as bearers of a new cultural politics, conveyed through bodily styles, and organized across unconventional and antiauthoritarian sentiments and practices. Poet Lernoud and other fellows called for a celebration of the coming of spring in Plaza San Martin, near the manzana loca. They invited all young men wearing long hair and requested that they "dress as [they] would dress if [they] lived in a free country." To the organizers' surprise, on September 21, 1967, about three hundred long-haired boys wearing colorful clothes showed up. Tanguito—among others—played the guitar and they all walked along the main commercial streets in downtown Buenos Aires, intermittently singing "La Balsa."[39] The "we" that these early rockers articulated was anchored in a common taste for rock music and in bodily styles—colored clothing and, chiefly, long hair. Borrowing on anthropologist Greg McCracken's apt expression, hair for these young men had become "transformational": it helped shape individual *and* collective identities.[40] For example, Tony— who did not attend Plaza San Martin—recalls that only two other boys and he wore long hair in his working-class neighborhood: "we were not friends," he says, "but we began first to say hello, then to listen to music, and finally to play together."[41] For these boys, long hair acted as a conduit to build up fraternal bonds and to express attitudes further cemented through rock music. Shaped and displayed in late-1960s Argentina, these styles, attitudes, and sociability involved contesting cultural and political authoritarianism.

In the spring and summer of 1967 and 1968, droves of long-haired boys became *náufragos*, developing a sociability based on hedonism and companionship. In Córdoba and Mendoza, for example, the main plazas served as places of congregation. Alvin, the "leader of the Córdoba beatniks," pointed out that his group of twenty boys wanted to transform the "sounds" of a city ruled by "priests and military bureaucrats"—a reference

Cartoon of *náufragos*. *Atlántida* No. 1213, December 1967.

to the main ideological and political alliance represented in the Onganía regime and also to a city famous for its clericalism and militarism.[42] In Buenos Aires, the Plaza Francia was the *náufragos'* reference point. They attracted some young women, like Silvia, who told the reporters that she had run away from her home, tired of her "father's tyranny." Silvia's story offers a glimpse of the difficulty that young women had in fully engaging with the emerging rock culture: without overtly confronting their parents, they had little chance of participating in rockers' street-based sociability. Young women comprised a minority of the three hundred "hippies" that, according to the press, gathered in Plaza Francia or in Plaza San Martin every day. What did they do? In one onsite report with the *náufragos* at Plaza Francia, a journalist commented that the "eccentric youths," besides sharing cigarettes and food, chatted all night long and "played rock music" until they "fell asleep under the trees."[43]

The mostly homosocial routines of these *náufragos* resemble other eras in the history of masculinity. In turn-of-the-twentieth-century Buenos Aires, demographic, social, and cultural factors converged in the crystal-lization of an active street-based male sociability. Cutting across social strata and joining men from different national origins—40 percent of the population of Buenos Aires was foreign-born in 1910—that sociability was made of young men. Whether they were married or single, these young men spent their spare time in cafés, taverns, and on the streets, in the company of friends and occasional acquaintances. Among them, masculinity was defined vis-à-vis physical strength and sexual prowess, obliterating values such as responsibility and arenas such as the family.[44] By the 1920s, that sociability had begun to vanish. New sociodemographic and cultural conditions favored the spread of a form of domestic life in which the ideal of masculinity revolved around attaining the ability to support "well-constituted" families. For the working and middle classes, being a "good" breadwinner required learning the obedience, responsibility, and respect for hierarchies that the dynamics of boys-will-be-men aimed to instill. Some of the old sociability did persist, though. The corner cafés, which could be found in most neighborhoods by midcentury, served as the institutions for informally upholding masculine ideals, sites where old and young men gathered to discuss football and "women's issues," as tango and literary pieces portrayed.[45] That was a confined sociability, which supplemented domestic life centered on the roles of husband and father and the labor arenas that consecrated the figure of the responsible worker. As those nostalgic of the bygone era complained, even the cafés and the groups of friends who congregated on street corners were disappearing in the 1960s, when the *náufragos* re-created a type of all-male sociability. Theirs was nonetheless premised upon the questioning of the domestic ideal of masculinity in the authoritarian context of the 1960s.

The *náufragos'* sociability and their bodily styles were markers through which they turned into a target of harassment and repression, just as in other countries at the same time, like Italy and Mexico.[46] On November 30, for example, *La Razón* informed its readers that a "group of 21 loud hippies" had been detained at Plaza San Martín after neighbors complained about their "scandalous songs and behavior." In the first weeks of January, at least 120 youths were detained not only in the "hippie enclaves" of downtown Buenos Aires but also in lower-middle-class neighborhoods of the city, such as Paternal and Villa Crespo.[47] Some *náufragos* also stated that young men known as the "Pompeya group" (for living in that working-class neighborhood) often went to Plaza Francia and beat them. When twenty youths organized a "rock happening" in Mar del Plata, at least "one hundred short-haired boys armed with sticks and stones" launched their attack against them.[48] In addition, the tiny but visible Federación de Entidades Anti-Comunistas de la Argentina (FAEDA, Federation of Anti-Communist Groups) carried out a rally where they asserted that the "hippies" were part of a "worldwide network of Castroite guerrillas," and accused former Socialist deputy Juan Carlos Coral of helping free them from police stations. Coral replied that he would "never help a hippie" because "they were well-to-do, effeminate."[49] While Coral stressed the hippies' alleged class standing as the reason why he rejected them, he drew on a prevalent belief: federal police, the "Pompeya group," the "short-haired boys," and FAEDA, each employed homophobia to ostracize the long-haired boys.

The reaction against *náufragos*, hippies, or rockers—exchangeable terms in the late 1960s—was premised on homophobic sentiments. Over the months of intense police and "civilian" raids, for example, the lifestyle magazine *Siete Días* published fifty-two letters from readers addressing the "hippie" issue. An adult man initiated the series of letters when he wrote to complain that the "long-haired hippies" represented a threat to Argentine society because, he argued, "they are all homosexual." Responding to this letter, two young men, signing as "Adam Dylan" and "Oswald Lennon," claimed that the "hippies and rockers" were the "true representatives of the Argentine youth" because they carried the "message of peace and love" that the country needed.[50] Readers were split regarding these two stances: while eight backed "Dylan and Lennon," forty-three agreed that "hippies and rockers" were a homosexual menace. Among them were many youths, including Omar, age twenty, who argued that rockers could not be "good Argentines" by "smoking marijuana and being homosexuals," an argument with which Juan "totally agreed." Carlos, age nineteen, argued even more heatedly: "if the hippies want to help the fatherland," he wrote, "they should be courageous and abandon their music and stupid clothes."[51] Ironically, psychologist Eva Giberti, who since the late 1950s had advocated for democratizing intergenerational relations, reached similar conclusions. Commenting on a concert by Los Gatos, she cautioned her readers about how dangerous the "little cross-dressing games" were for young men, since they would "heighten the natural sexual confusion of their age."[52]

The homophobic reaction the rockers incited upon first entering into the public milieu was framed by anxieties over the transformation in gender relations taking place in Argentina. It had been young women who, in a practical rather than self-conscious fashion, initially marked the limits of the prevailing arrangements of domesticity and patriarchal authority by remaining longer in the education system, fully participating in the labor market, helping shape youthful leisure activities, daring to experiment with new courtship mores, acknowledging publicly that they engaged in premarital sex, and marrying older than before.[53] Until the mid-1960s, young women's experiences and expectations created a generation gap vis-à-vis their mothers' that did not have a parallel in the case of their male counterparts. In the second half of the 1960s, though, rock culture offered a contingent of young men an iconoclastic framework through which they challenged the dynamics for making "men" out of boys. By stimulating a sociability centered on hedonism, companionship, and leisured life, rockers questioned discipline, responsibility, and sobriety, which were the premises for the hegemonic ideal of masculinity. As Eve Kosofsky Sedgwick pointed out, when some sense emerges that the traditional ways of transmitting patriarchal power are broken, it can "take the form of ideological homophobia."[54] Old and young men—and women—created a homosexual menace out of rockers, whom they believed jeopardized the generational continuity of patriarchal power. The blend of these social responses with the threat of police repression—common to other Latin American experiences—politicized rock culture, shaping the ideological and gender dynamics of the rapidly growing movement.[55]

In the late 1960s, countless groups of boys launched themselves into rock music by playing and listening. The first evidence that young men were taking up the music was the impressive increase in the sales of certain musical instruments: the sales of electric guitars had increased by 260 percent between 1967 and 1970, base guitars by 180 percent, and drums by 120 percent. In early 1970, a journalist suggested that, in Buenos Aires alone, there was a rock band every four blocks.[56] The explosion of music playing came as a boom for the record industry. In fact, after the success achieved by "La Balsa," record entrepreneurs embarked upon a search for bands to emulate Los Gatos. In mid-1968, a producer for RCA visited rehearsals throughout the city, like the ones of Almendra, a quartet led by Luis Alberto Spinetta, who had just finished secondary school. Meanwhile, a new label named Mandioca was formed by participants in the group of náufragos at Plaza Francia and also by the publisher Jorge Alvarez.[57] Unable to attract Almendra, this label produced the trio Manal and was a preeminent organizer of concerts. Burgeoning across Buenos Aires, rock concerts were venues for further shaping rockers' fraternity in the face of police harassment that took place in obscure halls and larger theaters alike.[58] Police harassment and state prohibitions oftentimes even conflicted with the music business. As late as 1970, a famous radio DJ and RCA executives organized the would-be "Argentine Woodstock" in a district 120 miles away from Buenos Aires. Police did intelligence work and concluded that the organizers were "drug addicts, with dubious morality." The police decided not to authorize it two days before the festival was due to begin.[59] Police repression was crucial for setting antiauthoritarianism as the most significant ideological component of rock culture, and that repression also partially helps explain why the fraternity of long-haired boys largely excluded women.

In the early 1970s, there were only three women in the fifty-five bands and soloists that had recorded. Gabriela, Carola, and María Rosa Yorio shared two commonalities: they were vocalists and all were married to prominent musicians. The marginalization of women in the rock scene was a global episode. Women, as performers, found more room within the folk variants of the rock scene. At the same time that Joni Mitchell recorded her first LP, for example, Gabriela did the same in Argentina. She also tried to find a more "female" voice but, unlike Mitchell's, hers was not feminist. In her "Voy a dejar esta casa, papá" (I'm leaving this house, dad), for example, Gabriela asked a fictionalized father "to come off his wings" since there was "another man waiting outside." There were no elements in her poetics that allowed for an autonomous female experience. Moreover, being the most successful female performer did not mean that she was booming in the market: "rockers are *machistas*," Gabriela explained.[60] Carola and María Rosa Yorio also recalled their earliest experiences as unfolding in an unfriendly landscape.[61]

Equally important, the initial venues of sociability like plazas and streets and then concerts were not a welcoming space for many young women. As a middle-class young woman, Hilda recalled that it was hard for girls to go to rock concerts: "We were afraid of the police, but our parents were more afraid."[62] Even when they were willing to attend, young women found it hard to negotiate with their parents: concerts were associated with disorder, not suitable for girls. Many girls, though, did have a chance to attend some concerts, like the shows organized by a radio program to celebrate the end of the 1969 school year, where bands like Manal played.[63] For musicians and "true" fans, these shows represented chances for "money making" and not for "playing." Young women only participated in rock sociability in contexts that male rockers deprecated. This also held true for the rock band with which young women engaged the most: Sui Géneris. The duo first played acoustically and sold almost two hundred thousand copies of its first LP in early 1972, which was reportedly purchased by both boys and girls. When many rockers praised "electric" sounds, Sui Géneris, according to their own producer and La Pesada's leader, Billy Bond, "played like and for girls [nenas]."[64] Playing "like nenas" was as insulting as playing "for nenas": rock was supposed to bind together a fraternity of boys.

Although young women were excluded from the fraternity of rockers, song lyrics were flush with representations of them. These representations oscillated between two poles: either a reverential attitude toward young women as the epitomes of tenderness and love or an aggressive posture towards supposed female superficiality. As in other countries in the 1960s, rock poets traded in imagery about "hippie princesses." Tanguito and Lernoud, for example, wrote of a "golden princess" who was ethereal, motherly, "perfect." This deferential attitude toward "princesses" reverberated in myriad lyrics related to love and sexuality. In one of the most poetically sophisticated lyrics of Argentina's rock, Spinetta sang to the "girl with honey breasts," asking her to "wait to dusk" while he built a "castle" with her "belly." Duo Pedro y Pablo deployed similar language when depicting "blonde Catalina" as a tender giver and taker of sexual pleasure.[65] Yet many rock lyrics constructed representations of women as mere sexual objects. Two years after writing on the "honey-breast" girl, Spinetta wrote the misogynistic "I like that pussy," and he also sang to the "foolish girl" who just wanted to be "suntanned." La Pesada, for their part, made use of an old childish rhyme addressing chores like sewing. While acidly criticizing domestic stereotypes of women, the song posited that it was hard to find a "lady who knows how to think," a verse that led one journalist to dub it as "rockers' antifeminist, or antifeminine, manifesto."[66]

Besides unveiling a *machista* sentiment, perhaps the antifeminine attitude rampant among some rockers comprised one way through which they tried to counter the homophobic claims against them. As scholars have noted for other contexts, rockers shaped their own sense of masculinity by expelling "the feminine," mainly when they were targets of homophobia.[67] In Argentina, slander of the feminine formed a key divide of the rockers' fraternity that opposed Almendra and Manal. Spinetta's leadership provided Almendra with poetically sophisticated lyrics as well as exquisite music that drew on fusion, notably with tango. Manal localized blues and relied on Javier Martínez's poetry, focused on narrations of rude, mostly working-class landscapes.[68] Scholars have assessed the opposition in class terms: Manal would have aimed at interpellating a working-class audience, while denying that Almendra belonged to a rock culture based upon claims they were mere "middle-class boys."[69] Yet the members of both bands came from middle-class families and, as Mario Rabey—former manager of Manal—recalls, both attracted a cross-class audience to their concerts. "Almendra was softer," he sarcastically recalls, "while Manal was a boys' thing." In the opinions of some of Manal's fans, the trio sounded "more macho."[70] The rockers' fraternity was misogynist on its own terms and helped to incite a discussion about what Argentines expected from the boys-will-be-men dynamics as well as about the significance of "manners and morals" in an authoritarian context. Embedded within a transnational repertoire of ideas, sounds, and images, rockers' iconoclasm cut across class barriers to encompass an ever-growing mass of middle- and working-class men.

Three Times Hair: Beat, Rock, and Counterculture

In March of 1970, the movie *El extraño de pelo largo* (The Long-Hair Stranger) became a hit. By drawing on the symbolism of long hair, the movie epitomized the implosion of "beat" styles that pervaded the visual and sonic spheres. In that year, also, the first rock magazine in Argentina appeared, tellingly titled *Pelo* (Hair). *Pelo* was crucial for creating labels to assess what rock meant vis-à-vis beat, including the notion of authenticity, which it applied to Almendra, Manal, and Los Gatos—all of which disbanded in 1970, at the height of their popularity. *Pelo* also organized annual festivals where the rockers' fraternity gathered en masse, one of the key elements of the "second-stage" of Argentina's rock culture (ca. 1970–75). In 1971, Argentines saw their version of Gerome Ragni and James Rado's musical *Hair*. Criticized because of its links to the entertainment industry, the experience of *Hair* nevertheless allowed for members of its cast to start communal living. The three variants of hair revealed different articulations of masculinity. The youth attracted to rock helped modernize the contours of masculinity by helping to expand the aesthetic parameters of how men could look, and, more crucially, by insisting on a cultural politics that allowed for reimagining experiences of love and family.

The first invocation to "hair" refers to the success of *El extraño de pelo largo*, which was premised on the beat wave. That phenomenon fueled a renewed expansion of the music industry, which was directly involved in shaping and marketing the bands. Record production expanded dramatically: while in 1967—the year of "La Balsa"—15.5 million records were produced and sold, in 1969 that number rose to 27 million, and in 1971 to 40 million. Business reports showed that, between 1968 and 1970, 70 percent of local records belonged to beat music.[71] Targeted as a beat band, for example, Almendra sold one hundred thousand copies of its single "Muchacha (ojos de papel)" and twenty-five thousand of its LP. Yet the figures pale when compared to the success achieved by Los Náufragos, whose singles sold three hundred thousand copies. The case of Los Náufragos illustrates the shaping and marketing of these bands. By appropriating the notion of *naufragio* (shipwreck), entrepreneurs at CBS determined the selling-point for these long-haired boys. CBS also hired professional musicians to compose and play the music and songwriters to create the lyrics. The record company secured broad media promotion as well. Lifestyle magazines and papers ran numerous interviews with the beat band, where they propagandized a sugary image of nonconformism, happiness for being young, and satisfaction with conveying their "music and feelings."[72]

Calling to mind the qualities of youth and dynamism, the beat style was a conduit for diversifying the options of how men—both young and adult—could look. Its major impact was, in fact, on menswear and hair style. For instance, color began to appear in men's dress shirts: in 1970 only 30 percent of the shirts sold were the "[traditional] white, sky blue, or grey." Also in 1970, the stylish clothing store Casa Modart opened a branch in Buenos Aires wholly dedicated to "youth clothes," but the most prominent costumers, according to a report, were "middle-aged men."[73] Though exaggerated, the report offers a glimpse of the juvenilization of menswear, along beat lines. Equally important were the changes in hair style. While in 1967 the *náufragos* recognized themselves as wearers of long hair, three years latter it could hardly act as a marker for unconventional cultural grouping. Although people on the streets still shouted homophobic remarks to long-haired boys, many employers refused to hire long-haired workers, and school principals endorsed the wearing of short hair, a growing minority of men let it grow.[74] A barber in a working-class neighborhood commented that young boys and also some "middle-aged men" went to his shop with pictures of "modern singers" to have their haircuts modeled after them. In fact, the figure of the long-haired young man had become accepted in the larger public culture.[75]

As it happened in other countries in the early 1970s, the beat style that pervaded Argentina's mass culture represented a vehicle for updating beliefs about the aesthetics of masculinity. The youth that, since the mid-1960s, participated in the making of a rock culture did so in bodily terms. They combined a taste for rock music with a particular sociability and certain bodily practices, which were the keys to produce and convey a criticism against the sites and institutions that punctuated the boys-will-be-men dynamics in authoritarian Argentina. At the same time that old and young men and women reacted against the *náufragos* by deploying homophobic claims, their bodily styles infiltrated music and fashion. In becoming a mass culture phenomenon, those styles—now labeled "beat"—paved the way for new forms of fashioning, and of performing, masculinity for young and middle-aged men alike. Casualness, "color," and a celebration of individuality were the new mandates.[76] Those mandates potentially conflicted with the notions of respectability and respect for hierarchies that premised the hegemonic construction of masculinity. They promoted a certain degree of egalitarianism—in terms of age and class—and they tolerated a more relaxed positioning of men in their everyday interactions. However cosmetic or apparently superficial they were, the beat styles made visible and helped define broader societal tolerance with alternative forms of producing and experiencing masculinity.

Reacting against the wave of beat fashion and trying to recapture the symbolic potential of hair for a fraternity of "true" rockers, in February of 1970 the first issue of *Pelo* appeared. *Pelo*'s explicit objective, an editorial stated, was to differentiate "what is honestly authentic from what is just commercial merchandise."[77] Unlike other youth magazines, *Pelo* was devoted to rock: it represented a crucial step for the autonomy of Argentina's rock culture and reinforced its gendered dynamics. As Daniel Ripoll, *Pelo*'s creator and director for thirty years, recalls, the readership for the magazine was almost totally male, including many "amateur music practitioners." The magazine rapidly sold 150,000 copies monthly, and was exported to other South American countries. From the outset, it carried updated information about rock worldwide. When rumors about the separation of The Beatles spread, for example, Ripoll himself traveled to London to gather "precise information" to deliver to his readers.[78] *Pelo* also included information about novelties in equipment, and like rock magazines such as *Rolling Stone* and *Melody Maker*, participated in the cult of "guitar heroes." Emerging as the epitome of rock, guitar players were expected to combine "virtuosic display, bodily flamboyance, and control of technology."[79] *Pelo* promoted that variant of masculinity, tied to the notion of creativity and authenticity.

Pelo's most pressing concern was to establish criteria for differentiating the "authentic" from the "commercial," criteria framed into gendered language. *Pelo* crafted a vital dichotomy: *complacientes* (complacent) and *progresivos* (progressive). The former were the bands whose creative decisions depended on the record business. The *progresivos*, in contrast, were the bands engaged in a search of more sophisticated musical and poetical forms, which would find little echo within the record business. By using these categories, *Pelo* mapped out Argentina's musical landscape, gathering data on fifty-three bands. Thus, Los Náufragos were unquestionably placed into the *complacientes*, while Manal, Los Gatos, and Almendra ranked high among the *progresivos*.[80] This dichotomy was the way in which *Pelo* coded the opposition between pop and rock, as shaped in the 1960s and 1970s worldwide. As happened with that opposition, *Pelo*'s dichotomy was gendered. Like any "pop star," the *complacientes* were depicted as having a female audience and endowed with attributes related to the feminine: weakness, passivity—regarding the music industry—and superficiality. As "true" rockers, the *progresivos* occupied the male and superior position: active, moving forward, and creative.[81] In endorsing *progresivos* alone, *Pelo* uplifted these perceived male values, which would ideally bind a renewed fraternity of rockers.

The fraternity of rockers that *Pelo* sought to enact was bound by a search for authenticity, and it continued to exclude women. While *Pelo* might have merely reflected the marginalization of women from rock's performances, it also contributed to those dynamics. In its first two years only one report focused on women: it was devoted to the fans, or "groupies." The report argued that these women hardly knew about music: they dreamt of being a musician's romantic partner, including "ironing their pants before the concerts," as one groupie told a reporter.[82] In so doing, *Pelo* assimilated women to caring mothers, at best, or superficial fortune seekers, at worst. In any case, young women did not fully belong to the "authentic" fraternity. As Pablo Vila has noted, the quest for authenticity was crucial for defining Argentina's rock: rather than qualifying good or bad music—as in the Anglo-Saxon context—it was the criteria to belong and stay. Musicians complied with the quest for authenticity in myriad ways, beginning with the fact that when they were at the peak of their popularity—when they were becoming stars—they disbanded.[83] When Almendra disbanded and rumor spread that Manal and Los Gatos would do the same, *Pelo* foresaw an auspicious future: the *progresivos* would avoid the commercial trap, create new bands, and move forward. Equally important, *Pelo* delved into rockers' personal styles to assess their pledge to authenticity. When interviewing Los Gatos, a journalist noted that they looked "un-prolix": they were not "stars but street boys, as we are."[84] *Pelo*'s project revolved around shaping a fraternity without distinguishing musicians from audiences, enacting what sociologist Simon Frith has dubbed the "folk myth" fueling rock's claims of authenticity and community. As one editorial stated, "For the first time, a link ties an entire generation," and explained that, "Now, musicians don't wear shiny suits; now, there are less idols, and more human beings."[85]

The imagery of an age-based fraternity of male "equals" was at the core of Argentina's rock culture, highly visible in the occasions of its public gathering such as the three successive annual Buenos Aires Rock (BAROCK) festivals. The refusal to validate any project of stardom came along with the praise of authenticity—as opposed to superficiality and commercialism—and of a vague yet nonetheless undeniable celebration of "human individuality." Alongside the prevalent antiauthoritarianism, these values—humanism, authenticity, equality—informed the effort to build community ties that would ideally transcend class differences and would express an alternative version of masculinity, centered on loving friends, romantic partners, and fathers. These were the images that the national press selected to portray the BAROCK festivals that *Pelo* organized beginning in 1970. The festivals showed that the rockers' fraternity had enlarged considerably since the days of "La Balsa." The organizers estimated that six thousand people attended each of the five afternoons when the festival took place in 1970, a figure that tripled in the years that followed.[86] Reporting on the 1971 festival, journalists agreed that it was "musically poor" but striking in terms of attendance. A journalist wrote, in an impressionistic fashion, that the audience was composed of "boys from suburbia, wrapped in long, waving hair," noting that the "fuel to rock culture" came not from "the pseudo-hippies of Barrio Norte" but from the "industrial belt of Buenos Aires." Similarly, others signaled that the audience was made of "secondary school and long-haired boys from the workshop floors."[87] The BAROCK served to gather a cross-class fraternity in search of the "authentic" experience of rock.

Perhaps because of the ubiquity of rock, in 1971 two entertainment impresarios decided that the time was ripe to bring the acclaimed rock musical *Hair* to Argentina. *Hair*'s impact was felt before and beyond its actual theatrical performance. *Hair* had played off-Broadway in 1967, though it quickly moved to Broadway and became the "first love-rock musical," in

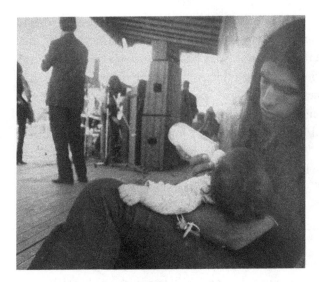

A new fatherhood,
Buenos Aires Rock
Festival, 1971. Archive
Diario Clarín.

which youths danced and sang the now memorable lyrics of the "Age of Aquarius." *Hair* achieved immediate success and elicited debate, chiefly about its theatrical characteristics and the decision to show nudity.[88] Scandal accompanied *Hair* worldwide. Buenos Aires was not an exception. The local producers, like their counterparts in other countries, also pursued their casting call by unconventional means; that is, they posted ads in record stores and at rock concerts rather than in theater schools. For the casting call, five hundred youths competed for thirty-five acting positions, and at least ten of the selected ones belonged to the "rock world." When the rehearsals began, members of the cast "took over" the theater and its adjacent streets and turned them into a "hippie enclave."[89] *Hair* attracted self-identified hippies to the area. Former *náufrago* Mario Rabey, for example, recalls that he followed his girlfriend—an actress and dancer who had been selected as a cast member—and began to live in a cheap hotel on the same block where the theater was located: "everything was crazy there," he recalls, "people arrived, played music, danced, chatted. It was a liberated zone." Most of the initial cast, however, did not make it to the premiere: after clashing with the impresarios, many were fired and headed toward other places to initiate communal living. Rabey's group, for example, went to Patagonia. Some months after the premiere, director Roberto Villanueva, choreographer Marilú Marini, rocker and music director Carlos Cutaia and his wife Carola—one of the few female rock performers—headed to Córdoba province to set up a short-lived "artistic commune."[90] While the staged musical incited criticism focusing on its failure to account for "Argentina's reality," its "soft" treatment of sexual and political issues, and its representation of the hippies, *Hair* had served, unintentionally, as an experience from which overt countercultural practices emerged.[91]

The hippie countercultural experiments articulated around *Hair* were neither the first nor the only ones in Argentina, though. The rock band Arco Iris, for example, began a project of urban communal living in early 1970. A former beat quartet, Arco Iris had recorded one single with RCA and achieved instant success in 1969 when they found their muse: a young woman named Danais Wynnika, aka Dana. She was trained in yoga and acquainted with Eastern religions and so became the band's spiritual leader. Arco Iris rented a house in a suburban neighborhood where they followed a quite monarchal routine. As the band's voice and guitar player, Gustavo Santaolalla, explained, they woke up early, took shifts doing the domestic chores, and together thought up their music and lyrics. They performed yoga exercises, quit smoking, and became vegetarians.[92] As the 1970s wore on, the band familiarized itself with imagery related to indigenous communities, which reverberated in its most remembered record, *Sudamérica, o el regreso de la aurora* (South America, or the Return of Dawn). They became more radicalized in their rejection of the "commercial machinery" of the music business and organized alternative circuits for producing and distributing records. Yet they also radicalized their spiritual claims: like some religiously inspired communes in the United States did, the members of Arco Iris also abandoned sexual activity to lead all energy to create. "Our Civilization," Santaolalla stated, "has succumbed to sexual desire and narcotics."[93] These antisexual and antidrug claims did not inform other countercultural experiences.

In addition to Arco Iris, one of the lasting communal-living experiments was La Cofradía de la Flor Solar, in La Plata. This city hosted the second largest public university in the 1960s as well as a School of Fine Arts, which attracted a vast student population from all over the country. In 1967, several art students abandoned classes and paying jobs to rent a house. When a group of musicians from Entre Ríos joined them, La Cofradía de la Flor Solar was born, naming both the commune and the rock band the musicians created. By late 1969, Mono Cohen, age twenty-six, told a reporter who visited the "hippie house" that they spent their days working on artisan goods and the evenings discussing "how to modify our limited environment." The group made a living through the sale of artisan goods, the painting they did in the neighborhood, and the money the band received when it performed. In 1971, Cohen was interviewed again, this time about whether or not the group practiced "free love." He responded that they were "freer than the rest of the population, but not promiscuous."[94] More recently, Meneca Hiquis, who engaged in La Cofradía in 1971, clarified that sex was free to the extent that it took place between couples not formally married, but there was not "group sex." In addition, she recalled that the group only occasionally used "LSD or acid," because even when they would have desired it, it was expensive and hard to get in Buenos Aires. The same held true for the commune that former La Cofradía's members and Miguel Cantilo built in El Bolsón in 1974.[95]

These experiences sought to materialize the utopias of hippie countercultures worldwide: to create a community from the onset, endowed with rules and values separated as much as possible from those of the "mainstream society." These experiences heightened some of the values that articulated rockers' fraternity, such as the praise for equality, respect for "human individuality," and search for authentic expression. Unlike rockers' fraternity, these experiences did include young women. The available testimonies suggest that some of the commune's men upheld a "hippie princess" approach that—as one strand of rock lyrics did—confined young women to the roles of ethereal lovers. Those beliefs, as scholars have studied for the United States, did not entail the pursuit of sexual equality but did lessen the more overt forms of machismo that cut across other youth cultural and political realms.[96] In comparison to the hippie experience in the United States and Mexico, likewise, the experience in Argentina was more limited and less dependent on a psychedelic imagery related to drug use. The multilayered hippie trends in the United States attracted a "hard core" of almost eight hundred thousand youths who, in 1970, had had some communal living experience. American hippies crossed the border and helped enlarge communes in Mexico as well, where local and foreign hippies engaged in psychedelic trips with hallucinogens.[97] Hallucinogenic drugs were hardly available in Argentina and—as Arco Iris showed in an extreme fashion—drugs were not a reference point for the building of identities. Similarly, it is evident that the "hard core" of the Argentine hippies comprised a tiny minority of youths. Miguel Grinberg—manager of the rock band La Cofradía—stated that by 1970 about two thousand youths had engaged in "removing energies from the system."[98]

To help shape the removal of energy from the system, Grinberg launched the magazine *Contracultura*, which offers insight into the ideological materials on which some groups drew as well as, fundamentally, on the challenges that any countercultural effort found in appealing to a broader constituency. An active cultural organizer, Grinberg translated and published documents from experiences abroad—and some local—that, he believed, could be useful to invigorate a radical movement. *Contracultura* published fragments of Guy Debord's "situationist" texts, the "thirty theses" that French students agreed on in May of 1968, and some lectures by Herbert Marcuse on "student power" along with texts of the antipsychiatry movement, the manifesto of the Living Theater group, and even a document drafted by Third World priests in 1969. Grinberg also pushed to create communes as venues for "fighting here and now." As he had done in *Eco Contemporáneo*, he sought to carve out a space between the commercialized and the politicized youth. Grinberg expressed a reaction against the politicized groups as they existed in Argentina: "Those of us who, by principle and will, cannot be Leninist," he stated in an editorial, "do remember that the duty of any revolutionary is to create alternatives and defend them as liberated zones."[99] In early 1970s Argentina, the hippie groups in particular and rock culture at large were neither the only nor the most influential discourses and practices to interpellate youth. They represented one layer in a broader culture of contestation articulated through the notion of "liberation"—in its collective and/or individual inflections. The overtly political subset of that culture, epitomized by the revolutionary Left, claimed a political and ideological definition to the "unaffiliated" young men attracted to rock culture, whose rebellion was viewed as insufficient.

A Time for Definitions

In May of 1969, a series of popular revolts spread through several Argentine cities, including Corrientes, Rosario, and especially Córdoba, and marked the beginning of the political finale of the Onganía regime. It was only in June of 1970, though, after the Peronist guerrillas, the Montoneros, kidnapped and killed former president General Pedro Aramburu, that Onganía finally resigned. Guerrilla activities had caught up with a broad and radical societal politicization. In that process, rising numbers of young people engaged with revolutionary projects aimed at forging a Socialist future—either in its classless, Marxist form or in its national, Peronist version, which reached its height between 1972 and 1974. In that biennium elections were called, and in them a Peronist formula triumphed, allowing Juan Perón to return from exile, becoming president until his death. That was also the juncture in which rock gained momentum: in 1972 thirty-two records were launched, the highest number thus far and for the ten years to follow. How did rock culture interact with the dynamic of politicization of increased numbers of youth? While each constellation of discourse and practice developed their own ways of appealing to youth, there were points of overlap. Although many leftist intellectuals and militants did not deploy a harsh criticism of what some began to call "rock *nacional*"—rather the opposite was true—they did ask rockers to clarify their ideology and abandon their sensibility, a claim that was all in all more intense with the "hippies."

Many left-wing intellectuals and young activists plainly rejected what they understood as the "hippie" phenomenon. In the late 1960s and early 1970s, as intellectuals in Mexico or Chile did, some Argentines also thought that the hippies in the "central countries" represented a progressive movement against consumerism and bureaucratization, but discredited their counterparts in the periphery as a bad copy: "what *there* means healthy unconformity," an essayist wrote, "*here* is alienating marginality."[100] Two other intellectuals explained that "the Latin American hippie movement is fueled by clothing firms" and argued that the pacifist slogans just distracted youth from "more effective rebellions."[101] These intellectuals viewed the local hippies as emulative, fabricated, and politically demobilizing. These arguments reverberated among many politicized youths as well. In 1972, in a roundtable with secondary school students, for example, a young woman affiliated with the Montoneros-oriented Juventud Peronista (JP, Peronist Youth) argued that the local hippies were "all snobs, the product of the *cipaya* [sold-to-imperialism] propaganda." A Trotskyist boy, age sixteen, said that through the hippies "the *yanquis* colonized youth and make them drowsy."[102] These youths amplified the stereotypes of the *náufragos* in the days of "La Balsa," yet they adapted the criticisms to represent the hippies as obstructive to a revolutionary project.

However, as some memoirs allow us to infer, there was a zone of intersection in which some youths articulated their political activism with their involvement in countercultural projects and practices, and vice versa. For example, the journalist Martin Granovsky recalls that one of his best friends, Pablo, was a militant with the ERP at the same time that he was a rock guitar player. Trying to reconstruct his friend's life before being kidnapped by the military, Granovsky found that Pablo, while hiding from state repression, spent nights within a "hippie house" where he found not only a refuge but access to a creative, musical life. It bears noting that the ERP leadership and many of its militants were strict in their judgments of both the "hippie" and rock lifestyles: as former members recall, they were sanctioned as "petit bourgeois and escapist" when going to rock concerts, which did not prevent many youths—like Pablo—from being attracted to them.[103] The historian Alejandro Cattaruzza recalls also an experiment of communal living in Santa Fe, wherein a dozen youths participated in artistic endeavors while engaging with the JP or the Communist Youth.[104] The line between activism and countercultural projects was crossed from the other direction as well. In 1973 the "hippie artisans" who had poured into Buenos Aires plazas organized a union affiliated with the JP. They argued that instead of "peace-and-love hippies," they were "creative workers" producing apart from the "imperialist circle."[105]

Yet even broader than the encounter between hardcore countercultural projects and political militancy was, at least for a time, the intersection between rock culture and political activism. In their memories, some former young militants created a life narrative characterized by a passage from "rebellion" to "revolution" in which rock had an important role. Thus, Carlos recalls that in the late 1960s he crafted his "rebellion" through wearing long hair, playing in a rock band, and attending "Manal concerts," where he "ended up in jail several times." He was already "a rebel," he says, when he found his path to a "sophisticated revolutionary thought" and affiliated with a Trotskyist group. While he kept attending rock concerts, he quit playing and had his hair cut "for security reasons."[106] Other former political activists shaped different memories. Luis Salinas, for example, ironically recalls that, in the early 1970s, "I wanted to be exactly what I was: a blend of guerrilla and Rolling Stone." There was not a passage from rock-rebellion to politics-revolution: as a former member of Fuerzas Armadas Revolucionarias (FAR, Revolutionary Armed Forces) and as a "fan of *música progresiva,*" Luis believes he embodied both. Yet Luis is self-reflective regarding the limits of the zone of intersection he inhabited. He comments that, on the one hand, the FAR's leaders were "very strict with discipline," especially as related to the prohibition of drug use. On the other hand, Luis asserts that *el circo* (the circus)—as the unaffiliated rockers were known—was "hermetic and skeptical with politics."[107] These stories illustrate the possibilities and limits of the encounters between rock culture and political activism. Security reasons, party discipline, and self-discipline conditioned the involvement of militants with rock culture as the 1970s went on. In a context of intense politicization, revolutionary militants were required to "define" themselves by privileging their allegiance to one of the strands that constituted the youth culture of contestation. The "circus" was also required a definition.

The "circus" did not easily fit into how the political was conceptualized in the early 1970s, and some left-wing intellectuals and journalists asked them to "ideologize" their practices. Rock poets and musicians, in fact, insisted on labeling rock as "a new sensibility," the dominant idea unifying an anthology of rockers' testimonies published in 1970. Commenting on that anthology, left-wing intellectual Germán García found that by identifying rock as sensibility, rockers avoided ideology, which they conceived of as "vulgar." García pointed out that the testimonies were flush with political metaphors such as "we live in a dictatorship of hypocrisy," which ultimately emptied the meaning out of the political language they deployed.[108] What was at stake in the dichotomy opposing sensibility vs. ideology was a battle over how to get the politicization of unaffiliated rockers along with a consistent effort to "ideologize" what both García and the influential rock journalist Jorge Andrés already dubbed "rock *nacional*." In his music columns for the prominent daily *La Opinión*, for example, Andrés constructed a schema for analyzing records in which he evaluated, primarily, the degree of "ideological definition." Thus, he plainly rejected the work of Arco Iris, which he took as example of the "dreamlike attitude" that characterized rockers' "ideological emptiness." He valued instead the projects showing an "evolution toward ideological clarification," such as the duo Pedro y Pablo's work. Andrés thought that rockers should clarify their positions, which meant removing themselves from the domain of "dreaming" to enter that of the one of "ideology." Musicians' and poets' definitions were all the more important to Andrés because he saw that rock attracted a massive constituency. As seekers of some sort of "liberation," he wrote, rockers had "marginalized themselves from the political process" and, in doing so, they limited "the scope of their liberationist attitude."[109]

Rock musicians' and poets' responses to\the request for "ideologizing" their practices were diverse. In fact, some had long participated in a "protest" trend within rock music. That was the case with duo Pedro y Pablo, whose "La marcha de la bronca" (The Hatred March), denounced police and military violence, cultural censorship, and "social exploiters" alike. The single of "La marcha de la bronca" was a hit, selling eighty thousand copies in three months, to the point that *Pelo* stated that the song had replaced "La Balsa" as the anthem for rockers.[110] Moreover, filmmaker Raymundo Gleyzer—linked to the ERP—chose the song as the soundtrack for the images of the 1969 popular revolts in his film *Los traidores* (The Traitors, 1972), a prime example of militant cinema. As the 1970s went on, other rockers "ideologized" their practices, usually through making political references in the song lyrics. The jazz-rock band Alma y Vida dedicated a song to Che Guevara, and soloist Roque Narvaja—ironically, the former leader of the beat band La Joven Guardia—also wrote a song to Guevara and Camilo Cienfuegos and another one to Luis Pujals, a leader of the ERP killed in 1971.[111]

In March of 1973, amid the euphoria incited by the triumph of a Peronist ticket in the presidential elections after an intense campaign carried out by the ever-growing JP, time seemed ripe for celebrating in a "youth way" and testing rockers' keenness to engage in political endeavors. Alleging that a majority of the "rock boys" had voted for the Peronist ticket (which was possible because 50 percent of the voting population had done so), rock producer Jorge Alvarez organized a mega-festival to celebrate the triumph and to honor president elect Héctor Cámpora as well as to express "rockers' wish for a return of Juan Perón to the country soon." On March 31, all the major rock bands were onstage, including Luis Alberto Spinetta with Pescado Rabioso, Sui Géneris, La Pesada, and Pappo's Blues. Although it was a rainy evening, twenty thousand people attended the "Festival of Liberation." In attendance were "boys from every working- and middle-class corner of Buenos Aires," as Jorge Andrés depicted them, also noting that while the JP tried to draw chants from the audience, the "rock boys acted as if they were untouched by the political overtones of the festival."[112] A rather atypical episode, this nonetheless demonstrated the eagerness to articulate the strands that made a youth culture of contestation under the umbrella of left-wing Peronism, as well as the attendant difficulties of doing so.

Intellectuals and journalists with the Montoneros-oriented JP combined a respectful attitude vis-à-vis rock culture and its male constituency and requests for its "ideological definition." The Montoneros, like other Latin American revolutionary groups, developed a cultural politics centered on the vindication of the aesthetics of "the people," which in musical terms entailed the appreciation of folkloric traditions and the politically committed "New Song" movement.[113] Soon after Cámpora won the election, some Montoneros leaders participated in the writing of lyrics to songs that narrated their history through vignettes focused on their guerrilla activities. Recorded by the folkloric group Huerque Mapu, the LP titled "Montoneros" was presented at a festival that the JP organized to celebrate the end of 1973, which included the performance of a folk ballet.[114] These political and aesthetic preferences did not preclude the attention of journalists who wrote for the Montoneros' daily *Noticias* and valued rock culture. Commenting on a recital by Aquelarre, one journalist wrote that the band "represented the best of our rock," pointed out the quality of the music, and praised the "boys in the audience," who were "attentive and demanded quality." He nonetheless criticized Aquelarre and Arco Iris because of their "irrational lyrics."[115] Montonero intellectuals were perhaps not confident about the rockers' chances of "overcoming ideological weaknesses" while recognizing that rock was the best venue to reach youths' attention. Because of that, a group of Montoneros intellectuals themselves produced a single geared to secondary school students. One of its songs called on them to "use their youth to struggle against dependence" and help to "our country's liberation."[116]

While not "ideologized" in ways in which leftist intellectuals and militants wished, many rockers did "define" themselves at a crossroads marked by the keywords "liberation" and "revolution." Hence, they were called to give their opinions in mid-1973, when promises of "national and popular" liberation seemed close to fulfillment. Spinetta, for example, stated that rock had enabled many youths like himself to begin a process toward liberation, albeit a liberation from "the patriarchal and social process of edu-castration in which we were raised."[117] Spinetta appropriated the notion of "liberation" but used it to signal the significance, which he thought of as ineludible, of both personal and eventually generational reactions against deep-seated and repressive "castrations." An editorialist for *Pelo*, meanwhile, stated that the Argentine rockers who stood for revolution pursued "a total reorganization of the world: a Psychic Revolution, a revolution of mores, of values."[118] This proposal for a "total revolution" received the support of many readers. Some of them stated that the new political juncture could be a good "starting point" because the police would not "harass us anymore," or because of its promise of enhancing "social justice." Yet it was not "enough."[119] The "circus" was faithful to the search for "authenticity" that had fueled rock culture. Their pervading antiauthoritarianism, the vague pacifism, and the commitment to carve out individual forms of liberation may have prevented many young men from engaging with the guerrilla-oriented revolutionary Left.

In turn, the revolutionary Left in Argentina largely refused to seriously consider the demands for "micro" or "individual" liberations as well as other politics that could center on erasing patriarchal (or other) forms of "castration." As scholars have shown with regard to the emergent feminist and gay-rights movements, while the revolutionary Left in Argentina advocated for an abstract notion of equality, it downplayed gender and sexual politics as legitimate sites for organizing and belonging.[120] The revolutionary Left's explicit positions vis-à-vis rock culture worked similarly. That is, it did not recognize the legitimacy of rock culture's antiauthoritarian claims that gave an individually and culturally inflected meaning to the notion of liberation. In contrast to what happened with its Mexican or Chilean counterparts, however, the Argentine revolutionary Left (especially that of Peronist origins) did not accuse rock culture of representing the "tip of the iceberg" of cultural imperialism. This speaks to the success that rock musicians, fans, and journalists achieved in linking rock to other forms of popular music. Equally important, militants and intellectuals discerned that rock culture was a cross-class mass phenomenon. While acknowledging its "national" credentials and its potential for articulating protest, intellectuals and militants denigrated rock as a form of cultural politics. The request for "ideologizing" rocker's practices merged with their belittling of the sensibility that it entailed. Yet loopholes existed between the mandates and rules set within the revolutionary Left and the practices of many young people. Youths participated with different degrees of commitment in revolutionary politics and rock culture, the crucial cornerstones that made the basis of a youth culture of contestation in Argentina. The zones of overlap and the very possibility of forging a culture of contestation decreased as a rightist backlash that started in 1974 put an end to the promises of "liberation" in its multiple meanings.

▶ Beginning in 1974 and escalating with the imposition of the last and most dramatic military dictatorship (1976–83), a wide-ranging "authority-reconstitution" project started, whereby state institutions and a broad range of civilian actors tried to put an end to the threats of social, cultural, and political disorders epitomized in the youth culture of contestation. Rock's basic contribution to that culture of contestation in the late 1960s and early 1970s related to the ways in which it gave expression to young people's discontent with authoritarianism at the same that it offered them a symbolic space for shaping fraternal bonds while challenging patriarchal arrangements and enacting alternative forms of "being a man." The fraternity of long-haired boys appropriated strands from transnational, music-based countercultural practices and bodily styles and created forms of sociability centered on leisure and enjoyment. This was at odds with the cultural conservatism that crossed through the Argentine 1960s and the values that premised the hegemonic arrangements of masculinity. The rockers' fraternity neither unanimously endorsed an egalitarian vision of gender relations nor avoided misogynist and ultimately hierarchical views of women. It did, however, offer many young men the possibility of deploying alternative models of masculinity that centered on the figure of the *pibe*. It also focused on the notions of creativity, authenticity, and "human individuality," which were the basis for making of Argentina's rock a cultural politics.

In building a rock culture, young men confronted in practice the values enforced in the boys-will-be-men dynamics as well as the rules governing "manners and morals," the keystones for preserving a hierarchical and patriarchal order. As cultural critic Lawrence Grossberg points out, there is nothing intrinsically political in rock music: "rock's politicization resulted not from its own activities but from the attacks which it elicited: rock was politicized behind its back."[121] Rock in Argentina became the site of a cultural politics that privileged the pursuit of hedonism, individual "liberation," and expression while it met and faced a pervasive societal and state-led authoritarianism and repression. Amid that process, the performance of rock music expanded and diversified. Rockers—journalists, fans, musicians, and poets—created their own, also gendered, hierarchies to categorize their movement; and rock culture kept attracting a vast and cross-class constituency composed of, largely, young men.

"In my collection, I had Almendra's and [Uruguayan "protest" singer, Daniel] Viglietti's records and on my bookshelf I treasured Artaud and Perón: it was such a mix, wasn't it?," Emilio, a former member of the JP, asks rhetorically when he recalls "all these images that we had around us."[122] Emilio's "we" refers to his fellow secondary school militants within the JP. Just like other youths, Emilio and his friends participated, with differing degrees of commitment, in both the sensibilities encapsulated in rock culture and the practices and groups that made the revolutionary Left. They may have felt the tensions between disciplining oneself to favor a collective project of social liberation and the desires of carving out forms of "liberating oneself, one's Eros, one's mind," as Luis Alberto Spinetta argued while commenting that this liberation did not have any "ideological sign whatsoever."[123] Respecting rock culture and its constituencies, militants and intellectuals within the revolutionary Left strove for "ideologizing" its practices: they witnessed its potential for articulating social protest and for giving expression to young people's antiauthoritarianism, but they belittled what rock represented as cultural politics. Meanwhile, many rockers within the "circus" would have no doubt about deeming as authoritarian or decidedly militaristic those practices and values that the revolutionary Left endorsed, especially after mid-1974 when the ERP and Montoneros resumed armed struggle. By that time, as I will discuss in Chapter 8, a broad and dreadful Rightist backlash had been activated that targeted young militants and rockers alike as supposed links in a chain that included, in the Rightists' perception—and in the eyes of many Argentines—drug consumption and "subversion."

6 ▸ Close to the Revolution

THE POLITICIZATION OF YOUTH

How did young women and men become involved with the most radicalized variations of Argentine politics in the late 1960s and early 1970s? Which ideas and images helped propel and shape that involvement? And, finally, why was Peronism the political movement that seemed to benefit the most from the politicization of youth? There is a common theme that cuts across the possible answers to these three overarching questions, namely, the ways in which middle- and working-class youth questioned the ideological and political bases of the dynamics of sociocultural modernization that Argentines went through in the 1960s. The cohort of youth that engaged with politics had been exposed to expanded educational and labor opportunities, the rising cosmopolitanism of Argentina's cultural life, and the concomitant chance of participating in a transnational repertoire of ideas, images, and sounds. Their experiences were also shaped by the pervasiveness of authoritarianism in the intimate, cultural, and political milieus epitomized by, but by no means confined to, the regime of General Juan Carlos Onganía (1966–70). Yet while the young men attracted to rock culture iconoclastically confronted the cultural and gendered components of the modernizing project, the young women and men that embraced revolutionary politics contested the narrative of a socially modern and egalitarian Argentina that they perceived as unreal and unjust. For these youths, Argentina belonged to the Third World, and for its "liberation" it required an urgent and drastic process of revolutionary change.

In the late 1960s and early 1970s young people became key political actors and the bearers of a new, revolutionary political culture marked by Third World perspectives. This chapter begins by reconstructing the situation of 1968–69 to show that it was in the context of the concatenated popular revolts in Corrientes, Rosario, and Córdoba in May of 1969 when young people, chiefly university and secondary school students, became visible political actors. Those revolts made apparent profound political and ideological transformations that cut across the student movement that had risen after the 1966 coup d'état. The new student activists were even more connected with the most radicalized Peronist unions and, in some cases, infused with the renovated ideas and practices stemming from the Second Vatican Council. They did not recognize themselves in what they perceived were the motives of their European counterparts. One year after the French student uprising of May 1968, when the Argentine students were engaged in popular revolts, many of them posited the sentiment that "ours is different." The difference, as student leaders explained, consisted of how the local students were subsumed into "the people."

The centrality of "the people" formed part of the political culture that young people helped build when embracing revolutionary projects. Shared beliefs, values, vocabulary, and representations of the past broke through a broad spectrum of political groups and reached young people at large, sometimes propelling them to engage in political activism.[1] One crucial component of that political culture was the political and cultural assimilation of Argentina to the Third World. That identification both allowed for the confrontation of the modernizing narratives of an egalitarian country and intermingled with it a pervading sense of imminence that, as cultural critic Diana Sorensen has argued when analyzing the 1960s in Latin America, entailed "an anxious, sometimes optimistic sense of arrival about to take place, or to be voluntaristically ushered in."[2] For the youths who participated in that political culture, given that the revolution was increasingly close at hand, armed struggle became not only "necessary" to push the military but also to pave the way for a liberated, Socialist fatherland. Many young people in Argentina, as many others throughout Latin America in the 1960s and 1970s, endorsed armed struggle as a means to start a society anew in the shortest possible time. People in their twenties were the bulk of the combatants within the five national guerrilla groups that had surfaced by 1971, when the last president of the so-called *Revolución Argentina*, General Alejandro Lanusse (1971–73) initiated negotiations with the exiled Juan Perón to resume democratic rule.

If there was a political movement that "benefited" the most from the politicization of young people, it was Peronism. It was within this political space that youths were more forcefully framed as political actors and as a category, and it was within Peronism that a generational language served to codify and enact ideological and political disputes. The youths that strove to "connect with the people" believed that Peronism was the natural venue for that encounter. Yet the engagement of young people with revolutionary trends within Peronism was anything but natural. At its most basic level, Perón understood that "youth" meant the chance of transcending the temporal limits of his movement, and since the mid-1960s he had called for a *trasvasamiento generacional* (generational transference) to infuse Peronism with "new blood" and ideological vitality. For many young people, that call for ideological and generational change implied the chance of conceiving of Peronism as the incarnation of a "national liberation" movement and as the national road toward Socialism. By the early 1970s, youth took up an ideological position as well, reflecting the radicalized young people who embraced Peronism while identifying with the Montoneros. A generational interpellation served to codify political and ideological battles within Peronism. Those battles turned more dramatic once elections were held in March of 1973 and Perón was given a last chance to make his comeback as president until his death in July of 1974. The disputes within Peronism were shaped like a dramatic family romance, in which the "young" would try to share power with the "old," while everyone depended on the authority emanating from the only father-like figure, namely Perón himself.

The Argentine May and the Politicization of Youth

In July of 1969, Perón compared the events of May of 1968 in Paris with the revolt in Córdoba province in May of 1969. He quoted graffiti that appeared on Parisian walls, chiefly one that read, "we are the guerrillas against the air-conditioned death they want to sell us with the name of future." Perón believed that the spirit of struggle against cultural and political conformism was rampant among Córdoba rebels. He foresaw, too, the beginning of a "global revolution" in which Argentine youth was destined to take the lead (*tomar el rabo*).[3] For rising numbers of youth, mostly students, the message of the exiled leader was growing in significance. Ironically, only a few of them would have agreed with his comparison. As protagonists of the interwoven popular revolts in Corrientes, Rosario, and Córdoba, many youths saw theirs as incomparable to the French events. In the Argentine May of 1969, young people tried to erase markers of youthfulness, chiefly their student condition, in order to merge with "the people." Yet for most observers, as for Perón, the May events broadcast an unequivocal meaning: the emergence of youth as a political actor.

In 1968, the Argentine press informed its readers about the revolts sweeping across the world, while it showed surprise at the apparent calmness domestically. Student leaders Rudi Dutschke and Daniel Cohn-Bendit became household names after appearing in many news reports while images of barricades in cities that upper- and middle-class Argentines had long conceived of as cradles of culture, such as Paris, dominated the newsmagazines and television newsreels.[4] Local journalists strove to explain to their readers how and why the "student" revolts were happening. Some analysts focused on what they believed were attitudes of ethical rebellion and wrote about the new humanism, the refusal to follow the rules of a technocratic-oriented society, and the vindication of values related to the creation of a "new man." Some observers also scrutinized new sexual mores, interpreting them in the light of the position that Herbert Marcuse achieved among the "antiauthoritarian, antirepressive youth."[5] In that seemingly chaotic scenario, some journalists were embarrassed when observing the apparent stolidity of the local students. "How could it be possible," a journalist asked, "that in the country which shaped the possibility of student participation in politics [the Reform Movement] things are so calm?" His answer pointed to the depoliticizing effects of the military intervention in the universities that the Onganía regime carried out in July of 1966.[6] Far from deterring students, however, the intervention intensified and transformed their political engagement.

In the second half of the 1960s, Catholic and Peronist student groups came to occupy the prominent place that Reformism had previously occupied. Catholic groups had begun to make inroads in public and private universities in the late 1950s, but they gained momentum primarily in the aftermath of the Second Vatican Council (1962–65). In mid-1968, the "Humanists" at the Universities of Buenos Aires and Littoral and the Integralistas at the Universities of Córdoba and the Northeast joined in the Unión Nacional de Estudiantes (UNE, National Student Union). Its president claimed that the only requirement for membership was "to be a revolutionary: to be a student is a trivial fact" and posited that the intervention had positively pushed students to reach out to the "proscribed people," a reference to Peronism.[7] In that encounter they also met the students who, coming from Marxism, created the Federación de Estudiantes Nacionales (FEN, National Student Federation), key to "Peronizing" the student movement.[8] Whether Catholic, Peronist, or Marxist, the most prominent groups rejected what they perceived as the main legacies of Reformism: the focus on the university as a site for generating social reform and the belief that democratizing university life would pave the way to democratizing the country. In June of 1968, on the occasion of the fiftieth anniversary of the launching of the Reform Movement, while the UNE celebrated the end of the "dream of the university as a democratic island," the students with the FEN and with the Partido Revolucionario de los Trabajadores (PRT, Revolutionary Workers' Party) reached more nuanced conclusions. They noted that "initially the Reform was an important link in the movement for democratic reforms," led by the Radical president Hipólito Yrigoyen, the first elected after the passing of the law of secret, mandatory, and universal male suffrage. However, the FEN pamphlet argued, "the reformists isolated themselves in the University." The Reform represented "the past" and, now, the FEN and the PRT wanted the students to build "bridges to the people."[9]

A similar drive of creating "bridges to the people" fueled the Catholic students. Together with their specific organizations, the most radicalized students had the journal *Cristianismo y Revolución* as a reference point. Launched in 1966 by a former seminarian, Juan García Elorrio, its first editorial noted that the journal would reflect "the feeling, the urgency, the forms, and the moments of Christian commitment to the revolution." The journal—whose readership numbered as many as forty thousand—published frequent reports on the situation in war-torn Vietnam because, as one editorial predicted, "we, the oppressed in Latin America, will be the 1970s Vietnam." It also promoted materials authored by local clerics who founded the Third World Priests Movement. The journal likewise served as the nexus for two dozen activists who founded the Camilo Torres commando—and who latter on would create the Montoneros guerrillas.[10] The commando was named for the Colombian priest turned guerrilla (assassinated in 1966), an inspirational figure for the journal's staff and followers. In its second issue, for example, *Cristianismo y Revolución* published a letter addressed to students, wherein Torres reminded them that they were privileged in "underdeveloped societies." If they wanted to become revolutionary, Torres asked them to "ascend to the masses and share their poverty." Paraphrasing Torres, the Movimiento Ateneísta, from Santa Fe, urged their members to "engage with the poor and persecuted people."[11]

The articulation between the new student groups and "the people" crystallized, in particular, in the experience of the Confederación General de Trabajadores de la Argentina (CGTA, General Labor Confederation of Argentina). Founded in March of 1968, the CGTA was the outcome of cleavages within the labor movement caused by the differing positions vis-à-vis the Onganía regime. The unions that coalesced into the CGTA represented those workers most affected by the regime's economic policies and those who had long opposed the bureaucratic tendency of the labor movement.[12] Led by Raimundo Ongaro—a fervent Catholic and Peronist representative of the print workers—the CGTA called for the creation of a worker-based, democratic, and anticapitalist alliance to oppose Onganía. Although short-lived, this experience served as a point of encounter between the working class and radicalized artists, intellectuals, professionals, and students. The FEN and the UNE, for example, used the CGTA headquarters in Córdoba, Buenos Aires, and Rosario to hold meetings and helped with administrative and press tasks, while they participated in the permanent "worker-student" committee. The identification of the new student groups with this experience was so strong that the "bureaucratic" unionists mocked the CGTA by labeling it "the students' CGT."[13]

In 1968, when the global revolts were unleashed, the Argentine student activists questioned their "status" and university politics alike. Sharing similar perceptions with left-wing students in Mexico and Brazil, the Argentines did not take heed of the notion that their European equivalents also tried to "bridge the gaps" with the working classes, as was evident in the demonstrations in Paris and in the joint occupations of university and factory buildings in Turin.[14] Even though from today's vantage point former young people tie the Mexican Movement or the Argentine May to a global wave of rebellion in which most protagonists were young, in 1968 and 1969 that scope was denied and oftentimes the commonalities rejected.[15] In 1968, for example, a popular magazine surveyed Argentine youth about their opinions of the "youth revolt" in Europe and many responded that they did not agree with demands "centered on their problems." Another survey, seeking to elucidate the circulation of Marcuse's ideas, showed that "his influence is minimal." In fact, the interviewees disagreed with Marcuse's statement regarding the student revolutionary status in societies where the working class had presumably lost its vanguard role. "If that thesis works for Europe, it does not for us," one student argued. The UNE's leader was more emphatic: "Marcuse can go to hell."[16] The FEN's leader clarified that, in Argentina, "those who think that the workers would follow the students are dreaming of Paris, when the revolution is taking place in [the working-class suburb] Avellaneda or in Tucumán."[17] "Our" rebellion would sharply differ from the European: "here" students would always go behind the workers.

In May of 1969, however, when a series of popular revolts erupted in Corrientes, Rosario, and Córdoba, students were in fact the leading force alongside workers and broad segments of the local populations. Unlike the blend of antiauthoritarian, cultural, and political claims that the students in France, Italy, and Germany enacted through a renewed repertoire of collective action, the Argentine students did not expressly deploy generational rhetoric nor did they question received methods of processing authority and power in the educational system or within the family.[18] The unifying thread of the Argentine May was political, although articulated around economic and social demands. The intensity of the revolts signaled a deep-seated discontent with a political order that had excluded, since 1955, the representation of the majority forces and that, since 1966, had closed up all political channels. Most immediately, popular unrest responded to the repressive policies upheld by the Onganía regime, dramatically enacted in May. Some exceptions aside, the studies of that May have focused on the revolt in Córdoba, which quickly came to be known as the *Cordobazo*. As sociologist Francisco Delich noted in his canonical analysis, the violence and decisiveness shown by Cordoba's workers (the "best paid in the country") was as unexpected as it was virulent and showed changes in who made up the workers and what their ideology and practices were.[19] By studying the *Cordobazo* through mid-term changes centered on that province, however, most of these studies have overlooked that it comprised the last and most striking link of a chain of popular revolts. Yet through examining how May unfolded in terms of the interaction of popular activism, government reactions, and press coverage, it is apparent that after that May, "youth" and "rebellion" became linked referents.

The beginning of the Argentine May occurred in Corrientes province, at the University of the Northeast (UNNE). Created in 1959, the UNNE was one of the smallest national universities (it had seven thousand students in 1969), and it had been one of only three whose authorities had not opposed the military intervention in 1966. Opposition to the Onganía regime did escalate among the students. In mid-1968, some groups had begun to mobilize against *limitacionismo*, the attempts to set limits to the enrollments according to student test scores. A Catholic group issued a communiqué denouncing *limitacionismo* as part of a broader plan set by Rudolph Atcon, a former member of the State Department's think tank for higher education who visited Argentina on invitation from the government. Catholic students censured Atcon's arrival because it signified, for them, "a way through which this regime, a local ally to *yanqui* imperialism, tries to prevent our liberation."[20] In April of 1969, not only the radicalized Catholics but also many other groups joined to oppose a more localized problem: the university administrators had increased the price for meals in the student canteen. The students improvised canteens and meeting places at the CGTA headquarters and in local parishes. In early May, students carried out silent marches after the rector refused to receive them. On May 15 the police imprisoned dozens of students, raided their houses, and shot to death Juan José Cabral, age nineteen.[21] The popular anger incited by Cabral's death was heightened by the untimely response of the minister of interior, who accused the students of "working for international extremists."[22]

The events initiated in Corrientes made visible the fact that repression was the only way the regime coped with dissent, which was rampant among broad segments of Argentines; and that the students could effectively forge alliances with the "people." The student-"people" alliance was particularly successful in Rosario, which was the epicenter of popular revolts between May 17 and May 22. On May 17 around four hundred students met at the canteen of the local university to then march to the city center. One of these groups, composed of two young women and a young man, was followed to the entrance of a shopping gallery. There the police shot to death Alfredo Bello, a twenty-two-year-old law student. The governor and the police chief accused Bello's group of having threatened the policemen, yet witnesses wrote to newspapers to state that this was not true. Students and workers affiliated with the CGTA agreed to organize a rally on May 21, and they received the support of the local chapters of most unions, professional groups, and business associations.[23] On that day, four thousand secondary school and university students took to the streets and were accompanied by workers and other city residents. The police did not allow them to march, and many groups opted for organizing sit-ins. It was at a sit-in where the police shot to death a metalworker named Luis Blanco who was only fifteen. When news about his death spread, the revolt generalized: "at every corner," a reporter wrote, "homemakers, children, all helped keep bonfires burning."[24] Bonfires and barricades lasted until 2:00 A.M., when the government declared Rosario a "military zone" subject to military justice, including the death penalty for those "resisting authority." The city was paralyzed when, on May 23, a general strike was declared and people overtly challenged government policy.[25]

The regime's *pax*, which had thus far constituted its main source of legitimacy since it represented itself as a guarantor of social order, had been unequivocally broken, and the students had been the main force initially fueling that crisis. In that context the press tried to uncover whether the revolts were spontaneous or not. When interviewed, the student leaders of UNE and FEN recognized that, in Rosario at least, the rank-and-file students surpassed any directive and were eager to "stone the police." Bringing the memories of European protests and comparing the two Mays, they rightly pointed out that "there, people did not die in the streets, while here—as in Mexico—people did," and insisted that "ours is different, we are fighting for, and alongside the people."[26] In fact, in the wake of the massive rebellion in Rosario, where "the people" had joined in what at first was a student-led protest, most student leaders noted that it had been insufficient. A representative of a Maoist group stated that the students should insert themselves into a "process of liberation led by the workers" if they did not want to be protagonists of "isolated episodes." A Peronist spokesperson, meanwhile, stated that the students should become involved with the "only national movement that allows for the people's liberation."[27] Consistent with the motto guiding student activism, the leaders downplayed the significance of any student-led revolt. For them, as for most observers then and now, the *Cordobazo* was the turning point.

The *Cordobazo* was distinct in that the labor movement was the force leading the popular revolt. As scholars have shown, the most immediate dynamics driving the workers' massive involvement were grievances related to working conditions, which created an opening for airing the most diverse grievances within the labor movement.[28] After several partial strikes, the workers called for a general strike in the city on May 29. Gathered in massive meetings (of about eight thousand people), the students discussed whether to participate, and if so, how, and on May 29 most went into the streets.[29] The usual chronology of the *Cordobazo* divides the day into three moments. The first moment (until noon) was marked by the presence of unionized workers accompanied by students. Coming largely from the automobile plants in the suburban areas, the workers marched toward the city center in columns. Their leaders were at the front—notably Augusto Tosco, from the Power Workers Union. The police tried to prevent the columns from arriving at the central plaza, and, in doing so, they shot to death a worker named Máximo Mena. The second moment (the afternoon) was the time of generalized rebellion, which involved not only the strike spreading around the city but also the active incorporation of larger segments of the local population. Groups of people battled with the police and set fire to the Development Bank, the Jockey Club, and the Citroen and Xerox stores, among other buildings targeted as belonging to the "oligarchy" or to imperialist businesses. At 5:00 P.M., when the government decided to militarize Córdoba, a third moment began. Most workers abandoned the streets, some of them hiding from the military. The epicenter thus shifted to the student bastions in Barrio Clinicas and Barrio Güemes, which were both barricaded. While the military went house to house, some snipers from the "Santiago Pampillón" commando fired shots throughout the night, intending to distract rather than kill the soldiers. Of the fourteen people who were killed, most were students and workers, and only one was a soldier. Moreover, three hundred and fifty were arrested and five thousand were wounded.[30]

The *Cordobazo* was the core event of the Argentine May, a synecdoche for the entire uprising. As scholar Carlos Altamirano has pointed out, it rapidly became mythic in that it encoded both the promises and drawbacks that "insurrection" represented for a revolution that to many seemed imminent.[31] At the level of the regime, the month of May in general and the *Cordobazo* in particular, prompted the beginning of the end of the so-called *Revolución Argentina*. After the *Cordobazo*, everyone in the president's cabinet resigned, although Onganía did not do so until June of 1970 when the Montoneros, in their baptism of fire, kidnapped and executed former resident Pedro Eugenio Aramburu. That event was significant because it succinctly represents the dynamics of Argentine politics by 1970. These new actors, the guerrilla groups, in part legitimated their raison d'être in the conditions that prevailed in May 1969, namely the popular readiness to struggle against the regime, the limits of "popular insurrection" to fight back the army, and the violence "from above" that they wanted to respond to "from below."[32] If, for the workers, May represented the endpoint of traditions of struggle and a "combative" consciousness dating back to the mid-1950s, it also inaugurated a new era. Unlike the experience of "68" in Mexico and Brazil, which ended with tragic repression (such as the Massacre of Tlatelolco) and repressive legislation (such as the infamous Acta Institucional 5, or Al-5), the Argentine May paved the way for a dynamics of societal mobilization dominated by the emergence of new political actors: the guerrillas, for sure, but in interconnection with the politicization of a new cohort of young activists.

After the Argentine May, youth came to embody a new, ideally revolutionary, political era. While in the 1960s different actors projected onto youth their hopes for the "rise of rationality" in all spheres of social life, including politics, by 1970 the imagery of a prudent youth was broken. As sociologist Juan Carlos Torre has pointed out, after the *Cordobazo* it became apparent that many youths no longer trusted the political institutions or the likelihood of forging individual careers. "Repeatedly frustrated and deprecating what society had to offer them," Torre concludes, many young people—chiefly from middle-class backgrounds—began a "movement to the People."[33] In fact, the student activism that emerged after the 1966 coup d'état initiated the "movement to the people" long before the Argentine May, which perhaps helps explain its scope and intensity. The political time inaugurated by the Argentine May, in any case, generalized that movement and located youth as a critical political category and actor that actively helped amplify and shape a political culture in which Argentina became associated with the Third World—and, as a "Third World" nation, it would liberate itself by any means possible.

Feeling a Third World Argentina

In a new introduction to his *Sociology of Modernization* (1971), Gino Germani challenged those who identified Argentina with the Third World. He argued that, in contrast to countries in Asia and Africa—his shorthand for the Third World—Argentina was "a 'middle-class' nation at an international scale of development and modernization." Forgetting this distinction, Germani cautioned his readers, "is a cause of political and ideological mistakes."[34] Founder of the so-called scientific sociology in the 1950s, Germani also popularized some of the most significant concepts through which many citizens of that "middle-class nation" grasped the sociocultural transformations that they lived through, such as "modernization." By 1970, Germani might have felt satisfied: signs of modernization seemed to flourish in Argentina's enduring urbanization (65 percent of the country's population lived in cities), improving literacy rates (which reached 82 percent), and ongoing expansion of enrollment in secondary schools and universities.[35] Situating Argentina within the prevailing paradigms of the Third World required effort. How and why, then, were educated youth—those who apparently benefited the most from belonging to a "middle-class" nation—so willing to identify their country as part of the Third World?

The political socialization of young people in the late 1960s and early 1970s Argentina occurred within and was shaped by a renewed political culture in which the assimilation of Argentina to the Third World constituted a key component. Scholars have tended to explain the rise of a "New Left" throughout the 1960s in terms of both the growing acceptance of armed struggle as a means for achieving national and social liberation as well as the ways in which left-wing intellectuals and militants reevaluated the Peronist movement as a potential road to Socialism.[36] Although these novelties were indeed crucial, often overlooked—and perhaps naturalized—the Third World framework created commonality among politically and ideologically divergent groups, who attributed to the concept two basic meanings. First, the Third World was defined as a political geography highlighting the importance of decolonization of Asia and Africa and the need for similar transformations in "neocolonial" Latin America, which was depicted as economically and military dependent on the "imperialist centers" but, thanks to the success of the Cuban revolutionary process, ever more conscious of the opportunities of liberation. Second, the local uses of the Third World concept stressed the scope and intensity of social oppression, which required the systemic use of violence that usually came in the form of military rule. Along both lines Argentina would belong to that geography.[37] A lexicon dominated by keywords such as dependency, systemic violence, and social oppression spread to Catholic, Peronist, and Marxist groups and pointed to the pervasiveness of the Third World framework in that New Left. The embrace of that approach also entailed connecting the local New Left with its counterparts in France or Italy, who were opening up their agendas to address anti-imperialism in displays of solidarity with the peoples in Asia, Africa, and Latin America—as demonstrated in the pantheon of heroes that presided over the rallies in 1968.[38] The Argentine New Left did not aim at merely expressing solidarity but also at claiming that Argentina belonged to the Third World in its own right.

Far from being an "ideological and political mistake," the assimilation of Argentina to the Third World was a template for creating a political culture whose mobilizing ability was related to the shaping of emotions such as indignation. As some anthropologists and cultural historians have recently argued, indignation is a collectively shaped emotion that potentially fuels political action since it is tied to how groups trace the limits of "the unbearable." Its definition involves the certainty that rights are being violated and that the unjust situation merits urgent reparation.[39] Defining "the unbearable" in Argentina implied highlighting the country's Third World status. Hence, many cultural and political actors—ranging from the CGTA to the PRT—focused on the contrasts between a supposedly cosmopolitan and modern Argentina that grew at the price of the persistence of extreme poverty and social oppression. Illuminating that "hidden" Argentina was a pressing task. Typified in numerous reports within the leftist press, the focus on the "hidden" Argentina was perhaps best exemplified in one of the most quoted documents on the dynamics of political radicalization of the late 1960s: the May Day Manifesto of the CGTA, which was authored by journalist and writer Rodolfo Walsh in 1968. While calling for the articulation of a broad anti-imperialist and anti-Onganía bloc, it pointed out that in Argentina:

> The rate of infant mortality is four times that of the developed countries, twenty times in districts of Jujuy where one out of three children dies before his or her first year of life. One half of the population suffers from parasites in the northern littoral. Fifty percent of our children quit school before finishing the primary level, 83 percent [quit] in Corrientes, Santiago, and El Chaco. . . . There is no city without its belt of *villas miseria*, where water and electricity consumption is only comparable to the interior regions of Africa.[40]

Based on this panorama, how could anyone see Argentina as a modernizing country? The activists and intellectuals within the CGTA, as many others within other spaces, sought to place these contradictions at the center stage of political attention. Drawing on hyperbolic depictions and metaphors (such as "only comparable to the interior regions of Africa"), the implicit goal was to convince skeptics about the Third World nature of the country and the need for urgent action. From CGTA's *Semanario* to the PRT's *El combatiente*, the leftist press was flush with reports that emphasized on the nonindustrial working class, lamenting for example the health, housing, and living conditions of the cane-, wood-, and cotton-cutters and the dwellers of the *villas miseria*.[41] The coverage made use of disciplinary tools of the "scientific sociology" in an effort to challenge the modernizing narrative that Germani and others invoked. For example, academic and journalistic commentators used to point out the expansion of university enrollment as a sign of the sociocultural modernization of Argentina in comparison to other Latin American countries. A series of reports in the *Semanario* charged that enrollment had stagnated after 1966 and that the previous expansion, while real, had served to veil a deeper trend: "the 70 percent illiteracy rates in Corrientes and Santiago."[42] The statistics built up a "contrasting effect" aimed at showing the structural inequalities that resulted from the country's "neocoloniality," which went hand in hand with the promotion of activism beyond Buenos Aires, Rosario, or Córdoba.

The province of Tucumán became a critical marker of Argentina's status as a Third World nation and a focal point for cultural and political activism. Tucumán was a showroom for both Onganía's economic policies and the CGTA's ability to articulate political discontent at a national level. In late 1966, one of the regime's first economic initiatives was to discontinue subsidies to the sugar mills, a decision justified on the grounds of efficiency, but whose most immediate result was more unemployment among the already impoverished sugar workers. Endowed with a combative unionist tradition (the PRT dubbed them the vanguards of Argentina's revolution), the sugar workers responded with hunger strikes and rallies—actions that were severely repressed, including the police shooting of a worker named Hilda Guerrero.[43] Tucumán would also become a key symbolic space for the interplay of artistic and cultural projects. In 1968, avant-garde artists worked together with sociologists and literary critics to put together an exhibition titled *Tucumán Arde* (Tucumán Burns). *Tucumán Arde* was complete with statistical data on wages, literacy, and health as well as historical descriptions of sugar production, all visual materials that hung on the walls and from the roof or that were screened on television sets. Exhibited in the CGTA headquarters in Rosario and Buenos Aires, it instilled the "contrasting effects" in epicenters of modernizing Argentina; in doing so it illuminated its most "hidden" and allegedly "truest" reality.[44]

In the late 1960s and early 1970s, young people could interact with cultural and political materials showing the "hidden" Argentina and, furthermore, many attempted to encounter it literally. In 1970, the historian and journalist Félix Luna wrote about what he termed "neo-tourism" by commenting on how many youths had broken with the "family-vacation paradigm" to explore unconventional destinations. Luna believed that the drive fueling the "tide of young pilgrims" was their "willingness to know our country, assume that is theirs, and try to change it."[45] The figure of the backpacker typified that "pilgrim." Already in 1966, journalistic reports informed readers that fifty thousand backpackers, largely young men between the ages of fifteen and twenty-five, had overwhelmed the country's limited camping facilities and argued for establishing a "backpacker identification card" to assist "safe hitchhiking."[46] A 1970 government study indicated that 10 percent of young women and men in the age group eighteen to twenty-five from Buenos Aires, Córdoba, Rosario, and Mendoza that traveled that year were not "in the company of family members." The study further noted that half of them went to destinations other than the conventional ones (the Atlantic Coast and Córdoba), and contrasted those "traditional" tourism practices with the images of the backpacker jumping from trains in Bariloche and Tucumán.[47] Entry points to Patagonia and the Northwest, these two cities nevertheless represented different aesthetic, cultural, and political options; to generalize, while youth attracted to countercultural movements headed to Patagonia, those in the process of involving themselves in revolutionary politics opted for the Northwest.

Already an important tourist destination, young visitors endowed Northwest Argentina with heightened cultural and political significance in the 1960s and 1970s. None other than Ernesto "Che" Guevara had traversed the Northwestern corridor (the provinces of Tucumán, Santiago del Estero, Salta, and Jujuy) in 1950, prior to his first grand continental trip, fueled by the desire to find "revelations of hidden aspects of social reality."[48] In the decades to follow, thousands of chiefly middle-class youth pursued similar encounters. Interviewed for a report on backpacking in 1968, one female history student noted that visiting the region had broadened her knowledge of the country and "its most humble people." In 1971, a group of university students from La Plata concurred when describing their journey, which included stops in "every single village from Tucumán to Jujuy."[49] Similarly, Cacho Narzole recalls that, along with his girlfriend, he made two trips to the Northwest: "while discovering the beauty of the landscapes," he wrote, "we were shocked by the social reality of extreme poverty and the inhuman exploitation." Hugo Macchi experienced an analogous "shock" in a journey that also included Bolivia and Peru, when he "immersed himself in conditions of misery and suffering."[50] For Hugo and Cacho, as for many other youths, these experiences were integral to a broader process of discovery, including their rising interest in revolutionary militancy—they both became militants with the PRT.

The political dimension was evident in the second kind of travel many youths undertook. Within a climate marked by the rising commitment of Catholics to social justice, hundreds of youth—sometimes immediately following secondary school graduation—carried out social work in the most impoverished regions of the country, such as the Northwest and the Northeast. This was the case, for example, with the Camilo Torres commando (which included subsequent founders of the Montoneros) that spent the summer of 1966 in a small town in northern Santa Fe where they conducted literary campaigns, taught the gospel to children, and helped workers with their daily chores.[51] In the same region, Catholic students with the Movimiento Ateneísta performed similar tasks with the *hacheros* (woodcutters) and, upon their return to college, reported that sharing the *hacheros'* daily life constituted "an accelerated class on the nature of dependency and neocolonialism."[52] Those travel experiences, however, were not restricted to Catholic, middle-class university youth. On one side of the social spectrum, Alejandro, a former upper-class youth from Córdoba, recalls that when he was a secondary school student he used to spend the weekdays and most of his time in company of his "social equals"—playing rugby, attending parties, or simply hanging out. When he began to develop a "social consciousness" and despite being "secular," he decided he would accompany a priest to do social work in a little town in Misiones upon graduating in the summer of 1967: "witnessing so much poverty and suffering," he wrote, "basically drove me crazy." At the same time that he abandoned his leisure activities, he joined the PRT.[53] On the other side of the social spectrum, José, a former working-class boy who in 1970 went with his parish fellows to Santiago del Estero, recalled, "That little town did not have anything: no doctor, no potable water, no gas or power. People worked hard for not having anything to feed their children with." As other former travelers, José depicted his as an eye-opening experience: "We took a practical class on social injustice, to say the least."[54] For them, such journeys served both as a political-pedagogical initiative and as direct evidence of Argentina's Third World condition.

In addition to travel, these Third World perspectives were shaped and conveyed through cultural practices that altered the country's traditionally European-oriented cultural landscape. In the overtly politicized sociology department of the University of Buenos Aires, for example, a cohort of professors taught undergraduate-level courses (the *cátedras nacionales*) and created the journal *Antropología 3er Mundo* with the goal of challenging the Eurocentric orientation and theories of modernization that shaped the interpretations of Argentina's past and present endorsed by Germani and others. They taught classes on the "history of the popular struggles," where they exposed the students to the work of Frantz Fanon and of "national thinkers" such as Juan José Hernández Arregui and Juan Perón. In 1969, one professor explained that the goal was to produce the "mental liberation" of the "ideological vanguard of the middle classes" (i.e., students), and he viewed the outcome so far in positive terms, since "they have begun to think nationally and to conceive of our country as a Third World nation."[55] In a similar vein, another professor taught a seminar in the 1971 school year on the choice between rural or urban guerrilla, for which he made required reading works by Guevara and interviews with the Fuerzas Armadas Peronistas (FAP, Peronist Armed Forces) and the Uruguayan Tupamaros published in 1970 by *Cristianismo y Revolución*—which included a section titled "Bulletin of the Third World."[56] Yet young people other than the overtly politicized students at the most radicalized schools joined the tide of Third World perspectives through their reading options. A survey of bookstores in 1972 showed that younger readers chiefly purchased political and historical books authored by "national thinkers" and "Latin American writers" such as Paulo Freire and Eduardo Galeano as well as the year's main bestseller, Martha Harnecker's *Conceptos elementales del materialismo histórico*, a "mandatory textbook" for politicizing youth.[57]

Third World music, and especially that of Latin America, pervaded the musical consumption of many youths as well. As in other Latin American countries, the "New Song" movement gained a certain prominence. The precursors of the movement, Atahualpa Yupanqui and the Chilean Violeta Parra, shared a willingness to represent "the people," usually in their lyrics and in their use of certain instruments of indigenous origins that recovered the styles of folkloric projection.[58] Leading that renewal, the singer Mercedes Sosa embodied the link of "the interior"—chiefly her hometown, Tucumán—with the "true" Argentina, imagined as tied by history and will to its neighboring Latin American countries. In the making of her persona and repertoire, Sosa celebrated the "America *morena*" (darker America) and its presumed common destiny of liberation. Although she captivated the mass market in the early 1970s, Sosa's association with the Communist Party was detrimental to her appeal to groups of youth attracted to revolutionary Peronism, who used to criticize her for an alleged "reformism."[59] They had plenty of other options, though. In 1971, one business report showed that the records by the Chileans Inti Illymani and Quilapayún and the Uruguayan Daniel Viglietti had become popular among college students. That constituency might have been the one crowding Buenos Aires' Luna Park stadium in August of 1972 to listen to Viglietti and the Venezuelan Soledad Bravo—another important "New Song" artist—while chanting slogans about "Cuba and the Socialist fatherland."[60] Some youths mingled their taste for the aesthetics and politics of the "New Song" with their taste for rock music and culture.[61] In contrast, other youths, mostly women—who had been excluded from rock culture—favored the New Song. As Mabel, a student who joined the JP recalled, the New Song was "the soundtrack" of her life: she was attracted to "songs about the landless peasants, the Latin American revolution."[62]

The dissemination of cultural practices associated with the identification of Argentina with the Third World was only one part of the story. In fact, for those in the process of committing themselves to revolutionary militancy, the making of a Third World Argentina implied also the emergence of a new political sensibility dominated by a sense of urgency. For the young women and men who traveled to see the country's Third World nature for themselves, the experience of finding that "hidden truth" helped shape indignation. The military, for many of these youths, represented the transient incarnation of powerful enemies—the "oligarchy," for example—who, since the nineteenth century, had been responsible for creating a neocolonial society whose result was *that* Argentina. Masked in "bourgeois" parties, or "unmasked" as military, the enemies controlled the state and repressed or outlawed "popular forces."[63] A new cohort of political activists had no confidence that change was possible within the limits of the "system" and thought that only a radical change would be sufficient to overcome the conditions making *that* Argentina possible. Change was imminent: the Argentine May and the struggles in other "Third World" countries showed that the time was ripe and that there was only one method for change: armed struggle.[64]

At the time that the first guerrilla groups became visible they attracted broad support among young people. In late 1969, a sociologist conducted a survey on the political socialization of secondary school boys in Buenos Aires. He crafted the category of "nominal revolutionaries" to define the 18 percent of boys who thought that "a revolution was the only solution for creating a socially just country."[65] This survey was conducted before the most important guerrillas surfaced: the Montoneros, FAP, FAR, and PRT-led ERP. In this respect, the survey conveys insight into the positive expectations that some middle- and working-class boys projected onto the role of violence for "changing the country." In late 1971, once guerrilla groups had begun to act widely, an oft-quoted survey conducted by Investigaciones Políticas y Sociales de la Argentina (IPSA, Argentina's Social and Political Research) showed that 45 percent of those consulted in the Greater Buenos Aires area, 51 percent in Rosario, and 53 percent in Córdoba thought their actions were "justified." As historians have suggested, these favorable views were determined by the actions that guerrilla groups carried out from 1970 to 1973, mostly in the form of armed attacks. The guerrilla groups targeted property rather than people, selected their targets carefully, and cultivated their ties with "the masses" by distributing food and toys, for example.[66] But the heroic figure of the guerrilla and armed struggle as a method continued attracting youth sympathy after the 1973 elections had already passed. A survey of secondary school boys and girls showed that 30 percent had a "positive view" and 22 percent had a "tolerant view" of the guerrillas, who were perceived as the only "guarantee for change to happen."[67]

Supporting armed struggle represented, for many youths, supporting the "revolution" tout court. That new cohort of activists and militants set the tone for a conjuncture of the claims for radical change and the backing of radical means to achieve it that marked indelibly the Argentine political scenario. That shift in beliefs and practices had, if anything, a generational component. Although it is likely that, as one essayist recently put it, they represented a statistical minority of those aged eighteen to twenty-five, rising numbers of young people in the early 1970s were confident that "the revolution" was pending.[68] That certainty meant many wanted to be a part of an irreversible process. In a roundtable with the winners of the essay contest on youth and politics, Antonio Brailovsky, age twenty-two, briefly argued that "Youths have two options: either following the *caminito* [little road] that an unjust system has traced for us, or following the *camino* [road] toward a different, new society."[69] The belittled *caminito* implied, perhaps, the possibility of upward mobility and the integration into a "bourgeois" life, which modernizing thinkers thought possible throughout the 1960s and which many youths opted for. The *camino*, in contrast, was the promise of a "different," better society: "I feel confused," wrote Viviana, age sixteen, "but I learned that the Revolution is the only possible *camino*."[70] Many youths joined the *camino* by involving themselves in political activism in the student, party, or guerrilla groups they helped create in what seemed to be their hour.

The Hour of Youth

When recalling his political experiences, a former schoolboy noted that he circulated among different groups, including Marxist groups, before settling on the Peronist UES. "The other groups were alien to the people and, if the revolution was to happen, it would happen through Peronism: it was natural," he said.[71] Rather than natural, the engagement of young people with revolutionary Peronist trends was at the junction of at least three interrelated phenomena. In the first place, Peronism represented itself as the most suitable venue to connect with and mobilize "the people," a claim that student and youth groups (not only in Argentina) increasingly valued throughout the 1960s. Second, Perón and his younger followers learned to situate that movement into new ideological and cultural coordinates, notably within a Third World framework. Finally, Peronism was in fact the major beneficiary of a larger youth participation in the entire political spectrum. The fragmented Radical Party witnessed the growth of its two youth branches, and youth also flooded into left-wing parties that did not endorse armed struggle, such as the Socialist Workers' Party. Even the pro-Soviet Communist Party started to slowly recover young militants after having lost 50 percent of its youth constituency in 1967, chiefly to pro-Chinese groups.[72] Meanwhile, the most important non-Peronist force endorsing armed struggle, the PRT-ERP, created its youth branch (the Guevarista Youth) in 1973, but the calls for reorganizing it as late as 1975 suggest that the initiative was not successful. While the PRT-ERP's constituency was indeed young, it was not organized by using a generational interpellation.[73] On the contrary, in Peronism "youth" was a category that reflected the young people who embraced that movement while identifying with the Montoneros, indicating a generational and ideological positioning.

Although youth groups did exist at the end of the first Peronist government, their political importance grew after the 1955 coup d'état and especially by the mid 1960s, when Perón spoke of *trasvasamiento generacional* (generational transference).[74] As it happened with the "Peronist left" at large, Perón vindicated the actions of youth groups when the "bureaucratic" Peronist trends threatened his authority. In one of these contexts, in 1965, he called for a *trasvasamiento generacional* through which youth should prepare to infuse new blood into the movement. Endorsing deeply rooted tropes within the left-wing sectors, he insisted that youth should develop an "anti-imperialist, anticapitalist, antioligarchic attitude" and realize that the "coexistence between the exploiters and the exploited" was impossible. From his perspective, youth should fight against the exploiters "even if they infiltrate our movement."[75] It is not surprising that Perón manipulated a rhetoric based on presumed anticapitalist stances. What is surprising is that he chose youth as the addressee for his rhetoric, which located youth as the harbinger of an ideological, if also generational, renovation. It was not accidental, then, that radicalized young people who engaged with Peronism in the late 1960s referred to this letter as their foundational text: it showed a leader willing to make of Peronism a "national liberation movement" akin to others in the Third World.[76]

Perón's messages helped shape the new young addressees, many of whom, by the early 1970s, supported guerrilla groups. In the context of negotiations with the military regime to call elections, Perón doubled his efforts to court youth. Significantly, his recognition of the role of the "special formations"—his euphemism for the guerrillas—came in a cassette to be played in a meeting of university students in 1971. After thanking "the wonderful youth who know how to fight," he reiterated his plea for *trasvasamiento generacional* without delay: "this is the hour of youth," he said.[77] Responding to Perón's order, youth groups coming from different ideological backgrounds coalesced in 1972. The unified JP tried to keep shared positions regarding what youth stood for. In practical matters, they all agreed that the members of JP should be under thirty years old. Moreover, they all rejected the "bourgeois" definition of youth as a "golden age"; instead they viewed youth as a "political fact" meant to infuse Peronism with "ideological vitality."[78] Yet they disagreed about what kind of political fact and ideology youth embodied. The discrepancies were apparent in the JP foundational event, when only one leader supported the "special formations." By embodying the allure of armed struggle among youth, however, Montoneros rapidly rose as the dominant force. In fact, the JP organizational structure mirrored the Montoneros': it was divided into seven regional units, and its cadres were appointed directly by the Montoneros' leadership.[79]

The radicalized JP channeled and reflected the rapid Peronization of youth. Leader of street rallies, the JP was also the first group to side with Perón when he chose his delegate in Argentina, Héctor Cámpora, to run for the presidency in the elections to be held in March of 1973. While all candidates courted the three million youth who had never cast their vote, a survey showed that "four out of six will elect Cámpora."[80] The Peronist ticket received 49.5 percent of the vote, including most of the youth vote. Cámpora's government did partially recognize the importance of the JP and Montoneros in the process leading to the elections. In fact, his cabinet was composed of all the factions converging in Peronism, ranging from Perón's private secretary, the rightist José López Rega (appointed minister of social welfare and soon-to-be-founder of the parapolice group Argentine Anti-Communist Alliance, or the Triple A) to three JP allies in the Ministries of Education, the Interior, and Foreign Relations. The JP only had eight representatives but gained influence in Córdoba, Salta, Mendoza, Buenos Aires, and Santa Cruz. On May 25, when Cámpora was sworn in, the JP had reasons to celebrate. In his inaugural address, Cámpora thanked the "wonderful youth" and asked, "How could this triumph not belong to the youth who gave everything—family, friends, life—for a Peronist fatherland?"[81]

Under the slogan "to support, defend, and control the popular government," the Montoneros and the JP embarked upon an organization of mass fronts soon to be known as the Revolutionary Tendency, in which a youth interpellation prevailed. Supporting the government, a communiqué explained, meant also defending it against "external and internal enemies" and controlling how it fulfilled "the popular will." As scholars Silvia Sigal and Eliseo Verón have argued while analyzing this document—as well as the editorials in JP's weekly *El Descamisado*—the youth groups, like other "vanguards," positioned themselves as spokespersons of "the people" and claimed the right to indicate who the traitors and the loyalists were, two prerogatives thus far reserved for the "primary word" of the Peronist discursive space: that of Perón himself. The Tendency strove in vain not to lose ground within a movement that was conceived of as a venue for accessing "the people" they aimed to speak for and organize.[82] Notably, it strove to organize the "people" by appropriating a youthful framework, perhaps because they viewed their place within Peronism as coded generationally. Aside from the JP, the most important fronts were the Juventud Trabajadora Peronista (JTP, Working Peronist Youth), the UES, and the Juventud Universitaria Peronista (JUP, Peronist University Youth). Their actions were determined by their willingness to belong to a movement that soon after the elections turned to the right. They were, though, the largest youth organizations ever in Argentina, both affirming and neglecting "youth" as political actor.

Launched in April of 1973, the JUP helped amplify the Peronization of university students initiated in the late 1960s. Unlike previous Peronist student groups, the JUP valued the university as a legitimate site to battle "cultural and economic dependency" following overarching tenets. First, the JUP suggested that all students, no matter their majors, should conduct both manual and intellectual work in an effort to acclimatize themselves to a future society in which the divide would no longer exist. Second, the JUP proposed to reinforce the funding for "priority schools or careers" like engineering and veterinary medicine that would ideally help overcome "economic dependency."[83] Third, the JUP did not evaluate university autonomy positively: inasmuch as the universities were not to be "islands" but dependent on the broader political situation, they agreed that the government might rule them, beginning with the appointment of their authorities.[84] Although as early as February of 1974 that position vis-à-vis university autonomy would help to pass a law that would be used against the politicized students, during Cámpora's term the JUP was influential enough to lobby the government over the appointment of rectors, notably the UBA's, historian and "national thinker" Rodolfo Puiggrós.

The UBA was one of the strongholds of the Tendency, a site to enact

Juventud Universitaria Peronista rally, Buenos Aires, September 1973.
Archivo Fotográfico, Archivo General de la Nación, Box 883, File 15.

imagined and material battles and to build a "liberated fatherland." The
first enemy that the JUP sought to battle was *continuismo*, that is, the continuity of practices and personnel from the military regime. While *continuismo* was battled in all schools, it was perceived as intolerable at the
law school, since many professors had collaborated, as advisers and judges,
with the creation of a legal system to repress militants. As soon as Puiggrós
was appointed rector, students took over the law school and other school
buildings—as a part of a tide of "takeovers"—to prevent "antipopular" professors and staff from entering.[85] In those days, both the educational authorities and the UBA's rector passed a series of political-administrative
changes to fulfill the motto of "opening the university to the people." The
minister of education—an "ally" of the JUP, Dr. Jorge Taiana—resolved to
shelve all restrictions on admissions to the universities. As a result, enrollment increased from a total of 280,000 in 1972 to 390,000 in 1974, when,
at the UBA alone, 80,000 new students registered.[86] Puiggrós was rector
for only four months, but made the decision to support classes teaching
"national liberation," including mandatory classes on popular movements.
He also discontinued the subsidies granted by "*yanqui* foundations," and
enacted the ban on holding professorial positions along with jobs in "multinational companies."[87]

For the students attracted to the JUP, these actions and measures seemed to pave the way for recrafting the role of the university and the students in the "liberation process." In 1973 and early 1974, the endeavors for "connecting the university to the people" were the ones which both generated further student engagement and allowed for larger recruitment for the JUP. In the School of Humanities and Social Sciences at the UBA, for example, the Peronist professors, authorities, and students negotiated an agenda to relate each discipline to the "people and the popular government." While at the School courses on "Latin American Revolutionary Thought" and "History of the Popular Struggles" prevailed, the sociology students worked in government agencies and as consultants for unions; the anthropology students helped create a Third World Museum; the educational science students conducted literacy campaigns and contributed materials to adult schooling; and the psychology students did practical outreach in the Greater Buenos Aires area.[88] Many of them alternated their student- and university-based militancy with political work at the locales the JP opened in working-class neighborhoods. In Lanús, medical students staffed first-aid clinics and psychology students gave psychological advising and family counseling. The students at the University of Córdoba pursued analogous initiatives, with a focus on vaccinations and literacy campaigns as well.[89]

Similar drives for "connecting with the people" inspired the creation of the second student-based organization of the Tendency: the UES. Peronist groups had been active among secondary school students since at least 1971 when, during a teachers' strike, there was rapid Peronization in a realm thus far dominated by the Communist Youth.[90] Like their university counterparts, the secondary school students within the UES also strove to validate the school as a legitimate arena for activism. In contrast to the university students, who did not have examples to emulate, the ones affiliated with the UES held idyllic images of what the first Peronist governments had implied in terms of cultural changes and student organization. "We want to re-create the student experience of the 1950s," one boy from La Plata argued, "when they learned a true democratic culture." The UES often compared that imagined landscape with the one that the students had inhabited since 1955 "when the schools became training camps for obeying the system through military-like discipline and anti-national content."[91] To begin deconstructing that school system and repudiate *continuismo*, the UES students also took over schools. At the Colegio Nacional in La Plata, for example, the students requested the principal's resignation, financial aid, and the establishment of a tripartite government of students, teachers, and staff. Neither they nor the almost one thousand students who occupied two technical schools in San Nicolás succeeded in their demands.[92] Some of the takeovers, however, did result in profound changes, such as the one in the Belgrano School, where the students gained the right to appoint a new principal. It would be hard to overestimate the feeling of empowerment these adolescents may have experienced: as one student put it, "until yesterday, we were 'good-for-nothing' kids, now we have a voice."[93]

The new government gave the secondary school students a voice at the same that it tried to transform the curriculum. The minister of education discontinued the Democratic Education class imposed after the 1955 coup d'état, replacing it with Study of Argentine Social Reality, and mandated "nationalization" to cut across all disciplines: language classes should strive to "deter English neologisms," while history classes might reinforce the "learning of national history."[94] The transformation of content did not exhaust the ways in which the schools, to the authorities, might serve to forge new citizens for the "nation's liberation." In this respect, they thought that it was a student's right to participate in the schools' decision-making process, crucial to fostering "active, risk taking, caring youths." To that end, the minister discontinued a decree passed in 1936 prohibiting student politics and encouraged the creation of student centers. The authorities further believed that supporting student involvement was not enough to end the well-entrenched authoritarian practices at schools. Although more difficult to actualize than the student centers (which mushroomed in 1973), the authorities advocated "building horizontal relations," and they suggested ways to "ensure that dialogue and equality [are] prevailing in the relations between teachers and students, parents and children."[95] The antiauthoritarian ethos permeating this proposal was unusual, since it combined a politically "liberationist" overtone with an emphasis on undoing hierarchical relations. Similar to other promises of the "popular government," this one went unfulfilled because teachers refused to discuss it and because the mobilized students did not consider it a pressing political issue either.

Like the JUP's, the UES's politics were animated by the motto of "connecting with the people." This included enlarging its constituency by organizing working-class students. In contrast to the university student body, which was presumed to be composed of middle-class youths, the secondary school student body had expanded significantly since the 1950s to include even more working-class adolescents. Thus "going to the people" meant organizing students other than the ones in the traditionally middle-class schools where the UES first grew. The Colegio Nacional de Buenos Aires exemplified this: a stronghold for the children of enlightened middle-class professionals, the UES recruited more than one hundred fifty students there in 1973. Former students recall that, in the years that followed, the UES leaders asked them to move to different schools, yet the task of mobi-lizing students seemed difficult: "we did not have any idea of how to engage with the girls," recalls one student sent to organize in a teacher-training school, "they were interested in telenovelas and boyfriends."[96] However, the UES's main targets were the technical schools, sites for engaging with working-class boys. A police report, for example, noted that one hundred delegates from schools in the Greater Buenos Aires area agreed to priori-tize the technical students in a meeting held in late 1973. Although re-cruitment figures are missing, the UES was likely relatively successful in recruiting technical students. As a former activist recalls, they were re-luctant to discuss but always ready to act: "they were the first wanting to plant bombs."[97]

As happened with the Tendency at large, the UES also embarked upon a series of social work endeavors that amplified the practices many youths had developed since the late 1960s. Among the tasks developed by the UES, those related to vaccination campaigns, literacy campaigns, and children's recreation prevailed. In the city of Santa Rosa in La Pampa province, for example, the UES students ran seventeen "literacy circles" to improve adult education, and they also ran twelve daycare centers. Moreover, the stu-dents with the UES were proud to help paint and to do maintenance work at schools and hospitals in their respective districts.[98] These activities co-alesced into what was the UES's largest venture, the "Operativo Güemes." In January of 1974, five hundred students from all over the country went to Salta province to help build roads, canals, and schools. These activi-ties resembled the eye-opening travel practices of Catholic youths: as one student argued, he was encountering an impoverished Argentina that he "could not believe existed." Unlike the youth in the 1960s, these were nonetheless confident: they were helping fulfill the "national reconstruc-tion mandated by the popular government."[99]

In the summer of 1974, when Perón and the Peronist right-wing sec-tors intensified their backlash against the Tendency, "national reconstruc-tion" initiatives and other deployments of Third World status flourished. The Ministry of Education launched a program of student trips to "his-torical and political sites" in the Argentine Northwest, Bolivia, and Peru.

Three contingents of about two hundred students and professors then traveled from Tucumán to Cuzco in January and February of 1974.[100] State-sponsored, these experiences emulated those gained by thousands of backpackers who had traveled to the "hidden Argentina" since the late 1960s. The most common travel options that summer were the operations of "reconstruction" for most youth who traveled with the Tendency. The UES carried out its projects in Salta and also conducted fourteen more, most of which involved the deployment of large youth contingents to impoverished areas in the northern provinces like Santiago del Estero, Santa Fe, Chaco, and Formosa. As one leader of the JP argued, the operations had two goals: "to share the lives of our poorest compatriots" and "to help materialize reconstruction promises" by solving their most urgent needs, such as "first-aid clinics or classrooms."[101] Gradually more critical of the Tendency for its willingness to stay in a movement turning to the right, the weekly *Militancia*—representing the revolutionary group Peronismo de Base—sarcastically criticized the operations when it asked, "What do these *Operativos* offer to elevate popular consciousness? They take 'reconstruction' as brickwork."[102]

In many ways, *Militancia* rightly perceived a common thread unifying the practices of the JUP and UES: the literalness with which they enacted slogans. Interpreting that the 1973 election results had initiated "national liberation," young Peronist groups alternated between fighting against the "old regime" (i.e., *continuismo*) and mobilizing "the people." This combination of promises and threats was the backdrop against which rising numbers of young people affiliated with the Tendency, which appropriated powerful slogans, such as "connecting with the people" and "national reconstruction." In the dynamics of 1973, the JUP and the UES acted on these slogans in myriad ways. In doing so, many youths shaped and channeled attitudes of social solidarity and extreme will—*voluntarismo*—and sometimes they may have experienced a previously unknown sense of entitlement. Yet acting out slogans did not ensure their fulfillment: "national reconstruction" did not mean brickwork, nor did "connecting with the people" result in what many youths would have imagined when, for example, they did social work in working-class neighborhoods. Acting out slogans, however, did result in the numeric growing of the UES and the JUP, which became protagonists of at least six mobilizations in which the Tendency drew between fifty thousand and one hundred fifty thousand people, and far more to the Ezeiza airport to welcome Perón back to the country. Their tragedy, as historian Richard Gillespie has noted, was that Perón was not impressed by their numbers.[103]

Parricide, Filicide, and the Peronist Family Romance

In engaging with Peronism, many youths confronted their familial and cultural backgrounds. Some former students recall, for example, how their middle-class parents opposed their militancy based upon entrenched anti-Peronist claims, often by remembering the first Peronist governments and Perón's "tyranny."[104] While it is likely that these confrontations were more widespread among middle-class families, some militants from working-class origins also faced them. That was the case of Mabel, who joined the JUP while she was a student at the School of Humanities and Social Sciences at the UBA. Her parents were "nominal Peronists," that is, "they identified themselves with Peronism and voted Peronist when possible," however they opposed the radical overtone of her militancy.[105] In many respects, thus, the youth with the Tendency modified their inherited ways of conceiving of and interacting with politics. As Juan Carlos Torre has suggested, in their "movement toward the people," youth carried out a symbolic "parricide."[106] The metaphor is all the more important, since the political and ideological disputes within Peronism were coded in that language: framed and enacted as a family romance, they set discussions about authority and patriarchy as well, chiefly between Perón's return to the country and his death in July of 1974.

On June 20, 1973, the Ezeiza airport became the stage of an ongoing drama in Argentina's politics. The right-wing Peronist sectors, relegated to the sidelines in Cámpora's administration, were the leading forces organizing the event to welcome Perón back to the country, including the mobilization of about three thousand heavily armed civilians recruited from a pool of ex-policemen and body guards of the most prominent unions. Led by an infamous torturer from the first Peronist governments, Colonel Jorge Osinde, and funded by the Ministry of Social Welfare, these forces controlled the stage and its adjacent areas, attempting to prevent the Tendency's columns from being visible to Perón. The Tendency had made of that would-be celebration an occasion to literally show Perón its capability of mobilization: although there are no exact figures, observers agreed that half of the almost one million people rallied under the Tendency's banners. Yet the plane bringing Perón back never landed in Ezeiza, and the

Waiting for Perón's return, Ezeiza airport, June 20, 1973. Archivo Fotográfico, Archivo General de la Nación, Box 3166, File 38.

Tendency's columns never got close to the stage. As they approached, the right-wing forces fired shots at them, killing thirteen (three members of the JUP and UES) and wounding three hundred. The Ezeiza events set the stage for the rise of the Peronist right within Argentina's politics. Perón himself, in this first message to the country, threatened: "to the disguised enemies, I just recommend ending their attempts because when the people exhaust their patience, they *van a hacer sonar el escarmiento* [are going to teach them a lesson]."[107]

Although other political forces soon understood that the Ezeiza events and Perón's ensuing message were meant to begin the dismantling of the Peronist revolutionary sectors, the Tendency developed a defensive reading focused on "hedge theory." The PRT-ERP (which, unlike the Montoneros, decided not to abandon armed struggle once the elections had passed) was perhaps the one that most emphatically indicated that Perón had come back to "reconstruct the bourgeois bloc," a task that implied barring the revolutionary sectors in his political force. For that reason, the PRT-ERP suggested that their "brother Peronist groups" leave a movement that would not be willing to include them.[108] Far from that, the Tendency crafted an interpretation geared to both justify their place in "the move-ment" and safeguard Perón. As for Ezeiza, the Tendency claimed the pres-ence of CIA agents acting alongside the "bureaucratic" unionists paid by the minister of social welfare had caused the massacre. Minister López Rega epitomized the "hedge" circling Perón, which prevented his real encounter with "the people." For the Tendency, breaking that hedge was imperative and it asked its constituency, "the people," to mobilize so that Perón could listen to them without intermediaries, as when eighty thousand youths visited Perón's house in July.[109] The "hedge theory" allowed the Tendency to create an imaginary occurrence: Perón would not be in Argentina until the desired encounter with "the people" took place.

Yet Perón was indeed in Argentina, unleashing a war in the "Peronist family." After Ezeiza, two disparate but leading intellectuals drew on fam-ily metaphors to grasp the political scenario. An intellectual hero for young Peronists, the "national thinker" Arturo Jauretche wrote an opinion piece echoing Freud's *Totem and Taboo*. As the "primitive horde of brothers" in the Freudian text, he argued that "the young" embodied a revolution that "would devour the elderly fathers" who were unable to adapt them-selves to new times. A member of the "older" group himself, Jauretche asked his generational peers, including Perón, not to "become sad wid-ows."[110] While Jauretche endorsed a political parricide, the psychoanalyst Arnaldo Rascovsky spoke of "filicide." Since the 1960s he had researched the meanings of what he believed were extended practices of assassination and symbolic mutilations of children and youths at the hands of their el-ders. These filicidal practices at the same time reversed and reinforced the parricide that psychoanalytical theory recognized as essential to the indi-vidual's psychic configuration and to the building of civilization: filicide, for Rascovsky, was equally constitutive.[111] Perhaps acquainted with these ideas, *La Opinión* asked him to write a piece about Ezeiza. Perón's call for a *trasvasamiento generacional*, Rascovsky asserted, had caused "expectations among the youth who anxiously waited for the leader, who would support the unfolding of their developmental possibilities." Yet Ezeiza incited a "reaction of the elder: it was a sacrificial ritual through which filicide was accomplished." And he further dramatized: "all filicide practices incite par-ricide sentiments."[112]

Both Rascovsky's theory of filicide and Jauretche's invocation of par-ricide, as applied to the disputes within Peronism, erased the ideological meanings of "elders" and "children," but these categories do stress the family and, most notably, the generational language in which the disputes were framed. Between September of 1973 and May of 1974, Perón deployed generational-based language to "purge" his movement from its revolutionary sectors in three decisive conjunctures. Soon thereafter Cámpora was forced to resign and Perón decided to run with his third wife, Isabel Martínez, in the elections to be held in September of 1973, Perón met the "elder" and asserted that "the youth branch is questioned." Moreover, he reminded "the young" that the "elder"—namely, the unionists—should not be attacked. The attacks nevertheless continued.[113] In fact, some days after Perón won the favor of 62 percent of the voting population, the CGT secretary, José Rucci, was killed. Although the Montoneros had officially abandoned armed action, they were soon (and correctly) blamed, and Perón talked of "purging" the youths who "beneath a Peronist T-shirt" were "Marxists." The purge had several ramifications. First, rightist groups such as the Triple A escalated their violence against the Tendency, beginning by killing JP militant Enrique Grinberg in early September of 1973. In two months, five other left-wing Peronists had been killed and dozens of JP locals shot.[114] Second, the purge entailed barring the sites in which the Tendency had mostly grown up, like the university. Perón requested the resignation of the UBA's rector, and the violent attacks against the university buildings and the JUP militants continued.[115]

The second moment when Perón made use of generational-based language and settings took place in early 1974, which ended with his expelling the "youth" revolutionary sectors. The starting point for these events was marked by the PRT-ERP's attempt to take over a military battalion. In that context, Perón asked the population to stand against Marxism and to promote a reform of the penal code so as to tighten repression: not only the PRT-ERP but also revolutionary Peronist groups—and their "ally"—were the targets. In January, the governor of Buenos Aires was asked to resign, over a period of only four days right-wing groups shot up nineteen locales of the JP, and police forces raided the headquarters of the JP's weekly.[116] In that context, Perón called for a meeting with "youth delegates." The leaders of the JP tried unsuccessfully to exclude the right-wing groups. In a press conference, the Montoneros' leader Mario Firmenich claimed that the Tendency's delegates would not "be seated with the ones who shot our locales." At the meeting, Perón replied, "I prefer an honest leader with ten people behind him to a traitor with ten thousand," and asked the "traitors" to leave.[117]

"Yesterday we were the *muchachos* and the boss of the movement greeted us and honored our dead," the editorialist of the JP's weekly stated, "and now, because we are as Perón wanted us to be, we became Socialists or infiltrators."[118] This editorial dramatized the situation that the Tendency faced when Perón expelled them and the rationale of the decision that many young people performed when engaging with Peronism to "connect with the people." While most may have carried out a symbolic parricide when confronting their familial and cultural backgrounds, a father figure stood: Perón. By inserting themselves as the "youth" in the Peronist movement, thus accepting the place that Perón reserved for them, these revolutionary sectors were also involved in a family romance. As historian Lynn Hunt has pointed out in her analysis of the French Revolution, "notions of familiar order underlie revolutionary politics," leaving room for imagining relations of authority and power modeled after those between fathers and sons, among others.[119] In the Peronist family romance, the sons indeed wanted to share power with the father, who had contributed to their initial empowerment. In contrast to the "elder"—who accepted being the primus inter pares—the *muchachos* forged their particular brotherhood out of their vindication of armed struggle and refused to comply with the authority of the father when he came back to the country to expel them. "Nobody can throw us out of Peronism," the editorialist stated, and that "nobody" was Perón himself. The editorialist turned Perón's words around: because "we are as he wanted us to be," he betrayed "us," the *muchachos*. Yet how to guarantee the persistence of the *muchachos* when their family name was neglected? As scholars Sigal and Verón have noted, the JP acted as if he was already dead months before Perón died.[120]

There would be, however, a final chapter of the Peronist family romance: the May Day celebration of 1974. As recounted in memoirs and scholarly works, the Tendency believed that the first May Day celebration with Perón as president would be like the ones they imagined happening in the 1940s and 1950s: meetings where the leader listened to "the people" and held a dialogue with them. Columns identified under the banners of JP, JUP, UES, and Montoneros arrived at the Plaza de Mayo chanting, "*Aquí están los Montoneros que mataron a Aramburu* [Here are the Montoneros who killed Aramburu]." When Perón went out to the balcony to address the crowd, the Tendency forced the dialogue, beginning by chanting "*qué pasa General / que está lleno de gorilas el gobierno nacional?* [What happens, General / that the national government is full of gorillas?]." The General replied, speaking highly of the "union organization, kept alive over twenty years, despite the stupid [people] who shout!" while the Tendency chanted "*se va a acabar / la burocracia sindical* [The union bureaucracy / will end]."

Resuming his argument, Perón went on, "The union organization has remained alive, and now it happens that some of the unbearded [*imberbes*] who shout want to have more merits than those who have struggled for twenty years!" and he called on everyone to pay homage to the "prudent union leaders . . . who have seen how their fellows fell killed" and once again spoke about "*hacer sonar el escarmiento*" [teaching them a lesson]." When he finished his words, the *imberbes* were not listening: in one of the most astonishing events in Argentina's politics, they abandoned the Plaza.[121]

What did this abandonment of the Plaza represent? Scholar Carlos Altamirano argues that the Tendency's columns went to the Plaza to "force the end," that is, to deploy the apocalyptical component organizing their practices and imaginaries.[122] Coupled with this plausible analysis, if viewed from the perspective of the family romance, this event marked the impossibility of the Tendency's "killing" the father figure and moving away from a hierarchical relation other than in exclusively literal terms. They could not literally "kill" the father figure but they did challenge his authority while showing a still powerful brotherhood, tied to their vindication of Montoneros' baptism of fire. However, whereas their chants at that event focused on their opposition to the "bureaucrats" and their identification with armed struggle, these groups seemed to have avoided representing themselves as the *muchachos* while emphasizing that they represented "the people."[123] Perón cast no doubt: to downplay them and boost the "elders," he positioned the Peronist revolutionary sectors as youth. The *muchachos* turned into the *imberbes* who shouted. This rhetorical makeover of "youth" as the belittling *imberbes* (defined by their "lack" of maturity, of beard, of virility perhaps) would allow him and the "elders" to recover their political and symbolic authority: the *hacer sonar el escarmiento*—like what parents said to threaten their children when they misbehave—indicated that this would have an even more dreadful overtone. Perón died two months after May Day, having left to the "elders"—the right—the task of recovering their authority and to the "young" the void that his father figure represented.

▶ The "authority-reconstitution" project upon which the Peronist right embarked in 1974, which I discuss in detail in Chapter 8, was a response to the destabilizing effects that the politicization of youth had represented in Argentina. I do not mean to imply either that all young people engaged in radical politics or that all who engaged in radical politics were young people, but that the emergence of a revolutionary political culture was sustained by the decisive involvement of young people and by the making of youth as a political category. It was Peronism that offered a way through which youth signified a positive political category, as well as a bridge for young people to "connect with the people." This was something that the new student activism emerging after the 1966 coup d'état claimed as necessary and which many more began to feel both "real" and imperative since the Argentine May of 1969.

The Argentine May made apparent the profound transformations cutting across student activism since 1966 and marked the emergence of young people as political actors. Decentering the narrative from the *Cordobazo* to include it as the last episode of a series of revolts allows for the unraveling of how students had initially constituted the leading forces of the popular revolts in Corrientes and Rosario. Although able to crystallize the desired "worker and student" union, many student leaders understood that the revolts would fall short unless the "working class" led them, and thus they downplayed their own political significance. In this respect, the *Cordobazo* fulfilled the young activists' hopes when the students— and youth at large—mobilized alongside yet "behind" industrial workers. While for activists the massive and unprecedented engagement of workers in Córdoba's streets was a promising surprise, for most observers at the time—the press and Perón himself—the radical novelty came from the visibility of young people.

The youth who came of age, politically, in the aftermath of that May did so by participating in a revolutionary political culture dominated by the assimilation of Argentina with the Third World. A project articulated in the political press and manifestos and disseminated through a broad range of cultural practices, building up a "Third World Argentina" involved the mobilization of emotions—such as indignation—as well as more traditional ideological components. The belief that the country belonged to a geography marked by "neocolonialism" and "liberating forces" became commonsensical by the early 1970s, which had several effects. First, it allowed for a multilayered confrontation of the narrative indicating that Argentina was socially egalitarian and exceptional vis-à-vis its Latin American neighbors. Contrasting the modernizing epicenters—largely the urban, middle-class cities—to the pockets of social oppression was the "revealing" mechanism whereby the so-called real Argentina was uncovered. In an ethical, political, and emotional move, politicizing young people came to refuse what the "modern" Argentina had to offer them in order to change the conditions that made the "real" Argentina possible. Second, then, that seemingly unbearable real Argentina, in their view, could only be transformed through radical means. The identification of Argentina with the Third World paved the way for naturalizing armed struggle as the appropriate venue for social and political transformation.

The making of youth as a political actor and the configuration of a revolutionary political culture were not the only novelties of the 1960s and early 1970s. As a number of scholars have noted, a key development of this period was the engagement of young people—mostly of middle-class origins—in the ranks of Peronism. This engagement was neither "natural" nor could it be taken for granted. At a very basic level, it is obvious that not all young people who engaged in radical politics did so via revolutionary Peronism. Other options, such as the PRT-ERP, amassed a cross-class youth constituency as well, although it was not organized across generational lines. In contrast, Peronism provided a referential frame through which to interpellate young people as "youth" and through which to codify political and ideological differences in generational terms. This entailed both the reaffirmation of "youth" as a legitimate political category and the making of young people as crucial political actors. However, it also implied the possibility of enacting a family romance in which issues of authority were at stake. In that romance, the revolutionary sectors (whether composed of young people or not) were positioned as "youth." In 1973, Rodolfo Ortega Peña was almost alone when he insisted that "the revolutionary transcends the generational" and recommended that the Tendency "revise how to engage with Peronism."[124] He perhaps understood that political and ideological disputes, when coded in generational terms, would potentially carry heightened effects. Toward 1974, when the resolution of the Peronist family romance occurred, not only the revolutionary sectors (whether Peronist or not, whether young or not) but also young people at large would suffer from the "authority-reconstitution" project that the "elders," the right, dreadfully endorsed.

7 ▸ *Poner el cuerpo*

THE YOUTH BODY BETWEEN EROTICISM
AND REVOLUTIONARY POLITICS

In preparation for the coming of the spring of 1966, an ad for Sportline jackets addressed a male readership with a challenging and alluring statement: "only if you brought together a guerrilla's audacity and a playboy's affluence, would you be ready to dress Sportline." Six years after that ad, *Para Ti* introduced its young female readers to the changing fashions for the summer of 1972. It produced a photographic report in which two models exhibited new dress items (high-heeled boots and tight short pants) and colors, notably brown and olive green. The title for the report could not have been more explicit: that summer "Guerrilla Fashion" was "in." These are only two examples of the ways in which youth, eroticism, and revolutionary politics were woven together in Argentina, a dynamics that this chapter aims at unraveling. In doing so, I follow the suggestion of feminist scholar Elizabeth Grosz, who proposed understanding the body as both a "surface on which social law, morality, and values are inscribed" and as a lived experience.[1]

In the late 1960s and early 1970s Argentina, *poner el cuerpo* (to put one's body on the line) acquired manifold, sometimes competing meanings, which taken together help explain how and why youth as a category and young people as actors became so fundamental to defining the politics, culture, and sexuality of the era. Youth, for example, "put the body" at the service of a profound renewal of fashion trends, which reformulated notions and practices of eroticism as well as debates over the limits and meanings of sex and authority. The youthful, largely female body that stood at the center stage of an extended commercialized eroticism was also located at the center of political debates over sex and revolution wherein new actors participated, from the emerging feminist and gay rights groups to the most varied groups of the revolutionary Left of the 1970s. Perhaps not deserving the "revolutionary" adjective (as it was understood at the time), most young women and men did participate in deep transformations of prevailing sexual arrangements, which included a practical redefinition of the legitimate age and sites for sex and the incipient, although embattled, struggle for sexual equality among men and women. Radical social equality was, without a doubt, the central component of the revolutionary projects of the time. As they unfolded in a political culture tied to armed struggle and reliant upon "action," those projects practically required the shaping of resilient bodies. Young, largely male, and heterosexual, those bodies would be the carriers of a new revolutionary consciousness and the avenues that paved the way for a new time, which many youth envisioned as impending.

Between Display and Disguise

As in most Western countries, in Argentina during the second half of the 1960s new fashion and advertising practices located the young, "nude" body at the center of attention. John Berger, in his essay on the representational traditions of the body, famously concluded that to be nude "is to be seen naked by others, to be on display . . . to have the surface of one's own skin, the hair of one's own body, turned into disguise."[2] Berger's idea carries deep implications for reading the body. First, it allows for viewing a continuum, albeit symbolic, between dress and nudity, conceptualizing them as relational rather than oppositional terms. In the 1960s and 1970s, the intermingling of dress and nude paved the way for new senses of eroticism, whose attainment depended on meeting cultural mandates regarding slenderness and fitness, chiefly addressed to young women.[3] Second, Berger noted that it was always the female body on display for, presumably male, viewers. Feminist scholars have long analyzed how the female body became a spectacle or, as Laura Mulvey has put it, an object for visual pleasure.[4] In Argentina, it turned into a venue for discussing overly public morals as well, which illuminates the scope and limits of authoritarian censorship in an era of transnational, market-oriented eroticism. Third, amid that pervading "commercialization," Berger's ideas introduce the interplay between nudity, dress, and disguise. Although formally reacting against the prevailing fads, the young women who engaged with revolutionary politics drew upon clothing items marked by eroticism. Dress, nudity, and eroticism were then part of their disguise for performing the "guerrilla woman."

Well before the first guerrilla groups came to the surface, however, the

Miniskirts in Buenos Aires
c. 1967. Archivo Fotográfico,
Archivo General de la Nación,
Box 850, File 25.

increased display of young women's bodies was triggered by the spread of new fashion items, the most legendary of which was the miniskirt. In early 1966, the traditionalist women's magazine *Para Ti* informed its readers of the imminent arrival of the miniskirt and invited them to prepare their legs (through gymnastics and depilation), while at the same time predicting it would be a transient fad. Local fashion designers made the same predictions: spring and summer collections of 1966–67 displayed the miniskirt in vacation resort settings but gave little consideration to the idea that it could be worn in everyday contexts, with the exception of the most "snobbish youth." In fact, right after the military coup d'état led by Juan Carlos Onganía in 1966, only a few exclusive stores sold miniskirts in Buenos Aires. The first consumers were young women involved in avant-garde aesthetic movements or to intellectualized milieus, with the students at the School of Humanities and Social Sciences at the University of Buenos Aires credited as the "initiators."[5] One year later, however, the miniskirt had reached even the most remote working-class neighborhoods in the metropolitan areas. A survey conducted in July 1967 in Buenos Aires, Córdoba, and Rosario showed that 65 percent of young women had purchased at least one miniskirt in the past year. Some of the young women polled reckoned they had felt ashamed when wearing the miniskirt for the first time and had feared of awakening "flirtatious remarks" (*piropos*) from men.[6]

In July 1967, an advertising campaign for miniskirts and blue jeans, the two most important items in youth fashion, incited a small scandal over the perils of over-sexualizing young women's bodies. The ad for the local brand Lady Far West showed two young women combining "dress" and "nudity": with their backs turned to the viewer, they wear a denim miniskirt and a denim pant, while their bodies are naked from the waist up. In the week that followed the launching of the ad, moral watchdog organizations complained. The League of Mothers went as far as organizing a public demonstration against a catwalk where young women showed miniskirts and pants, and its representatives wrote an infuriated letter to the mayor of Buenos Aires to have the Lady Far West ad banned.[7] Mayor Eugenio Schettini, one of the most conservative officers within the Onganía regime, readily agreed to ban the ad. In his efforts to "moralize" the city, he had passed an advertising Code increasing the penalties for ads that "damage public morals," and applied it for the first time to the Lady Far West ad. The ad disappeared from billboards and periodicals, while the advertisers had their license briefly removed.[8] Despite his efforts, Schettini could not prevent young women from wearing jeans or miniskirts. Yet the mayor and most of the (male) "public opinion" that newsmagazines insistently surveyed coincided at one point: the new fashion items had an unusual "sex appeal."[9]

Wearing the new fashion items involved further display of the body, which young women attempted to keep thinner. Not by accident, the dissemination of jeans and the miniskirt coincided with the growth of dieting practices, which echoed similar developments worldwide. As the cultural critic Susan Bordo has noted, the idealization of the slender body in the twentieth century coded the tantalizing ideal of a well-managed self through deploying self-management techniques, like dieting and exercising.[10] In Argentina, these dynamics exploded in the 1960s. While in 1958 *Para Ti* recommended to its youth readers that the ideal weight for those five feet four inches tall was 132 pounds (60 kilos), in 1968 it had dropped to 119 pounds (54 kilos). Like other magazines, *Para Ti* also began to carry advice on dieting practices; and young women wrote letters to complain about how hard it was for them to fit the new ideals.[11] It very likely was hard: according to survey data for 1965, the average dieter in urban areas took in 3,450 calories per day, making slenderness difficult to attain.[12] Moreover, as journalistic reports showed, sports were only just beginning to be popularized among young women, who would rather "resist tempta-tions [and] suffer to fit into their tight pants and skirts."[13] For observers of daily life, however, changes in actual bodies were apparent. Dr. Florencio Escardó, for instance, compared how young women looked in the early 1950s and in the late 1960s and concluded: "in elegant and humble streets, they show themselves thinner and more confident in their bodies, yet it takes them considerable effort."[14] Wearing the new fashions involved the effort to construct and meet a new ideal of beauty.

The debate about changing fashions and patterns of female beauty in-tersected with a second set of concerns, which revolved around the men-ace of "unisex dress" to the blurring of gender identities and the concom-itant feminization of young men. Sociologist Julio Mafud, for instance, argued that one sign of the "Argentine sexual revolution" was the rising resemblance of young women and men in the realm of dress and hair-style. To Mafud, that resemblance involved both a promise to "level the sexes" and a risk of "forgetting who the man and the woman are." He asked women to be prudent and keep clear gender barriers.[15] More tolerant, the psychiatrist Isaac Lubchansky asserted that the "ambiguity of dressing" was related to "the search for new styles, common to the sexes: long hair and jeans are the symbols of the 'unisex' youth world." Other accounts focused on how young women's new dress practices implied an "aggressive invasion" into the world of men, who "counterattacked" by wearing long hair and colored clothes.[16] Thus, in contrast to the debates on how the jeans and miniskirts "oversexed" young women's bodies, the discussions of the "unisex fashion" addressed anxieties about young men's sexuality. At the most extreme level, the police raided bars and rock concerts and either imprisoned or scared young men with a "hippie" look, including blue jeans, colored shirts, and long hair. The imagery that informed those actions went as far as conceiving of unisex as an issue of national security because it prevented the police from identifying men from women.[17] The "confusion" theme appeared in other milieus as well. A survey on "unisex fashion" published by the lifestyle magazine *Siete Días*, for example, incited a flurry of letters, pointing to the connections between dress, long hair, and "uncertain" sexuality.[18]

Both inciting and addressing anxieties with the new fashions, adver-tisements played with the "unisex" yet "sexy" characteristics of youth dress items. In fact, jean ads were the ones that most helped to eroticize the visual culture of late 1960s and early 1970s Argentina, since they heavily relied on the interaction between nude and dress (as the ad for Lady Far

West had done) and, consequently, on the articulation of new patterns of eroticism. As Abigail Solomon-Godeau has noted, it is the feminine image that "operates as a conduit and mirror of desire, reciprocally intensifying and reflecting the commodity's allure."[19] Certainly, young women's bodies became the emblem and lure of blue jeans. In 1972, one ad for Levi's went as far as to show a picture of a nude young woman and to single out her left buttock, imposing over it an "imaginary" pocket. In large font, the ad announced that "The legitimate Levi's is recognized in this way." While in small font it indicated the technicalities of the actual jean, the message was clear: only Levi's guaranteed a perfect (that is, almost total) display of the female, privileged, erogenous zone. This was the lure Levi's offered to women and, especially, men.[20] Significant in its literality, this ad was nevertheless unique. Other ads for jeans showed mixed-sex couples wearing the same clothes (although female bodies were supposed to catch the viewer's eye and dominated the sexed-up atmosphere conveyed by blue jean consumption). Dynamic, joyful, and sexy: These were the sorts of attributes advertisers competitively strove to associate with blue jeans and youth consumption.

How do we explain that, while in 1967 the mayor banned an ad for miniskirts and blue jeans, only five years later (and still under military rule) an ad for Levi's could occupy the third page of the most widely read lifestyle magazine? Advertising, in fact, is the key to unraveling the limits of censorship. Formally, in the 1960s and 1970s, the "censor ideology" relaxed for just a few months during the governments of Héctor Cámpora and, transitorily, Juan Perón. As I showed in Chapter 1, over those two decades, national, provincial, and municipal boards flourished and new legislation mounted. The rationale informing censorship entailed blockading the diffusion of "politically subversive" and "morally harmful" materials. Yet the enforcement of censorship was inconsistent, with books and films being the most monitored. Not surprisingly, as part of the "democratic spring" of 1973 Cámpora appointed a filmmaker as head of the Board of Film Qualification and soon authorized the release of movies that had long been prohibited, like Pierre Paolo Passolini's *Teorema* (1968) and Bernardo Bertolucci's *Last Tango in Paris* (1972). As the humoristic monthly *Satiricón* put it, "our liberation begins when we can see nudity."[21] Before and after this short "spring," however, other materials were far more elusive. Market forces were as powerful as moralistic forces and, as an advertiser stated, "sex sells nowadays."[22]

"Sex" entailed primarily the display of the young female body within the most widespread representational realms: advertisements and lifestyle magazines. The year 1967 not only signaled the attempt to control advertisements in Buenos Aires, but also, more lastingly, it was a turning point for the industry at a national level. First, investment grew 50 percent in comparison with 1966, the largest inter-annual growth for the booming decade 1964–1974. Beginning in 1967, there was a solid recovery of the investment in printed advertising, presumably because lifestyle magazines incorporated color printing for ads.[23] Second, amid the 1967 boom (and helping triggering it) an "erotic tide" hit the ads to the point that a journalist reported that "75 percent of the ads" relied on the "exposure of women's bodies" to sell all type of products.[24] Perhaps foreseeing the economic losses that censorship would have cost to their industry, in 1969 advertisers passed their own ethical code and promised to avoid showing "anything which goes against Argentine morals, or stimulates sensuality and obscenity." Vague and formal, the code was dead upon arrival.[25] A similar story happened with magazines. In the summer of 1968–69, *Siete Días* updated its self-promoting techniques: like many illustrated magazines in the West, it began to carry "cover girls" wearing bikinis. Concerned with the "tide of pornography," Minister of the Interior Guillermo Borda threatened the directors of the most widely read weeklies with a ban for not only the display of female (semi) nudes but also for any article questioning marriage and parental authority over youth. Although they complained, the weeklies tried to comply with his prescriptions.[26] Yet as soon as Borda resigned as a consequence of the popular revolts that erupted in May of 1969, the weeklies resumed their "hunting" for "sexy" cover girls.

Amid the sweeping tide of political radicalization initiated in May of 1969, however, almost no sphere of cultural and social life remained untouched, including fashion and clothing. At the most obvious level, fashion models created a union, which attempted to provide training, regulate working conditions, and discuss the role of fashion "in a changing society."[27] In 1972, models and journalists promoted a series of discussions on the relationships between fashion, dressing practices, and politics. Some claimed that, in a context of dependent capitalism, fashion represented still another arena where "neocolonialism" worked. In Argentina, they argued, the only "fashion" not colonized was that of the Peronist workers in the 1940s and 1950s, those who "Evita named *descamisados* [shirtless]." Fashion models, journalists, and psychologists concurred in a 1972 roundtable that fashion entailed individual and social oppression, "to be deterred in a future Socialist fatherland."[28] Yet these overt discussions constituted only one venue of the politicization of fashion. Most fundamentally, as they became involved in radical politics, young people rearticulated their dress practices.

Testimonies of young women who engaged in political activism alluded to the paramount importance changes in dress had, which they narrated as part of a conversion process. A former militant with the PRT-ERP named Pola, noted that her decisions regarding fashion and her body were particularly important. She was seventeen when she attended her first meeting with a political comrade from the party and decided to dress herself so as to better impress him: she wore a miniskirt, an elegant blouse, high-heeled shoes, and make-up. "Are you sure you want to become a militant?" he asked without waiting for an answer. Pola was sure and, after some weeks had passed, she asked for a second meeting. Meanwhile, Pola underwent her bodily conversion, attending the new meeting in "blue jeans and olive-green shirt." Laughing about herself, she concluded that it was then, when changing clothes, that she formally became a "party activist."[29] Pola depicted a conversion involving the rejection of what was regarded as fashionable. In doing so, she and other young activists embraced a new ideal of femininity, which tended to reinforce simplicity and to downplay the markers of eroticism and desirability.

Ironically, however, the requirements of revolutionary militancy sometimes implied staging performances in which the female body was called on to conform to prevalent notions of femininity and desirability. As happened in Brazil, newspapers and magazines were flush with stories of dangerous and alluring young women participating in armed action.[30] Even though exaggerated, those representations were premised on the fact that some young women did utilize their "sex appeal" to facilitate armed actions like car or bank robberies and assaults on military garrisons and police stations (which were the most prevalent actions and targets from 1969 to 1972).[31] Young women of "singular beauty," who "looked like fashion models" and wore miniskirts and tight jeans as well as abundant makeup overflowed the chronicles.[32] In July of 1970, for example, a Montonero cell made up of eight young men and three women took over a small town in Córdoba. The press reported that "a beautiful Amazon with a 38-caliber gun" had "initiated everything."[33] Interviewed by a television channel, the policemen of the small town indicated that the "beautiful, refined" young woman had entered the police station to ask for help because she said she had been "molested" on the streets.[34] The policemen and the media felt deceived: they, "as anyone else," would have been betrayed in their encounter with such a seemingly vulnerable, pretty, young woman.

Links between deception and sexualized bodies were further emphasized in some particular actions that other young women performed. In 1971, for example, the most widely read newspaper in Argentina, *La Razón* (in its daily column titled "Guerrilla Chronicles") informed its readers of the actions of a PRT-ERP cell geared to get cars and money. Reinforcing the spectacular traits of the actions, the report focused on the main character, "a blonde woman about twenty years old, beautiful face, wearing a sophisticated, modern outfit: red mini shorts with a red blouse."[35] The young woman had apparently dressed in the most sexual fashion possible, including mini shorts, which had elicited controversy regarding morality, nudity, and femininity.[36] The young woman appropriated the mini shorts, which unexpectedly became a politicized tool aimed at generating surprise. The gas station employees where the young woman initiated the action, for example, told the reporters that they would surely have yelled *piropos* at her on the street. When they realized she was a guerrilla, they thought, "We cannot trust anyone, anymore." The strategies of self-presentation that exploited the sexualized body pointed to both lure and neutralize potential male witnesses or "victims."

These strategies suggested the quandaries that young women may have faced when coping with the bodily requirements of revolutionary militancy, since the hyperbolic uses of sexualized fashions spoke of the logics of the disguise. As Georg Simmel noted in his classic study of secret societies, the disguise marked the bifurcation of their participants' self, torn apart between the values of the secret and those of the open society.[37] The revolutionary groups that embraced armed struggle in Argentina were, in some respects, secret societies—literally, from 1969 to 1972, and then again after 1974, when they went clandestine. Navigating the secret/open divide involved the negotiation of gendered and sexual understandings for members of these organizations. They were negotiating through the logics of disguise. At a general level, both women and men disguised in the sense that the Brazilian guerrilla Carlos Mariguella mandated when he wrote that "the urban guerrilla is an expert at blending in with the masses. . . . He wears the same clothes as any street man, and has a full time job."[38] There are abundant examples of men crafting their public personas according to the stereotypes of physicians, workers, or policemen. Women, instead, either drew on "traditional" images (faking indicators of motherhood, passing as nurses) or, more prominently, focused on associating themselves with markers of desirability attached to the most commodified variants of feminine sexuality.[39] The insistence on that disguise perhaps indicates not only a rational manipulation of sexual stereotypes for political purposes but also the persistence of well-entrenched ideals of sexual attractiveness among revolutionary militants: armed actions were the occasions for performing those sexualized roles and at the same time for serving the revolution.

Sex and Revolution

"Sex" and "revolution" were keywords of a larger lexicon of the 1960s and 1970s that included terms such as "emancipation" and "liberation." Part of a transnational movement associated with emergent cultural and political actors (youth cultures, feminism, gay rights movements, to name just a few), the most radical variants of sexual revolutionaries questioned the patriarchal family, gender- and age-based inequality, and heteronormativity. In North America and some countries in Western Europe, the mobilization of feminists and gay liberation groups crystallized in new legislation such as the decriminalization of homosexuality and the legalization of abortion.[40] In Latin America at large and Argentina in particular, these actors were less relevant for defining the connections of "sex" and "revolution." Disentangling the contested meanings of those terms entails going beyond the bodies on display or in disguise. In fact, the condemnation of the commercial aspects of eroticism was the only point of agreement among gay rights activists, feminists, and "new leftist" groups. They differed notably, however, in arguing for the very plausibility of a "sexual" revolution alongside a social and national revolution, which most deemed as ongoing. However, more resilient than these raucous claims, a "discreet revolution" unfolded among youth at the time, consisting of the disengagement of sex and marriage.

The commercialization of sexuality and the market-oriented display of the female body were the most evident aspects of the transformation of Argentina's sexual culture, representing a key concern for emergent feminisms. The Unión Feminista Argentina (UFA, Feminist Argentine Union), Movimiento de Liberación Femenina (MLF, Female Liberation Movement), and Muchacha, among others, aimed at revitalizing a movement that, in their view, had been dormant between the 1920s and the 1970s. All of these groups tried to build up horizontal organizations and create "consciousness-raising" groups similar to the ones in Europe and the United States.[41] They also established personal ties with American feminists: they invited, for example, Socialist-feminist Linda Jenssen to give lectures in Buenos Aires, which resulted in the growing media visibility of the admittedly small local groups.[42] With about fifty members in 1972, the MLF (like the UFA) recruited its members among middle-class adult women. Muchacha, instead, targeted secondary school and university students. Perhaps because its audience was presumed to be young, Muchacha's first communiqué was titled "[We are] No [longer the] objects at the hands of men and society" and revolved around the need to struggle against the "oppression articulated through consumption and its mediations (advertising, women's magazines, fashion)."[43] Besides denouncing the inequality in educational and job opportunities between women and men as well as the degradation of "invisible" domestic work, Muchacha focused its criticism on the persistent sexual double standard and the "commercialization of women."[44]

Short-lived, these groups had difficulties in creating a feminist network and in establishing alliances in a political milieu whose dominant actors were unwilling to recognize feminist claims as "political." Unlike what happened with gay rights groups, feminist groups could not create a network and carried out just a few activities in common. For example, they went to the streets together only twice. In October of 1972, the groups agreed on the distribution of pamphlets to protest against the commercial and "idealizing" underpinnings of Mother's Day, an occasion that also served to reiterate the claims for access to contraception, abortion, and day care systems. Two months later, the three most important groups promoted a protest at Femimundo, a fair of fashion and cosmetics dedicated to "the young woman."[45] Yet the rallies went almost unnoticed: sexual politics, and other feminist demands, seemed restricted in the political atmosphere of the early 1970s.[46] A roundtable joining a member of Muchacha with two left-wing Peronist women illustrated that atmosphere. While the feminists strove to assert that by no means were feminist and Socialist struggles irreconcilable, Peronist women dominated the discussion, insisting that they were indeed incompatible: "in dependent countries," they argued, "feminism and the much-propagandized sexual revolution are other ways in which neo-colonialism acts."[47] Most groups identified with the revolutionary Left used those terms to reject an overt inclusion of gender and sexual politics in their agendas, and they were applied to both feminist and gay rights groups.

Founded in 1971, the Frente de Liberación Homosexual (FLH, Homosexual Liberation Front) served as an umbrella for joining various gay and lesbian groups. Activists and historians alike single out the groups Nuestro Mundo (Our World) and Eros as the ones propelling the creation of the FLH. Héctor Anabitarte, a former Communist militant and post office worker, created Nuestro Mundo in 1968, and the group attracted working- and lower-middle-class men concerned with the rising repression to which homosexuals were subjected during the Onganía regime. Unlike Nuestro Mundo, Eros represented the most radicalized segment of the gay rights groups: its members advocated for "unleashing the libido," which they viewed as intrinsically revolutionary and liberationist. Led by Néstor Perlongher, a would-be major anthropologist and poet, Eros was instrumental in organizing university youth and in trying to bridge gaps between the FLH and revolutionary Peronist groups.[48] As it happened with the feminists, the relationships of the FLH and the revolutionary Left, mainly that of Peronist background, were tense. In 1973, when Cámpora was sworn in and the promises of national and social liberation seemed close at hand, the FLH participated in Peronist rallies and sent letters to representatives in Congress to state that in "the struggle for liberation" they participated by "dismantling bourgeois morality based on machismo and the ensuing domination of women and rejection of homosexuals." They never received positive responses: in 1974, in a pamphlet titled *Sexo y revolución*, the FLH recognized that their attempts at linking the sexual to the "social revolution" had been unsuccessful, largely because, they argued, "the revolutionary militants are part of a reactionary sexual culture."[49]

Drawing on ideas circulating transnationally, the FLH strove to describe the country's sexual culture, which they regarded as blending a Catholic (or traditional) morality with a "morality of replacement." In the "traditional moral" paradigm, they wrote, the patriarchal family was the basic cell of society: it was the site for the building of men's economic, political, and sexual prerogatives as well as for enacting women's subjugation. The patriarchal family was also the primary agency for confining the libido through the negation of infant sexuality, crucial to the disassociation of pleasure and sex. Such a repressive structure, the FLH believed, had met a "morality of replacement" disseminated through the "pro*yanqui*" media, which enhanced and controlled sexual gratifications. That moral entailed "commodified eroticism," whereas women continued being "neurotic objects of display" to gratify men, who were turned into passive agents of their own gratification. Sharing premises with lesbian and gay activists worldwide, the FLH argued that the "morality of replacement" had created further allure to the "traditional" patriarchal sexual culture. It had likewise created its own "totems," such as the idealization of the companionate heterosexual couple. Gays and lesbians were excluded from the "new accepted parameters," which further questioned the alleged novelties of the "new" sexual culture.[50] Unless sexual drives were liberated, the FLH argued, there would not be a revolution of any kind.

In the early 1970s, left-wing militants and intellectuals, for the most part, conceived of the sexual as a "false" revolution. *Moral y proletarización*, an oft-quoted document crafted by a PRT-ERP leader in 1972, is one of the few preserved pieces of prescriptive and programmatic thoughts and rules for shaping an ideal militant. It aimed at constructing a moral code according to what it deemed the proletariat morals, that is, an anti-individualistic, antibourgeois, new consciousness that would produce a new subject on the way to Socialism. Significantly, *Moral y proletarización* produced a reflection on sex, and on couple and family relations, based on Friedrich Engels's *The Origin of Family, Private Property, and the State.* Following Engels, it advocated for the superiority of the monogamous family. That admittedly bourgeois form, the document pointed out, was nevertheless to be kept at times when "bourgeois morality seems to revolutionize itself through what some labeled the 'sexual revolution.'" In a statement that gay and feminists could have shared, *Moral y proletarización* cautioned its readers that this was a "false" revolution since it maintained—and reinforced—the "objectification of human relations and the subjection of women to men." That revolution, it went on, reduced love to the "animal instincts of sex," and made women into "images to be sold in the marketplace." Along with this statement, yet, *Moral y proletarización* asked its readers to displace sex from the center of couple's relation: sex was not the marker of "harmony" but rather the communion of ideals and the mutual consecration of a project geared toward the building of a Socialist project.[51] As I will discuss next, this moralistic understanding of sex permeated the shaping of the militants' bodies within the PRT-ERP, who often labeled as petit-bourgeois individualism both consumption and sexual behaviors that deviated from the ideal of the monogamous heterosexual couple.

The PRT-ERP's members were hardly alone, however, when it came to downplaying sex as a possible domain for "revolution" and "liberation" and for condemning the ongoing eroticization of public life. In 1967, Francisco Urondo, a leading poet and would-be member of the FAR, when referring to the uses of female nudity in 1960s movies, asserted that eroticism in late capitalism resembled "mere pornography." Moreover, he argued that sex represented a "false alleviation" of cultural and political crises, a means for "escaping from reality."[52] Liliana Hecker, one of the most renowned leftist writers at the time, reached similar conclusions when she participated in a roundtable addressing literary eroticism. She asserted that "perhaps before"—in an undetermined past time—sex might have had a "political side" because talking about sex meant breaking established rules, but "now, in 1971 Argentina," it meant "diverting energies" from political ways of opposing the social order. Since the "real danger" was elsewhere, Hecker concluded, "society" imbued sex with "pretended oppositional tinges" but delivered only "pornography."[53] For his part, when writing for one pan-leftist journal, psychoanalyst Augusto Klappenbach further theorized the connections between politics and the "erotic tide." By appropriating Herbert Marcuse's ideas, he claimed that the rising publicity of eroticism undermined the critical potential of Eros through its confinement to the "safe realm of sexuality." That was the key to understanding the "counterrevolutionary revolutions" which, he posited, were merely ways of "praising more or less subtle forms of prostitution." However, in contrast to other leftist intellectuals (and, at this point, closer to the FLH's proposals), Klappenbach predicted that in a noncapitalist future, Eros would be unleashed to pervade human experience but, for this utopian moment to come into being, the "true revolutionaries" could not entertain themselves with the eroticism that consumer capitalism sought to "impose" on them.[54]

Far from the strident claims and slogans of revolution, many young women and men in Argentina were protagonists in lasting transformations of sexual attitudes and practices. As I discussed in Chapter 4, by the mid-1960s it was plain that a new attitude toward sex had spread, mainly among middle-class youth: this attitude tied sex to love and responsibility and eventually to the horizon of marriage, thus presenting itself as both "modern" and prudent. This dynamic had brought about a practical questioning of female virginity as the marker of young women's "honesty" and prowess. As historian Isabella Cosse has put it, the erosion of the "taboo of female virginity" was at the core of the "discreet sexual revolution" that Argentines would have lived through in the 1960s.[55] In 1972, in fact, a journalist wrote in the humor magazine *Satiricón* that recalling what virginity had meant for girls entailed doing "archeological work."[56] While exaggerated, this vignette contributes insight into the normalization of heterosexual youth intercourse. The novelty of the early 1970s, in any case, meant that youth helped disengage sex from the possibility of marriage, thus challenging the respectable idea of *premarital* sex.

Some surveys indicated that both middle- and working-class youths were becoming sexually active earlier, which suggested the spread of a new attitude vis-à-vis sex and marriage (or its promise). A large survey conducted in 1973 of 1,200 women, for example, showed that 46 percent of those from twenty to twenty-four years old responded that they first had sex when they were adolescents. Among single university students the same age, moreover, the survey found that 80 percent had had "sex at least once."[57] Also in 1973, a survey among 252 secondary school students showed that 70 percent of the boys had their first sexual relations at the age of sixteen, and 80 percent of them had done so with "girls of the same age." Interpreting this finding, Dr. Octavio Fernández Mouján, an adolescent psychoanalyst, suggested that boys and girls in the working-class neighborhoods where he worked had not only had sexual intercourse at that age but also "lived sexuality in an unprejudiced way."[58] Although imprecise, these interpretations and studies point to the normalization of the practice of sexual intercourse among youth as well as to the extension of these practices and attitudes beyond the intellectualized middle classes.

In this respect, one recurrent topic in 1970s popular culture and in memories as well was the recrafting of the *piba de barrio* (neighborhood girl). A sociologically lax category that usually evoked working- and lower-middle-class girls in their late teens, the *piba de barrio* had long captivated the imagination of poets and essayists, who made it the epitome of sexual repression and middle-brow superficiality. In a superb poem published in 1924, "Exvoto: To the Girls from Flores," Oliverio Girondo wrote about the girls from that neighborhood who "walk together arm in arm, broadcasting their trepidation, and if anyone looks them in the eye, they press their legs together, for fear their sex would fall out on the sidewalk." Sexually desiring and desired, the "girls from Flores" strove anxiously to get rid of desire. In 1964, for his part, essayist Juan José Sebreli blamed the "hypocritical petit-bourgeois man" for making his daughter (the *piba de barrio*) a "half virgin who masturbates her boyfriend in the movie theaters."[59] Ten years later, however, one journalist wrote for *Satiricón* that the *piba de barrio* was one of the "species in extinction." Dressed in tight blue jeans and wearing "lots of makeup," the neighborhood girls, she asserted—and some of the interviewees concurred—did not have major problems with their parents with regard to flirts and boyfriends. Most vitally, these girls thought of sex as "something natural" and conceived of virginity as a "burden."[60] The portrayal may have been exaggerated, but memories of "neighborhood youth" in the early 1970s point to the profound, yet embattled, transfiguration of sex mores among girls and, subsequently, boys. That is the case in an autobiographical novel about the coming of age of a boy in Lanús, who narrates his sexual experiences with his "neighborhood girlfriend." The story revolves around Jorge and Mariana's "first time" and chiefly around how both overcome the fact that they do not want to marry: they fear the "stigma" over her, yet as the narrative goes by, they not only leave the neighborhood but also learn that "at least as it comes to sex, we are equal."[61]

"Sexual equality" was, nevertheless, an incomplete project. While both the vanishing of the figure of the *piba de barrio* and the studies on the age of the first sexual intercourse suggest an incipient disengagement of sex from marriage, a double standard persisted nonetheless. That was one of the subject matters of two roundtables organized by the youth magazine *La Bella Gente* with working and student young men. They all concurred that having sexual intercourse with their girlfriends was "normal" and insisted that they did not make distinctions between "girls for sex" and "girls for dating" anymore. A university student, however, brought to the forefront the fact that "we are asked to have as many sexual relations as possible: this means machismo." Young men discussed machismo and expressed anxieties regarding a new (self)-requirement: "quantity" as a marker of sexual prowess.[62] Meanwhile, some young women and girls, while recognizing that the "taboo" of virginity had somewhat disappeared, insisted that young men "at the bottom of their consciousness, still want a girl to be a virgin," as Norma, a shop worker, age twenty-two, stated in another roundtable. Norma and the other young women agreed, pointing out the persistent "veiled forms of machismo" that related not only to how youth sexuality was negotiated at an "intimate" level but also to the ways in which "this erotic tide shows only female bodies."[63] In practical terms, these young women captured the gendered dynamics and inequality that pervaded Argentina's changing sexual culture in the early 1970s. In that context, young bodies were also the main carriers of projects that ideally would erase all forms of inequality. For these projects, other young bodies were required.

Consciousness in the Body

While exiled in Mexico, the Argentine intellectual Héctor Schmucler produced one of the first reflections about the relationship between political subjectivity and the body, as he thought it unfolded among revolutionary groups in the early 1970s. He claimed that the revolutionary Left came to conceive of politics as a technique performed on the margins of other, manifold human experiences. The revolutionaries, hence, would have replicated the capitalist-based fragmentation of experience, in their case through splintering the "desiring man" and the "political man." In doing so, they postulated the hero as the ideal political subject and assumed the revolution as an ideal as well, which then turned into a "monster to be served." The ideal political subject, the heroic figure, obliterated the corporeal "everyday, concrete man."[64] Ironically, Schmucler's piece was informed by the persistence of presumed gender-neutral categories, like the universalizing "man."[65] As in other Latin American countries where revolutionary projects were tied to armed struggle, the ideal political figure in Argentina was built upon masculine standards centered on courage and resistance, sometimes depicted as a process of overcoming obstacles related to class origins and ideological or physical weaknesses—Che Guevara being the main example. The combatant was praised as the most courageous and conscious, as the "best among ourselves."[66]

Rather than focusing on the combatant and the attendant discussions of the "death cult" and martyrdom that have thus far attracted well-deserved scholarly attention, I scrutinize the larger militant culture to which that figure belonged, a culture characterized by the confidence on the body as a carrier of consciousness.[67] First, while the glorification of the heroic guerrilla spread among most militants and helped them assess their prowess vis-à-vis the ideal, only a few gained the status of combatants: revolutionary militancy, for most, meant the restless activism through which their aptitudes and commitment were evaluated. A type of resilient body, culturally linked to youth and masculinity, appeared as the most suitable for engaging with that style of militancy that focused on "action" per se and that, unlike previous leftist traditions, denigrated ideological and political debate, dubbing it as "feminine." Second, the creation of that resilient body brought different meanings for women and men. Women found it hard to comply with the requirements of the activist style of militancy. Along with the undeniable machismo "impregnating" the Left (and Argentina's culture), the presumed nonideological link of militancy to activism was gender-based and in turn reinforced gendered hierarchies. A young, usually male, heterosexual body that was, in addition, able to domesticate its own sexual and other desires was the (self-)requirement.

The praise of an activist style of militancy expressed the fervor to hasten the political times for a revolution that many regarded as impending. That style presupposed and required a resilient body, capable of enduring the seemingly endless activities to which militants were assigned and according to whose performances their commitment would be evaluated. Although with different modalities and intensities, the enforcement of that style swept across the most important revolutionary groups. In late 1971, an obituary for the recently killed PRT-ERP leader Luis Pujals, for example, evaluated his political consciousness by invoking his ceaseless activity: "days and nights, he took hours from resting, from eating, from sleeping." In 1973, another portrayal detailed what Pujals's activities entailed: when he was initiating his political militancy (that is, before becoming guerrilla) he "would, at 6:00 A.M., be at the entrance of a factory plant, at noon in another, at the evening in a meeting; without sleeping, he would then write and print pamphlets that he would himself distribute at the factories in the day that followed."[68] The steps that Pujals followed in order to climb the party's ladder, which in his case included military command, had nonetheless been punctuated by restless political activism.

The PRT-ERP drew upon and amplified previous leftist traditions, particularly Trotskyism, to forge a distinctive militant style that centered on the vindication of patience, humility, tenacity, and self-sacrifice. All of these were part of a "proletariat moral" that would assure that the militants gave themselves in "soul and body to the revolution."[69] For the middle-class youth attracted to the party, this entailed crossing sociocultural boundaries and creating new routines. Written by his brother, an obituary portrayal for Eduardo Capello, a twenty-four-year-old young man murdered in the 1972 "Massacre of Trelew," pointed to the changes involved in the making of a revolutionary militant "out of a petit-bourgeois kid." Eduardo attended a commercial secondary school and wanted to become an accountant. By the mid 1960s, moreover, Eduardo "didn't miss Saturday night dances and soccer matches on Sundays, and he was a sexual conqueror on a daily basis." It was only in 1968, upon joining the Party, when his life changed dramatically. Although his parents had been affiliated with the Socialist Party in the 1950s, they had been "café militants"—the term that 1970s revolutionary militants used to denigrate their predecessors for their alleged inaction. In any case, his parents were astonished by Eduardo's restless activities since he "barely ate or slept, all his time went to his militancy."[70] Perhaps trying to "compensate" in a short amount of time for a previous life of relative affluence, Eduardo overloaded himself with multiple activities, which the Party's leadership deemed crucial to develop a new morality.

Although without framing it into the "proletarian morals" that the PRT-ERP aimed to carve out, the revolutionary Peronist groups also promoted an activist style militancy. That became apparent, for example, in the portrayals they made out of their particular heroic figure, Eva Perón. Along with highlighting her identification with a "perennial" revolutionary Peronist ethos and her unconditional loyalty to Perón, most memories pointed out the intensity of her will to "give herself to the People."[71] The portrayals of her life were flush with descriptions of superhuman activity and illustrated with pictures of either a smiling young Eva with untied hair ("Evita Montonera") or, by other images that showed her working with tied hair, usually at dusk, and with bags under her eyes.[72] The reports depict the side effects of Eva's "giving everything to the people," namely illness and death. Further, the Peronist press did point out certain side effects in portrayals of less famous militants as well, as happened with Manuel. In 1972, the Montonero leadership sent Manuel to politically organize a district thus far overlooked, Rosario: "Manuel did the work of ten people," the portrayal read, "he was desperate to undertake everything: pamphleteering, military training, street rallies." Yet the portrayal shows that he suffered from the consequences: "his health and his marriage deteriorated, since Manuel viewed them as secondary." Ironically, however, at the same time that the portrayal recognized the side effects of Manuel's activist style of militancy, it suggested that Manuel (as everyone else) could only overcome the situation by "doubling his efforts."[73]

Coupled with the lure of these heroic figures, the eagerness to speed up the political times helped condition a style of militancy that required a resilient, youthful body. In their memories, former militants convey the corporality of their engagement. For example, one militant with the Peronist Unión de Estudiantes Secundarios (UES, Secondary School Student Union) narrates her involvement in terms of a passage from laziness to the complete use of her body. She portrays herself as a "neighborhood girl" who, after joining the UES, became "a machine of doing," which included political agitation at schools, social work in slums, and eventually military training. Like other militants in revolutionary organizations, she also recalled that climbing the ladder at the UES (being "promoted") was the result of the evaluation of her performance doing many activities which, in turn, strengthened her daily commitments.[74] Looking from the vantage point of adulthood, another former Peronist militant recalled that her activities began at 7:00 A.M. and ended at 11:00 P.M. By combining nostalgia with estrangement, she noted that such devotion was only possible for a "young, healthy body."[75] In fact, physical resistance and health accounted for two attributes linked to young bodies.

The association of resilience with the young body was also unbridled among older militants that engaged with revolutionary politics. While the key innovation in Argentine (and worldwide) politics in the late 1960s and early 1970s was indeed the involvement of young people, this has often erased the fact that adults also participated and sometimes "followed" their children. That was the case with Coty and Ramona, who engaged with the PRT while in their fifties. Mothers of two known guerrillas, they first volunteered to fix food and help the families of those who were imprisoned. As the 1970s went on, both committed to a more intense militancy: "for their strength and vitality," one memoir recalls, "they looked twenty-something."[76] The links among resilience, youth, and action were also prominent in the case of the poet Francisco Urondo, who joined the FAR after his daughter, when he was in his forties. Commenting on his commitments, he stated that he had abandoned his "sedentary life" to assume "a gymnastic" routine that rejuvenated him.[77] This entailed the attainment of the slenderness and fitness that the youthful body signified in consumer culture. Idealized in ads, that body was also at the center of the requirements of elder but "new" revolutionary militants, like Urondo.

Urondo's engagement with revolutionary politics and with armed struggle is paradigmatic of how the mandate *poner el cuerpo* created a dichotomy between "action" and "intellectualism." In the late 1960s, the always-incomplete autonomy of the cultural and intellectual fields had vanished. The validation of artists and writers in those fields depended on extrinsic rules, such as their positioning in debates including, for example, the self-reflexive "role of the intellectual in politics."[78] Intellectuals like Urondo understood that their "role" involved abiding by corporeal requirements. Although by no means all of them made Urondo's radical decision, in 1968 about fifty of the most renowned writers and artists wrote a letter to pay homage to Che Guevara. Besides praising his anti-imperialism and internationalism, they argued that Guevara was a hero because he had left "intellectualism" aside and had showed that Latin America was "ripe for what counts: action."[79] Although it had been part of the Peronist tradition from the 1940s onwards, this anti-intellectualism pervaded the entire "New Left" in the early 1970s and was key to the socialization of a new cohort of militants, who differentiated their involvement in politics from the one of previous leftists—"café militants," as Eduardo's parents were dubbed. At times critically, former militants recall the scarce attention they gave to ideological and political formation vis-à-vis their literal praise of action. Luis Salinas, a former Peronist militant, for example, recalls that "there was not much interest in political formation, neither when [you] entered nor afterwards, in fact." He continues that "not even our own periodicals were important in our militancy: the real thing was action."[80] Action was a polysemous term, although "armed action" resounded as its most sublime meaning.

In a militant culture that hyper-valorized action, political preparation was at times conceived as feminine. One former militant with the PRT-ERP, for example, recalls that the (all male) leadership made her responsible for teaching strategy in a school for cadres. Instead of viewing this as a "promotion," she experienced it as an exclusion from other, more pressing political and military-oriented activities. In fact, *Moral y proletarización* helped set the feminization, and essentially the demeaning of political preparation, when it prescribed that pregnant women or recent mothers should "study to compensate" for their inability to perform other activities.[81] Hence, a reversal of the Cartesian mind/body dichotomy occurred among revolutionary militants. The "activities of the mind," which had long been associated with the masculine and became the dominant in a dichotomist relation with the body, were practically transferred to the feminine. While some intellectuals predicted that in a looming revolutionary society the divide mind/body would disappear altogether, it had neither vanished nor lost its capability of evoking and setting gendered hierarchies in the early 1970s.[82] In the same movement in which the "activities of the mind" were linked to the feminine, they lost preeminence in favor of the resilient body, the marker of activity and action tout court, which was supposed to be masculine.

The emphasis on an activist style of militancy and its attendant type of body helped produce and reinforce gendered hierarchies among revolutionaries, an occurrence that should not obscure a crucial novelty of the 1970s: the substantial involvement of young women in politics. Although exact figures are missing, the most prudent estimates state that, in 1973, women represented 25 percent of all the groups embracing armed struggle, yet one scholar argued that in that year they made 30 percent in the Montoneros-oriented groups and another scholar indicated that, in 1975, women accounted for 40 percent of the PRT-ERP members.[83] These figures are relatively high if compared with other groups in revolutionary political cultures in 1960s and 1970s Latin America. For example, women made up no more than 5 percent of Fidel Castro's forces in the late 1950s, and, ten years later, in the context of the radicalized Brazilian Left, they made up 20 percent. The percentages for Argentina, hence, are closer to the 30 percent of female militants and combatants who fought with the Nicaraguan Sandinistas in 1979. As it happened in late 1960s Brazil and late 1970s Nicaragua, the young women joining the Argentine leftist groups were also more educated than the "average" young woman and than many of their male counterparts.[84] The PRT leaders recognized that young women attracted to the party did not come from working-class origins and needed "reeducation" in "proletarian morals." As one former militant recalls, the PRT (as other political forces, she claims) undervalued the fact that so many women "broke with the middle-class dreams in which we had been raised" to participate in an uncertain political dynamics.[85] Their massive engagement in revolutionary politics configured a crucial indicator of the changing experiences and expectations that young women underwent throughout the 1960s and 1970s, which however did not significantly modify the organization of gender hierarchies.

Even when most 1970s revolutionary groups upheld equalizing rhetoric, in practice women and men enforced standards of militancy associated with male, youthful bodies, which resulted in the perpetuation of men's leadership. Just a few women, in fact, held leadership positions: only two had seats within the PRT-ERP's Central Committee and none in the national Montoneros leadership. Some women did hold middle-range positions in both groups, and the Montoneros went a step further in creating the Agrupación Evita, which focused on organizing women at a neighborhood level, at the same time reinforcing "traditional" female roles as homemakers and providing them with a space for speaking of problems linked, for example, to domestic violence. But this experience was short-lived and limited in terms of membership.[86] As the failed attempts of the PRT-ERP to create "a woman's front" suggest, the Agrupación Evita was also an unappealing front for most male and female militants: it was devoid of the appeal of the factory and student fronts, not to mention the military one. Only a few women, however, made it to the military fronts in both groups. In late 1975, when embarked upon a rural guerrilla experience, the PRT-ERP announced it received women "in the forest." While depicting that women and men shared the same responsibilities and daily activities, reports in the ERP press evaluated that the experience was positive because "women have helped ameliorate the living conditions, mainly issues of order and hygiene . . . and they also improved the language men use and all became more affectionate."[87] Women's contributions, then, were associated with their most "traditional," home-like roles and with their so-called natural tendencies to be emotional. Yet promoting the experience in itself signaled the rarity of the occurrence. Women comprised a minority of those performing the most vaulted form of action among 1970s revolutionary militants, that is, armed action. This happened partly because those receiving guerrilla training were chosen among those who proved themselves by being tireless activists. As a practical standard, it worked more effectively than any overt sexist statement to exclude women.

At a basic, quotidian level, the requirement to be a tireless activist proved harder to sustain for women than for men, reverberating deeply rooted cultural dynamics. Although over the 1960s middle- and working-class young women had achieved greater autonomy, most were still monitored. In contrast to countries where a campus culture existed, in early 1970s Argentina the experience of living alone or with roommates was just beginning to make inroads among single youth.[88] Most young women engaging in political activism lived with their parents, and that was definitively the case with secondary school students. In 1973, the all-male leaders of the principal groups active in secondary schools concurred that girls faced "many problems" in becoming activists. The UES's leader, for example, stated that parents set tight controls over the girls' schedules, making it hard for them to "assume commitments."[89] However, many women in their twenties, single or engaged, also faced troubles within their families. Mabel S., for example, recalls that her involvement with the JUP generated several conflicts with her parents, both workers at a textile factory in the Greater Buenos Aires area. Her parents opposed less her "revolutionary ideas" than the fact that her militancy led her to spend "all day, every day, out of the home."[90] She moved from her family home after much effort and negotiation, but it is likely that other young women could not afford such an alternative. Therefore many young women were less active than they wanted to be. That was the situation with women, young or not, who were principal caregivers. As recalled in widespread testimony, while the explicit mandates within the revolutionary groups emphasized the ideal that men and women share the domestic chores and childrearing practices, women continued to be in charge of both.[91] In this way, the equalizing rhetoric clashed with the day-to-day militant practices, centered on the production and display of resilient bodies.

In the production of those resilient bodies, suitable for revolutionary militancy, the attempts at codifying sexual behaviors and attitudes figured prominently—showing both the limit and the scope of formal mandates. With significant particularities, the ideal resembled the one upheld by most youth in the early 1970s. The PRT and the Montoneros-oriented groups endorsed the monogamous, heterosexual couple as the best antidote against sexual "liberalism." According to a letter written by a highly admired Brazilian guerrilla (and published in a pan-leftist magazine), that couple was "in touch with the moral standards of the day" from which revolutionaries could not deviate since it prevented them from "forgetting politics for sex."[92] The leaders of Peronist and Marxist groups alike were called on to comply with that ideal by sticking to the monogamous couple and, if possible, the stable family. A portrayal of a Montonero leader, hence, highlighted the fact that he had been married for twenty years and "never even looked at another woman," while reportedly the PRT's maximum leader, Roberto Santucho, had to submit to a Party's tribunal and discontinue an extramarital affair.[93] The existence of that tribunal signals one particularity of the ways in which revolutionary groups handled sexuality, namely, the moving of "intimate" affairs to the party level. Former PRT-ERP militants recall, for example, that adultery or casual sex (outside of a "formal" couple) were serious issues. Understood as individualistic deviations, they could entail grave results, such as political degradation. They could be also used as ammunition against competing factions or individuals. As expected, stories of arbitrariness and hypocritical attitudes run rampant in today's memoirs, as one case that occurred in a Montonero cell acting in a working-class neighborhood. A former militant recalls that her "political superior," who had been involved in a "secret adulterous affair" for years, was especially harsh with others' adultery, and never submitted himself to his subordinate fellows' "justice."[94]

Alongside the pragmatic use of "sex as ammunition" and the ideologically based downplay of sex and eroticism as sites of liberation, the revolutionary groups may have tightened their preoccupations and regulations to adapt to the life conditions of most of their members by 1974, when they went clandestine. Some former militants recalled with surprise, for example, how they could occupy the same house, even the same bed, with fellow militants and "nothing happened." As a former young woman concluded when commenting on one of those situations, "perhaps we had internalized the rules, or we were too afraid to be erotically moved."[95] Nonetheless, tenser situations took place as well. In his memoir, a former PRT-ERP militant narrates that he shared a so-called "operative house" with his wife and a younger female, with whom he fell in love. When the "triangle exploded," his political superiors sent him to a "reeducation program": they removed him from the most cherished front, the military front, and sent him to work at a meatpacking plant, with the hope that he would learn from the idealized proletariat.[96]

For his part, in a telling autobiographical novel Martín Caparrós depicts the relations of the members of a Montonero "triangle" composed of an adult male, a former university-student woman, and a boy coming of age. The novel is set in 1975, after the Montoneros had passed their second normative code for disciplining members, which prohibited sexual relations outside the "constituted couple." This was allegedly to prevent the leaking of information in what the Montoneros viewed as wartime and also, perhaps, to strengthen morale. In any case, the knot of the novel revolves around how the trio, living in an "operative house," prepares to kill a "union bureaucrat." The underlying narrative thread centers on sexual anxieties, capturing the tension between self-control and desire.[97] The novel sets its characters against a backdrop of imminent death and suggests coding this tension as one between Thanatos and Eros—represented as a drive to life not confined to hetero- or homosexual desire.

It was not coincidental that homosexual desire was represented in fiction—as in Manuel Puig's memorable *El beso de la mujer araña* (1976)—yet went unmentioned in party literature. The revolutionary groups did not escape from the homophobia pervading Argentina's culture. Rather the opposite was true. Homophobia was a venue to regulate their own members' sexuality, and sometimes acted as way to offset any "blackmail" to which the right-wing sectors subjected the Left. Recalling their experiences as revolutionary militants, three gay activists depicted their strategies to cope with their respective groups' mandates. One of them, a psychology student affiliated with the PRT-ERP, recalls that he never "got out of the closet." Daniel, another PRT-ERP militant, did communicate to his superiors that he was homosexual and he was referred to a party psychologist who insisted that it was an "individualistic deviation." Luis, a former student with the Peronist Youth, recalls having a better reception among his fellows, who pretended not to notice his sexuality.[98] Luis, however, may have been fortunate: while unverified rumors spread that the PRT-ERP leaders "only" expelled homosexual militants, a journalist assures that the Montonero leaders executed two because they were not "trustworthy."[99] The Montoneros leaders' actions would have been informed by the myth regarding the vulnerability of gays, that is, that gays were targets of blackmail and/ or unable to tolerate the hardships of clandestine life, perhaps because of their "uncontrolled" sexuality. Without "moral" and physical resistance, the men whose sexual practices did not meet the heterosexual mandates were deemed unfit to bear the resilient bodies that the activist style of militancy required as proof of consciousness.

Through blending overt prescriptions and practical mandates, thus, militants delineated the male, heterosexual, young body as the most suitable for carrying out a revolutionary process. That was not a given body but one that had to be carved out, which entailed regulating corporeal practices. A portrayal of two militants with the Fuerzas Armadas Peronistas (FAP, Peronist Armed Forces) who were killed by the police in 1971 illustrates how some of these regulations were imagined. A friend of Manuel Belloni, age twenty-three, and Diego Ruy Frondizi, age twenty-two, wrote a public letter to his friends to pay them homage. He commented on how Diego, especially, used to enjoy "plentiful meals" and "beautiful women," and on how hard it was for him to learn to shoot a gun properly. Diego had overcome his "weaknesses": he had not only learned how to shoot but also how to "control his appetites"—referring to both the eating and sexual aspects—when preparing "for action." Diego and Manuel represented the triumph of revolutionary will: their youthful male bodies were a surface over which they had worked hard. "I try to adopt your discipline of young and courageous men," their friend said to them and concluded, "revolutionary militants: what else could a guy like me ask for?"[100]

This letter may help reframe what Schmucler intuitively posited regarding the splintering of the revolutionaries between a "political" (ideal) and a "desiring" (concrete, corporeal) man. First, even though in this portrayal it is possible to view that desire or "appetite" was regulated, it is also possible to infer that it was directed to an ideal: "young and courageous men, revolutionary militants," the letter writer asked, "what else could a guy like me ask for?" Second, there was a particular type of body that served as the conduit for reaching that ideal. Mutually conditioning, the revolutionary militancy in the early 1970s required and produced resilient bodies, and young men, such as Diego and Manuel, were culturally better prepared to shape them. Third, the styles of militancy and the parameters for political promotions that the revolutionary militants endorsed revolved around the praise of action and were shaped according to the potentials and possibilities of young men. An eminently practical creation that took elements from mass culture—such as the celebration of the young, slender, and healthy body—the shaping of the resilient bodies also helped materialize the feeling of imminence that swept across the revolutionary political culture of the early 1970s, with all its celebration of action and its rejection of intellectualism. In this culture, the ideal combatant was one that had surpassed daily proofs of activism, which were also the markers to assess his consciousness. The body was made the carrier of consciousness.

▶ Both as a surface and as lived experience, the youthful body was at the center of Argentina's culture and politics in the late 1960s and early 1970s. The unprecedented explosion of the youthful body in the public sphere (from magazine covers to fashion catalogues to street demonstrations and plazas) went hand in hand with the further renewal of the mores and options ruling the "when" and "how" of its display and interaction in the most intimate spheres. Both movements, in fact, brought significant transformations to the ways in which eroticism, sexuality, and politics were "embodied" through *poner el cuerpo*. To begin with, the young woman was the one who became the protagonist of new patterns of eroticism as they related, for example, to the ubiquitous interplay between dress and nudity. I tried to consistently avoid that word "liberation" to define this dynamic inasmuch as, among other things, the ideals and notions of beauty and desirability that many young women upheld (and advertisers and fashion designers decisively reinforced) implied a new kind of bodily exposure and a new ideal body, which required and shaped the techniques of self-management necessary to produce it. In many ways, thus, the expansion of female bodily exposure brought about incipient mandates for internalizing capillary forms of self-control. As the local feminists and gay rights groups as well as left-wing intellectuals soon pointed out, the eroticization based upon the rising display of the young female body to a large degree implied its reification. Doubtlessly, this is the major reason why the word "liberation" is not the most suitable. Although further study is needed, it is possible to argue that this dynamics of eroticism did not necessarily have "disempowering effects" for young women either: it did not make women *more* subjected to male power, as one radical feminist has argued when analyzing this process for England—partially because assuming that entails overlooking the ways through which eroticism was connected with other transformations of sexuality.[101]

Less visible yet perhaps more lasting than the exposure of the youthful body in the public scene, that body was at the center of changing sexual mores and practices. In this respect, the normalization of premarital sex that had occurred in the 1960s paved the way to an incipient new understanding: the disengagement of (hetero)sexuality from marriage or its impending marriage. This implied a relocation of the legitimate site for heterosexuality, and set in motion a (sometimes surfacing) debate about sexual equality between men and women, about the persistent double standard. While these new arrangements about heterosexuality seemed to have cut across young people at large, sex did attain different meanings among the revolutionary militants, especially since it was moved from the intimate to the party or group milieu. In some cases, the individual's political moral (his or her commitment to a revolutionary project) could be measured against the backdrop of his or her sexual mores and behaviors. In the most Puritan models, the "normal" excluded behaviors accepted in segments of the broader sexual culture (for example, sex outside the established, heterosexual couple). In any case, revolutionary groups endowed their militants with formal and informal mandates for regulating sex as well as other bodily practices.

Revolutionary militants produced a resilient body, conceived of as young and, largely, masculine. The youths who engaged in revolutionary politics were hardly alone in "disciplining" their bodies to fit into an ideal: they shared the "disciplining drive" with their generational female peers who pursued, for example, dieting practices to fit into their tight blue jeans. The particularities of the resilient body consisted in that it crystallized a series of practices and incarnated values related to commitment and will. The resilient body was nothing if not gender-based: amid deep-seated cultural understandings about the "role" of women in the public and political spheres, young women—especially—found it hard to comply with the requirements of producing that sort of body. In a political culture that validated, above all, activism—vis-à-vis "intellectualism," for example—most women were steadily excluded from leading positions, from escalating to the "sublime" way of *poner el cuerpo* among revolutionary militants, that is, of becoming a guerrilla combatant. As the 1970s went on, the state repression over revolutionaries did not discriminate between "guerrillas," "militants," or "activists": they all put their bodies on the line, they were all targets of parapolice, police, and military repression.

8 ▸ Youth and the "Authority-Reconstitution" Project

In late 1975, when the civilian government of Isabel Martínez de Perón had already authorized the military to repress social and political activities, groups of neighbors from Buenos Aires and from the distant city of Comodoro Rivadavia wrote to the minister of the interior asking for more security in their communities, which they viewed as threatened by youths engaged either in "subversive actions," "drug consumption," "sexual orgies," or all of the above.[1] They created a link between youth, sexually and culturally deviant practices, and subversion—the main characteristics of the "enemy within" that jeopardized the fabric of the national body that the military, in March of 1976, was supposed to restore. This chapter looks at the unfolding of a project destined to "reconstitute authority," which promised to reverse the cultural, political, and sexual changes that Argentines had lived through as part of the modernizing dynamics that, since the 1950s, privileged youth as its key embodiment.

Beginning in 1974, a broad arc of conservative actors pushed for a hierarchical restructuring of Argentina's society, thus reversing what they envisioned as the lost authority of parents, teachers, and politicians at the hands of their children, students, or "unprofessional" militants. In their view, that reconstitution was pressing, and it was the only guarantee for preventing what they hyperbolically depicted as the final dissolution of Argentina's society. Deeply embedded in the Cold War imagery surrounding national security were actors who made youth the "enemy within." Not all young people conformed to the emerging image, but the face of that "enemy" was young: the guerrilla woman or man, the "drug addict," the so-called sexual deviant. In this respect, new legislation regarding the distribution of contraception, political participation in schools and universities, and drug consumption, all passed throughout 1974, led toward the shaping and containment of that figure, whereby also setting limits to the sociability, sexuality, and political organizing of flesh-and-blood young women and men. That legislation served to create and amplify the trope of deviancy surrounding youth and helped create consensus for increasingly authoritarian projects that promised to restore "order" to every sphere of social life.

Although the "authority-reconstitution" project started before March of 1976, the military junta that imposed Argentina's last military dictatorship (1976–83) added new, dramatically refocused, overtones. The military imposed its authoritarian order through enforcement of the basic mechanism of state terror: the systematic kidnapping, torture, and "disappearance" of their so-called enemies. The victims of state terror were overwhelmingly young: the young men and women that had made the ranks of the student, party, and guerrilla groups that renewed Argentina's politics in the late 1960s and early 1970s. Less because of their young age, they became the targets of the military's deadly project because they had belonged to revolutionary movements. This does not preclude the fact that the military set the stage to discipline youth at large, which in their view was the key to preventing another "subversive generation" from spreading. The responses of young women and men to these disciplining attempts varied greatly. Although further study is needed, the last segment of the chapter begins to tackle some of these responses.

Neither Sex nor Drugs . . . nor Politics

The "authority-reconstitution" project started as soon as Juan Perón came back to the country in June of 1973 and was forcefully crystallized throughout 1974, first with Perón and then after his death on July 1 with his wife Isabel as president. That project involved the revamping of Argentina's society, culture, and politics in ways that touched upon the experiences and expectations that young people had carved out throughout the 1960s and early 1970s. In 1974, legislative developments restricted the distribution of the birth control pill and prohibited the dissemination of information regarding contraception; increased penalties for the trafficking and consumption of so-called illegal drugs; and stopped schools and universities from being legitimate sites for political activism. By the end of that year, an imposed state of siege (that would last until 1983) closed the possibilities of legal political activism and restricted youth sociability. Although it did not preclude the broadening of extralegal repression, a façade of legality allowed the state and a broad range of political actors to delineate the figure of the "enemy within," as historian Marina Franco has recently studied.[2] That façade covered the "authority-reconstitution" project during the biennium 1974–75: its scope and pitfalls in those years forecast and shaped what came next.

The "authority-reconstitution" project crafted a sexual politics that repositioned conservative Catholic groups at the forefront of decision-making bodies. In January of 1974, the League of Mothers asked the police to interrupt the circulation of novels such as Manuel Puig's *The Buenos Aires Affair*, because they "violated the sense of morals." While it is likely that one year earlier the league's claim would have gone unheard, now, as in the "old days with [Gen. Juan Carlos] Onganía," one report indicated, the police entered bookstores, threw the novels away, and imprisoned booksellers and editors.[3] The police deployed similar raids vis-à-vis gay sociability and fads, to the extent that the Frente de Liberación Homosexual (FLH, Homosexual Liberation Front) distributed a pamphlet cautioning readers on the "police efforts to reimpose a Cary Grant image" by cutting young men's hair and obligating them to change shoes and colored clothes for more sober and "manly" items. The FLH rightly understood that this campaign was part of a broader backlash geared to prevent "social and political revolution from spreading."[4] Along the same lines of the campaigns and the censorship of books, in mid-1974 the never-dismantled Board of Film Qualification appointed a new president, the film critic Miguel Paulino Tato, who in only six months prohibited the release of sixty-one movies, "whose sexual or political content," he argued, "would damage the already weakened 'internal front.'"[5] Explicitly, sex and politics intermingled in his mind, as they did in the rationale informing other major public decisions.

Framed by a larger concern about "Argentina's secular depopulation," Perón and his minister of social welfare, José López Rega, passed a decree that made it more difficult to acquire contraception, notably the "Pill," and prohibited public hospitals from promoting any birth-control methods as of March 1974. As historian Karina Felitti has shown, evidence suggests the decree was unevenly enforced, and it is likely that it affected chiefly poor women, who relied on the public health system—in contrast to middle- and upper-class women, who relied on the less supervised private system.[6] In any case, the rationale for that policy is significant since it allowed for the rearticulation and broader dissemination of a discourse permeated by gender and sexual concerns in the public milieu of the mid-1970s. Utilizing a common argument among conservative Catholic groups, the decree stated that birth control had "distracted young people from their natural duties as protagonists of the future of the fatherland, and denaturalized women's maternal role."[7] Birth control represented the pernicious effects of "liberalizing" trends, which were embodied in young people's sexual mores and ended up by subverting the gender order tout court. Right-wing Peronists and conservative Catholics did not cast doubts: young people potentially "subverted" the sexual, gendered, and political terrain. In their view, that dynamic corroded the "future of the fatherland" and could only be countered by returning sex to its "legitimate" role and site: procreation and marriage within a stable family.

The appeal to "family values" helped create consensus over repressive solutions. In late 1974, the Ministry of Social Welfare organized a large conference titled "First Encounter of the Family." In his inaugural address, Minister López Rega pointed out that "guns, drugs, and pornography are annihilating our nationhood," which could be recovered, he said, only through the "reconstitution of the family." Rather than being a policy-making forum, the event set the scene for staging a conservative discourse that touched on politics, culture, and sexuality as they related to youth.[8] Most directly, the meeting was the background for the launch of an Episcopal pastoral for the years 1975 and 1976 on "Marriage and Family," an endeavor that came about when the Catholic hierarchy unleashed a campaign to silence the voices of the radicalized laypeople and the Third World Priests.[9] For the depurated Catholic community, the defense of "society's basic cell" seemed all the more urgent since, as the archbishop of Rosario argued in a well-publicized letter—replicating the ministry's tropes—"our families are losing their youth to political violence, promiscuity, and drug addiction."[10] Like all conservative Catholics and right-wing Peronists, he believed that the family was defenseless and in need of the state as a key agent for activating an "authority-reconstitution" project on three fronts: politics, sex, and drugs.

The "drug problem" was linked to national security through the passing of Law 20771 on narcotics, also in 1974. Up to that year, that "problem" had grown slowly. In contrast to the rising interest it garnered in the United States and Western Europe, by the mid-1960s, the media in Argentina only focused on an experiment that a group of psychoanalysts had developed with lysergic acid, one of the components of LSD. This practice was legendary, in part because actors, filmmakers, and some left-wing intellectuals underwent it, although, as one report noted, the group comprised "no more than three hundred people." By 1967 it was hard to obtain the drug from laboratories, and the experience was discontinued.[11] Also in 1967, some reports began to refer to "marijuana." Besides explaining the characteristics of cannabis and the fact that Argentines imported it from Brazil and Paraguay, the weekly *Primera Plana* organized a "smoking session" and concluded that "it does not create addiction" and reminded readers that it was neither "an alkaloid (it does not produce secondary effects)" nor "a narcotic (it does not produce habit)." That last note was significant: technically, marijuana did not match the two kinds of substances that the Penal Code considered illegal. Further, a would-be controversial reform of that code in 1968, which augmented the penalties for drug trafficking, stipulated that the possession of one dose of any drug for personal consumption was not to be penalized.[12]

In 1971–72, however, the public perception of the "drug problem" began to change significantly, and this included the emergence of new actors and regulations as well as an increased media focus. Although the press quoted police officers who asserted that it was necessary to "prevent [drug consumption] rather than alarm" the population, the reports that insistently popped up in lifestyle magazines helped build persistent and dramatic tropes. One of them was the "spiraling model," that is, the belief that youth who used amphetamines and marijuana initiated a process that would lead to their use of "hard drugs." Cases of dubious authenticity were cited to show how "miscommunication" and "breakdown" prevailed among families of drug users. Only "well-constituted" families could keep their youth safe by exercising a "discreet" yet permanent surveillance over them.[13] Alongside the media, other actors played key roles in the "drug problem," such as the federal police, which in 1971 publicized the birth of its Narcotics Division through several spectacular raids.[14] According to police statistics, as soon as the Narcotics Division was born, drug-related detentions multiplied, notably among the labile category of "detainees in prevention" (those in the company of "traffickers") which went from 1,410 in 1970 to 2,610 in 1971, including 619 underage boys and 405 girls. Police data showed, in addition, that the trafficking of marijuana had skyrocketed over a two-year period: while 9 kilos had been seized in raids conducted in 1969, 57 kilos were seized in the first six months of 1971.[15] In this respect, the officers with the Narcotics Division insisted on including marijuana in the official list of prohibited drugs, a demand supported by editorialists and legal specialists alike.[16] It was in mid-1971 when the Ministry of Social Welfare endorsed a decree prohibiting the sale of amphetamines without medical prescription and making marijuana an "illegal drug."

The Ministry of Social Welfare became a leading actor in the shaping of the "drug problem," and it forged new alliances, notably with the U.S. Bureau of Narcotics and Dangerous Drugs (BNDD). In the summer of 1972, the minister of social welfare, Captain Francisco Manrique, announced the creation of the Comisión Nacional de Toxicomanía y Narcóticos (National Committee of Narcotics and Toxicology). Chaired by the minister and composed of delegates from the Narcotics Division and the School of Medicine at the University of Buenos Aires (UBA), the committee's purpose was to coordinate policies that stopped drug trade and consumption. Its creation was fueled by the arrival of representatives of President Richard Nixon's administration.[17] They were neither the first nor the last. As historian Paul Gootenberg has shown, the Nixon administration played a key role in recasting hemispheric relations in terms of a "drug problem," promoting the creation of copious ad-hoc committees.[18] Hence, having identified Argentina as a transshipment point for "hard narcotics" to the United States (substantiated by repeated seizures of heroin coming from Marseille to Argentina, with the New York City as final destination) the BNDD established in Buenos Aires its headquarters for South America. According to the report filed by U.S. officers, who visited Latin America to map governmental responses to the "narcotics problem," Argentina ranked high. It was the only country which had thus far signed a "bilateral treaty of understanding" with the United States, under which the minister of social welfare and the U.S. ambassador presided over a bi-national committee on the "drug problem" and under which the U.S. government committed itself to providing training, equipment, and other "material and human resources."[19]

Beginning in 1973, the understanding about drugs reached between the Ministry of Social Welfare and the U.S. Embassy had powerful effects. The ultra-rightist minister López Rega signed a treaty with U.S. ambassador Robert C. Hill to gain access to resources for expanding "the intelligence aspects to stop the internal and external drug trade." In a press conference, the minister publicized things that perhaps had to remain in the shadows: "our mutual commitment," he said, "is to struggle against drugs and subversion alike."[20] López Rega's direct involvement in the "drug problem" had at least two major consequences. First, the Ministry of Social Welfare began to receive funds other than those assigned in annual congressional budgets. The ministry did not have to account for these extra funds, either in Argentina or to the U.S. authorities. Rumors suggested that some of the anti-drug intelligence funds provided in the form of U.S. aid were funneled into the creation of the later notorious Argentine Anti-

Communist Alliance (Triple A), a parapolice group that, as l briefly discuss below, violently attacked left-wing militants and activists.[21] Second, that understanding allowed López Rega to create a legal, drug-related means for repression. In this respect, the Narcotics Division, which in 1975 turned into a department, acquired an even more prominent role and most of its members received training in the United States.[22] Moreover, the increased funding received by the ministry made the creation of the Centro Nacional de Reeducación Social (CENARESO, National Center of Social Reeducation) possible. Between 1973 and 1975, CENARESO functioned as a pro-ministry entity. Its director was an obscure doctor named Carlos Cagliotti, who participated in the making of Law 20771 on "narcotics."[23]

Congress passed Law 20771 in September of 1974, helping create a legal link between youth, deviancy, and subversion. Strongly influenced by CENARESO's proposals and information, the Executive Power urged representatives to help "stop the wave of addiction" that, the bill stated, had "increased 500 percent in two years." The representatives responded positively. Besides rising penalties for the production and distribution of all "narcotics and psychotropic drugs," the law dubbed as "aggravated offenses" those committed by people who encourage consumption by underage youths. The law included three other novelties. First, it mandated that all drug-related offenders would be subjected to federal justice. Second, it stipulated that drug possession, "even if it is for personal use," was to be penalized by one to six years in prison. Finally, the law specified that any offenders proven to have "physical or psychic addiction to drugs," might be mandated to undergo obligatory rehabilitation as part of their penalties.[24] In the months that followed the passage of the law, the most debated issue was the subjection of drug-related offenses to federal justice, that is, to the highest judicial system in the country. One defendant of the novelty explained that this decision was based on the fact that "drug addiction" was related to national security: in pursuing their addictions, he added, young people could fall into transnational delinquent and "extremist networks."[25]

This legal framework established links between youth, drugs, and "subversion" and materialized in new conditions for youth sociability and politics. First, in illegalizing consumption and endorsing a reinforcement of police monitoring over sites of youth interaction, Law 20771 criminalized youth leisure patterns. In the summer of 1975, for example, the chamber that joined the owners of entertainment locales—dance clubs, concert stadiums, and night clubs—wrote letters to the minister of the interior to complain about the visits of the Narcotics Division to their establishments. They pointed out that policemen deployed "large weapons" and "harassed men and women," while they searched for drugs, an occurrence that had led the youth clientele to refrain from going out at night. Throughout 1975, numerous reports likewise spoke of police raids at schools, plazas, and concerts. In the case of rock music, police monitoring resulted in fewer performances and this created hardships for musicians. Some, like Claudio Gabis, Moris, and Pappo, went abroad to acquire professional training or create new bands. In any case, the rock scene began to evaporate.[26] In addition, some of the youth harassed in those sites probably were charged as "offenders" and sent to rehabilitation. Dr. Cagliotti proudly announced that, in mid-1975, the CENARESO had received "1,425 boys between sixteen and twenty-one."[27]

The second connection between youth, drugs, and politics as framed by the "national security" ideology implied the involvement of radical political militants, notably guerrillas, in drug trafficking or consumption. As early as 1970, for example, *La Razón* insisted that Montonero leader Mario Firmenich was trafficking in drugs to get money and weapons.[28] Although groundless, these reports tried to endow rumors with a halo of credibility. This was the case of newspaper reports detailing "spectacular" actions that the guerrillas carried out. In January of 1974, for example, the ERP attacked an army battalion in Azul, Buenos Aires. There several members of the military and one dozen guerrillas died. In its coverage of the episodes, the press focused on the conclusions of a supposed psychiatric report of "seventy young guerrillas" that claimed the ERP had planned the attack by timing the effects of amphetamines over the fighters. Yet because of a "miscalculation," the psychiatrists went on, the guerrillas ended up in the battlefield "depressed and feeling all the possible side effects of the drugs: they became their worst enemies."[29] Rapidly, radical political groups publicized their opposition to drug use (while they tightened rules for preventing their militants from using them) and tried to dismantle what they dubbed a "propaganda operation orchestrated by the CIA and right-wing Peronism."[30] Regardless of their efforts, the link between political and cultural "subversion" embodied in youth became commonsensical, helping pave the way for increasing repression.

Beginning in January of 1974 and accelerating in the months to follow, the political scenario disappeared and the spaces for youth politics vanished. In fact, Perón unleashed his "counter-subversive war" right after the ERP attacked the army battalion. He ordered the resignation of the governor of Buenos Aires (an ally to left-wing Peronism) and mandated a reform of the Penal Code so as to increase penalties for a whole range of political activities now dubbed subversive. He also restituted repressive legislation discontinued in the short "democratic spring" of 1973.[31] This was the context in which he expelled the pro-Montonero Revolutionary Tendency from his movement, accusing them of being "Marxist infiltrators." Furthermore, Perón promoted the passing of a new law to regulate public universities, which was one of the last pillars of left-wing Peronism. The student movement at large, and the JUP in particular, were marginalized from the accords that Perón reached with other politicians.[32] Passed in March, the law tightened governmental control over the universities as it gave the Executive Power the right to name rectors. It also diminished the power of alumni in the university government (and increased the staff's) and, most basically, outlawed "politics from the classrooms."[33] Convinced that the new law would serve as a repressive tool, the JUP abandoned its submissive politics (they had tried not to confront Perón's decisions) and joined the Communist and Radical students to protest. It was too late: Perón's government not only left the law untouched but also prohibited rallies and imprisoned three hundred students.[34]

In launching its "authority-reconstitution" project, the Peronist government focused on the secondary schools as well. Perón named new authorities for the 1974 school year, which set as their most pressing goal the achievement of order and discipline in schools across the country. In a widely distributed memo, the new authorities hyperbolically depicted the experience of student organizing as "chaotic" and oriented to the "subversion" of all hierarchies within and potentially outside the schools. Appealing to teachers and parents, they stated that their highest priority was to "avoid indiscipline by any means," especially when "student political groups" carried it out. To that end, authorities asked principals to notify them and the police of any "suspicious movement," to prevent its spread and "contagious effects," whether those movements implied sit-ins or strikes. The memo forcefully concluded that the teachers' and principals' authority should be upheld "at any cost."[35] Intimidating in its tone, the memo incited reactions. While part of the press concurred with the "efforts to discipline the rioting adolescents," others called for combining "sticks with at least one carrot"—such as curriculum changes.[36] As their university counterparts, the Peronist and Communist groups in the secondary school student movement tried to mobilize against the "repressive regulations" and promised to organize rallies and a round of "school-to-school battles." Reporting to his political superiors, a Communist student acknowledged that after "that infamous memo" there was no chance of mobilizing.[37]

As 1974 went on, the education institutions became unfriendly spaces for young activists. When Isabel Martínez de Perón was sworn in, the ultra-rightist sectors of the Peronist movement gained even more positions of power within her government. One epitome of that ultra-right was the minister of education, Dr. Oscar Ivanissevich—a veteran Peronist militant, who had already occupied that position during Perón's first presidency. In a speech transmitted on all radio stations and television channels (something unusual for a minister of education, which signaled the significance of his position at that juncture) he questioned the "youth who deprecate what their parents and the country give them." He stated that the only goal of his administration would be to "deter the climate of subversion from the secondary schools and the university."[38] To accomplish his goal, he ordered universities to be closed until they were "normalized," which included both intervention as well as the resumption of barriers to entry. As for the secondary level, the minister also ordered intervention in schools where the principals were not willing to "recover their authority" vis-à-vis the students, and he mandated the closure of the student centers at the beginning of the 1975 school year.[39] At that point in time, though, the government had already passed a decree establishing a state of siege, which restricted most civil rights and limited the legitimacy of any political practice—let alone the illegal activity of the revolutionary groups like the ERP and Montoneros that endorsed armed struggle.

Alongside the changes in legal frameworks, the repressive policies initiated in 1974 took on ever more violent forms. Between 1974 and 1976, parapolice groups such as the Córdoba-based Comando Libertadores de América and the Triple A, which functioned at a national level, acted broadly. In a sort of division of labor, while the regular security forces—the police and, since 1975, also the military—fought against guerrilla combatants both urban and rural, the parapolice forces focused on social and political militants, including many students. As early as March of 1974, Hugo Hanssen, a student at the University of Lomas affiliated with the JUP, was killed by an "unidentified group," as a police report observed. He was participating in a takeover of the university building meant to oppose the appointment of a rector identified with the previous military regime and to protest against the new university law.[40] In August of that same year, the Triple A took credit for the assassination of eighteen-year-old Eduardo

Beckermann, a leader with the Peronist UES. They were but the first two student victims of ultra-rightist violence. Prudent estimates suggest that these parapolice organizations assassinated nine hundred people between late 1973 and early 1976: one half of the victims were members of Peronist Youth and almost two hundred were women.[41]

The "guerrilla woman" epitomized the sexual, cultural, and political meanings of subversion in mid-1970s Argentina, when the armed forces were getting ready to fix what many depicted as chaotic violence coming from both left and right. Doubtless, however, when the armed forces thought of the enemy, the image was just such an irregular leftist "army" that also included young women. Brigadier General José D'Odorico, a leading counterinsurgency expert trained in France and the United States, alerted his comrades about what to know about "them." He posited that "she" was the final product of an ideological and political task through which a ubiquitous "Communist enemy" took advantage of female traits such as "sensibility, tenacity, tolerance to pain, and passionate commitments." In doing so, he argued, the enemy "emptied her spiritual and cultural content, creating a humanoid." The "guerrilla woman" had lost any trace of humankind and, specially, of womanhood. Talking to an imaginary peer, D'Odorico urged him to understand that "in front of you, or more likely on your back, you will see a being that only keeps the empty body of a woman." The conclusion was plain: the military might break their gender prejudices and, simply, shoot first.[42] The armed forces prepared themselves for barring with all prejudices in order to struggle against such an "enemy" that, in their perception, and in that of large portions of Argentina's society, promised to erode all sense of order.

Youth and the Production of "Order"

On March 24, 1976, in a climate that the media dubbed as chaotic, a long-awaited military coup d'état took place. The lifestyle magazine *Gente* (one of the most committed advocates of the new regime) published a half-page picture of four boys painting a wall, titled "Pongamos la casa en orden [Let's put the house in order]," three weeks after the coup. "No, they are not members of a political group," the caption explains to readers. "They are students from a technical school who decided to paint their school walls, which were full of graffiti of calls to meetings and rallies . . . this is a symptom, and a good one, that some youth understood that *el orden empieza por casa* [order begins at home]."[43] In a few weeks, the caption suggests, the ef-

PONGAMOS
LA CASA
EN ORDEN

No, no son
miembros de nin-
gún grupo político
ni están pintando
leyendas en la pa-
red. Son alumnos
del colegio Otto
Krause que, por
propia determina-
ción, decidieron
blanquear el
frente de la es-
cuela. Allí había
cartelones con
frases de tono po-
lítico, fechas, lla-
mados a reunio-
nes o huelgas.
Ahora sólo ha
quedado un muro
prolijo y blanco.
Como debe ser.
Como debió ser
siempre. Este
gesto de jóvenes
argentinos es un
síntoma, un buen
síntoma. Algo que
nos hace pensar
en eso de: "El or-
den bien enten-
dido empieza por
casa".

"Let's put the house in order." *Gente* No. 560, April 15, 1976, 17.

fects of the new regime had begun to spread even to the most "disorderly" milieu. The four boys had engaged (of their own accord, the caption clarified) in the making of the order that *Gente* and thousands of anonymous people claimed. While many civilian institutions (the Catholic Church's hierarchy, the dominant media, and business boards) actively endorsed the new regime, broad segments of Argentines deployed what scholars call "reactive consensus": a silent but real carte blanche for the military to "restore order."[44] That restoration implied reversing the modernizing sociocultural dynamics unfolding in the 1960s and early 1970s, which had helped shape youth experiences. Janus-faced, youth came to epitomize disorder and the potential for producing a new, "counter-subversive" order.

Like most Latin American military groups, the junta in Argentina deployed and was informed by a strategically vague notion of subversion. Taking root among the security forces trained in the national security doctrines, the notion of "subversion," or "subversive Communist action," was embedded in an enemy that from the early 1960s was regarded as already "within" the geopolitical space of the West. Under those doctrines, the security forces had the right and the duty of waging an irregular war against an enemy who, as they imagined, acted on manifold battlefronts.[45] Attuned to the most conservative Catholic ideas as well, the military leaders in Argentina proposed to unleash a "missionary war" that was to be played out in the bodies and minds of those who were already, and those who potentially could become, enemies. One week after the coup, President Jorge R. Videla (1976–81), defined what the junta took for subversion: "it is not only planting bombs in the streets" but also "all social conflict, the struggle between parents and children."[46] The restoration of the principles of hierarchy and discipline was deemed crucial to winning over such a ubiquitous enemy and it required enlisting all those who held positions of authority: parents, teachers, employers. Besides framing the enterprise, the junta assigned the security forces the tasks of carrying out the bodily aspects of the mission.

The Argentine version of state terrorism prioritized the mechanism of kidnapping, torturing, and finally "disappearing" people.[47] That mechanism reached its highest point in the biennium 1976–78 and its main target was an "enemy" who in terms of age was young. The military justified their "war" on the grounds of a total struggle against the guerrilla. According to a plausible estimate, though, in 1975, when reaching their maximum capacity, the combatants for all the guerrilla groups numbered no more than twelve hundred. By late 1975, likewise, the guerrilla groups had been almost dismantled and a majority of combatants were dead. In any case, they constituted only a small fraction of about twenty thousand "disappeared" in the 340 clandestine detention centers that the security forces created throughout the country.[48] Those thousands of disappeared victims of state terror had been part of a network of militants and activists coming of age politically in the 1960s and early 1970s. As the report by Argentina's National Commission on Disappeared People noted, whether they were students, employees, or workers, 69 percent were between sixteen and thirty years old at the time they were kidnapped.[49] By pointing this out, I do not claim that they were killed for being young: scant evidence supports the idea of a generational war, as one scholar has posited recently. Rather, as historian Steve Stern has argued for Chile, the term "politicide" seems appropriate for labeling also the Argentine junta's resolution of annihilating one segment of the population defined less by their age than by their involvement in revolutionary projects.[50]

The fact remains, however, that the military amplified the "authority-

Para
la Juventud
siempre hay un
camino nuevo.
Pongámonos
en marcha.

"For youth there is always a new path. Let's follow it." Advertisement for Flecha sneakers. *Gente* No. 578, August 19, 1976, 18.

reconstitution" project, marked by an effort to reverse the modernizing dynamics that had shaped youth experiences as well as youth visibility. While in the 1960s and early 1970s youth had occupied a prominent position in Argentina's visual culture, as soon as the military imposed the coup, youth vanished from one key visual realm: advertising. Off the record, one advertiser confessed to political scientist Guillermo O'Donnell that he did not dare to portray youth.[51] Regardless of the reliability of the fears, available data do show that in the most widely read lifestyle magazines, *Siete Días* and *Gente*, ads for jeans and sneakers (which relied on representing their main target) were discontinued in the first months after the coup. The timing speaks for itself, since these advertisers used to increase their investments in the fall and winter seasons, that is, from March to August. It was only in August when the local brand of sneakers, Flecha Juventud, resumed its campaigns, though they sharply differed from previous years. In its campaign for 1975, for example, Flecha Juventud first showed shots of three young women and men in their early twenties and localized them vis-à-vis the product per se, without further slogans. In August of 1976, the ad showed a group of adolescents at a distance and carried an unusually long slogan: "For youth there is always a new path. Let's follow it."[52] Tacitly mobilizing memories of a "rebellious" youth, the ad conveyed the idea that a supervised new youth would deserve another chance: one to follow the "correct path" the previous cohort had not pursued.

Youth centralized the conversations over the cultural conditions that, many argued, had made "chaos" possible. Across conservative Catholic lines, military ideologues had long linked the emergence of "chaos" with the effacement of authority principles within the family. As one leading officer with the air force wrote, the family institution was being "corroded" by a list that included "young people equipped with ideas of individual and sexual liberty; and adults with a demagogic desire for cultural renewal."[53] Likewise journalists in the pro-regime media wrote that the "chaos" Argentines had lived through had not begun in the "revolutionary 1973" but in the 1960s, "when one culture replaced another" by exposing the younger generation to "badly digested psychoanalysis; ideas of a generation gap; and images of adultery mixed with cries of liberation of the oppressed."[54] By focusing on the stereotypical aspects of the 1960s, military ideologues and their spokespeople in the media imagined a future when authority at the state and family levels would reinforce one another.[55] Time seemed not ripe for such an entwinement. The first minister of education, José Bruera—a civilian—in his inaugural speech of the 1977 school year argued that, since the "family has lost its educational role due to pseudo-psychological discourses that neglect the duties of the parental authority," the state should act as a surrogate father for youth and assume extra responsibilities to lead the "authority-reconstitution" project.[56]

Not surprisingly, the education system was key to the "authority-reconstitution" project. While formally the military just continued the demobilizing politics initiated in 1974, it set the stage for massive persecutions at the university and the secondary levels. Convinced that those levels had been the recruiting grounds for revolutionary militancy—something containing a kernel of truth—the educational authorities, whether they were civilian or military, took special effort in creating rules to prevent that from happening.[57] A widely distributed memo delineated a step-by-step method to "detect subversive infiltration" in the classrooms. It assigned principals and deans the task of monitoring classes, readings, and conversations among educators, staff, and students. The memo explained to readers that they should be warned of how "subversive content" might infiltrate in myriad ways. As examples, it listed "any attempt to modify traditional values (religion, tradition) or to damage known notions of family and patriarchal authority," along with the most obvious references

The "Authority-Reconstitution" Project 235

to words such as "liberation and revolution." In case of finding such offenses committed in the school, the principal was obligated to denounce "the subordinate" to his or her "superiors."[58] Although the memo surely reinforced a sense of fear, there is no sign that the principals made widespread denunciations. Perhaps envisioning a failure, the would-be second president of the junta, General Roberto Viola, involved himself directly in Operación Claridad in mid-1978. This was an operation orchestrated at the Ministry of Education (headed by the right-wing Catholic nationalist Juan J. Catalán). Besides systematizing lists with prohibited textbooks, the officers in charge of the operation promoted the firing of eight thousand teachers, professors, and staff members from the public education system.[59]

The politically and ideologically motivated expulsion of educators went hand-in-hand with larger sociocultural and economic processes that, crystallizing in the late 1970s, produced the overall shrinking of the education system. Generations of Argentines had viewed the system as a legitimate and affordable ladder of social mobility. Key to the imagining of an inclusive, modernizing nation, the secondary and university levels of education had greatly expanded in the 1950s and 1960s, opening youth to new experiences and expectations. Beginning in the mid-1970s, the seemingly never-ending inclusionary movement was interrupted. At the secondary level, the total enrollment grew 27 percent from 1970 to 1975 and only 3 percent from 1976 to 1980. Meanwhile, the university level experienced a decrease in its student body from 530,000 in 1976 to 400,000 in 1980.[60] As part of its project for "reordering" Argentina's society, the junta's neoliberal economic plan had a depressing effect on education. In an effort to cut back the state budget, in 1977 the government decided to charge tuition fees in the public universities, for the first time violating the free-of-charge (*gratuidad*) tenet that had been instituted during the University Reform Movement. Although fees were not as costly as in private colleges, they were imposed just as unemployment rates were growing. Coupled with the decreasing allure of the universities as spaces of sociability, these economic limitations might have prevented a youth cohort from enrolling.[61] Similarly, rising levels of unemployment among the industrial working classes help explain the stagnation of the secondary level. From 1975 to 1980 commercial and technical schools, which attracted working-class children, were those that shrunk the most.[62] In sociocultural and economic terms as well, the military regime put an end to the modernizing dynamics that, chiefly in the 1960s, had youth as a privileged actor and education as a pivotal territory.

Increasingly restrictive, the education system would ideally serve to forge a disciplined new generation in the military's project. While memos and operatives pointed to the "cleaning" of so-called subversive people and ideas from the university and secondary school levels, professors, teachers, staff, and students made up a large segment of the "disappeared." At the same time that the government increased police surveillance and students were required to show their identification cards to gain access to the universities' buildings, droves of students were taken to detention centers. Prudent estimates indicate that 1,500 faculty, students, and recent graduates of the UBA "disappeared" (including 105 students at the Colegio Nacional de Buenos Aires), a staggering figure, accompanied by 750 students and professors from the University of La Plata and 170 from the National and Technological Universities of Rosario.[63] As Mabel, one student formerly affiliated with the JUP recalls, "How was it possible to take classes, to enter the building when so many of your friends were not there?" Her memories invoke silence and fear: like other former militants, she quit.[64] Secondary school students could not make those decisions, although probably many had wanted to. Like universities, secondary schools were sites where "task forces" searched for "subversives." At least 600 teachers "disappeared," along with 120 recent graduates and 130 students, a tragic figure that included 10 young women and men taken from their homes on September 16, 1976, in La Plata—the infamous "night of the pencils."[65]

In the military's project, disciplining the new generation started by "disappearing" what they viewed as its already-lost segment and continued by imposing new rules and values on the rest. In his programmatic definitions of the goals of the education system, formulated as early as April of 1976, Minister Bruera displaced academic objectives from the junta's priorities to focus instead on the "restoration of order and hierarchies."[66] As the education sociologist Juan Carlos Tedesco has aptly put it, that overarching goal was less translatable in a pedagogical discourse (for the most part emptied and traditionalist) than in the enforcement of "ritualistic signs" of obedience.[67] At the secondary level, the main curricular change was the discontinuation of a class introduced in 1973, the Study of Argentina's Social Reality, which was replaced with Civic and Moral Formation. This class reversed the secularist tradition of Argentina's education: it included religious ideas as organizing principles for discussing topics such as "the nature of men" and the family. The latter was conceived of as a natural institution, based on an irrevocable pact (marriage), and endowed with procreative and "formative" roles under the "supervision of the father."[68] The content for this class was meant to act as ideological ammunition for viewing an immutable and hierarchical order that "began at home" and should continue at school. The educational authorities insisted on keeping the school buildings "clean," especially of political and cultural graffiti. In addition, they were consistently preoccupied with the students' dress practices. Girls were forbidden from wearing pants and make-up and should have their hair tied and their skirts below the knees. Young men were required to wear grey pants, ties, and shoes, besides having their hair cut eight centimeters above their shoulders. They could not address educators informally (for example, by using the *vos* or *tu*) and had to stand up when teachers and principals entered the classrooms.[69] From the perspective of the educational authorities, these "ritualistic signs" would mold a generation respectful for hierarchies, discipline, and authority.

The ideal of youth that the educational authorities, the dominant media, and, perhaps, broad segments of Argentina's population wanted to enforce, would combine discipline, respect for hierarchies and authority, and also patriotism. In this respect, while the military regime made demobilization a crucial policy for society at large, there was one particular episode of programmed mobilization whose target was youth. The National Gendarmerie, endowed with the task of monitoring the national frontiers, launched the campaign *Marchemos a las Fronteras* (Let's Go to the Frontier), an endeavor that involved the redeployment of five thousand boys from secondary schools in the large cities to interact with their frontier counterparts. The first campaign, carried out in late 1979, was preceded by fund-raising efforts of secondary school students to purchase the food and school supplies that they would take to the frontiers—efforts that involved more young people than actual travelers, who were apparently chosen because they had shown "leadership abilities" at their schools. Formally launched at the River Plate stadium, in a ceremony with the regime's highest authorities (including Videla), the first *Marchemos a las Fronteras* represented a political success. It showed a fraction of the "new youth" willing to participate in an initiative overtly associated with the regime and framed into a patriotic and militaristic rhetoric that included a solidarity component (the students would aid their impoverished peers).[70] The initiative was successful *and* limited, allowing us to further interrogate how young people responded to the mandates of integration into an "orderly" society.

There Is Life in the Shadows

In a pioneering work, sociologist Pablo Vila produced what would become a canonical interpretation of the relationships between youth and the dictatorship, as seen through the prism of the changes of rock culture. Vila argued that rock, as culture and movement, came to replace previous political affiliations by acting in itself as a form of politics associated with countercultural practices. As such, it constituted an avenue for cultural and political resistance to the dictatorship, which positioned youth as an actor at the core of new practices of solidarity and anti-authoritarianism. It is difficult to overestimate Vila's contribution. Published in the immediate aftermath of the dictatorship, his work has provided a periodization of the relations between rock culture and the regime. It also recognized how rock culture diversified its constituency by incorporating youths coming from different cultural and political backgrounds and pointed out the emergent "tribes" and styles among rockers. Lastly, it signaled the political dimensions of countercultural practices. Not randomly, Vila's work had influenced most essays on youth and dictatorship.[71] However, Vila's work introduces three key problems. First, it posits a clear-cut divide between political activism and rock culture in the pre-1976 era, which permits it to view the convergence between rock and politics after as a novelty. Second, his work is based on a chain that equates youth to rock and both to resistance, which obliterates other cultural and political responses that young people might have developed vis-à-vis the authoritarian conditions reinforced after 1976. Finally, Vila's work disregards the uneasy yet persistent efforts to politically organize youth. Although further study is needed, the relations that youth developed to the conditions set by the military were neither subsumed into the (certainly crucial) history of rock culture nor into the dichotomy resistance versus conformity.

From the viewpoint of the military, rock music and culture occupied an ambivalent, while changing, position. The hyper-atrophied censorship apparatuses that the regime set up to control cultural production did not impose on rock artists and records as many restrictions as they did, for example, against folkloric music. In 1977, the office of the State Secretary of Intelligence created and distributed a report on how popular music had supposedly served (and continued serving, in their view) the unfolding of a "Marxist psychological war over youth's consciousness." The report included a list with twenty-five recordings available in record stores that were deemed potentially subversive. Only one album belonged to the rock world, duo Pedro y Pablo's *Conesa* (1972), which had been part of the "protest" trend of rock music.[72] Along with the scarce attention that censors paid to rock music and artists, in the biennium 1976–77 (at the height of state terrorism) the military also allowed for the organization of concerts, such as one at the Luna Park in July of 1976 whose lineup included all the "stars" that remained in the country and attracted eleven thousand youths. Luis Alberto Spinetta's band Invisible attracted thirteen thousand people at another concert in August, in the same venue.[73] Furthermore, the pro-regime media made copious room for artists such as Spinetta. Profiling this writer and musician as a "good son"—when he was already a father of two—*Gente* went as far as quoting him saying that his main advice for fans was to "really listen to what your parents have to tell you."[74] Yet the making of rock musicians into "role models" for youth lasted a short time. In late 1977, Spinetta had songs banned from radios and spent days in prison, while artists such as León Gieco joined the contingent of exiles. As if a symbolic exchange were taking place, when the severest time for the repression of political militants was coming to a tragic end, the most repressive time for rockers began.

The critical biennium of 1978–79 was transformative for rockers—musicians, poets, and fans—and for the status of rock culture in the broader cultural and political framework. In this respect, the representative of the navy in the first junta, Admiral Eduardo Massera (whose force ran the deadliest clandestine detention center, the Escuela de Mecánica de la Armada), set the tone for rock culture's rising persecution. In late 1977, he stated that young people "create a private universe," endowed with its own "rites, as shown in their clothes and the music." While at first rock culture led youth towards "supine pacifism," Massera thought that it could turn them to the "terrorist faith, a predictable deviation of the sensorial spiral."[75] Once the military leaders located rock culture within these coordinates, they required its surveillance and repression, which translated into the resumption of police raids in concerts, ideological and political monitoring of musicians, and the disbanding of most existing formations. In terms of Vila, rock culture became privatized: it "hibernated" in small groups of friends who, through practices such as exchanging records and listening to music together in private homes, kept alive a sense of solidarity and the antiauthoritarian ethos linked to the "we" that they recon-figured.[76] For analysts and members of rock culture alike, those practices epitomized how rock served as a culture for "resisting," on the margins, au-thoritarianism and cultural repression. As Eduardo, one former working-class young man, recalls, "purchasing a cassette was more than that." The extra value of the purchase implied, in his memory, the "discussions I had with friends over the details of rock music . . . the practice of discussing things."[77] In his memories, rock favored not only the ability to discuss and criticize (which neither the school nor the public culture endorsed) but also a sense of community.

As had happened since rock's debut in Argentina, the rockers' "com-munity" did not preclude aesthetic and cultural differences. Rock fans and artists in the late 1970s built up a sense of community through appealing to a common past. Exchanging records was an occasion for sharing stories about rock *nacional*, which allowed for the creation of intercohort bonds that surfaced, for example, in 1980, when youths in their twenties and others in their teens crowded stadiums to attend reunion concerts of two legendary bands, Almendra and Manal (both disbanded in 1970). Secret po-lice agents monitored Spinetta's former quartet prior to authorizing them to perform. While Córdoba province police evaluated that "the damage that Almendra can create for youth through the promotion of drugs and sensuality" was too serious to allow them to play, officers with the Buenos Aires police disagreed and the quartet performed in La Plata and Mar del Plata, to the joy of thirty thousand people.[78] Many of them then attended the concerts of Almendra's former archrival, namely, the trio Manal. The organizer of the event, Pedro Pujó, recalls that they took advantage of the "little window opened in late 1979" to infuse "rock *nacional* with new force." In the attempts to reinvigorate rock culture, then, rockers looked back to create a sense of community, postponing "old and silly disputes."[79] Yet the "little window" also allowed new bands to form, and spots to play proliferated in 1978 and 1979. These marginal experiences paved the way for the emergence of would-be major bands (such as Patricio Rey y sus Re-donditos de Ricota) and for the chance to appreciate novelties: punk, ska, and reggae. Equally important, these experiences incited discussions of the "commercial" versus the "alternative" so central to the countercultural practices articulated in relation to rock.[80]

Overtly countercultural practices related to rock culture had a major forum: the monthly *Expreso Imaginario*. First appearing in August of 1976, *Expreso Imaginario* played a key role in the making of a countercultural "we." As other scholars have noted, the profusely illustrated and well-edited monthly led by poet Pipo Lernoud and journalist Jorge Pistocchi could intelligently sidestep censorship because it avoided references to politics and sexuality. When assuming a critical stance, it did so in tacit ways: for example, there is no reference whatsoever to the 1978 Soccer World Championship when many Argentines went crazy about the event.[81] Political in its own terms, *Expreso Imaginario* reached in 1978 a readership of fifteen thousand people attracted, perhaps, not only to the rock section of the monthly but also to its "Practical Guide to Living on this Earth," which included macrobiotics and yoga as venues for creating alternatives to a "system" deemed physically and psychically oppressive. "Alternative" was also the qualifier for all other practices the magazine endorsed, ranging from communal living and independent journalism to ecological tourism.[82] The dichotomy "alternative" versus "system" pervaded the readers' pages as well. As Vila has superbly analyzed, those pages motivated the desire of youth to develop a community—however virtual it was. As happened with Eduardo's friends, who talked endlessly about music and exercised their abilities to discuss and criticize, the readers' pages were forums to define the ideal world for the "we" they helped create. The letter writers wanted an "authentic" world, rid of hierarchies and inequalities. Unlike previous eras in rock culture, for example, young women did not only participate as members in their own right but some of them openly criticized their male peers for being machistas.[83] Young women and men, most fundamentally, delineated the parameters of belonging to an "authentic" world by rejecting the authoritarianism of the "system" embedded in the figure of the *careta* (masked).

In the late 1970s, the term *careta* entered the lexicon of youths involved in rock culture to pejoratively refer to most of their generational peers, whom they dubbed as conformist, submissive to the "system," and superficial. In 1978, after the release of *Saturday Night Fever* (dir. John Badham, 1977), *careta* was the term used to describe the qualities of the movie's main character, John Travolta's Tony Manero: a responsible and submissive worker on weekdays, whose identity was played out in how he dressed up, danced, and consumed during the weekends. Writing the movie's critical comment, Pipo Lernoud depicted the "Saturday-Night-Fever" mood as "a contagious temperature of cerebral drowsiness dancing to the rhythm of modern consumption." A quintessential counter-figure to *Expreso Imaginario*'s culture, Lernoud understood that the fictional Manero embodied an entire generation that "is totally sold out."[84] Drawing on metaphors resonating in rock cultures worldwide, Lernoud—and, surely, many of the magazine's readers—believed that there was not a "we" sweeping across a generation, since one segment was "sold out" to a system that, in Argentina, inevitably evoked political overtones. In that respect, the figure of the superficial youth, the *caretas*, acquired new meanings. In the memories of a former student at the Law School of the UBA, it was "packed with *caretas*." When I asked what she understood by the term, she said: "the *caretas* were guys interested in the little things and who would never, but never, question anything: they did not care." In Marcela's memories, "they did not care" about "the content of the classes, the arbitrariness of the school, politics: they were the product of the *no te metás* [don't get involved] ideology."[85] The *careta* represented submission to "the system," which in late 1970s Argentina involved some degree of tolerance or tacit complicity with the military and the repression it embodied.

While the *careta* epitomized cultural superficiality, the figure also invoked the obstacles that politicized young people faced in organizing their generational peers. In mid-1980, some university and secondary school students in Buenos Aires, Rosario, and Córdoba might have had a chance to read the mimeographed periodical *Jotapé* (an acronym for Juventud Peronista or Peronist Youth). While during the early 1970s Peronist Youth did not explicitly discuss what "youth" meant—imagined as a homogeneous category—now *Jotapé* did so. Like *Expreso Imaginario*'s writers, those for *Jotapé* also viewed "youth" as divided into two halves, which they identified as the "revolutionary" and the "Pitman youth"—made of "thousands of *caretas*." Pitman was a chain of schools that offered one- or two-year degrees to prepare students for jobs as office clerks. As the recipient of a bad-quality education that promised material success, *Jotapé* noted, the Pitman youth had interiorized "what the military want from us: submission and individualism."[86] Although *Jotapé* was confident in the "revolutionary youth," who would help others overcome their own "passivity and conformity," former youth militants recall how difficult it was. Marcelo, for example, participated in the group that made *Jotapé* upon his return from exile in Mexico. A former member of the UES, he could barely believe how, "with such short notice, the regime had created a lobotomized youth." He recalls especially the political work that young Peronists did to "resuscitate the youth movement" in the context of openness initiated under General Roberto Viola's presidency (March to December, 1981), overlooking that other political forces had continued activating for most of the dictatorship.[87]

However successful they were in their efforts, some political forces took advantage of their semi-legal status to try to organize youth. While the Peronist Youth was almost dismantled (and, tragically, its militants were the bulk of the "disappeared"), the pro-Radical Franja Morada and the Federación Juvenil Comunista (FJC, Communist Youth Federation) kept working. The FJC went a step further. Since the Communist Party initially understood that the coup d'état had been carried out by the "most democratic sectors of the military," it attempted to promote a dialogue between young military officers and Communists via the weekly *Vamos*. Looking back from today's vantage point, one historian of the FJC deems the project as "embarrassing," and surely it was. At the same time that the army led state terrorism, for example, *Vamos* published a five-page interview with an adviser to President Videla, who argued that the government favored youth and was setting the stage for "a truly democratic new generation."[88] Regardless of their efforts in courting the military, the Communist rank-and-file was also persecuted. In a climate of generalized fear, the leader of the Communist secondary school students noted, the FJC had ceased to incorporate new members in August of 1976, a situation that began to change only by early 1978. In that year, in some schools in Buenos Aires and Rosario, the FJC started to create school committees to discuss with the authorities the selection of textbooks that were "too expensive" and to organize inter-school sport championships.[89] Full-fledged by the early 1980s, the school committees and the sort of activities they endorsed represented the only possibilities of gathering that the interested students had. One former secondary school student from the Greater Buenos Aires area recalls that soccer championships "were occasions to meet and address other things as well," including "information on more closed political meetings."[90]

Politicized youth, rockers, *caretas*: all coalesced in the mobilization ignited by the Malvinas War, from April to June of 1982. Scholars and observers alike have largely discussed the reasons why the regime, and chiefly the third junta led by General Leopoldo Galtieri (1981–82), decided to wage a war to claim Argentina's sovereignty over the islands. Most scholars agree that the military, cornered by human rights denunciations abroad and facing rising economic and political dilemmas at home that corroded its legitimacy, tried to regain momentum in proving itself capable of doing what the military always does (waging wars) and had a chance of gathering popular support for a cause that had long incited patriotic fervor. As soon as the invasion made the news, the regime collected demonstrations of support from the entire political spectrum and, perhaps for the first and only time, a majority of the population showed its willingness to participate in such an endeavor.[91] Youth, and chiefly young men, came to occupy the center stage. At the same time that a human rights organization publicized that at least 120 young men had been "disappeared" while fulfilling conscription in the period 1976–81, in mid-April of 1982 the military drafted 9,500 conscripts to go to the battlefront. Many of these eighteen-year olds, regardless of their political and cultural backgrounds, in a spirit of patriotism proudly accepted the mission assigned—at least until they reached the islands and found that the scarce food and clothing went to the officers, and that the chances of winning were almost nil.[92]

In the public culture of those intense months, the conscripts represented just the forerunners of a youth willing to defend the fatherland. The regime and the dominant media revamped the representations of youth, a category associated with traditional notions of self-sacrifice, idealism, and patriotism. Those actors projected onto the youth of the 1980s their own apparent success in instilling national values and respect for hierarchies and authority in the new generations, which appeared to be confirmed in other initiatives as well. During the war, rock impresarios and artists convened to assemble a mega festival titled "of Latin American solidarity." Carefully avoiding any direct association with the regime, rockers nevertheless collaborated with the "war effort," showing their solidarity with the conscripts. Like most of Argentina's citizenry, rockers onstage and off chanted against the British and, ironically, called for peace. When the news began to report the successive blows and the pro-regime media could not hide the disaster anymore, that pacifism turned into antidictatorship positions. The same conjuncture when the regime endowed youth with the task of "saving" the nation was the one that ended with the military's dreams of eternity. The military could not demonstrate any prowess on the battlefront, and their attempts at renewing their popularity failed badly. The military leaders did not pay the price of the attempts either: 650 out of the 800 dead in the battlefronts were eighteen-year-old conscripts.[93]

▶ In one of his most intuitive essays, the political scientist Guillermo O'Donnell claims that the last military dictatorship worked alongside a society that "patrolled itself." The authoritarian conception of authority, O'Donnell posits, was not exclusive of the state: dispersed in "micro-contexts," those who occupied positions of command at all levels of social life (family, schools, hospitals) were called on to enlist their efforts in reconstituting hierarchies and discipline. Produced in the wake of the dictatorship, O'Donnell's piece was meant to invite a reflection on the role of myriad social actors who welcomed and eventually benefited from a "macro" context, or framework, that allowed for unleashing the crudest forms of authoritarianism.[94] As provocative as it is, however, this piece leaves one key interpretative dimension intact: that project was neither initiated in 1976 nor acted out within a historical vacuum.

By focusing on the role that, both discursively and politically, youth had in the "authority-reconstitution" project, this chapter proposes that, strictly speaking, it started before the imposition of the military coup d'état. Already in 1974, leading conservative actors related to the Catholic Church and right-wing Peronism came to occupy prominent positions in decision-making bodies and "legally" set limits to the political activism, sociability, and sexuality associated with youth milieus. In their initiatives, these actors did not only have the blessing of broad segments of the media but also, seemingly, of increasingly larger portions of Argentina's citizenry who clamored for "order" in all spheres of social life. As it happened with the groups of neighbors from Buenos Aires and Comodoro Rivadavia, most identified youth as the carrier of multiple disorders. They projected onto youth their condemnation of the dynamics of sociocultural modernization that unfolded throughout the 1960s, blamed as responsible for the relaxation of mores, values, and hierarchies. The military represented their project as the most suitable to put an end to those chaos-generating dynamics. In this respect, they and the people that joined their "authority-reconstitution" endeavor were producing a dialogue with their immediate past and building a bridge with a romanticized era temporarily located in the first half of the twentieth century when, they imagined, "things were not out of place."

The enforcement of that past-oriented, reactionary project was based upon the *pax* of the clandestine detention centers, which permeated society at large and the ranks of young people in particular. Fear, political demobilization, and cultural restrictions configured the coordinates for the socialization of a new generation, allegedly free from the "subversive" ideas and practices of the past. Yet neither were historical breaks easily implemented nor the "authority-reconstitution" project completely imposed—however dispersed and accepted it was across "micro" and "macro" levels. While political groups kept acting in student milieus according to their limited possibilities, rockers and young people attracted to countercultural practices strove to create a sense of community based on the appeal of a common past that did not register in the post-1976 divide. The past associated with the libertarian and revolutionary movements of the 1960s and early 1970s was simply too close to produce a definitive break. The military tried hard, though, and in some respects, they achieved major success. Education, for example, would never recover the socially democratizing sheen that it had had up until the 1960s. Political activism and its connection with youth and change, moreover, would lose its utopian meanings, gone with the (youthful) bodies of thousands of people.

Conclusion

Soon after the imposition of the military junta in 1976, diverse organizations domestically and abroad started campaigning to denounce the massive, state-led violation of human rights. These organizations publicized the implementation of the mechanisms of kidnapping, torturing, and "disappearing" thousands of people. Amnesty International and the Argentine Commission on Human Rights abroad, the Argentine League for Human Rights and the incipient Mothers of Plaza de Mayo at home, all produced rosters listing "disappeared" people. They organized the rosters by occupational criteria (like disappeared lawyers or university students) and demographic data, including one of "disappeared adolescents." Both during the dictatorship and immediately after the resumption of democratic rule in 1983, human rights organizations downplayed the political commitments of the victims of state terrorism to focus on other aspects of their biographies.[1] Their appealing to age markers, notably of youth and adolescence, symbolically mobilized notions of innocence, idealism, and virtue.

In the aftermath of the dictatorship, the imagery surrounding the "young victim" galvanized public attention. A key example was the sweeping impact of the movie *La noche de los lápices* (The Night of the Pencils, dir. Héctor Olivera, 1985), which depicts the "true story" of ten secondary school boys and girls from La Plata, most of them affiliated with a Peronist youth group, all kidnapped from their homes on September 16, 1976. The movie and the two pieces on which it is based (a chapter of the Report of the National Committee on Disappeared People titled *Never Again* and María Seoane and Héctor Ruiz Núñez's journalistic essay of the same name) blurred the political dimension of their young lives and deaths, perhaps aiming at inciting a particular sort of public indignation. Since *La noche de los lápices* represented a lethal regime coming from nowhere to murder idealist adolescents, viewers could feel horror but rest in peace:

they had not had "anything to do" with what they saw. But the military regime did not come from nowhere and both built upon and heightened a widespread demand for "order" perhaps shared in 1976 by many of the viewers of the movie.[2] While it continued to permeate memory writings in the 1990s (through the romanticization of the "idealistic youth"), the building of the "young victim" as a strategic trope was fundamentally a product of the 1980s in both public culture and human rights activism.[3] That may have sensitized the population to dictatorial crimes, but it did little to captivate the historical dimensions of state terrorism whose main victims were defined less by their—certainly young—age than by their involvement in revolutionary militancy.

The last military regime, however, did mark an end to an age in which youth, as a category evoking change, and young people as actors had come to occupy the center stage. I would like to come back to the first moment when youth began to rise in the public arena as a device that helped shape the discussion of the scope, limits, and characteristics of the dynamics of sociocultural modernization in Argentina. Youth as a category gained ascendancy along with the collective perception that post-Peronist Argentina underwent a critical juncture marked by rapid political, social, and cultural change, a time of sweeping instability of institutions, values, and norms, which sociologists and the media, among others, encapsulated in the phrase "crisis of our time." In that context, myriad actors (Catholic leagues, psychological professionals, the media, and educators) maneuvered with the category of youth they were helping craft. Intensified in the voices of the Catholic leagues, one position conceived of youth as the epitome of the disorders that the "crisis" entailed in terms of the erosion of patriarchal authority; other voices, dominant in the public sphere, believed that youth had the potential to expunge authoritarianism from the familial, cultural, and eventually political milieus. As the psychological professionals repeatedly stated, through living their individual, "biologically based crisis" at a critical social and cultural time, young people would help erase the harsher forms of patriarchy and other "atavisms" and taboos. The category of youth was a key to discuss the future, an argument dominated by a paradoxical attitude toward change, both feared and, seemingly, longed for.

How did young people interact with the "change" that they, or the category they inhabited, symbolized in the public imagination? In reconstructing the daily experiences of young men and, chiefly, young women by looking at different milieus where they took place (families, schools, leisure spaces, political and cultural groups) and by looking at them through a gendered prism, it was possible to illuminate how embattled sociocultural change was. These findings complicate the usual narratives of a "society pushing for change" suffering from top-down "authoritarian blockades," which have pervaded the scholarly assessment of the Argentine 1960s. It is worth recalling, hence, the moral panic around the runaway girls early in that decade. In a heightened, dramatic fashion, that panic made apparent one central occurrence: it was young women who more fully embodied and shaped sociocultural modernization. They practically contested prevalent ideas of domesticity and destabilized deep-seated notions of patriarchal authority by remaining longer in the education system, fully participating in the labor market, helping shape entirely youthful leisure activities, and experimenting with new courtship conventions. The moral panic, which arose around the Penjerek case of 1963, stemmed from daily tensions that those changes in young women's expectations and experiences had generated in the familial and cultural milieus (that is, not from a "blockade" from above). That panic as well as successive "morality campaigns" served as occasions when a wide range of actors (Catholic leagues, for sure, but also myriad "unaffiliated" parents, cultural producers, and politicians) attempted to discipline young women and men by decreasing the autonomy that they were gradually gaining and thus recover what they regarded as their vanishing authority.

Unintentionally, that moral panic of the early 1960s also served to catapult discussions about youth and sexuality into the spotlight, making visible emerging attitudes and practices. The cohorts of women who came of age in the 1960s were the first ones to gradually voice their approval of premarital sex in the public arena, and—like many young men—they did so in the framework of a discourse connecting sex with love and responsibility, which represented the novelty as "modern" and prudent at the same time. In many respects, the young women and men who came to occupy the category of youth in the late 1960s and early 1970s built on the effects of these previous challenges to prevalent familial and sexual arrangements. As the debate over the extinction of the *piba de barrio* suggested, in the early 1970s middle- and working-class young women did not face the same degree of parental controls that their predecessors did, although it bears noting that (as many female political militants recalled) they did not have the same degree of freedom from parental supervision that their male peers had either. Meanwhile, premarital sex had become largely normalized in the broad public culture. An incipient new understanding spread among working- and middle-class youth, namely, the disengagement of sexuality from marriage or its horizon. This implied a relocation of the legitimate site for heterosexuality, which also helped set in motion a conversation about sexual equality and the extent of the persistence of a double standard. The emerging gay rights and feminist groups did denounce that persistence, as well as the development of a "moral of replacement" that ended by making patriarchy and male domination alluring and "sexy." Part of the voices that advocated for a "revolution"—in their case, a noncommodified sexual revolution—these groups were silenced when the "authority-reconstitution" project systematically started in 1974. Besides the imposition of restrictions to the access to contraception—framed in a conservative sexual politics whose practical results were uneven—in the sexual realm the "authority-reconstitution" project did not mark a shift. On this terrain, times had certainly changed.

In the late 1960s, however, what changed the most had been the ways in which many young women and men articulated a vocal, iconoclastic, and multilayered culture of contestation, which called into question different dimensions of the dynamics of sociocultural modernization. One of the avenues for that articulation was rock culture. Unlike the contestations to patriarchal authority and domesticity that young women and girls had produced since the late 1950s, the middle- and working-class young men attracted to rock culture produced an overtly oppositional questioning of the hegemonic construction of masculinity. Rockers' cultural politics revolved almost entirely around their criticism of the sites, institutions, and values that punctuated the boys-will-be-men dynamics in 1960s Argentina, including sobriety, responsibility, respect for hierarchies, and consumerism. Rockers' questioning was eminently practical and embedded into the bodily styles and daily practices through which they created a homosocial fraternity of long-haired boys. That fraternity incited an intense homophobic reaction when it erupted in the public arena, which conditioned the ideological and gendered components of rock culture. On the one hand, that reaction, as epitomized in the form of police and civilian harassment and persecution, helped consolidate antiauthoritarianism as a crucial element of rockers' ideology. On the other hand, the permanent threat of repression to rockers' cultural practices contributed to reinforce the perception that this was a male-only territory, unsuitable even for the young women who wanted to engage with it. Equally important, the exclusion of young women was also reinforced by a powerful misogynistic strand that cut across rock culture, which perhaps enabled rockers to symbolically assert their senses of masculinity while counter-ing the "homosexual blackmail" to which they were subjected. Yet it was within the countercultures connected to rock whereby some young men, and women, deployed their radical versions of gender egalitarianism. Lim-ited in their constituency and cultural impact, those experiences repre-sented one visible refusal to the modernizing expectations, heightening the anticonsumerism and antiauthoritarianism that swept across rock and its politics of cultural, while gendered, rebellion.

Rock culture was only one strand of the youth culture of contestation that burgeoned in the late 1960s and early 1970s. While there was a broad gray zone for their intersection, rock culture and revolutionary politics remained separate constellations of discourse and practice aimed at in-terpellating youth. However, viewed from the vantage point of the "age of youth" these can be connected as two strands of the vocal youth cul-ture of contestation. First, both strands contributed to the recrafting of the category of youth in public culture, associated ever more with radical change and cultural rebellion. Second, these two strands shared a lexicon of contestation, although rockers and revolutionary militants produced different meanings out of the keywords of that lexicon, "liberation" and "revolution." In Argentina, as these two key terms spread among young women and men, they signaled the expansion of the "properly political" subset of that youth culture of contestation. The youth that made up the base of Argentina's "New Left" in the early 1970s, neither viewed rock-ers' cultural politics as political nor thought seriously about their claims for expunging capillary forms of authoritarianism, as rockers proposed, even when they enjoyed cultural practices related to rock. Although from today's viewpoint we can conflate those strands as part of a "New Left," as historian Eric Zolov has proposed based on 1960s Mexico, the case of Ar-gentina shows that contemporaries drew a clear line between the cultural rebellion attached to rock and the countercultures and the quest for radi-cal sociopolitical change permeating the revolutionary militancy.[4]

The cohorts of young people that massively engaged with revolution-ary politics brought two key novelties that helped solidify the "newness" of the Left: the certainty that Argentina was part of the Third World and a willingness to *poner el cuerpo* in order to accelerate the political times for a revolution that many thought was impending. The association of Argen-tina with the Third World entailed a practical and ideological questioning of the narratives of modernization, chiefly the portrayal of Argentina as undergoing a homogenizing, socially democratizing, and forward-looking process toward social improvement. Being themselves the outcome of modernization, most youth in the process of becoming revolutionary militants emphasized instead the markers of the country's Third World status—the enduring and extreme social oppression, the regional and social inequalities, and the dependent nature of Argentina's economy and culture, for example. That project was predicated on the practical engagement with the geographical markers of Argentina's Third World nature (as youths who traveled to the northwestern regions of the country soon discovered) and with renewed cultural consumption, including reading, musical, and even fashion practices. The encounters with those cultural practices and, chiefly, with those geographies and their inhabitants were incorporated into a new emotional frame dominated by feelings such as indignation and hatred, which propelled many young people to "act." Along with these cultural and literal displacements, politicizing young women and men who were usually secondary school or university students tried to erase the markers of their youthfulness and their student condition to merge into the broader "people." Although they replicated similar developments worldwide, those participating in the Argentine May of 1969, for example, insisted on their originality vis-à-vis their European counterparts, who they viewed as politically self-centered and ultimately naïve. These claims remind us that even amid one of the most transnational junctures in the twentieth century ("1968"), events, interpretations, and actions were encoded into national or regional categories and preoccupations.[5] The Argentine May marked the beginning of mounting youth politicization, framed into a profound discontent with political authoritarianism and with social modernization. In the view of politicizing young people, that juncture acted as a reminder of the apparent need to prepare one's body and put it at the service of a revolutionary project to hasten political times and speed up social and national "liberation."

Peronism as a political force had both informed and benefited most from young people's politicization. It was in this realm where youth was most forcefully framed as a legitimate political category and where young people sought to find a bridge to "connect with the people." As a political category it reflected the increasing amounts of radicalized young people who entered en masse the ranks of the Juventud Peronista or its related organizations via their identification with the Montoneros. In the Peronist family romance that started when Juan Perón returned definitively to the country in mid-1973, the deployment of generational-based language allowed for the positioning of the revolutionary sectors (whether composed of young people or not) as "youth." The ideological and political disputes in that force carried heightened cultural and political meanings when coded as familial ones. Toward 1974, when the resolution of the family romance occurred, not only the revolutionary sectors (whether Peronist or not, whether young or not) but also youth at large would suffer from the "authority-reconstitution project" that the right-wing sectors (the "elder" in the family romance) unleashed. The passing of legislation on contraception and so-called illegal drugs as well as the restrictions on political activism in schools and universities, all pointed to the production of a figure of an "enemy within" that had a young face and conflated ideas of sexual, cultural, and political disorder.

One way or another, all the preceding chapters showed that between the midcentury and the mid-1970s, youth as a category, and young people as actors, stood at the center of discussions, and questionings, on how relations of authority were thought of, built up, and enforced at the familial, cultural, and political terrains. The enforcement of authority and hierarchies in the relations between parents and children, between women and men, between teachers and students, between high and popular culture, between the state and its (young) citizens, between the body and the "mind," all of them were called into question, often simultaneously. Youth offered a window to look at those questionings and to assess their multilayered effects on Argentina' society and culture. Over these two decades, youth stood for change, and the cohorts of young women and men that occupied that category experimented and crafted cultural, political, and sexual change. They were the last cohorts that embodied the dreams of generations of Argentines vis-à-vis the attainment of social and cultural improvement (for example, through ascending the educational ladder), dreams nurturing the image of an "exceptional" country amid its Latin American neighbors (a nation that was supposedly richer, whiter, and opener). When politicizing youth questioned those dreams and focused instead on collective projects of radical political change for Third World Argentina, they rejected the country's "exceptionalism" and, ironically, anticipated what the "authority-reconstitution" project accomplished.[6] The military junta came to put an end to those dreams and to most modernizing dynamics, including the dismantling of the education system as a ladder to social mobility.

In many respects, in amplifying the "authority-reconstitution" project initiated in 1974, the junta responded to the perception that, over the prior decades, youth had brought destabilizing (meaning disorderly and chaotic) effects to Argentina's politics, culture, and society. The regime was not isolated in that perception, since millions of anonymous Argentines believed the same in 1976, and—as political scientist Guillermo O'Donnell suggested—seemed willing to sympathize with initiatives that allowed them to reconstruct their "vanishing authority" at the most intimate levels of the family or the school.[7] The military certainly met opposition, in political and countercultural venues alike, although not all youth responded in the same way to attempts by the regime to discipline that segment of the population. Notwithstanding the thousands assassinated as victims of state terrorism, "authority-reconstitution" was an incomplete project. It was successful in one point, though: the "age of youth" reached an end when the words "order" and "chaos" replaced "change" in its attachment to the category of youth.

Notes

Abbreviations

AAF-BN	Archivo Arturo Frondizi, Biblioteca Nacional
AGN	Archivo General de la Nación
AICA	Agencia Informativa Católica Argentina
AO-UBA	Archivo Oral de la Universidad de Buenos Aires
CBS	Columbia Broadcasting System
CEDINCI	Centro de Documentación e Investigación de la Cultura de Izquierda
CEHPFA	Centro de Estudios Históricos de la Policía Federal Argentina
CENIDE	Centro Nacional de Información Documental Educativa
CGT	Confederación General del Trabajo
CNNAF	Consejo Nacional de la Niñez, Adolescencia y Familia
DIPPBA	Dirección de Inteligencia de la Policía de la Provincia de Buenos Aires
FLH	Archivo del Frente de Liberación Homosexual
FYL	Facultad de Filosofía y Letras Archive
JVGA	Instituto del Profesorado J. V. González Archive
JWT	John Walter Thompson Company Archives, John Hartman Center for Sales, Advertising, and Marketing History, Duke University
LMF	Liga de Madres de Familia Archive
MPDH	Museo Pablo Ducrós Hicken Archive
OPJ	Obra de Protección de la Joven Archive
PCA	Partido Comunista Argentino Archive
RCA	Radio Corporation of America
RECEM	*Revista de la Escuela de Comando y Estado Mayor de la Fuerza Aérea Argentina*
SISBI-UBA	Biblioteca del Sistema de Información y Bibliotecas, University de Buenos Aires

Introduction

1. "Informe sobre la juventud," *Confirmado* No. 65, September 15, 1966, 34–37.

2. For reformism as a cultural and political identity for the "progressive" middle classes, see Sigal, *Intelectuales y poder*, 63–80; for general accounts of the University Reform Movement in 1920s and 1930s Argentina, see Biagini, *La Reforma Universitaria*.

3. For the transnational reverberations of that figure, see Modern Girl around the World Research Group, "The Modern Girl"; for Buenos Aires, see Cecilia Tossounian, "The Argentine Modern Girl."

4. For a vivid picture of the *petiteros*'s sociability and fashion, see Goldar, *Buenos Aires*; for insights into sociability in social clubs as it is related to football, see Archetti, *Masculinities*.

5. For those metaphorical capabilities, see Passerini, "Youth as a Metaphor for Social Change."

6. Torre, "A partir del Cordobazo," 21.

7. Cattaruzza, "El mundo por hacer."

8. For the pioneering psychological and anthropological studies of adolescence and youth, see Hall, "Initiation into Adolescence"; and Margaret Mead, *Coming of Age in Samoa*. For an overview of social science discourse on youth, see Bucholtz, "Youth and Cultural Practice."

9. Mintz, "Reflections on Age."

10. Mannheim, "The Problem of Generations," 291.

11. See, for example, Sirinelli, *Les baby boomers*; Austin and Willard, *Generations of Youth*; Roseman, *Generations in Conflict*. For a discussion of the heuristic validity of "youth" vs. "generation," which informed my own reflections, see Jobs, *Riding the New Wave*, 7–9.

12. Medovoi, *Rebels*, 216.

13. David Viñas offers his portrayal of that "frustrated generation" in his novel *Dar la cara*.

14. Gillis, *Youth and History*; Fass, *The Damned and the Beautiful*.

15. See Torre and Pastoriza, "La democratización del bienestar."

16. Jobs, *Riding the New Wave*.

17. For discussions of youth and sexuality in British Canada and Tanzania, see Adams, *The Trouble with Normal*; and Ivaska, "Anti-Mini Militants Meet Modern Misses."

18. Herzog, *Sex after Fascism*; Sohn, *Âge tendre*; Bailey, *Sex in the Heartland*.

19. Cosse, *Pareja, sexualidad y familia*.

20. Herzog, *Sex after Fascism*, 153–70; Collins, *Modern Love*, 134–60.

21. Parsons, "Age and Sex," 89–102.

22. Fowler, *Youth Culture in Modern Britain*, 126–36; Gorgolini, "Il Consumi"; Osgerby, *Youth in Great Britain*, 30–49; Palladino, *Teenagers*, 97–115; Sohn, *Âge tendre*, 79–90.

23. I take the notion of the transnational as "units that spill over and seep through national borders" from Seigel, "Beyond Compare."

24. For Mexico, Brazil, and Chile, respectively, see Zolov, *Refried Elvis*; Dunn, *Brutality Garden*; and Barr-Melej, "Siloísmo and the Left in Allende's Chile." Two recent doctoral dissertations are in the process of becoming books: Barbosa, "Insurgent Youth," and Langland, "Speaking of Flowers."

25. See especially O'Donnell, *Bureaucratic Authoritarianism*; De Riz, *La política en suspenso*; and Altamirano, *Bajo el signo de las masas*.

26. Hilb and Lutzky, *La nueva izquierda argentina*; Terán, *Nuestros años sesenta*; Sigal, *Intelectuales y poder*; Altamirano, *Peronismo y cultura de izquierda*.

27. Among the most important, see Brennan, *Labor Wars in Cordoba*; Gordillo, *Córdoba en los '60*; Pucciarelli, *La primacía de la política*. For the histories of the most prominent guerrilla groups and their connected political branches, see Gillespie, *Soldiers of Perón*; Sigal and Verón, *Perón o muerte*; Pozzi, *Por las sendas argentinas*.

28. See especially Vezzetti, *Sobre la violencia revolucionaria* and *Pasado y presente*; the essay on Montoneros in Sarlo, *La pasión y la excepción*; and Calveiro, *Política y/o violencia*.

29. Sorensen, *A Turbulent Decade Remembered*, 7.

30. King, *El Di Tella*; Sigal, *Intelectuales y poder*; Castagna, "La generación del 60"; Longoni and Mestman, *Del Di Tella a "Tucumán Arde"*; Sarlo, *La batalla de las ideas*; Giunta, *Vanguardia, internacionalismo y política*; Gilman, *Entre la pluma y el fusil*; Aguilar, "La generación del 60."

31. Pujol, *La década rebelde*; Podalsky, *Specular City*; Varela, *La televisión criolla*.

32. Feijóo and Nari, "Women in Argentina during the 1960s"; Nari, "Abrir los ojos, abrir la cabeza"; Vasallo, "Movilización, política y orígenes"; Barrancos, *Mujeres en la sociedad argentina*; Felitti, "La revolución de la píldora"; Cosse, *Pareja, sexualidad y familia*.

Chapter 1

1. Telma Reca de Acosta, "Las jóvenes generaciones en un mundo de cambios acelerados," *Revista de la Universidad de Buenos Aires* 7.3 (July–September 1962): 405.

2. Torre and Pastoriza, "La democratización del bienestar," 298–99; Ministerio de Educación y Justicia, *La enseñanza media (1914–63)*, vol. 1, 58–59, 283.

3. David Wiñar, "Aspectos sociales del desarrollo educativo argentino, 1900–1970," *Revista del Centro de Estudios Educativos* No. 4 (September 1974): 14.

4. Dussel and Pineau, "De cuando la clase obrera entró al paraíso," 107–43.

5. Carli, *Niñez, pedagogía y política*, 305–6; Rein, *Politics and Education in Argentina*, 51–52; Caimari, *Perón y la Iglesia Católica*, 281–82; Plotkin, *Mañana es San Perón*, 163–64; Leonard, *Politicians, Pupils, and Priests*, 132.

6. Torre, Introduction to *Nueva Historia Argentina*, 8:58.

7. Koon, *Believe, Obey, Fight*, 148–51.

8. *Perón y la juventud*, 9, 21.

9. Juan Domingo Perón, "Mensaje Presidencial a la Asamblea Legislativa," *Diario de Sesiones de la Cámara de Diputados* No. 1, May 1, 1955, 18, 26–27.

10. "Mensaje a la juventud," *Mundo Peronista* No. 86, May 15, 1955, 28.

11. "Inauguró hoy las monumentales obras de la UES," *La Razón*, January 16, 1954, 1.

12. The CGU was created in 1950 and opened chapters in most faculties. In 1954, a survey of the faculty of engineering at the University of Buenos Aires showed that the reformist center had 4,000 members and the CGU only 200. See Walter, *Student Politics in Argentina*, 139.

13. Mangone and Warley, *Universidad y peronismo*, 10–38, Kleiner, *20 años de movimiento estudiantil reformista*, 103–19.

14. "¡Vayan a bañarse!," *Mundo Peronista* No. 48, August 15, 1953, 13.

15. Acha and Ben, "Amorales, patoteros, chongos y pitucos."

16. "Una residencia presidencial para los estudiantes," *Mundo Peronista* No. 45, July 15, 1953, 35–36; "El regalo del General para las estudiantas," *Mundo Peronista* No. 51, October 1, 1953, 25–28; "Una nueva sede para estudiantes," *Mundo Peronista* No. 55, December 1, 1953, 7–9.

17. "Una juventud que se maneja a sí misma," *Mundo Peronista* No. 56, December 15, 1953, 10; "Gracias a Perón y a Eva Perón vemos cristalizados nuestros sueños," *Mundo Peronista* No. 58, January 15, 1954, 21.

18. "La UES es la Nueva Argentina," *Mundo Peronista* No. 78, December 15, 1954, 18.

19. Ibid.; see also Santiago Giralt's nonfiction novel, *Nelly R.*; and Kriger, *Cine y peronismo*.

20. "La Residencia Presidencial, sede de una alegre estudiantina," *Esto Es* No. 11, February 9, 1954, 6–9.

21. *La Unión de Estudiantes Secundarios* (Buenos Aires: Secretaría de Prensa y Difusión, 1955), 15–19; "La fiesta de la UES," *Mundo Peronista* No. 68, July 15, 1954, 26–29.

22. Scarzanella, "El ocio peronista," 65–85.

23. For a vivid description of the dance halls, see Goldar, *Buenos Aires*, 139–40.

24. Ads appeared in *La Razón*, February 28, 1954, 2, and March 2, 1954, 3. On the habit of drinking Coke, see Goldar, *Buenos Aires*, 24.

25. "Recibió el saludo de un grupo de estudiantes de todo el país," *La Razón*, March 4, 1954, 3.

26. Bianchi, *Catolicismo y Peronismo*, 149–67; Caimari, *Perón y la Iglesia Católica*, 292–310.

27. "Los estudiantes somos y seremos libres" and "El Tero No. 44," in Lafiandra, *Los panfletos*, 173–74, 185.

28. "¡Estudiante!," in Lafiandra, *Los panfletos*,, 235–36.

29. "La doctrina peronista ante la reacción político clerical," *Mundo Peronista* No. 76, November 15, 1954, 10–11; "¿Qué está haciendo Perón con la UES?," in Lafiandra, *Los panfletos*, 181.

30. Marcilese, *30 días en la UES*, 13–15, 27, 61, 144–48.

31. The president was Dr. Carolina Tobar García, a renowned childhood psychiatrist, and the three secretaries were Gilda Lamarque, who would become one of the organizers of the School of Education at the UBA, Carmen Aguirre de Victoria—her husband, Marcos, was appointed as the first chair of the Psychology

Department at the UBA—and Delfina de Ghioldi, the wife of Américo Ghioldi, a Socialist Party leader. See *Casos de la Segunda Tiranía: La UES*, 6.

32. *Libro Negro de la Segunda Tiranía*, 137, 9.

33. Comisión Provincial por la Memoria (Area Archivo), Public Interview with former Conintes prisoners (1955–63), La Plata, May 30, 2008. I thank Laura Elhrich for sharing this source with me.

34. Poder Ejecutivo Nacional, "Decreto No. 7625: Crease la materia 'Educación Democrática,'" *Boletín Oficial*, December 30, 1955, 6, 36–43.

35. For the emergence of a Peronist Youth identity and militancy in the late 1950s, see especially Elhrich, *Rebeldes, intransigentes y duros*, Chapter 3.

36. The description and calculation is based on *La Razón*, from January 1, 1958, to December 30, 1961. *La Razón* used to transcribe the contents of those events, and it sold an average of 450,000 copies a day, according to the Instituto Verificador de Circulaciones, *Diarios*, 1960, 1965, 1970.

37. Germani, *Política y sociedad*, 233–34; on the work of Germani and his idea of crisis, see Blanco, *Razón y modernidad*, 83–186.

38. Germani, *Política y sociedad*, 262–64.

39. Plotkin, *Freud in the Pampas*, 84–85.

40. "Psicología Evolutiva II—Programa 1960," Box 724, File 3756/59 and "Telma Reca de Acosta, 1961," Box 725, File 12965, FYL; Fendrik, *Psicoanalistas de niños*, 3: 61–109.

41. In 1964, the center offered psychological treatments to 1,250 adolescents—a category defining boys and girls between thirteen and twenty-two years old. See Reca, *Temas de psiquiatría y psicología*, 489.

42. Plotkin, *Freud in the Pampas*, 108–14; Cosse, "Argentine Mothers and Fathers," 180–202.

43. Interview with Dr. Eva Giberti. To explain her success, Giberti added that she came as a novelty herself: "a young female professional, mother of a little boy, divorced and re-married with a man who was 25 years older than I was . . . I was the change myself."

44. "El hijo no es un hombre que está solo y espera," *La Razón*, May 22, 1957, 7; "El mundo de la adolescencia", *La Razón*, December 22, 1959, 13; "Actitudes del joven frente a la vida," *Nuestros Hijos* No. 68, September 1960, 8–10; "¿Es su hijo normal?," *Leoplán* No. 656, December 6, 1961, 11.

45. "Los adolescentes actuales y el amor de siempre," *Vosotras* No. 1271, April 14, 1960, 10–11; "La moderna dinámica familiar," *La Razón*, September 9, 1961, 15; "Los años difíciles," *La Razón*, March 21, 1962, 7; "Papá es un hombre antiguo," *La Razón*, June 16, 1963, 11.

46. Medovoi, *Rebels*, 30.

47. On the ways sociologists in the 1950s and 1960s engaged with the study of youth under the lens of "subculture" and "deviancy" theories, see Cohen, *Folk Devils and Moral Panics*; Piccone-Stella, *La prima generazione*; and J. Gilbert, *A Cycle of Outrage*, 127–42.

48. Bianchi, *Catolicismo y peronismo*, 164–6.

49. "Carta de la familia," *Boletín AICA* No. 66, September 13, 1957, 7–8.

50. "El joven vive una etapa intermedia, se refugia en la tierra de nadie y espera que los padres lo ayuden a vivir," *La Razón*, June 17, 1958, 13; "¿Qué pasa con la juventud?," *La Razón*, July 18, 1959, 7; "Academia del amor," *La Razón*, November 11, 1959, 11; "Dimensión de la juventud de hoy," *Nuestros hijos* No. 59, December 1959, 13–15.

51. "Apertura del Congreso Mariano," *Boletín AICA* No. 230, November 5, 1960, 1–5.

52. Barbanti, "Cultura cattolica, lutta anticomunista," 173–90.

53. *Actas de la Escuela para Padres* No. 1, November 2, 1963, n.p., Escuela para Padres File, LMF; *Nuestra Escuela para Padres*, Comité Central File, LMF.

54. *Actas de la Escuela para Padres* Nos. 2 and 3, May 14, 1964 and August 29, 1964, n.p., Escuela para Padres File, LMF.

55. Loaeza, "Mexico in the Fifties," 138–60; McGee Deutsch, "Christians, Homemakers, and Transgressors."

56. *Organización y propósitos*, 1962, Comité Central File, LMF.

57. Altamirano, *Bajo el signo de las masas*, 50–67.

58. Frondizi, *Mensajes presidenciales*, 1: 18, 31.

59. *Consejo Nacional de Protección de Menores: Antecedentes, Ley Orgánica y su reglamentación* (Buenos Aires: Poder Ejecutivo Nacional, 1960), 24, 31, 33. For a history of the institutional developments prior to the Consejo Nacional, see Guy, *Women Build the Welfare State*, 83–119.

60. For the notion of "permissive moment," see Weeks, *Sex, Politics, and Society*, 190–210.

61. Collins, *Modern Love*, 134–60; Herzog, *Sex after Fascism*, 153–60.

62. Jáuregui, *La homosexualidad en la Argentina*, 163–67; Sebreli, *Escritos sobre escritos*, 263–65.

63. "Se pide una medida nacional contra las publicaciones inmorales," *Boletín AICA* No. 99, May 25, 1958, 3; "La campaña de moralización," *Boletín AICA* No. 176, October 23, 1959, 2; "Manifiesto de la juventud de Acción Católica," *Boletín AICA* No. 189, January 1, 1960, 8–9; *Actas del Consejo Nacional de Menores* 2, No. 9, February 25, 1959, 239–40; ibid., No. 30, August 12, 1959, 76–77; ibid., No. 32, August 26, 1959, 26–28; ibid., No. 46, February 26, 1960, 248–51, CNNAF.

64. "El problema de la televisión," *La Razón*, June 8, 1962; "Conclusiones del Primer Seminario sobre la Función Social de la TV," *Criterio* No. 1491, January 13, 1966, 64.

65. "Reglamentación del decreto ley 15460/57," *La Nación*, November 17, 1965, 2.

66. *Actas del Consejo Nacional de Protección de Menores* 1, No. 53, June 6, 1962, 259–61; No. 55, June 27, 1962, 288–90, CNNAF.

67. Poder Ejecutivo Nacional, "Decreto 8205: Creación del Consejo Nacional Honorario de Calificación Cinematorgráfica," *Boletín Oficial*, October 3, 1963, 3.

68. I quote from the notifications that the board sent to distributors, reproduced in Goti Aguilar, *La censura en el cine*, 81, 135.

69. "Coeducación," *Boletín de Informaciones de la Universidad de Buenos Aires* No. 1, May 1958, 7–8.

70. "La coeducación reclama diálogo y experimentación," *La Razón*, June 10,

1958, 7. See also "Encíclica Divinis Illius Magistri," *Revista Eclesiástica Argentina* No. 2, April–May 1958, 60.

71. "El Ministro MacKay recibe a los padres de familia," *La Nación*, June 23, 1958, 6.

72. "En la Escuela Normal No. 4," *Boletín AICA* No. 176, October 23, 1959, 2; "Comunismo en la educación: Liceo 3," *Boletín AICA* No. 178, November 3, 1959, 4.

73. "Informe del estado actual de la Facultad de Filosofía y Letras relacionado con la Escuela Normal No. 4," Box 817, Archivos y Colecciones Particulares, AAF-BN.

74. Eva Giberti, "Las opiniones de los hijos," *La Razón*, November 21, 1960, 13. She came back to the issue in "Cambios en la dinámica familiar," *La Razón*, March 5, 1963, 11.

75. The previous calculation is based on *La Razón*, from January 1, 1962, to December 31, 1965. From 1963 to 1966, Giberti published an average of one and a half columns per week, whereas before she had published three. When I asked her why her column was discontinued, she answered that she did not know exactly but "all in all, the task was done." Interview with Eva Giberti.

76. Aguilar, "La generación del 60," 82–98; Castagna, "La generación del 60"; Feldman, *La generación del sesenta*.

77. Kuhn (1934–1987) narrated his cinematographic interests and influences— including, largely, Antonioni—in several interviews compiled in Peña, *60/90 Generaciones*, 160–63.

78. *Los jóvenes viejos*.

79. Jorge Couselo, "Cierta juventud en un importante film nacional," *El correo de la tarde*, June 6, 1962, 9; Agustín Mahieu, "Los jóvenes viejos," *Tiempo de cine* No. 9, May–July, 1962, 6; Ernesto Schóo, "'Los jóvenes viejos': Triunfo del nuevo cine argentino," *Vea y Lea*, June 13, 1962, 9; "Los jóvenes viejos," *La Prensa*, June 6, 1962, 17; press clippings in "Los jóvenes viejos" Folder, MPDH.

80. Viñas offers his own "testimony" of that frustrated generation in *Dar la cara*; the last quote is on "Un cross a la mandíbula: Reportaje a David Viñas," *Che* No. 7, February 2, 1961, 20.

81. Jaime Potenze, "Superficialidad nuevaolera," *El Principe*, July 1962, 107–8, press clipping in "Los jóvenes viejos," MPDH.

82. Sebreli, *Buenos Aires*, 97.

83. "La juventud, un problema para la juventud," *Che* No. 27, November 3, 1961, 10–11.

84. "Los jóvenes viejos," *Juventud* 14.10, June 25, 1962, 9; "Cosmonautas en Palermo," *Juventud* 17.9, June 15, 1964, 16.

85. Jobs, *Riding the New Wave*, 184–86.

86. On that intellectual generation, see Terán, *Nuestros años sesenta*, 129–49.

87. Alvarado and Rocco-Cuzzi, "'Primera Plana"; Mochkofsky, *Timerman*, 90–143; Podalsky, *Specular City*, 150–63.

88. Sara Gallardo, "Argentina 1980: Entre la incomunicación y el miedo vive la generación del futuro," *Primera Plana* No. 19, March 19, 1963, 22–24.

89. Máximo Simpsom, "Adolescentes 1965: Los hijos de la libertad," *Panorama* No. 25, June 1965, 44–48.

90. "Informe sobre la juventud," *Confirmado* No. 65, September 15, 1966, 34–37.

91. Ibid., 36.

92. "La juventud argentina realiza el segundo congreso de Tucumán," *Panorama* No. 38, June 1966, 38–44.

93. "Los que nacieron aquel día," *Extra* No. 4, October 1965, 62–66.

94. "Los ejércitos del terror," *Panorama* No. 13, June 1964, 30.

95. "Universidad: La dramática alternativa," *Confirmado* No. 26, October 28, 1965, 18–20.

96. Mariano Grondona, "Los jóvenes," *Primera Plana* No. 146, August 24, 1965, 7.

97. Eichelbaum de Babini, *Estatus socioeconómico y crianza de niños*, 89–105.

98. Regina Gibaja, "Actitudes hacia la familia entre los obreros industriales argentinos," *Revista Latinoamericana de Sociología* 3.3 (November 1967): 411–29.

99. "¿El fin de la familia 'nueva ola'?," *Atlántida* No. 1183, September 1965.

100. Grossberg, *We Gotta Get Out of This Place*, 176.

Chapter 2

1. In 1970, a scholar reported 133 pieces of research on the Latin American students, most of them conducted before the interest awoken by the international student upheaval in 1968. See John Petersen, "Recent Research on Latin American University Students," *Latin American Research Review* 5.1 (Spring 1970): 52–58.

2. See especially Sigal, *Intelectuales y poder*; and also Sarlo, *La batalla de las ideas*.

3. Ministerio de Educación y Justicia, *La enseñanza media (1914–1963)*, vol. 1, 58, 63, 77–78, 161 299–300, and vol. 2, 407–9; Ministerio de Educación y Cultura, *La educación en cifras, 1963–1972*, 2: 5.

4. Consejo Federal de Inversiones, *La educación secundaria* (Buenos Aires, 1968), Table 3, n.p.

5. Germán Rama, "Educación media y estructura social en América Latina," *Revista Latinoamericana de Ciencias Sociales* 4.3 (September 1972): 109.

6. Ministerio de Educación y Cultura, *La educación en cifras, 1961–1970*, 143; *La educación en cifras, 1958–1967*, 17.

7. Ministerio de Educación y Cultura, *La educación en cifras, 1958–1967*, 61; Gallart, "The Evolution of Secondary Education," 148.

8. Consejo Nacional de Desarrollo, *Origen socio-económico y otros factores*, 42–51.

9. "Educación," *Revista Eclesiástica Argentina* No. 2, March–April 1958, 86; Ministerio de Educación y Cultura, *La educación en cifras, 1963–72*, 2: 13.

10. *Resoluciones del Congreso Internacional de Enseñanza Media, 6 al 13 de julio de 1957*. Buenos Aires: n.p., 1958; Leonard, *Politicians, Pupils, and Priests*, 174–76.

11. "Congreso General de Segunda Enseñanza," *La Prensa*, August 15, 1958. 6.

12. Gilda Lamarque de Romero Brest, "Problemas actuales de la educación juvenil y de la adolescencia," *Revista de la Universidad de Buenos Aires* 7.3 (June–July 1962): 428.

13. Dussel, *Currículum, humanismo*; Suasnábar, *Universidad e intelectuales*, 137–42.

14. Ministerio de Educación y Justicia, *Planes de estudio*, 3–6.

15. Ministerio de Educación y Justicia, *Reglamento general*, 37.

16. Nicolás Tavella, "Algunas reflexiones sobre los problemas de la escuela media," *Revista de Educación* 2.10 (October 1957): 110; "Los educadores," *La Razón*, May 13, 1959, 9; Etcheverry, *El adolescente y la escuela secundaria.*

17. Robert J. Havighurst Papers, Box 157, Folder 1, Special Collections Research Center, University of Chicago Library.

18. Special issue with *Revista del Mar Dulce* No. 2, October 1956, 5; Ofelia Ferreiroa, "Experiencias realizadas en una escuela secundaria," *Revista de Psicología* No. 5, 1967, 38.

19. Daniel Muchnik, "Cinco años perdidos," *Panorama* No. 34, March 1966, 65.

20. Interview with Gerardo.

21. De Raffo, *Dejar crecer*, 80–84, 89–90; "La edad ingrata," *Para Ti* No. 2141, July 23, 1963, 20.

22. Silvia Rudni, "Adolescentes, la hora de la verdad," *Primera Plana* No. 309, November 30, 1968, 70–73; "Melenudos del mundo, uníos," *Panorama* No. 101, April 1, 1969, 10–11.

23. "Vida intelectual del adolescente," *Revista de Educación* 2.10, 1957, 50–58; "Adolescencia," *Revista de Educación* 2.12, December 1957, 605–16; Sastre de Cabot, *La formación del profesor de enseñanza media*, 18–19.

24. "Problemas de la adolescencia," *La Razón*, June 1, 1964, 14; Leguizamón, *La disciplina en la escuela secundaria*, 11.

25. "La concentración en Plaza de Mayo," *La Nación*, September 16, 1958, 16. On the foundation of Tacuara, see Gutman, *Tacuara*, 67–74.

26. "La Federación Metropolitana de Estudiantes Secundarios," *Revista del Mar Dulce* No. 8, June–July 1958, 28; I. Gilbert, *La Fede*, 353–60.

27. "Las agitaciones estudiantiles," *La Nación*, September 6, 1958, 13; for a detailed account of the *laica o libre* episodes, see Manzano, "Las batallas de los laicos."

28. Mesa "A," Factor Estudiantil, Folder 2, #11, DIPPBA.

29. "Los colegios ocupados en la provincia," *Clarín*, September 30, 1958, 20.

30. "Un grupo de alumnas visitó nuestra redacción: Una denuncia" *La Razón*, October 2, 1958, 2.

31. Ministerio de Educación y Justicia, "Resolución 5279" and "Informe Inspector—Sarmiento," Box 815, Colecciones Particulares, AAF-BN.

32. FJC, Balance General—1962, Folder 50, PCA.

33. Ministerio de Educación y Justicia, "Clubes Colegiales," *Boletín de Comunicaciones* No. 545, October 3, 1958, 354; "Reglamento de clubes colegiales," *Boletín de Comunicaciones*, Nos. 577–78, May 15, 1959, 335.

34. Dirección de Enseñanza Secundaria, Circular No. 7/961, June 16, 1961; No. 26/961, August 28, 1961; No. 22/962, April 26, 1962; No. 74/962, September 11, 1962, JVGA.

35. Verbitsky, *Una cita con la vida*, 35, 37.

36. Dirección de Enseñanza Secundaria, Circular No. 943/962, September 5, 1962; No. 21/963, April 15, 1963; No. 26/963, May 12, 1963; No. 12/964, April 12, 1964, JVGA.

37. Interview with Carlos.

38. Interview with Eduardo F.

39. For the century-long confidence in education, see Adamovsky, *Historia de la clase media*.

40. Torrado, *Estructura social de la Argentina*, 93.

41. Buchbinder, *Historia de las universidades argentinas*, 178–90.

42. Tedesco, "Modernización y democratización," 274–75; Ministerio de Educación y Cultura, *La educación en cifras*, 1963–72.

43. Ríos, *The University Student and Brazilian Society*, 7; Castrejón Díez, *La educación superior en México*, 49.

44. Germani and Sautu, *Regularidad y origen social de los estudiantes universitarios*, 14.

45. Cano, *La educación superior en la Argentina*, 46. In Mexico, in 1970, only 9 percent of the age group 18–24 was enrolled. See Castrejón Díez, *La educación superior en México*, 50.

46. Universidad de Buenos Aires, *Censo general de alumnos 1968* (Buenos Aires: UBA, 1969), 9; Klubitschko, *El origen social*, 19.

47. Universidad de Buenos Aires, *Censo General de Alumnos 1968*, 4, 103.

48. Terán, *En busca de la ideología argentina*, 194–253.

49. "Estudiantiles," *Centro* No. 3, September 1952, 52–7; "El Centro," *Centro* No. 4, December 1952, 52; "El Centro," *Centro* No. 7, December 1953, 52.

50. Buchbinder, *Historia de la Facultad*, 187–92; Neiburg, *Los intelectuales y la invención del peronismo*, 233–38.

51. "Actas de elecciones estudiantiles al Consejo Directivo," Box 731, File 204; "Actas de elecciones de alumnos a Juntas Departamentales," Box 733, File 7341; Box 734, File 11951; Box 732, File 15038; Box 736, File 18269; "Cambio de composición del centro de estudiantes," Box 732, File 15889/62, File 19989/63, FYL.

52. Universidad de Buenos Aires, *Memoria 1960*, 148, Unpublished Manuscript, SISBI-UBA.

53. Interview with Juan Azcoaga by Pablo Yanquelevich, October 29, 1987; Interview with Enrique Butelman by Nora Pagano, June 23, 1988, AO-UBA; "Concurso de Introducción a la Psicología," Box 725, File 8427/60, "Informe de los estudiantes," Box 725, File 15051, FYL.

54. Interview with Mirtha Lischetti; Buchbinder, *Historia de la Facultad*, 196.

55. Interview with Eduardo F.; Interview with Ana Lía K.

56. In 1964, 72 percent of the student body at that school worked full or part time, 6 percent above the average for the total student population at the UBA. Universidad de Buenos Aires, *Censo general de alumnos 1964* (Buenos Aires: Universidad de Buenos Aires, 1966), 231, 241.

57. Interview with Blas Alberti by Patricia Funes, February 19, 1989, AO-UBA.

58. Interview with Elena A.

59. During 1960, the student center organized a cine club and a theater club. See "Carta de la Comisión Directiva del CEFYL al decano," Box 731, File 10710, FYL.

60. Giunta, *Vanguardia, internacionalismo y política*, 144–52, 210–15; King, *El Di Tella*.

61. "Entrevista con Beatriz Sarlo," in King, *El Di Tella*, 301–2.

62. Carlos Correas, "La narración de la historia," *Centro* No. 14, December 1959.

63. Consejo Directivo de la Facultad de Filosofía y Letras, Resolución No. 60, December 24, 1959, Box 729, File 7487; AUDE al Consejo, April 19, 1960, Box 731, File 7227, FYL.

64. Carta del Juez Buero al Decano Morínigo, May 1960; Box 729, File 7487, FYL.

65. Interview with Jorge Lafforgue.

66. "¿Revolución sexual en la Argentina?," *Confirmado* No. 16, August 18, 1965, 32–35.

67. "Escuela Normal 4," *Boletín AICA* No. 176, October 23, 1959, 3; "Gino Germani," *Boletín AICA* No. 216, July 29, 1960, 3; "Definición en la Universidad," *Atlántida* No. 1148, October 1962, 31.

68. On the Ejército Guerrillero del Pueblo, see Rot, *Los orígenes perdidos*.

69. "Episodios del 9 de junio," *Gaceta de Filosofía y Letras* 2.5 (July 1964): 8–11.

70. "Reportaje al terrorismo argentino," *Confirmado* No. 18, September 2, 1965, 14.

71. Seymour Lipset, "University Students and Politics in Underdeveloped Countries," *Minerva* 3.1 (Fall 1964): 53.

72. Burgos, *Los Gramscianos argentinos*, 83–93.

73. "Discurso del Rector Risieri Frondizi al inaugurar los cursos," *Revista de la Universidad de Buenos Aires* 4.1 (January–March 1959): 110.

74. On the Latin Americanism of the Reform, see Portantiero, *Estudiantes y política*, 65–75.

75. David Viñas, "Good Bye, Mr. Haya," *Che* No. 9, March 9, 1961, n.p.

76. Sigal, *Intelectuales y poder*, 163–71.

77. Robert J. Havighurst Papers, Box 144, Folder 12, Special Collections Research Center, University of Chicago Library.

78. "Repercusiones por Cuba," *La Razón*, April 19, 1961, 1. For Mexico and the United States, see Zolov, "¡Cuba sí, yanquis no!"; and Gosse, *Where the Boys Are*.

79. See Tortti, *El "viejo" Partido Socialista*, 206–10; and Ferrero, *Historia crítica*, 79.

80. Carlos Barbé, "Entre la Universidad y el miedo," *Che* No. 14, May 17, 1961, 8.

81. "Inauguración de cursos 1964: Discurso del alumno Emilio Colombo," *Gaceta de Filosofía y Letras* 2.5, July 8, 1964, 2.

82. Sigal, *Intelectuales y poder*, 81–83; Sarlo, *La batalla de las ideas*, 72–74.

83. "Construyamos un frente anti-imperialista, May 1965," Box C15/5–4, Student Movement Collection, CEDINCI.

84. "Reunión con entidades estudiantiles," *Boletín Informativo Semanal de las Actividades de la CGT* No. 10, May 19, 1963, 4; "Estudiantes concurrieron a la central obrera," *Boletín Informativo Semanal de las Actividades de la CGT* No. 62, May 18, 1964, 24. On the "hard-core" Peronist labor unions, see James, *Resistance and Integration*.

85. Brignardello, *El movimiento estudiantil argentino*, 216–7; Zarrabeitia, *Militancia estudiantil*, 128–29; Ferrero, *Historia crítica*, 108–9.

86. Coronel Horacio Quero, "Acción comunista en el campo educacional," *Revista Militar* No. 663, 1962, 59–69; see also Genta, *Guerra contrarrevolucionaria*.

87. "El cardenal Caggiano denuncia la infiltración comunista en las universidades," *Boletín AICA* No. 215, July 22, 1960, 1; "El estudiantado sirve al comunismo," *Boletín AICA* No. 253, April 13, 1961.

88. "La otra cara: Estudiantes y obreros en una nueva batalla común," *Confirmado* No. 2, May 14, 1965, 7; "Según ACIEL, la indisciplina reina en la Universidad," *La Prensa*, June 23, 1965, 7.

89. *Diario de Sesiones de la Cámara de Diputados*, vol. 4, August 23, 1965, 2456-57.

90. "Marxismo teórico y violencia práctica," *La Nación*, June 16, 1966, 6.

91. Mazzei, *Medios de comunicación y golpismo*.

92. O'Donnell, *Bureaucratic Authoritarianism*.

93. "Cambióse el regimen de las universidades," *La Nación*, July 30, 1966, 1; "Los detenidos en las universidades han sido indagados por un juez," *La Nación*, July 31, 1966, 9.

94. "US Informs Argentina of Its Concerns," *New York Times*, August 2, 1966, 10.

95. "Terror in Argentina," *New York Times*, August 1, 1966, 16.

96. "University Teachers Begin Leaving Argentina," *New York Times*, August 19, 1966, 16; "Operación transplante" *Confirmado* No. 63, September 1, 1966, 20-21; "Esto es destruir y no modernizar," *Análisis* No. 290, October 3, 1966, 14.

97. See the testimonies in Rotunno and Díaz de Guijarro, *La construcción de lo posible*; Morero, Eidelman, and Lichtman, *La noche de los bastones largos*; and Candelari and Funes, "La Universidad de Buenos Aires."

98. "Encuesta de opinion pública No. 10," March 1967, Colección José Enrique Miguens, Colecciones Especiales y Archivos, Biblioteca Max von Buch, Universidad de San Andrés.

99. Ministerio de Cultura y Educación, *La educación en cifras, 1963-1972*, 3: 49.

100. "Más de 2500 estudiantes reclamaron la autonomía universitaria," *La Voz del Interior*, August 20, 1966, 3; on one of the branches of the "sacred family," see Tcach, "Los Nores Martínez."

101. "Se pronunciaron entidades estudiantiles," *La Voz del Interior*, August 22, 1966, 3; "Operación desconcierto," *La Voz del Interior*, August 26, 1966, 5.

102. "Córdoba: Un remolino político," *Primera Plana* No. 192, August 30, 1966, 12-15.

103. "Las fronteras de la paciencia," *Primera Plana* No. 194, September 13, 1966, 12-14; "La explosión en Córdoba," *Análisis* No. 288, 1996, 12-14.

104. See Tedín Bravo, *Historia del Barrio Clínicas*, 272-78.

105. "La noche se volvió díaen el Barrio Clínicas," *La Voz del Interior*, September 10, 1966, 3; Roberto Aizcorbe, "Qué pasa en Córdoba," *Primera Plana* No. 195, September 20, 1966, 15-18.

106. "Adhesiones al duelo por la muerte del estudiante Pampillón," *La Voz del Interior*, September 13, 1966, 3; "Inhumaron los restos del estudiante Pampillón," *La Voz del Interior*, September 14, 1966.

107. "Programa de principios, 1965," Box C5/5-2, Student Movement Collection, CEDINCI.

108. Bourdieu, "Youth Is Just a Word," in *Sociology in Question*.

109. Bourdieu and Passeron, *The Inheritors*, 15.

110. Ley Universitaria 17245/67, Buenos Aires: Universidad de Buenos Aires, 1967, 3.

111. Ibid.

Chapter 3

1. "¿Es usted de la nueva ola?," *Para Ti* No. 2119, February 19, 1963, 19.

2. On the notion of the "juvenilization" of mass culture, see Sirinelli, *Les baby boomers*, 55–56.

3. Bourdieu, *Distinction*, 60.

4. Gorgolini, "Il Consumi," 213–54; Sohn, *Âge tendre*, 79–90; Osgerby, *Youth in Great Britain*, 30–49; Palladino, *Teenagers*, 97–115.

5. "El rock sacó, en estruendosa reunión, carta de ciudadanía," *La Razón*, February 1, 1957, 7.

6. On the United States and Italy, see Altschuler, *All Shook Up*; and Capussotti, *Gioventù perduta*.

7. Doherty, *Teenagers and Teenpics*, 56–79.

8. "Películas estrenadas: 1957," *Heraldo del cinematografista*, December 30, 1957; "Post-Perón Film Fest," *Variety*, January 8, 1958, 181.

9. In 1954, 67 million tickets were sold; in 1957 the figure jumped to 75 million; and in 1960, it decreased to 45 million. *Boletín Estadístico de la Ciudad de Buenos Aires* No. 7, 1962, 115.

10. UNESCO, *Statistical Yearbook* 1963, 426; "En la Capital y en el Gran Buenos Aires, todos concurren al cine, pues es la diversión menos costosa," *La Razón*, April 6, 1959, 13.

11. "Durante largas horas, el centro de la ciudad fue agitado por bailarines de rock," *La Razón*, February 21, 1957, 5; "También en Mendoza y en Córdoba," *La Razón*, February 22, 1957, 7.

12. "Vuelan mesas y sillas en una reunión de rock en Bahía Blanca," *La Razón*, March 12, 1957, 2; "Incidentes entre partidarios del rock y el tango en Mendoza," *La Razón*, February 28, 1957, 5.

13. "Fíjense normas para la realización de concursos, competencias y prácticas de la danza denominada 'rock and roll,'" *Boletín Municipal Buenos Aires*, March 1, 1957, 331.

14. McClary, "Same as It Ever Was," 29–30.

15. Martin and Sagrave, *Anti-Rock*, 27–67; Poiger, *Jazz, Rock, and Rebels*, 182–205.

16. "El centro, otra vez, copado por los amantes del 'rocko,'" *La Razón*, March 1, 1957, 5.

17. "Hablan los detenidos por el rock," *Clarín*, March 2, 1957, 13.

18. "Nuestros adolescentes, esos desconocidos," *Vosotras* No. 1778, July 3, 1958; "Poesía del rock," *Nocturno* No. 99, March 1959, 3; Francisco Valle de Juan, "Los antiquísimos bailes modernos son inofensivos," *Claudia* No. 45, February 1961, 24–25.

19. See the ads in *La Razón*, November 11, 1957, 9, and December 18, 1957, 5.

20. "Global Report on Rock and Roll," *New York Times Magazine*, April 20, 1958, 62.

21. Zolov, *Refried Elvis*; Tamagne, "'C'mon everybody.'"

22. Daniel Colao, "De cómo y con quiénes empezó la cosa en nuestro país," *Rock Superstar* No. 5, August 1978, 4–6; Pujol, *Historia del baile*, 235–37.

23. *Annual Report*, CBS, 1958, 43.

24. "Haley llegó para dislocar a la juventud porteña con el 'rocko,'" *La Razón*, May 6, 1958, 11.

25. "El rey del rock," *Para Ti* No. 1873, May 20, 1958, 34–35; *Antena* No. 1409, May 13, 1958.

26. Amalia Lucas de Radaelli, "Empleo de las horas libres y satisfacción de las necesidades del adolescente," *Revista de la Universidad de Buenos Aires* 7.3 (July–September 1962): 470–77; Eva Giberti, "El tiempo en blanco," *La Razón*, August 5, 1960, 13.

27. "Hablan los jóvenes," *Nuestros hijos* No. 68, September 1960, 6.

28. Interview with Mabel G.

29. See, for example, "Itinerario del boogie," *Esto es* No. 3, December 16, 1953, 6–7; "Cogoteros existencialistas," *Esto es* No. 13, February 23, 1954, 13; "Existencialismo, signo de nuestra época," *Nuestros Hijos* No. 44, September 1958, 21–22; "Nudistas en el Tigre y Dolce Vita en las playas de Olivos," *La Razón*, March 2, 1961, 8.

30. "La noche: Han caído los viejos baluartes," *Panorama* No. 2, July 1963, 54–57.

31. Troncoso, "Las formas del ocio," 285–86.

32. *Relevamiento de Industria, Comercio, Prestación de Servicios y Profesiones Liberales*, July 12–21, 1964 (Buenos Aires: Dirección de Estadísticas, 1966), 54.

33. Jorge Bergstein, "Informe rendido ante el Comité Central Ampliado de la Federación Juvenil Comunista, Buenos Aires, 1957," Folder 50, PCA; "Informe de la Federación Juvenil Comunista al Comité Central," Folder 54, PCA; "¿Dónde está la juventud?," *Juventud* No. 12, July 27, 1964, 5.

34. Gerchunoff and Llach, *El ciclo de la ilusión*, 256, 295.

35. Zolov, *Refried Elvis*, 20–26; *Annual Report*, CBS, 1959, 63.

36. *Annual Report*, CBS, 1961, 9; "Argentina: Strikes Curb Sales," *Billboard Music Week: Who's Who in the World of Music*, December 25, 1961, 112.

37. "RCA's 'New Wave' Disks Clicking in Argentina," *Variety*, October 26, 1960, 57.

38. *Billboard 1962–1963 International Business Industry Buyers' Guide*, 96.

39. "Gaucho libre, show biz booming," *Variety*, November 30, 1960, 13.

40. Cámara de Industriales de Artefactos para el Hogar, *El confort del hogar y sus testimonios*, 1969, 110; ads in *La Razón*, January 15, 1958, 5; December 19, 1961, 5; and February 13, 1962, 9.

41. Chamosa, *Argentina's Folklore Movement*; Vila, "Peronismo y folklore," 45–48.

42. Dirección de Enseñanza Secundaria, Circular No. 7/961, June 16, 1961; No. 26/961, August 28, 1961; No. 22/962, April 26, 1962; No. 74/962, September 11, 1962, JVGA.

43. "Hits of the World," *Billboard*, February 10, 1962, 23.

44. "El resurgir de la pasión folklórica," *La Razón*, January 19, 1962, 6; "El gran despiporro," *La Razón*, January 22, 1962, 4; "Faltan 25.000 guitarras," *La Razón*, January 24, 1962, 6.

45. "Guitarras vs. Twist," *La Razón*, February 7, 1962, 7.

46. "La vida en un campamento," pamphlet, ca. 1963, Folder 753, PCA.

47. Zolov, *Refried Elvis*, 71–81.

48. "Requiem para la nueva ola," *Siete Días* No. 7, June 27, 1967, 58.

49. "El clan de los mil millones, ¿qué se hizo?," *Gente* No. 66, October 27, 1966, 17–21.

50. On a youth media "network" in France, see Sohn, *Âge tendre*, 80–85.

51. UNESCO, *Statistical Yearbook*, 1966, 489–90.

52. Varela, *La television criolla*, 143–52.

53. "Pino up, Farrell to RCA," *Billboard*, February 2, 1963, 43; "LP at 1.40 Hits," *Billboard*, April 6, 1963, 61; "ASCAP Representative," *Billboard*, November 30, 1963, 36.

54. "Ortega, the Rage of Argentina," *Billboard*, August 21, 1965, 24.

55. *Billboard International Magazine—1964-1965 International Business Buyer's Guide*, 112.

56. Merkin, Panno, Tijman, and Ulanovsky, *Días de radio*, 265, 272.

57. "Qué suerte," Music and Lyrics: Palito Ortega and Chico Novarro, in *Violeta Canta*, RCA-Victor, 1964, © Sony/BMG.

58. Pederiva, *Jovem guarda*; Giachetti, *Anni sessanta comincia la danza*, 82–83.

59. "Telerradiografía de Johny Tedesco," *Antena* No. 1639, October 9, 1962; "Johny Tedesco, el ídolo de la nueva ola," *Así* No. 380, April 23, 1963, 16–17.

60. Luis Santagada, "Ídolos con pie de barro," *Panorama* No. 45, February 1967, 112–14.

61. "Un tucumano enloquece a la juventud," *Así Segunda* No. 12, July 20, 1963, 16–17; "Palito Ortega recuerda," *Antena* No. 1698, November 26, 1963; "Palito Ortega recuerda (Parte Dos)," *Antena* No. 1699, December 3, 1963; "Palito Ortega recuerda (Final)," *Antena* No. 1700, December 10, 1963.

62. "¿Cuánto cuesta ser Palito Ortega?," *Confirmado* No. 18, September 2, 1965, 26–28.

63. "Sandro: Nuestro iracundo número 1 se confiesa," *Antena* No. 1740, September 15, 1964, n.p.

64. Sandvoss, *Fandom*, 7.

65. "Adolescentes 1965: Los hijos de la libertad," *Panorama* No. 25, June 1965, 42–43.

66. Interview with Ricardo.

67. "Suspiros, grititos y todo lo demás," *Primera Plana* No. 154, October 19, 1965, 30–31.

68. Antonio Dup, "T.V., Hoy," *Juventud* 17.9, June 15, 1964, 10–11; "La publicidad," *Juventud* 17.12, July 27, 1964, 11; "Televisión y juventud," *Juventud* 17.13, August 10, 1964, 14–15.

69. "Cartas de lectores: Beetles, Mokinis, y biombos," *Juventud* 17.12, July 27, 1964, 7.

70. Sebreli, *Buenos Aires*, 91, 160.

71. *Pajarito Gómez, una vida feliz*.

72. See, for example, "Una ola de espuma y dinero," *Atlántida* No. 1166, April 1964, 23.

73. "Kuhn y Franciso Urondo entre Pajaritos Gómez," *Tiempos Modernos* No. 3, July 1965, 22–23.

74. Rivera, *La investigación en comunicación*, 28.

75. "El ídolo roto," *Primera Plana* No. 144, August 10, 1965, 58; "El irónico revés de la trama," *Confirmado* No. 15, August 12, 1965, 53.

76. Huyssen, *After the Great Divide*, 50–53.

77. "Tota," *Tía Vicenta* No. 246, March 13, 1963, n.p.; *Tía Vicenta* No. 251, June 17, 1963, n.p.

78. "Disk-Jockeys: Los padres de la histeria," *Primera Plana* No. 130, May 4, 1965, 30–31; "Adolescentes 1965: Los hijos de la libertad," *Panorama* No. 25, June 1965, 40–42.

79. Jensen, "Fandom as Pathology," 9–28.

80. Casullo, *Diccionario de voces lunfardas*, 144; Gobello, *Diccionario del lunfardo*, 135.

81. Landrú and Russo, *¡Landrú por Landrú!*, 46–47.

82. "La Página de Barrio Norte," *Tía Vicenta* No. 281, June 1964; No. 287, November 1964; No. 290, January 9, 1965; No. 296, February 21, 1965; No. 302, April 4, 1965.

83. "Primer Campeonato Mundial de Mersas," *Tía Vicenta* No. 294, February 7, 1965; No. 312, June 12, 1965; No. 315, July 4, 1965; No. 329, October 10, 1965.

84. "Redescubrimiento de la sociología," *Confirmado* No. 33, December 16, 1965, 28.

85. "La Página de Barrio Norte," *Tía Vicenta* No. 296, February 21, 1965; "Mirna Delma," *Tía Vicenta* No. 299, March 14, 1965; "Mirna Delma," *Tía Vicenta* No. 300, March 21, 1965; "La Página de Barrio Norte," *Tía Vicenta* No. 302, April 4, 1965.

86. "Emigran nuestros nuevaoleros," *Antena* No. 1782, July 6, 1965; "¿El ocaso de los dioses?," *Para Ti* No. 2275, February 16, 1966, 50–51.

87. Davis, *Fashion, Culture, and Identity*, 25.

88. Ad appeared in *Clarín*, September 1, 1958, 31.

89. For a history of Alpargatas during the first half of the twentieth century, see Gutierrez and Korol, "Historia de empresas," 401–24. For histories of jeans in the United States, see Sullivan, *Jeans*; and Gordon, "American Denim," 31–45.

90. The J. Walter Thompson Company arrived in Argentina in 1929, as part of a major international expansion. See Salvatore, "Yankee Advertising," 216–35; and De Grazia, *Irresistible Empire*, 226–83.

91. Shirley Woodell to Ms. D. Moran, March 11, 14, and 16, 1957, Office Files and Correspondence, 1943–1958 folder, Box 3, Shirley Woodell Papers 1943–58, JWT.

92. Giberti, *Escuela para padres*, 3: 242.

93. Interview with Carlos R.

94. Marta Bechís de Ameller, "Adolescentes de clase baja," *Revista de la Universidad de Buenos Aires* 7.3 (July–September 1962): 457–69. In 1950s Italy, sociologists and judges took jeans as a sign of "gangster behavior." See Piccone-Stella, *La prima generazione*, 156–59.

95. "El amor que no osa decir su nombre," *Panorama* No. 19, December 1964, 128–35.

96. Viñas, *Dar la cara*, 298–99.

97. See "El motor de la moda," *Panorama* No. 137, December 9, 1969, 30.

98. Asociación Argentina de Agencias de Publicidad, *Actas de la Primera Con-*

vención Argentina de Agencias de Publicidad, Mar del Plata, September 1963, 48–49; "Burbujeante atractivo de la juventud," *Análisis* No. 305, January 16, 1967, 62–66.

99. "Blue jeans para todos," *Primera Plana* No. 208, December 20, 1966, 41.

100. "Casi un millón de vaqueros vendidos en seis meses," *Aquí Latinoamérica* No. 2, September 1966, Newsletter Series 1917-83, JWT.

101. "Un aviso diferente," *Aquí Latinoamérica* No. 3, October–November 1966, Newsletter Series 1917-1983, JWT. One of the Alpargatas directors recounted the fiasco in "Las cosas por su nombre," *Mercado* No. 222, October 11, 1973, 40–44.

102. Bourdieu, *Distinction*, 56.

103. Material anthropologists have begun to analyze the meanings of imports in several contexts throughout the nineteenth- and early twentieth-century Latin America. See Orlove, *The Allure of Foreign*.

104. Kroes, "American Mass Culture," 82–105; Poiger, *Jazz, Rock, and Rebels*.

105. "1960: La moda es joven," *Claudia* No. 37, June 1960, 65; "La moda a los 18 años," *Para Ti* No. 2001, November 15, 1960, 39–42; "Ritmo y moda joven," *Para Ti* No. 2071, March 20, 1962, 37–47; "Para la juventud coqueta," *Para Ti* No. 2227, March 16, 1965, 58–60.

106. "15-18 años, esa edad maravillosa en que," *Claudia* No. 11, April 1958, 58; "Naturalidad, mucha naturalidad," *Para Ti* No. 2025, May 2, 1961, 51–53.

107. "Los pantalones se visten de mujer," *Claudia* No. 51, August 1961, 87–91. See the special issue, "De invierno, la sencillez de los pantalones," *Para Ti* No. 2029, May 30, 1961, 37–41.

108. "Ejemplar medida moralizadora en Rosario," *Boletín AICA* No. 79, December 13, 1957, 2.

109. Ministerio de Educación, *Reglamento General para los Establecimientos de Enseñanza Secundaria, Normal y Especial* (Buenos Aires: Poder Ejecutivo Nacional, 1957), 44–45.

110. *Consejos útiles para las chicas que quieren trabajar* (Buenos Aires: Sopena, 1964), 34.

111. See, for instance, the ads titled "Student's Day: Joy of Living, Joy of Wearing Authentic Far West," *Clarín*, September 15 and 16, 1962; and *Clarín*, September 15 and 16, 1963.

112. Ad of Far West, *Para Ti*, No. 1943, October 6, 1959, 19.

113. Interview with María Ester.

114. "Rita con Illia," *La Razón*, June 11, 1964, 11.

Chapter 4

1. Cohen, *Folk Devils and Moral Panics*, xii, 217–18.

2. Feijóo and Nari, "Women in Argentina during the 1960s"; Felitti, "El placer de elegir"; Barrancos, *Mujeres en la sociedad argentina*, 224–35; Cosse, *Pareja, sexualidad y familia*.

3. Míguez, "Familias de clase media"; Nari, *Políticas de maternidad*; Cosse, *Pareja, sexualidad y familia*, 116–28.

4. For the anxieties over the "modern girls" in Argentina and Mexico, see Tossounian, "The Argentine Modern Girl"; and Hershfield, *Imagining la chica moderna*.

5. Recchini de Lattes, *Los aspectos demográficos*, 62.

6. Cartas a la Srta. Elena Frondizi, Box 39, File 6; Box 49, File 4, AAF-BN.

7. Margullis, *Migración y marginalidad*, 78, 130–31. See also "Santiago, la del éxodo," *Claudia* No. 44, January 1961, 28–29.

8. *Actas de Asamblea de la Obra de Protección de la Joven* 1.4, April 6, 1956, 40; 1.7, April 30, 1958, 47, OPJ.

9. The institution "assisted" 1,077 women in 1959; 2,043 in 1960—its most active year—and 1,859 in 1961. See *Actas de Asamblea de la Obra de Protección de la Joven* 1.9, April 27, 1960, 68; 1.10, April 26, 1961, 79; 1.11, April 30, 1962, 94, OPJ.

10. See "Varios temas trató el Congreso General de Segunda Enseñanza," *La Prensa*, August 15, 1958. 6; Delia Etcheverry, "¿Existe crisis juvenil?," *Revista de Ciencias de la Educación—Universidad Nacional del Litoral* No. 2 (1961): 36–43.

11. In 1958, *Para Ti* listed the possibilities that girls had for pursuing their professional formation. Out of 120 entries, 55 were open to graduates from primary schools. See "¿A qué puedo dedicarme?", *Para Ti* No. 1860, February 18, 1958, 73–74; *Para Ti* No. 1861, February 25, 1958, 77–78.

12. Interview with Mabel S.

13. Ministerio de Educación y Cultura, *La educación en cifras, 1958–1967*, 61.

14. Luisa Goldemberg, "El ingreso a la escuela secundaria," *Nuestros Hijos* No. 4, March 1955, 4; Dr. Ulises, "Los padres y la adolescencia," *Vosotras* No. 1193, October 16, 1958, 60; Telma Reca, "Orientación del niño al terminar la escuela," *Nuestros Hijos* No. 54, July 1959, 5.

15. Morgade, "State, Gender, and Class," 81–103; Lobato, *Historia de las trabajadoras*, 64.

16. Hebe Boyer, "Lo que piensan los adolescentes," *Leoplan* No. 635, January 18, 1961, 47; "¿Es este su problema?," *Vosotras* No. 1112, March 29, 1957, 96; *Vosotras* No. 1194, October 23, 1958, 76; *Vosotras* No. 1249, November 12, 1959, 88; *Vosotras* No. 1282, June 30, 1960, 76; "Y ahora, ¿qué?," *Para Ti* No. 2110, December 18, 1962, 4–5.

17. Cartas a la Srta. Elena Frondizi, Box 39, Files 3, 6, and 7; Box 44, File 2; Box 47, Files 3 and 6; Box 49, Files 1–4, AAF-BN.

18. *Censo Nacional de Población, 1960*, 1:69; *Censo Nacional de Población, Familias y Viviendas, 1970*, 2:38.

19. Recchini de Lattes, *Dynamics of the female labour force in Argentina*, 37–38, 64.

20. "Su segura secretaria," *La Nación*, Sepember 5, 1966, 30; "Las secretarias somos así," *Para Ti* No. 2298, July 24, 1966, 43.

21. Ministerio de Cultura y Educación, *La educación en cifras*, 1963–1972, 3:43–44.

22. Universidad de Buenos Aires, *Censo general de alumnos 1968* (Buenos Aires: UBA, 1969), 9; Klubitschko, *El origen social de los estudiantes*, 32, 77.

23. Ministerio de Cultura y Educación, *La educación en cifras, 1963–1972*, 91–92; Barrancos, *Mujeres en la sociedad argentina*, 220–24.

24. Eva Giberti, "Su primer baile," *La Razón*, May 26, 1963, 13; "Una fiesta entretenida," *Vosotras* No. 1198, November 20, 1958, 63–65; "Quince años," *Vosotras*

No. 1170, May 8, 1958, 55; Telma Reca, "La pubertad y la adolescencia," *Nuestros Hijos* No. 11, November 1955, 9.

25. "¿Es este su problema?," *Vosotras* No. 1370, March 8, 1962, 82.

26. See Chapter 3; and Pujol, *Historia del baile*, 235–64.

27. Eva Giberti, "Un nuevo estilo," *La Razón*, April 19, 1960, 13. See also Mario Bernal, "A dónde van nuestras hijas," *Claudia* No. 2, July 1957, 55–58; "Hay que contemporizar," *Para Ti* No. 2062, February 13, 1962, 45; "Nace una mujer," *Vosotras* No. 1373, March 29, 1962, 46–47.

28. "¿Es ese su problema?," *Vosotras* No. 1165, April 3, 1958, 82; *Vosotras* No. 1374, April 5, 1962, 63. For similar letters, see also *Vosotras* No. 1142, October 25, 1957, 80; No. 1189, September 18, 1958, 82; No. 1215, March 19, 1959, 68; No. 1227, June 11, 1959, 76.

29. "Qué opinan los padres," *Nuestros Hijos* No. 70, November 1960, 4–8.

30. Cosse, "Probando la libertad," 31–47.

31. "Tribuna de la juventud," *Nuestros Hijos* No. 36, January 1958, 84; "¿Es este su problema?," *Vosotras* No. 1189, September 18, 1958, 76; "Secreteando," *Idilio* No. 477, March 14, 1958, 53.

32. Interview with Maria Rosa.

33. "Matrimonios jóvenes," *Vosotras* No. 1179, July 10, 1958, 64; "Voy a casarme," *Para Ti* No. 2052, November 7, 1961, 5. On housing during Peronism, see Ballent, *Las huellas de la política*.

34. Tomás Eloy Martínez, "Los de la mesa 10 y todos los demás," *La Nación*, October 2, 1960.

35. "¿Amamos así?," *Extra* No. 19, February 1967, 51–58.

36. Torrado, "Transición de la nupcialidad," 414.

37. María Mendoza, "El adolescente y la familia," *Revista de Ciencias de la Educación* No. 4 (April 1959), 99–108.

38. "Tribuna de la juventud," *Nuestros Hijos* No. 36, January 1958, 83; *Nuestros Hijos* No. 50, March 1959, 54; "¿Es este su problema?," *Vosotras* No. 1375, April 11, 1962, 82; "Secreto de Confesión," *Para Ti* No. 2186, June 2, 1964, 5.

39. "¿Amenaza su hijo con irse de casa?," *Nuestros Hijos* No. 60, January 1960, 33; Eva Giberti, "El comportamiento familiar," *La Razón*, March 21, 1963, 7.

40. Aída Romanos and Octavio Fernández Mouján, "Problemática del adolescente: Motivos de consulta," *Acta Psiquiátrica y Psicológica Argentina* 8.4 (December 1962): 317–23.

41. Sara de Jarast, "Autismo, negación maníaca y atracción impulsiva en el adolescente," in Rascovsky and Liberman, *Psicoanálisis de la manía*, 364–71.

42. For San Francisco and New York, see Fass, *Kidnapped*, 147–57; and Staller, *Runaways*.

43. Policía Federal, *Orden del día*, January 1 to December 31 of 1953, 1955, 1957, 1960, 1963, and 1965, CEHPFA. These are the only years for the time period 1950–1970 for which the information is complete.

44. In 1955, 20 percent of the cases were reported in the police stations of the neighborhoods of Once and Parque Patricios, followed by Barrio Lacarra, a slum in the outskirts of the city.

45. Guy, "Girls in Prison," 369–89. For working-class runaway girls in Mexico City in the 1920s and 1930s, see Bliss and Blum, "Dangerous Driving," 163–84.

46. In 1960 and 1963, the police stations of Barrio Norte, Palermo, and Recoleta ranked first.

47. Policía Federal, *Orden del día*, May 2, 1953, 4; October 23, 1957, 3; February 12, 1955, 6; March 14, 1955, 3; November 8, 1955, 4; December 12, 1963, 4, CEHPFA.

48. Interview with María Emilia.

49. "Así es la Dolce Vita," *La Razón*, March 8, 1961, 4.

50. See "Estragos de la Dolce Vita," *La Razón*, March 15, 1961, 7; Manuel Brihuega, "La juventud y la Dolce Vita," *Nuestros Hijos* No. 74, March 1961, 34–36; "Dolce Vita en erupción," *La Razón*, July 17, 1961, 9; Michel Brignac, "Los tenebrosos," *Nuestros Hijos* No. 77, June 1961, 14–16; Eugenio Reynal Arrigo, "¿Entró usted en la Dolce Vita?," *Vosotras* No. 1365, February 1, 1962, 58–59; "Dolce Vita en propiedad horizontal," *La Razón*, June 8, 1962, 7; "Contaba con 50 mujeres una organización de la Dolce Vita," *La Razón*, June 12, 1962, 5.

51. See Guy, *Sex and Danger*, 141–74.

52. "Las confesiones de la madre," *Así* No. 344, August 31, 1962, 6.

53. See "La muerte de la joven Penjerek y el antisemitismo," *Así* No. 345, September 7, 1962, 5. For Tacuara, see Gutman, *Tacuara*.

54. "Caso Penjerek: En vías de su total esclarecimiento," *Clarín*, September 5, 1963, 19.

55. "Adquiere gravedad extraordinaria la investigación por el crimen de la joven Penjerek," *La Razón*, September 25, 1963, 1; "Reportaje a un colmillo afilado," *El Mundo*, October 2, 1963, 5.

56. "Carta al lector," *Primera Plana* No. 46, September 24, 1963, 3; "Las adolescentes y la Dolce Vita," *La Nación*, September 22, 1963, 4; "La ribera de Quilmes: Emporio de la Dolce Vita," *Así* No. 403, October 2, 1963, 2.

57. "El estado de sitio," *La Nación*, September 23, 1963, 1.

58. "Redadas en la provincia," *La Nación*, September 29, 1963, 11.

59. Dirección de Enseñanza Secundaria, Circular No. 67/963, September 25, 1963; No. 70/963, October 1, 1963, No. 72/963, October 10, 1963, JVGA.

60. "Un documento de la Acción Católica Argentina," *Clarín*, October 9, 1963, 5.

61. "La juventud y el hogar," *La Nación*, October 5, 1963, 6.

62. See Chapter 1; and Giberti, *Escuela para padres*, 3:202–8.

63. Eva Giberti, "Defensa de la adolescente," *La Razón*, September 29, 1963, 17.

64. "La CGT," *Clarín*, September 28, 1963, 13; "Pantalla," *Liberación* No. 19, October 1, 1963; *Diario de sesiones de la Cámara de Diputados de la Nación*, December 11, 1963, 7:647.

65. "Lucha frontal," *La Razón*, September 19, 1963, 1; "Un documento patético," *Clarín*, September 24, 1963, 19; "La Dolce Vita y el comunismo," *La Razón*, September 23, 1963, 1.

66. See Breines, *Young, White*, 8–9; D'Emilio, "The Homosexual Menace," 226–33; Freedman, "'Uncontrolled Desires,'" 83–106.

67. Cohen, *Folk Devils and Moral Panics*, 219.

68. "Gran proceso público a la corrupción," *La Razón*, November 8, 1963, 5.

69. Manzano, "Sexualizing Youth."

70. Mafud, *La revolución sexual argentina*, 11.

71. For Western Europe, the United States, and Mexico, see Weeks, *Sex, Politics, and Society*, 252–56; Bailey, *Sex in the Heartland*, 75–103 and 200–213; Sohn, *Âge tendre*, 149–63; Herzog, *Sex after Fascism*, 123–30; Monsiváis, "El cinturón de castidad al condon," 163–86.

72. "Cursos de temporada," *Boletín Informativo de la UBA* No. 10, June 1959, 3–7.

73. Amalia Lucas de Radaelli and Sara Zac de Filc, "Problemática y desarrollo psico-sexual del joven," *Acta Neuro-Psiquiátrica Argentina* 7.3 (1961): 188–90.

74. "El desamparo de la juventud," *La Razón*, May 5, 1960, 19; "Problema de la juventud," *La Razón*, June 6, 1960, 13; "Hablan los jóvenes," *Nuestros Hijos* No. 68, September, 1960, 6.

75. Luisa Goldemberg and Alberto Merani, "Educación sexual del adolescente," *Nuestros Hijos* No. 6, May 1955; "Los problemas prematrimoniales," *Nuestros Hijos* No. 9, September 1955. On homosexuality, see "El problema de la homosexualidad," *Nuestros Hijos* No. 40, May 1958, 12–15; "Tribuna de la juventud," *Nuestros Hijos* No. 42, July 1958, 53; *Nuestros Hijos* No. 44, September 1958, 67. On masturbation, see Manuel Brihuega, "El pecado solitario," *Nuestros Hijos* No. 51, April 1959, 10–12; Marcos Weinstein, "No tiene la gravedad que usted supone," *Nuestros Hijos* No. 60, January 1960, 16–17; Dr. Manuel Farago, "Vida psico-sexual del adolescente," *Nuestros Hijos* No. 68, September 1960, 56.

76. Alberto Merani, "Los jóvenes y la continencia," *Nuestros Hijos* No. 50, March 1959, 36–38; "Las jóvenes y la continencia," No. 51, April 1959, 38–39. For letters regarding young men's difficulties maintaining continence, see "Tribuna de la juventud," *Nuestros Hijos* No. 44, September 1958, 56; *Nuestros Hijos* No. 45, October 1958, 68–69; *Nuestros Hijos* No. 47, December 1958, 70; No. 49, January 1959, 71.

77. Escardó, *Sexología de la familia*, 37–40; Giberti, *Escuela para padres*, vol. 2, 53–78 and *Adolescencia y educación sexual*, 582–6.

78. Escardó, *Sexología*, 50–51. On "petting" see Bailey, *From Front Porch to Back Seat*, 176–96.

79. Mauricio Knobel and Beatriz Scaziga, "Actitudes de los pre-adolescentes acerca de la menstruación," *Revista de Psicología* (Universidad de La Plata) No. 3 (1965), 75–79.

80. Eva Giberti, "Consultorio de adolescentes," *Revista Argentina de Psiquiatría y Psicología de la Infancia y la Adolescencia* 2.1 (September 1971): 110–19.

81. "Universidad y juventud," *Confirmado* No. 209, June 19, 1969, 38; Silvia Rudni, "Adolescentes, la hora de la verdad," *Primera Plana* No. 309, November 30, 1968, 73.

82. "Erotismo y ternura," *Extra* No. 3, September 1965, 17; "Frente al matrimonio," *Extra* No. 23, June 1967, 57; "Relaciones sexuales prematrimoniales," *Siete Días* No. 116, July 28, 1969, 53.

83. Adriana, "Proceso a la virginidad," *Siete Días* No. 152, April 6, 1970, 58–63.

84. E. L. G, "Cómo se aman los jóvenes," *Análisis* No. 422, April 15, 1969, 40–46.

85. Serrano, *Historia de los cambios*, 121; Mossuz-Lavau, *Les lois de l'amour*, 146.

86. "Sexo, ¿quién nos lo explica?," *La Bella Gente* No. 3, December 1969, 82–85.

87. "Tribuna de la juventud," *Nuestros Hijos* No. 46, November 1958, 69; No. 51, April 1959, 62.

88. "Preparación para una unión más verdadera," *Siete Días* No. 21, October 3, 1967, 20-22.

89. Padre Agustín, "Secreto de confesión," *Para Ti* No. 2313, November 7, 1966, 66; Padre Iñaki, "Secreto de confesión," *Para Ti* No. 2472, December 1, 1969, 76; *Para Ti* No. 2504, July 6, 1970, 89; Padre Bacioli, "Conciencia," *Siete Días* No. 5, June 13, 1967, 46; *Siete Días* No. 25, October 31, 1967, 53; *Siete Días* No. 73, September 30, 1968, 42; *Siete Días* No. 97, March 17, 1969, 57.

90. Padre Iñaki, "Secreto de confesión," *Para Ti* No. 2402, 22 July 1968, 66; *Para Ti* No. 2466, October 13, 1969, 90; Padre Bacioli, "Conciencia," *Siete Días* No. 28, November 21, 1967, 13; *Siete Días* No. 88, January 13, 1969, 53.

91. "Cuando los jóvenes golpean las puertas de los mayores," *La Razón*, November 2, 1967, 11; "Un ríspido debate juvenil," *La Razón*, November 20, 1967, 8.

92. Martín Yriart, "Anticonceptivos," *Panorama* No. 50, July 1967, 93-98; "Control de la natalidad," *Siete Días* No. 31, December 12, 1967, 22-26; "Usted y la píldora," *Para Ti* No. 2419, November 18, 1968, 10-13; "La verdad sobre la píldora," *Para Ti* No. 2497, May 18, 1970.

93. Felitti, *La revolución de la píldora.*

94. "La píldora está entre nosotros," *Panorama* No. 226, August 25, 1971, 30.

95. Bailey, *Sex in the Heartland*; Giachetti, *Anni sessanta comincia la danza*; Pieper Mooney, *Politics of Motherhood.*

96. Torrado, *Historia de la familia*, 336-37, Cosse, *Pareja, sexualidad y familia*, 90-91.

97. "Cómo hacer el amor," *Confirmado* No. 152, May 16, 1968, 46-47; Giberti, "Consultorio de adolescentes," 114.

98. "Las argentinas y la sexualidad," *Panorama* No. 325, August 2, 1973, 52.

99. Susana Torrado argues that "co-habitation" as an "entrance" or alternative to marriage began to extend to the middle class in the 1960s. See *Historia de la familia*, 268-75.

100. Ordenanza No. 16.374, July 20, 1960, *Resoluciones, Comunicaciones, Declaraciones y Decretos 1960* (Buenos Aires: Imprenta Municipal, 1960), 73-75.

101. *Actas del Consejo Nacional de Protección de Menores* 3.81, June 19, 1963, 254, CNNAF.

102. "La industria del amor," *Panorama* No. 34, March 1966, 73-76; "El albergue no es un bicho," *Primera Plana* No. 238, July 18, 1967, 44; "¿Amamos así?," *Extra* No. 19, February 1967, 53.

103. On the debates and meanings of the 1936 law, see Guy, *Sex and Danger*, 131-34.

104. *Diario de Sesiones de la Cámara de Senadores*, June 30, 1965, 1:255-56.

105. "Obligatoriedad del examen prenupcial para las mujeres," *La Prensa*, July 1, 1965, 9.

106. "Examen prenupcial: Las antesalas del amor," *Confirmado* No. 14, August 5, 1965, 51.

Chapter 5

1. "Detúvose a integrantes de un trío musical," *La Prensa*, August 1, 1966, 7.

2. Vila, "Rock nacional: The Struggle for Meaning"; Alabarces, *Entre gatos y violadores*; Díaz, *Libro de viajes y extravíos*. The histories of Argentina's rock have thus far been written by rock journalists. See Grinberg, *Cómo vino la mano*; Marzullo and Muñoz, *Rock en la Argentina*; Fernández Bitar, *Historia del rock en la Argentina*; Kreimer and Polimeni, *Ayer no más*.

3. Grossberg, *We Gotta Get out of This Place*, 156.

4. See Zolov, *Refried Elvis*; Dunn, *Brutality Garden*.

5. On the notion of hegemonic masculinity, see Connell, *Masculinities*, 38–39.

6. Ministerio de Educación y Justicia, *La enseñanza media (1914–1963)*, vol. 1, 58; Ministerio de Educación y Cultura, *La educación en cifras, 1963–1972*, 2:55.

7. Consejo Federal de Inversiones, *La educación secundaria*, Table 8, n.p. On the "technical-oriented" policy makers, see Suasnábar, *Universidad e intelectuales*, 145–50.

8. Dirección de Enseñanza Secundaria, Circular No. 37/969, June 4, 1969; Nota D-015/971, May 18, 1971, JVGA.

9. Silvia Rudni, "Adolescentes, la hora de la verdad," *Primera Plana* No. 309, November 30, 1968, 70–73; "Los profesores," *Cronopios* No. 1, October 1969, 85; "El contestador," *La Bella Gente* No. 25, February 1972, 89. See Chapter 2 for a full description of school routines.

10. Ministerio de Educación y Justicia, *Reglamento general*, 37; Circular 12/964, April 12, 1964; Circular 99/968, November 6, 1968, JVGA.

11. "Melenudos del mundo, uníos," *Panorama* No. 101, April 1, 1969, 10–11.

12. "Incidentes en el Colegio Mariano Acosta," *La Opinión*, August 18, 1971, 18; "La ropa que vos usáis," *Primera Plana* No. 478, March 28, 1972, 31; "Adolescentes, lo que vendrá," *Primera Plana* No. 495, July 25, 1972, 39–40.

13. Charly García, "Aprendizaje," in Sui Géneris, *Confesiones de invierno*, 1973, Talent, © Sony-BMG. On Sui Géneris see Alabarces, *Entre gatos y violadores*, 64–66.

14. "Empezó la guerra," *Pelo* No. 54, December 1974, 16–17.

15. Charly García, "Botas locas," in Sui Géneris, *Pequeñas anécdotas sobre las instituciones*, 1974, Talent, © Sony-BMG.

16. Rodríguez Molas, *El servicio militar obligatorio*.

17. Prasad and Smythe, *Conscription*, 1–2, 18, 25–26, 89–90.

18. *Boletín de Educación e Instrucción del Ejército*, No. 22, 1972, 120–23, 129–31, 143–45, 155–65.

19. See Pozzi, *Por las sendas argentinas*; Anguita and Caparrós, *La voluntad*, vol. 2; and especially "Reportaje a Hernán Invernizzi," *Lucha Armada* No. 8, 2007.

20. "Tú juzgarás" and "No, decididamente no," *Soldado Argentino* No. 695, July–December 1973, 4–6 and 43–44; for the ERP's depictions, see "La toma del comando de Sanidad" (ca. September 1973) and "Ante la toma del comando de sanidad" (ca. October 1973), available at the website: topoblindado.com (Fondos Documentales/ Ejército Revolucionario del Pueblo/Volantes).

21. See the pamphlets "Soldado" (ca. November 1974) and "A los soldados: Carta del Comandante del ERP, Roberto Mario Santucho, a los soldados de la clase 1954" (ca. April 1975).

22. "¿Para qué sirve el servicio militar?," *Siete Días* No. 102, April 21, 1969, 30–34; Kado Kostzer, "El servicio militar por dentro," *Panorama* No. 188, December 1, 1970, 45–50; "Todavía quieren confundirnos," *Soldado Argentino* No. 695, July–December 1973, 7–9.

23. Cantilo, *Chau Loco*, 19–20.

24. *Censo Nacional de Población y Viviendas, 1960*, 1:68–69; *Censo Nacional de Población, Familias y Viviendas, 1970*, 2:38–39.

25. Torrado, *Estructura social de la Argentina*, 127; Brennan and Gordillo, *Córdoba rebelde*, 30.

26. Miguel Cantilo, "Yo vivo en una ciudad," in Pedro y Pablo, *Yo vivo en una ciudad*, 1970, RCA © Sony-BMG. On rock poets and the city, see Díaz, *Libro de viajes y extravíos*, 101.

27. "El contestador," *La Bella Gente* No. 20, September 1971, 85; see also No. 21, October 1971, 87; No. 22, November 1971, 88–89; No. 23, December 1971, 91.

28. For North America, see J. Gilbert, *Men in the Middle*; and Dummitt, *Manly Modern*.

29. Sebreli, *Buenos Aires*, 67–84; Jauretche, *El medio pelo en la sociedad argentina*.

30. Altamirano, *Peronismo y cultura de izquierda*, 88; Adamovsky, *Historia de la clase media*, 384–88.

31. See Frith, *Sound Effects*, 249–68. See also Grossberg, *We Gotta Get out of This Place*, 144–48.

32. Tomás E. Martínez, "La familia que venderá su casa para comprar un auto," *La Opinión*, November 3, 1972, 8.

33. Javier Martínez, "No, pibe," in Manal, *Manal*, Mandioca, 1970 © Sony-BMG.

34. Archetti, *Masculinities*, 182–85.

35. Miguel Grinberg, "Cartas a la Beat Generation," *Eco Contemporáneo* No. 4, 1962, 14; "Mufa y revolución," *Eco Contemporáneo* No. 5, 1963, 9; "Anatomía del desorden," *Eco Contemporáneo* Nos. 8/9, 1965, 14.

36. King, *El Di Tella*, 138. See a description of the *manzana loca* in Podalsky, *Specular City*, 138–47; for the Zona Rosa, see Zolov, *Refried Elvis*, 135–37.

37. "Con la violencia de un cross a la mandíbula," *Confirmado* No. 51, June 9, 1966, 59.

38. Nebbia, *Una mirada*, 22–24; Grinberg, *La música progresiva*, 34–37.

39. "Así llegó a Buenos Aires la primavera," *Siete Días* No. 20, September 26, 1967, 12–14.

40. McCracken, *Big Hair*, 3, 61.

41. Interview with Tony C.

42. "Córdoba y sus beatniks," *Siete Días* No. 9, July 11, 1967, 29–31; Cousinet, *Extramuros*, 44–46.

43. "La marabunta en Buenos Aires," *La Razón*, November 11, 1967, 7; "Hippies de utilería," *Siete Días*, December 12, 1967, 32–33. The on-site report is José de Zer, "48 horas con los hippies," *Atlántida* No. 1209, December 1967, 42–46.

44. Gayol, *Sociabilidad en Buenos Aires*; Ben, *Male Sexuality*.

45. See Verbitsky, *La esquina*; and Kordon, *Reina del Plata*.

46. Policía Federal, *Edictos Policiales y Reglamento de Procedimientos Contravencionales*, 1970, 1–7; Poder Ejecutivo Nacional, "Decreto 333/58," *Boletín Oficial*, March 3, 1958, 2. For Italy and Mexico, see Giachetti, *Anni sessanta comincia la danza*, 128–37; and Zolov, *Refried Elvis*, 141–46.

47. "Hippies en Buenos Aires," *La Razón*, November 30, 1967, 13; "Hippies al calabozo," *La Razón*, January 10, 1968, 8; "La guerra anti-hippies," *La Razón*, January 23, 1968, 6.

48. "Tumultos en la misa negra," *Siete Días* No. 36, January 16, 1968, 15; "Descomunal desorden entre hippies y anti-hippies en Mar del Plata," *La Razón*, January 11, 8. On the "Pompeya group," see Pipo Lernoud's testimony in Pintos, *Tanguito*, 127.

49. "¿Será posible?," *La Razón*, January 12, 1968, 7; "Hippies," *La Razón*, January 24, 1968, 6. Several people wrote to back Coral. See "Correo," *Primera Plana* No. 265, January 23, 1968, 4; *Siete Días* No. 37, January 23, 1968, 15.

50. "Correo de lectores," *Siete Días* No. 18, September 12, 1967, 5; *Siete Días* No. 21, October 3, 1967, 7.

51. "Correo de lectores," *Siete Días* No. 31, December 12, 1967, 7; see also No. 36, January 16, 1968, 6; No. 44, March 12, 1968, 5.

52. "Hippies en Buenos Aires: ¿Al paredón o tolerancia?," *Gente* No. 116, October 12, 1967, 37.

53. See Chapter 4.

54. Sedgwick, *Between Men*, 25.

55. Debora Paccini Hernandez, Héctor Fernández L'Hoeste, and Eric Zolov, "Mapping Rock Cultures," in *Rockin' Las Americas: The Global Politics of Rock in Latina/o America*, ed. Fernández L'Hoeste, Paccini Hernandez, and Zolov (Pittsburgh: University of Pittsburgh Press, 2004), 7–9; Zolov, *Refried Elvis*, 102–5, 133–34; Barr-Melej, "Siloísmo and the Left," 778.

56. "La multiplicación de los instrumentos," *Mercado* No. 95, May 5, 1971,. 40; Jorge Andrés, "Los jóvenes fuertes," *Análisis* No. 464, February 2, 1970, 48.

57. "La vida es como un long play," *Análisis* No. 402, November 27, 1968, 52; Berti, *Spinetta*, 15.

58. "Bofetadas," *Análisis* No. 432, June 24, 1969, 84; "El día," No. 445, September 23, 1969, 81.

59. File 15,557, Mesa "Referencia," DIPPBA, 21–27, 41.

60. Gabriela, "Voy a dejar esta casa, papá," in *Gabriela*, 1971, Talent Phantom; "La supremacía masculina es notoria," *La Opinión*, January 26, 1972, 18.

61. See their testimonies in Oliveri, *Éramos tan hippies*.

62. Interview with Hilda L.

63. "Adiós al secundario," *La Bella Gente* No. 3, February 1970, 78.

64. Fernández Bitar, *El rock en la Argentina*, 52.

65. Tanguito and Pipo Lernoud, "La princesa dorada," in *Ramsés VII*, RCA, 1968; Luis Alberto Spinetta, "Muchacha (ojos de papel)," in Almendra, *Almendra*, RCA, 1970; Miguel Cantilo, "Catalina Bahía," in Pedro y Pablo, *Conesa*, CBS, 1972,

© Sony-BMG. On "hippie princesses" in the Britisth and North American contexts, see Whiteley, *Women and Popular Music*, 33–39.

66. Luis Alberto Spinetta, "Me gusta ese tajo," in Pescado Rabioso, *Desatormentándonos*, RCA, 1972; "Nena boba," in Pescado Rabioso, *Pescado 2*, RCA, 1973; Billy Bond y La Pesada, "Que sepa volar," in *Billy Bond y La Pesada* vol. 4, Music Hall, 1973. The comment on "Que sepa volar" is in Jorge Andrés, "Un LP de lúcido y corrosivo humor," *La Opinión*, January 29, 1974, 21.

67. See Coates, "(R)Evolution Now?," 54–57.

68. As examples, listen to Luis Alberto Spinetta, "Hoy todo el hielo en la ciudad," in Almendra, *Almendra*, 1970 © RCA, now © Sony-BMG; Javier Martínez and Claudio Gabis, "Avellaneda's Blues," in Manal, *Manal*, 1970 © Mandioca, now © Sony-BMG.

69. Vila, "Rock Nacional: The Struggle for Meaning," 12–13; Alabarces, *Entre gatos y violadores*, 49.

70. Interview with Mario Rabey; "El contestador," *La Bella Gente* No. 8, September 1970, 85.

71. Instituto Nacional de Estadísticas y Censos, "Discos fonográficos," *Boletín Estadístico Trimestral*, January–March 1973, 84; "En materia de discos, los jóvenes mandan," *Mercado* No. 35, March 12, 1970, 42; "Encuesta: Discos fonográficos," *Pulso* No. 208, May 5, 1971, n.p.

72. On the making of Los Náufragos, see "Desde el hit hasta lo imprevisible," *Mercado* No. 54, July 23, 1970, 132–34. For more on "beat promotion," see "Cómo es un joven beat," *Gente* No. 255, June 11, 1970, 36; "La música moderna y su joven guardia," *Clarín Espectáculos*, July 13, 1970, 3.

73. Horacio de Dios, "¿Los argentinos se afeminan?," *Atlántida* No. 1197, December 1966, 40; Oscar Caballero, "Qué compran y qué venden los jóvenes," *Mercado* No. 38, April 2, 1970, 40; "Camisas con apellido," *Mercado* No. 81, January 27, 1971, 39.

74. "De cabelleras y barbas," *Análisis* No. 469, March 10, 1970, 38–40; Eduardo Gudiño Kieffer, "Los argentinos y el pelo," *Gente* No. 358, June 1, 1972, 32–33.

75. "Con pelos y señales," *Siete Días* No. 212, June 7, 1971, 67; "Cosmética masculina," *La Bella Gente* No. 26, March 1972, 39; "Cuando los hombres se hacen la toca," *La Bella Gente*, No. 29, June 1972, 24–26; "Cuidado con la cabeza," *Primera Plana* No. 435, June 1, 1971, 26–28.

76. "Encuesta sectorial: Indumentaria," *Pulso* No. 176, September 22, 1970.

77. "Editorial: Bueno/Malo," *Pelo* No. 3, April 1970, 4.

78. Interview with Daniel Ripoll, June 27, 2007; "Pelo en Londres," *Pelo* No. 6, July 1970, 4.

79. Waksman, *Instruments of Desire*, 252.

80. "Música pop argentina," *Pelo* No. 1, February 1970, 3. "Los conjuntos de la música pop argentinos," *Pelo* No. 3, April 1970, xvii–xxiv.

81. McRobbie and Frith, "Rock and Sexuality," 373–77; G. Frank, "Discophobia."

82. "Las groupies argentinas," *Pelo* No. 3, April 1970, 48–49.

83. Vila, "Rock nacional: The Struggle for Meaning," 7; for the Anglo-Saxon context, Beebe et al., *Rock over the Edge*, 1–23.

84. "La crisis más severa de la música pop argentina," *Pelo* No. 8, September 1970, 6; "Los Gatos están cansados," *Pelo* No. 1, February 1970, 21.

85. "Editorial: Los súper hombres," *Pelo* No. 9, October, 1970, 6; Frith, *Sound Effects*, 30, 50–54.

86. "El festival para sacar cabeza," *Pelo* No. 10, November, 1970, 52; Interview with Daniel Ripoll.

87. "BAROCK II: Al fin y al cabo, nació para ser salvaje," *Panorama* No. 238, November 11, 1971, 46–47; "Beat, un estilo de vida," *Clarín—Revista de los Jueves*, December 2, 1971, n.p.

88. Wollman, *The Theater Will Rock*, 42–59.

89. "Hair en Buenos Aires: el amor, todo el amor, nada más que el amor," *Siete Días* No. 208, May 10, 1971, 46–48; "Una nueva cuadra loca," *Panorama* No. 213, May 25, 1971, 30.

90. Interview with Mario Rabey; Oliveri, *Éramos tan hippies*.

91. "Una obra hecha delirio," *Clarín*, May 9, 1971, 28; "Pese a todo, libertad," *Primera Plana* No. 433, May 11, 1971, 43; "Pelo para consumidores," *Confirmado* No. May 19, 1971, 47.

92. "Arco Iris: La música, complemento de la disciplina yoga," *Clarín*, February 2, 1970, Sección espectáculos, 2; "Vida cotidiana y meditación," *Pelo* No. 11, December 1970, 12–13. In the late 1970s Santaolalla moved to Los Angeles, where he had a highly successful career that includes two Academy Awards for Best Original Score for *Brokeback Mountain* (2006) and *Babel* (2007).

93. "La música joven del mundo también sacude a la Argentina," *Panorama* No. 239, November 23, 1971. On a religiously inspired commune in New Mexico, see Hollenbach, *Lost and Found*.

94. "La Cofradía de la Flor Solar," *Cronopios* No. 0, September, 1969, 15; "Los fuegos locales de la contracultura," *Clarín Revista*, May 16, 1971, 37.

95. Hiquis's testimony, in Castrillón, "Hippies a la criolla," 60; Cantilo, *Chau loco*, 70–92.

96. Cantilo, *Chau loco*; For the United States' experience, see Hodgdon, *Manhood in the Age of Aquarius*.

97. Zolov, *Refried Elvis*, 136, 150–54; David Farber, "The Intoxicated State/Illegal Nation," and Timothy Miller, "The Sixties-Era Commune," in Braustein and Doyle, *Imagine Nation*, 17–39 and 327–51.

98. Interview with Miguel Grinberg, September 11, 2007.

99. Equipo C, "Arde Argentina?," *Contracultura* No. 2, August 1970, 35–38; "Qué? Cómo? Cuándo?," *Contracultura* No. 3, October 1970, 46–48; "Crear dos, tres, muchos amaneceres" and "El miedo a los jóvenes," *Contracultura* No. 4, November 1970, 3–4.

100. González Trejo, *Formas de alienación en la cultura argentina*, 57; Barr-Melej, "Siloísmo and the Left," 747–84; Zolov, *Refried Elvis*.

101. Brea and Ratier, "La adolescencia, hoy," in *Enciclopedia del Mundo Actual*, 2:238.

102. "Hablan los jóvenes: Lecciones para adultos," *Panorama* No. 249, February 1, 1972, 36.

103. Garaño and Pertot, *La otra juvenilia*, 191–94; Pozzi, *Por las sendas argentinas*, 146.

104. Cattaruzza, "El mundo por hacer," 18.

105. "Una feria de artesanos persigue claros objetivos políticos," *La Opinión*, August 15, 1973, 16.

106. Interview with Carlos U.

107. Interview with Luis Salinas (b. in 1954), File 0260, Memoria Abierta Archive.

108. Kreimer, *Agarráte*; Germán García, "Los jóvenes frente al espejo," *Los Libros* No. 18, April 1971, 26–28.

109. "Paráfrasis beat sobre el Padre Nuestro," *La Opinión*, December 18, 1971, 23; see also "El grupo Arco Iris," December 24, 1971, 22; "Crítica a la deformación del lenguaje de Jesús," September 8, 1972, 18; "Desórdenes en el Luna Park frustraron un recital de rock," October 22, 1972, 11; "Pretensión y vaguedad son los síntomas del actual rock argentino," February 2, 1973, 21.

110. "La marcha de Pedro hacia la bronca," *Pelo*, No. 12, January 1971, 14–17.

111. Alma y Vida, "Hoy te queremos cantar," in *Alma y Vida* vol. 2, RCA, 1972 © Sony—BMG; Roque Narvaja, "Camilo y Ernesto" and "Balada para Luis" in *Octubre (mes de cambios)*, 1972.

112. "Con música de rock, 20.000 jóvenes celebraron el triunfo peronista," *La Opinión*, April 1, 1973, 1.

113. Reyes Matta, "The 'New Song,'" 447–61. For Mexico, see Zolov, *Refried Elvis*, 225–33.

114. "Diez canciones montoneras," *El descamisado* No. 31, December 10, 1973, 20–21; "Fervor político en un Festival de la JP," *Noticias*, December 30, 1973, 19.

115. "Buen recital de rock," *Noticias*, December 28, 1973, 17; "Arco Iris," January 28, 1974, 22.

116. "Discos para la liberación," *Noticias*, January 26, 1974, 15.

117. "Rock nacional: En busca de una definición," *Panorama* No. 317, May 24, 1973, 51–52.

118. Hugo Tabachnik, "Rock y revolución," *Pelo* No. 37, March 1973, 40–41.

119. "Correo," *Pelo* No. 38, April 1973, 82–83; *Pelo* No. 39, May 1973, 88–89.

120. Nari, "Abrir los ojos, abrir la cabeza," 15–21; Vassallo, "Movilización, política y orígenes," 61–88; Rapisardi and Modarelli, *Fiestas, baños y exilios*, 159–63.

121. Grossberg, *We Gotta Get out of This Place*.

122. Interview with Emilio C.

123. "Reportaje a Luis Alberto Spinetta," *Grito Joven* No. 3, September 1974, n.p.

Chapter 6

1. On the notion of political culture, see Sirinelli, "Éloge de la complexité," 437–38.

2. Sorensen, *A Turbulent Decade Remembered*, 7.

3. "Carta del General Perón," *Cristianismo y Revolución* No. 19, August 1969, back cover.

4. See for instance "Dutshcke y la santísima Trinidad," *Análisis* No. 372, April 29, 1968, 26–7 and "Fue expulsado de Francia Dani 'el Rojo," *Clarín*, June 14, 1968, 2.

5. "La rebelión de los estudiantes," *Análisis* No. 371, April 22, 1968, 52–55; "La crisis francesa," *Clarín*, May 24, 1968, 10; "Francia no retoma a la normalidad," *Clarín*, June 25, 1968, 10; "Los mil ojos del Dr. Marcuse," *Primera Plana* No. 283, May 28, 1968, 61.

6. "La segunda revolución francesa," *Primera Plana* No. 283, May 28, 1968, 25. And also, "Los estudiantes rebeldes," *Siete Días* No. 57, June 11, 1968, 24–7; "Argentina: Poder estudiantil," *Primera Plana* No. 285, June 11, 1968, 53–6. On the military intervention, see Chapter 2.

7. "La semana estudiantil," *Semanario CGT* No. 17, August 22, 1968, 5; "Los estudiantes y el evangelio de la violencia," *Panorama* No. 68, August 13, 1968, 14.

8. "Córdoba," *Semanario CGT* No. 20, September 12, 2.

9. "La Reforma, los estudiantes y las luchas populares," FEN pamphlet, June 1968; "1968: Cincuentenario de la Reforma," PRT pamphlet, June 1968, Student Movement Collection, C9/5–2, Centro de Investigación y Documentación de la Cultura de Izquierda (CEDINCI).

10. Juan García Elorrio, "El signo revolucionario," *Cristianismo y Revolución* No. 1, September of 1966, 2; "La misma guerra," No. 6–7, April of 1968, 3. On the journal and its links with would-be guerrillas Lenci, "La radicalización de los Católicos;" Donatello, *Catolicismo y Montoneros*.

11. Camilo Torres, "Carta a los estudiantes," *Cristianismo y Revolución* No. 2/3, November of 1966, 19; "Movimiento Ateneísta de Santa Fe," No. 14, April of 1969, 32.

12. See Brennan, *Labor Wars in Cordoba*, 123–34.

13. "Junio, movilización popular," *Semanario CGT* No. 6, June 6, 1968, 1; "La CGT de los estudiantes," *Siete Días* No. 61, July 7, 1968, 18–9. Ana Longoni and Mariano Mestman have studied how artistic groups worked within the CGTA; see *Del Di Tella a "Tucumán Arde,"* 24–30.

14. Sirinelli, *Mai 68*. On the reception of the French events in Argentina, see Tarcus, "El Mayo Argentino"; for other Latin American countries, see Gould, "Solidarity under Siege."

15. Taibo, *68*; Sarlo, *Tiempo pasado*.

16. "Made in France," *Gente* No. 152, June 20, 1968, 5–7; "Marcuse, el nuevo profeta de la izquierda," *Panorama* No. 73, September 17, 1968, 82; "Estudiantes, los fantasmas tienen nombre," *Panorama* No. 110, June 3, 1969, 14.

17. "Hablan los dirigentes estudiantiles," *Semanario CGT* No. 33, December 12, 1968, 3.

18. For "68" in Europe in terms of demands and actions, see Siegfried, "Understanding 1968."

19. Delich, *Crisis y protesta social*. See a discussion of Delich in Brennan, *Labor Wars in Cordoba*.

20. "Una visita que huele feo," *Semanario CGT* No. 32, December 5, 1968, 3; "Los integralistas junto al pueblo," *Cristianismo y Revolución* No. 17, June 1969, 5.

21. "Muere un estudiante en Corrientes," *Clarín*, May 16, 1969, 32.

22. "Borda habló de Corrientes," *Clarín*, May 16, 1969, 21; "Los sucesos de Corrientes," *Clarín*, May 18, 1969, 32; "El Ministro Borda está tranquilo," *Análisis* No. 427, May 20, 1969, 9–11.

23. "Muere un estudiante en Rosario," *Clarín*, May 18, 1969, 31; "Realízance manifestaciones," *Clarín*, May 20, 1969, 21; "Estudiantes, los muertos mandan," *Panorama* No. 108, May 20, 1969, 6–7; and press communiques quoted in Beba and Beatriz Balvé, *El 69*, 263–73.

24. Andrés Zavala, "La sublevación de los rosarinos," *Primera Plana* No. 335, May 27, 1969, 18–19; for further depictions, see "La rebelión universitaria," *Siete Días*, Special Issue, May 26, 1969.

25. "La semana trágica de Juan Carlos Onganía," *Primera Plana* No. 335, May 27, 1969, 8–11.

26. "Los frutos de la violencia," *Análisis* No. 428, May 27, 1969, 6–7.

27. "Dirigentes universitarios, después del desborde," *Panorama* No. 109, May 27, 1969, 16–17.

28. See Brennan, *Labor Wars in Cordoba*, Chapter 5; and Gordillo, *Córdoba en los 60'*, Chapter 6.

29. "Coordinación del movimiento estudiantil," *La Voz del Interior*, May 23, 1969, 20; Ramón Cuevas and Osvaldo Reicz, "El movimiento estudiantil," *Los Libros* No. 21, August 1971, 17.

30. This account was based on "Tiempo de conmoción," *Análisis* No. 429, June 3, 1969, 6–8; "Córdoba, el camino de los errores," *Confirmado* No. 207, June 5, 1969, 200–201; "La hora de la violencia," *Primera Plana*, June 3, 1969, 10–17; "La violencia asistió a la cita," *Panorama* No. 110, June 3, 1969, 6–11; "Mayo de corceles y de aceros," *Siete Días* No. 108, June 2, 1969, n.p.

31. Carlos Altamirano, "Memoria del 69," *Estudios* No. 4, July–December 1994, 9–13.

32. See, for instance, "Hablan los Montoneros," *Cristianismo y Revolución* No. 26, November–December 1970, 10–14; "A dos años del Cordobazo," *Estrella Roja* No. 3, June 1971, 3.

33. Juan Carlos Torre, "A partir del Cordobazo," *Estudios* No. 4, July–December 1994, 22–23.

34. Germani, *Sociología de la modernización*, 12, 14.

35. *Censo Nacional de Población, Familias y Vivienda*, 1970, 1:8; Torrado, *Estructura social de la Argentina*, 265–66.

36. Hilb and Lutzky, *La nueva izquierda argentina*; Terán, *Nuestros años sesenta*; Altamirano, "Peronismo y cultura de izquierda"; Tortti, *El "viejo" Partido Socialista*.

37. See Manzano, "Argentina Tercer Mundo."

38. Frank, "Imaginaire politique et figures symboliques internationals," 31–47; Giachetti, *Anni sessanta comincia la danza*, 321–47.

39. Fassin and Bourdelais, "Les frontières de l'espace moral"; Prochasson, "Le socialisme des indigneés."

40. "Programa del Primero de Mayo," *Semanario CGT* No. 1, May 1, 1968.

41. "Al gran pueblo argentino, salud?," *Semanario CGT* No. 5, May 30, 1968, 2; see

also "La explotación de los obreros rurales," *Semanario CGT*, No. 12, July 18, 1968, 4; "500.000 argentinos amenazados de exterminio," *Semanario CGT*, No. 39, February 20, 1969, 2; "Represión en Santiago," *El combatiente* No. 64, November 29, 1971, 3; "Luchas campesinas: El Chaco," *El combatiente*, No. 68, February 12, 1972, 11.

42. "La Universidad para ricos," *Semanario CGT* No. 24, October 10, 1968, 7; "Educación: Más analfabetos para Onganía," *Semanario CGT*, No. 30, November 21, 1968, 2.

43. "Tucumán: Doloroso espejo del país," *Semanario CGT* No. 5, May 30, 1968, 5; "La CGT dice presente," *Semanario CGT*, No. 8, June 20, 1968, 4. On the PRT, see Pozzi, *Por las sendas argentinas*, 96–97.

44. Longoni and Mestman, *Del Di Tella a "Tucumán Arde,"* 146–93. The complete sociological report is in "Porqué arde Tucumán," *Semanario CGT* No. 33, December 12, 1968, 7.

45. Félix Luna, "El neo-turismo," *Clarín*, February 19, 1970, 44.

46. "50 mil mochilas invaden el verano," *Confirmado* No. 76, December 1, 1966, 48–50; "Albergues para mochileros," *Análisis* No. 324, May 29, 1967, 27.

47. *Encuesta nacional de turismo 1970–1971* (Presidencia de la Nación, 1972), 17, 39, 59–62.

48. Elena, "Point of Departure," 27. On the Northwest as touristic destination, see Chamosa, *Argentina's Folklore Movement*.

49. "La importancia del dedo pulgar," *Siete Días* No. 91, February 3, 1969, 56; "Con el verano en la mochila," *Clarín*, December 19, 1971, 10–14.

50. "Hugo Macchi," *Estrella Roja* No. 64, November 17, 1975, 4; Narzole, *Nada a cambio*, 17–18.

51. See Graciela Daleo's testimony in Anguita and Caparrós, *La voluntad*, 1:26–29.

52. "Informe especial: Los hacheros," *Cristianismo y Revolución* No. 8, July 1968, 5–13; "Corrientes," *Cristianismo y Revolución* No. 9, September 1968, 9–11; "Tucumán: Informe de la Asociación de Estudios Sociales de Córdoba," *Cristianismo y Revolución* No. 10, October 1968, 7–11; Mauricio Fontan, "Informe sobre el noroeste argentino," *Antropología 3er Mundo* 1.1 (May 1969): 14–26.

53. Ferreyra Beltrán, *Memoria de los vientos*, 17–20.

54. Interview with José.

55. Gonzalo Cárdenas, "El movimiento nacional y la Universidad," *Antropología 3er Mundo* 2.3 (November 1969): 41–60; see also Alcira Argumedo, "Cátedras nacionales: Una experiencia peronista en la Universidad," *Envido* No. 3, April 1971, 58. For the *cátedras nacionales*, see Barletta, "Una izquierda universitaria peronista."

56. "América Latina: Los caminos de la revolución," Syllabus, March 1971, Student Movement Collection, SJMP/CMS R4/5-1, CEDINCI.

57. "El tema político canaliza las preferencias de lectura," *La Opinión*, October 24, 1972, 15.

58. On the "New Song" see Moore, *Music and Revolution*; and Reyes Matta, "The 'New Song' and Its Confrontation." On the Yupanqui, see Orquera, "Marxismo, peronismo, *indocriollismo*."

59. See, for example, Mateo de la Calle, "Dependencia cultural y cultura mil-

tiante," *Cristianismo y Revolución* No. 26, November 1970, 21–24; and Guillermo Gutierrez, "Pensamiento nacional y política," *Antropología 3er Mundo* 3.4 (September 1970): 1–11. On Sosa's making of her artistic persona, see Carrillo-Rodríguez, "Latinoamericana de Tucumán."

60. "Sonidos e ideas: La canción argentina de hoy," *Clarín*, September 26, 1971, 14; "Un recital de canciones, acontecimiento político," *La Opinión*, August 16, 1972, 8.

61. See Chapter 5.

62. Interview with Mabel S.

63. With variations, this narrative appeared in countless texts; see for example, "Historia de nuestra dependencia," *Cristianismo y Revolución* No. 5, November 1967, 4–6.

64. "Carta argentina: El Che Guevara y la revolución nacional y social del pueblo argentino," *Cristianismo y Revolución* No. 11, November 1968, 37–38.

65. Petty, "Political Socialization among Secondary School Boys," 165, 171, 184.

66. Gillespie, *Soldiers of Perón*, 110–13; Pozzi, *Por las sendas argentinas*, 23–24.

67. "Pensamiento del poder adolescente," *La Opinión Cultural*, September 22, 1973, 3.

68. Carassai, "Ni de izquierda ni peronistas, medioclasistas."

69. "Crítico pájaro de juventud," *Análisis* No. 458, December 23, 1969, 42; see also Brailovsky et al., *México y Argentina visto por sus jóvenes*.

70. "Cartas," *Nuevo Hombre* No. 25, March 1972, 12.

71. Interview with Daniel Burak, File 0139, Memoria Abierta Archive.

72. See Muiño, *La otra juventud*. On the Communist Party, see I. Gilbert, *La Fede*, 525–42.

73. "Sobre la Juventud," *El Combatiente* No. 175, July 30, 1975, 4; "Juventud Guevarista: Dos años de experiencia revolucionaria," *El Combatiente* No. 186, October 8, 1975, 15; see also Pozzi, *Por las sendas argentinas*.

74. See especially Elhrich, *Rebeldes, intransigentes y duros*.

75. Juan Perón, "Carta a la juventud peronista," in Baschetti, *Documentos de la resistencia*, 437–38; see also James, *Resistance and Integration*, 103–57, and "The Peronist Left."

76. For references to this letter, see "La discordia, una vocación," *Siete Días* No. 112, June 30, 1969, 24; "Perón no se va a jubilar," *Primera Plana* No. 225, August 17, 1971, 16.

77. "Perón habla a la juventud," *Cristianismo y Revolución* No. 29, June 1971, 8–10. On the negotiations between Perón and Lanusse, see De Riz, *La política en suspenso*, 108–26.

78. "Los herederos del líder," *Panorama* No. 248, January 17, 1972, 16–20; "El justicialismo aumentó su volumen de afiliación," *La Opinión*, January 2, 1972, 14; "Documento de información doctrinaria para la juventud," *Primera Plana* No. 487, May 30, 1972, 31–37.

79. Miguel Bonasso, "El mitín opositor de la juventud peronista," *La Opinión*, June 11, 1972, 8. On the organizational structure of the JP, see Bartoletti, *Montoneros*, 360–425.

80. "Los candidatos y los jóvenes," *La Opinión*, February 6, 1973, 19.

81. Héctor Cámpora, "Mensaje a la Asamblea Legislativa," *Diario de sesiones de la Cámara de Diputados*, vol. 1, May 25, 1973, 343; for the JP's influence, see Gillespie, *Soldiers of Perón*, 130–34.

82. Sigal and Verón, *Perón o muerte*, 136–37; "Comunicado de FAR y Montoneros: Apoyar, defender y controlar," *El Descamisado* No. 2, May 29, 1973, 3–4.

83. "Declaración del Congreso General de Estudiantes Peronistas," *Envido* No. 7, October 1972, 78–80; "Juventud Universitaria Peronista," *Envido*, No. 9, May 1973, 54–61; "Estudiantes de ingeniería," *Cuestionario* No. 2, June 1973, 13; "Ejemplo de colonización," *Cuestionario* No. 2, June 1973, 19.

84. "La Coordinadora se pronuncia sobre la autonomía," *La Opinión*, March 27, 1973, 16.

85. "El cuadro de convulsión estudiantil," *La Opinión*, June 14, 1973, 7, "Puiggrós," *Militancia* No. 5, July 12, 1973, 16–20; "La Universidad," *El Descamisado* No. 7, July 3, 1973, 10–11.

86. Consejo de Rectores de Universidades Nacionales, *Censo Universitario* 1972, 4; Ministerio de Cultura y Educación, *Cifras educativas*, 1974, 15.

87. "Resoluciones adoptadas por la Universidad Nacional y Popular de Buenos Aires," *Universidad: Aportes para la Reconstrucción Nacional*, No. 2, July 1973, 13–14.

88. *Filosofía y Letras en la Reconstrucción Nacional: Boletín Informativo*, October 1973, Student Movement Collection, SMJP/CMS C5/5-1, CEDINCI.

89. Interview with Elena A. (b. in 1940 in Buenos Aires), August 24, 2007; Mesa "Referencia," File 15.979, vol. 2, DIPPBA; "JUP: Comunicado," *El Peronista* No. 9, October 1973, 11.

90. "La hora de los pibes," *Panorama* No. 210, May 4, 1971, 14.

91. "La UES está presente, mi general," *El Descamisado* No. 18, September 18, 1973, 26–27; "La Coordinadora Secundaria Peronista propone reconstruir la vieja UES," *La Opinión*, May 5, 1973.

92. Mesa "A," Factor Estudiantil, Folder 48; "Ocupaciones de colegios, facultades y universidades," Vol. 4, R.15.979, DIPPBA.

93. Interview with Marcelo Schapces, File 0245, Memoria Abierta Archive; "Reestablecimiento de la normalidad en los colegios secundarios," *La Opinión*, July 5, 1973, 15.

94. *La escuela media para la liberación y la reconstrucción nacional* (Buenos Aires: Ministerio de Cultura y Educación, 1973), 9, 13–16.

95. *Boletín de Comunicaciones del Ministerio de Cultura y Educación* No. 2, June 30, 1973, 1–4. *Suplemento del Boletín de Comunicaciones*, July 1973, 1:4–7.

96. Interview with Laura Giussani, File 0113, Memoria Abierta Archive. Gabriela Alegre's testimony is in Guelar et al., *Los chicos del exilio*, 191–92.

97. "Unión de Estudiantes Secundarios," Mesa "A," File 13, DIPPBA; Robles, *Perejiles*, 41–42.

98. Gatica, *Tiempos de liberación*, 53–58; "Van a Salta y hacen falta," *El Descamisado* No. 34, January 1974.

99. "El día en que la UES hizo vibrar a toda Salta," *El Descamisado* No. 37, January 29, 1974.

100. "Excursiones para alumnos," *Noticias*, December 24, 1973, 19; "Turismo estudiantil en Perú," *Noticias*, January 3, 1974, 11.

101. "Unas ganas de construir que contagian," *Noticias*, February 3, 1974, 4; see also "Culminó la campaña de la JP," *Noticias*, December 18, 1973, 6; "Reconstrucción, otra campaña," *Noticias*, December 24, 1973, 13; "Nuevos operativos de reconstrucción," *Noticias*, January 20, 1974, 10.

102. "Las vacilaciones de la Tendencia," *Militancia* No. 33, January 31, 1974, 11. See also a more detailed criticism to the Tendency in "La política de conjunto," *Militancia* No. 20, October 25, 1973, 9.

103. Gillespie, *Soldiers of Perón*, 136.

104. Interviews with Daniel Burak, File 0139; Raquel Resta, File 0240; Vicky Kornblitt, File 0252, Memoria Abierta Archive.

105. Interview with Mabel S. See Chapter 7 for a discussion on the gendered, class, and cultural components of youth politics.

106. Torre, "A partir del Cordobazo," 23.

107. Verbitsky, *Ezeiza*, 64–65, 81, 120, 171–89, 283.

108. "La burguesía penetra en el campo popular," *El Combatiente* No. 90, September 14, 1973.

109. See "La CIA, la fuga de François Chappe y la OAS," *El Descamisado* No. 7, July 3, 1973, 23–28; "La JP y Perón: Encuentro permanente, sin intermediarios," *El Descamisado* No. 10, July 24, 1973, 2–3.

110. "Jauretche: Reflexiones sobre la victoria," *Cuestionario* No. 3, July 1973, 4–5.

111. Rascovsky, *La matanza de los hijos*, 9, 127, and *El filicidio*, 66. For an overview of Rascovsky's theory of filicide, see Plotkin, *Freud in the Pampas*, 99–101.

112. "El líder Perón y la lucha generacional," *La Opinión Cultural*, July 1, 1973, 12.

113. "La JP debe prepararse para tomar el relevo," *La Opinión*, September 11, 1973, 10; "Perón: Basta de grupos," *El Descamisado* No. 17, September 11, 1973, 4–5.

114. "El péndulo se detuvo," *Panorama* No. 333, October 4, 1973, 4; "Depuración," *Panorama* No. 337, November 11, 1973, 4–5; "La persistencia del terror," *Militancia* No. 25, November 29, 1973, 4.

115. "La JUP denuncia una ofensiva reaccionaria," *El Descamisado* No. 20, October 2, 1973, n.p.; "Asumen posiciones antagónicas grupos peronistas," *La Opinión*, November 13, 1973, 9.

116. "Para frenarla, habría que asesinar 500,000 militantes," *La Opinión*, January 29, 1974.

117. "Perón enfatizó que deben irse los dirigentes juveniles," *La Opinión*, February 8, 1974, 8; "El tema de la representatividad," *Noticias*, February 11, 1974, 6.

118. Dardo Cabo, "Porqué somos peronistas," *El Descamisado* No. 39, February 12, 1974, 2–3.

119. Hunt, *The Family Romance of the French Revolution*, xiii, 8, 14–15.

120. Sigal and Verón, *Perón o muerte*, 204–5.

121. The paragraph was informed by Anguita and Caparrós, *La voluntad*, 2:309–15; Sigal and Verón, *Perón o muerte*, 209–19; Gillespie, *Soldiers of Perón*, 148–51.

122. Altamirano, "Montoneros," in *Peronismo y cultura de izquierda*, 139–40.

123. "Evaluación de la JP," *Noticias*, May 6, 1974, 6–7.

124. "De lo generacional y lo revolucionario," *Militancia* No. 9, August 9, 1973, 6.

Chapter 7

1. Grosz, *Volatile Bodies*, vii; and "Feminism and the Crisis of Reason," 33.

2. Berger, *Ways of Seeing*, 54.

3. Perniola, "Between Clothing and Nudity," 237; Barcan, *Nudity*, 46.

4. See Mulvey, "Visual Pleasure and Narrative Cinema."

5. "Adopte sin complejos la falda corta," *Para Ti* No. 2286, May 5, 1966, 48–49; "¿Primavera con minifaldas?," *Primera Dama*, with *Primera Plana* No. 195, September 20, 1966, 2–3; "La consagración de la minifalda," *Siete Días* No. 86, December 12, 1969, 13.

6. "Anatomía de la minifalda," *Primera Plana* No. 236, July 4, 1967, 40.

7. Liga de Madres de Familia al Intendente, July 23, 1967, Letters Folder, Liga de Madres de Familia Archive. The ad for Lady Far West appeared in *Clarín*, July 20, 1967, 13.

8. "Código de Publicidad," *Boletín Municipal de la Ciudad de Buenos Aires*, June 1, 1967, 4467–90; "Las chicas del aviso audaz," *Gente* No. 105, July 27, 1967, 18.

9. "Erotismo: La idea fija," *Primera Plana* No. 201, November 1, 1966, 44–45; "¿Qué miran los hombres?," *Siete Días* No. 47, April 2, 1968, 30–35.

10. Bordo, *Unbearable Weight*, 199, 201.

11. "Para el verano," *Para Ti* No. 1903, December 17, 1958, 81; "Cuerpo sano," No. 2419, November 18, 1968, 81. For letters of complaint, see "Secreto de confesión," *Para Ti* No. 2405, August 12, 1968, 66; *Para Ti* No. 2440, April 14, 1969, 82.

12. The next comparable survey was for 1985, and the average daily calories had dropped to 2900. See Aguirre, *Estrategias de consumo*, 72, 76, 82, 84.

13. "Las escuálidas," *Atlántida* No. 1234, January 1970, 26–30; see also "La manía de adelgazar," *Confirmado* No. 138, February 8, 1969, 32.

14. Escardó, *Nueva geografía de Buenos Aires*, 82.

15. Mafud, *La revolución sexual argentina*, 49, 53–54.

16. "Adán y Eva cada vez más parecidos," *Panorama* No. 80, November 5, 1968, 37; "Los límites del sexo," *Confirmado* No. 271, August 26, 1970, 44.

17. See Chapter 5; and "Luz roja para adolescentes," *Mundo Policial* No. 13, September 1971, 20.

18. "Abajo la discriminación sexual," *Siete Días* No. 132, November 11, 1969, 30–37; "Correo," *Siete Días* No. 138, December 29, 1969, 18; *Siete Días* No. 141, January 18, 1970, 20; *Siete Días* No. 142, January 25, 1970, 20.

19. Solomon-Godeau, "The Other Side of Venus," 113.

20. Ad for Levi's is in *Siete Días* No. 268, July 3, 1972, 3; see also Manzano, "Blue Jean Generation."

21. Carlos Ulanovsky, "La censura madre que nos censuró," *Satiricón* No. 12, October 1972, 36–39; Avellaneda, *Censura, autoritarismo y cultura*, vol. 1, Chapter 1.

22. "De Luca, a toda máquina y sin mirar atrás," *Mercado* No. 42, April 30, 1970, 49.

23. Cámara Argentina de Anunciantes, *Estudio de inversión*, 4:19.

24. "Publicidad: la escalada del sexo," *Confirmado* No. 148, April 18, 1968, 28–29; and also "Publicidad, sigue la diversion," *Primera Plana* No. 317, January 31, 1969, 16–17.

25. "Código de ética para avisos," in Alonso Piñeiro, *Breve historia de la publicidad argentina*, 254–55.

26. "Cámaras rigurosamente vigiladas," *Siete Días* No. 95, March 3, 1969, 21; "Editorial: Moral no, moralina," *Análisis* No. 416, March 5, 1969, 16–17.

27. "Reclamos de bella gente," *Análisis* No. 528, April 27, 1971, 43; "Modelos, ¿por qué no?," *La Bella Gente* No. 2, November 1969, 78–81.

28. Beatriz Spinoza and Juan Carlos Martelli, "La moda no es inocente," *Primera Plana* No. 486, May 23, 1972, 3; "Enfoque interdisciplinario de la moda," *La Opinión*, September 26, 1972, 16.

29. Augier, *Los jardines del cielo*, 107–8.

30. See Langland, "Birth Control Pills and Molotov Cocktails," 308–49.

31. Mattini, *Los perros*, 2:78; Diana, *Mujeres guerrilleras*, 166.

32. See "Audaz golpe en Córdoba," *La Razón*, April 28, 1970, 12; "La célula de Mendoza," *La Razón*, October 28, 1970, 13; "Un comando extremista en La Plata," *La Razón*, February 2, 1971, 8; "Tres hombres y dos mujeres robaron 9700 pesos," *La Razón*, February 11, 1971, 1; "El asalto a la custodia del embajador alemán," *La Razón*, February 15, 1971, 6; "Golpe extremista en Turdera," *La Razón*, May 18, 1971, 13.

33. "Los detenidos en Córdoba son jóvenes de las mejores familias," *La Razón*, July 2, 1970, 1; "El calerazo y las guerrillas," *Confirmado* No. 264, July 8, 1970, 16–17; my last quote is from "Agitación: Las 48 horas que conmovieron al país," *Panorama* No. 167, July 7, 1970, 10–14.

34. Videos 22–24, Centro de Documentación Audiovisual, Universidad Nacional de Córdoba, Archivo Canal 10.

35. "Audaz golpe comando," *La Razón*, August 13, 1971, 12.

36. See, for example, "Mini Shorts: Sus claves secretas," *Clarín*, May 23, 1971, 6–7.

37. Simmel, "The Secret and the Secret Society," 347.

38. Mariguella, *Mini-manual of the Urban Guerrilla*, 48.

39. "Una semana de fuego," *Análisis*, No. 490, August 4, 1970, 16–17; "Buenos días, agente," *Panorama* No. 158, May 5, 1970, 13; "Fue asaltada la Prefectura del Delta esta madrugada," *La Razón*, April 12, 1970, 4; "La mujer 71," *Mundo Policial* No. 8, March–April 1971, 69–71.

40. On legislative change see Collins, *Modern Love*, 134–60; Herzog, *Sex after Fascism*, 53–60.

41. Nari, "Abrir los ojos, abrir la cabeza," 15–21; Vasallo, "Movilización, política y orígenes," 61–88.

42. "Feministas argentinas: La cosecha ideológica," *Panorama* No. 266, June 1, 1972, 33–37; Dionisia Fontán, "Los caminos de la libertad," *Siete Días* No. 265, June 12, 1972, 9.

43. "Muchacha intenta luchar contra la discriminación sexual," *La Opinión*, December 7, 1971, 8.

44. "Luchas por la reivindicación de las mujeres," *La Opinión*, April 23, 1972, 15.

45. "Femimundo 1972: Una muestra para el consumo," *La Opinión*, December 17, 1972, 18.

46. Barrancos, *Mujeres en la sociedad argentina*, 239–43; Vasallo, "Movilización, política y origenes."

47. "Ni hablar de estas mujeres," *Primera Plana* No. 491, June 27, 1972, 32–34.

48. Rapisardi and Modarelli, *Fiestas, baños y exilios*; Sebreli, *Escritos sobre escritos*. See also "Un grupo de homosexuales pide mayor comprensión," *La Opinión*, August 24, 1971, 20.

49. "Declaración del FLH," *Homosexuales*, July 13, 1973, 4; *Sexo y Revolución*, Pamphlet, November 1974, FLH.

50. "La moral sexual en la Argentina," Pamphlet, September 1973; the main reference was Kate Millet's "The Sexual Revolution Would . . ."; see also *Somos* No. 3, May 1974, FLH.

51. Luis Ortolani (signing as Julio Parra), "Moral y proletarización," *Políticas de la Memoria* No. 5, 2004–5, 99–100. It first appeared in a clandestine publication of the PRT-ERP militants who, like Ortolani, were imprisoned in Rawson, in 1972. It was reprinted in 1974, and its reading was mandatory for the incoming PRT-ERP militants.

52. Francisco Urondo, "Sexo y escapismo," *Extra* No. 25, September 1967, 39.

53. "Sexualización de la literatura," *Clarín*, September 23, 1971, 4–5.

54. "Sexo, erotismo y capitalismo," *Nuevo Hombre* No. 16, November 3, 1971, 18.

55. Cosse, *Pareja, sexualidad y familia*.

56. "Señoritas . . . y la virginidad," *Satiricón* No. 2, December 1972, 12.

57. "La mujer argentina y la sexualidad," *Panorama* No. 325, August 2, 1973, 50–53.

58. *La Opinión Cultural*, September 22, 1973, 2–3.

59. Sebreli, *Buenos Aires*, 74.

60. Alicia Gallotti, "Sociología barata: La piba de barrio," *Satiricón* No. 14, January 1974, 21–24.

61. Poggi, *Perdón por la letra*, 109.

62. "¿Qué es el conocimiento carnal?," *La Bella Gente* No. 29, June 1972, 28–32; "Los muchachos enjuician a las chicas," *La Bella Gente* No. 32, September of 1972, 35–38.

63. "Sexo y represión: Audacia ma non troppo," *Panorama* No. 210, May 4, 1971, 24–27.

64. Héctor Schmucler, "Testimonios de sobrevivientes," *Controversia* Nos. 9/10, 1980, 5.

65. For a feminist reading, see Ciriza and Rodríguez Agüero, "Militancia, política y subjetividad," 88.

66. See Saldaña-Portillo, *The Revolutionary Imagination*, 67–77; Cohen and Frazier, "Defining the Space of Mexico '68," 617–60; Sorensen, *A Turbulent Decade Remembered*, 14–41.

67. Among the most important works, see Vezzetti, *Sobre la violencia revolucionaria*, 131–196; Sarlo, *La pasión y la excepción*; and Calveiro, *Política y/o violencia*.

68. "Luis Pujals: Una biografía revolucionaria," *Nuevo Hombre* No. 23, December 12, 1971, 8–9; "Gloria a Luis Pujals," *Estrella Roja* No. 25, September 21, 1973, 3.

69. Pozzi, *Por las sendas argentinas*, 130–43; Ortolani, "Moral y proletarización," 99–100.

70. "Testimonio del hermano de E. Capello," *Liberación* No. 2, April 1973, 8.

71. For the construction of the myths of revolutionary Evita, see Gillespie, *Soldiers of Perón*, 72–74; Sigal and Verón, *Perón o muerte*, 188–97; Sarlo, *La pasión y la excepción*, Chapter 1.

72. See, for example, "Suplemento Especial Evita," *El Descamisado* No. 10, July 24, 1973; "Evita, bandera de lucha," *De Frente con las bases peronistas* No. 11, July 25, 1974, n.p.

73. "Un jefe Montonero no se entrega," *Evita Montonera* No. 12, February–March 1976, 26; see also "Rodolfo Rey, peronista y Montonero," *Evita Montonera* No. 2, January–February, 1975, 20–22.

74. Robles, *Perejiles*, 46–50.

75. "Tina," in Diana, *Mujeres guerrilleras*, 47.

76. Mattini, *Los perros*, 2:27.

77. Montanaro, *Franciso Urondo*, 112.

78. Gilman, *Entre la pluma y el fusil*; Sigal, *Intelectuales y poder*. Also see the survey "Los temas que preocupan a los intelectuales," *La Opinión Cultural*, October 31, 1971, 8.

79. "Carta Argentina: El Che Guevara," *Cristianismo y Revolución* No. 11, November 1968, 37–38.

80. Interview with Luis Salinas, File No. 0260, Memoria Abierta Archive.

81. "Peti," in Diana, *Mujeres guerrileras*, 69; Ortolani, "Moral y proletarización," 101.

82. Augusto Klappenbach, "Cuerpo, alma, mente," *Nuevo Hombre* No. 13, October 13, 1971.

83. Moyano, *Argentina's Lost Patrol*, 106; Grammático, *Mujeres montoneras*, 50; Pozzi, *Por las sendas argentinas*, 70.

84. Ridenti, *O fantasma da revolução brasileira*, 196, 206; Kampwirth, *Women and Guerrilla Movements*, 2, 42–43.

85. "El papel de la mujer," *El combatiente* No. 157, March 3, 1975; Augier, *Jardines del cielo*.

86. Grammático, *Mujeres montoneras*.

87. "Las compañeras en la guerrilla," *Estrella Roja* No. 65, December 1, 1975, 18–19; "Carta de una compañera a sus padres," No. 66, December 15, 1975, 18–20.

88. "Los que se van de casa," *La Bella Gente* No. 33, October 1972, 30–34.

89. "La escuela secundaria y sus líderes," *La Opinión Cultural*, September 22, 1973, 4.

90. Interview with Mabel S.

91. See Diana, *Mujeres guerrilleras*, 60–61 and 163–71.

92. "Cartas de Carlos Lamarca a Iara Iaverlberg," *Nuevo Hombre* No. 14, October 20, 1971, 9.

93. "Marcos Osatinsky," *Evita Montonera* No. 9, November 1975, 23. For a fictionalized account of Santucho's trial, see Mattini, *Cartas profanas.*

94. Gómez, *Montoneros de Morón,* 111–12; for the PRT, see the testimonies in Carnovale, "Moral y disciplinamiento interno."

95. Actis et al., *Ese infierno,* 37, 45–46.

96. Diez, *El mejor y el peor de los tiempos,* 56–57.

97. Caparrós, *No velas a tus muertos;* see also Montoneros, "Código Penal Revolucionario—1975," *Lucha Armada* No. 8, 2007, 124–27.

98. See Rapisardi and Modarelli, *Fiestas, baños y exilios,* 159–63.

99. Sebreli, *Escritos sobre escritos,* 337.

100. "Carta a Manuel Belloni y Diego Frondizi," *Nuevo Hombre* No. 21, December 8, 1971, 8–9.

101. Jeffreys, *Anticlimax.*

Chapter 8

1. "Adriana Sesto y otros al Ministro del Interior," File No. 160785, Box 26; "Marina Santos y otros, Villa Crespo, al Ministro del Interior," File No. 172222, Box 13, Expedientes Generales—Sección Intermedia, AGN.

2. Franco, *Un enemigo para la nación.*

3. "La denuncia de una Liga de Madres impulsó a la Policía," *La Opinión,* January 9, 1974, 15.

4. "Comunicado del Frente de Liberación Homosexual," *Somos* No. 1, December 1973; "Falta Onganía," *Somos* No. 2, February 1974, FLH.

5. "Un Nuevo calificador en la cinematografía," *Clarín,* September 16, 1974, 36; "Películas prohibidas," *La Nación,* March 3, 1975, 8.

6. Felitti, *La revolución de la píldora.*

7. Poder Ejecutivo Nacional, Decreto No. 659/74, *Boletín Oficial,* March 3, 1974, 2.

8. "El Primer Encuentro Nacional de la Familia," *La Razón,* November 26, 1974, 1; "El Primer Encuentro Nacional de la Familia clausuró sus deliberaciones," *La Razón,* November 28, 1974, 12.

9. "Programa de acción pastoral: Matrimonio y familia," *Boletín AICA* No. 956, April 17, 1975, 25–39; for the "silencing" of the Third World Priests, see Obregón, *Entre la cruz y la espada.*

10. "Peligro de dominación marxista," *Boletín AICA* No. 981–82, October 16, 1975, 140–46.

11. "Paraísos artificiales," *Panorama* No. 46, March 1967, 35–39; for an overview of that experience see Plotkin, *Freud in the Pampas,* 172–75.

12. "¿Hacia la generación de la marihuana?," *Primera Plana* No. 254, November 7, 1967, 46–49; Millán and Fontán Ballestra, *Las reformas al Código Penal: Ley 15.567,* 205–10, 266–74.

13. See, for example, Leo Gleyzer, "Única solución: amor," *Gente* No. 293, March 4, 1971, 86–87; "Diario de un drogadicto," *Primera Plana* No. 420, Febru-

ary 17, 1971, 32–37; Elsa Jascalevich, "Buenos Aires visita al infierno," *Clarín*, November 7, 1971, 10–105; "Los caminos de la muerte blanca," *Siete Días* No. 270, July 17, 1972, 40–43.

14. "Graves revelaciones sobre el tráfico de alucinógenos en el país," *Clarín*, March 4, 1971, 24.

15. Policía Federal Argentina, *Superintendencia Técnica* (Buenos Aires: 1972), 83, 85.

16. "Marihuana, el revés de la trama," *Mundo Policial* No. 5, July 1970, 62; "Código y drogas," *Clarín*, March 7, 1971, 12; López Bolado, *Drogas y otras sustancias*, 84–92.

17. "Se constituye hoy la comisión contra el tráfico de drogas," *La Opinión*, February 2, 1972, 10.

18. Gootenberg, *Andean Cocaine*, 308–9.

19. U.S. Senate, *The World Narcotics Problem*, 35.

20. "Se firmó un tratado bilateral de lucha contra la droga," *Clarín*, August 20, 1973, 12.

21. Verbitsky, *Ezeiza*, 42–43.

22. Policía Federal, *Memoria, 1975*, 221–22, 268–69, unpublished manuscript, CEHPFA.

23. Weissman, *Toxicomanías*, 90–91, 153–61.

24. *Diario de Sesiones de la Cámara de Diputados*, September 19, 1974, 2:2856–68.

25. "Drogas, ¿qué pasa en la Argentina?," *Gente* No. 503, March 12, 1975, 64–67; for a similar explanation, see "Editorial: Drogas y subversión," *Clarín*, May 12, 1975, 12; and Moras Mom, *Toxicomanía y delito*, 149–58.

26. "Cámara de empresarios de locales de expansión nocturna al Ministro del Interior," File 16610, Box 15, Expendientes Generales, AGN; "Redadas en Plaza Irlanda," *Clarín*, March 15, 1975, 22; "Drogas, los tentáculos de la corrupción," *Siete Días* No. 445, December 12, 1975, 90.

27. "Adolescencia y drogas," *Actualidad Psicológica* No. 4, July 1975, 1–3.

28. "Habría conexión entre extremistas y traficantes," *La Razón*, September 27, 1970, 6; "Las drogas y la política," *La Razón*, August 23, 1971, 6.

29. "Procedimientos antisubversivos: Informe psiquiátrico," *La Razón*, January 30, 1974, 1.

30. "La propaganda contrarrevolucionaria," *El Combatiente* No. 106, February 6, 1974, 10; "La CIA y las drogas," *Liberación* No. 20, May 15, 1974, 32.

31. Servetto, *73/76*, 193–208.

32. "Modifican el proyecto de ley universitaria," *Clarín*, February 21, 1974, 9.

33. *Diario de sesiones de la Cámara de Diputados*, March 13–14, 1974, 7:6212.

34. "La JUP convocó a la movilización," *Noticias*, March 16, 1974, 11.

35. Dirección Nacional de Enseñanza Media y Superior, *Circular* No. 12, February 22, 1974, CENIDE.

36. "A estudiar," *La Nación*, March 9, 1974, 6; "Disciplina estudiantil," *Clarín*, March 10, 1974.

37. "UES: Críticas," *Noticias*, March 26, 1974, 11; "Balance Nacional Secundarios 1974," Patricio Etchegaray Collection, PCA.

38. "Discurso pronunciado por el Dr. Oscar Ivanissevich," Folder 042-I93, CENIDE.

39. Resolución 51/74, *Boletín de Comunicaciones del Ministerio de Cultura y Educación* No. 12, October 15, 1974, 9; Resolución 41/75, ibid., No. 18, January 31, 1975, 3.

40. "Universidad de Lomas de Zamora," Mesa "A," Factor Estudiantil, File 011, DIPPBA.

41. Gillespie, *Soldiers of Perón*, 216; García, *El drama de la autonomía militar*, 65.

42. Comodoro José C. D'odorico, "La mujer en la guerrilla," *Revista de la Escuela de Comando y Estado Mayor de la Fuerza Aérea Argentina* No. 78, October of 1974, 39–55.

43. "Pongamos la casa en orden," *Gente* No. 560, April 15, 1976, 17.

44. On "reactive consensus" see Palermo and Novaro, *La dictadura militar*, 24–5, on the Church's hierarchy and the media, Obregón, *Entre la cruz y la espada* and Blaustein, *Decíamos ayer*.

45. Pion-Berlin, "Latin American National Security Doctrines: Hard-and Soft-line Themes," 411–29; Perelli, "The Military's Perception of Threat in the Southern Cone," 93–106.

46. "El primer mano a mano con el presidente," *Gente* No. 560, April 15, 1976, 4.

47. For a description of that deadly mechanism see Calveiro, *Poder y desaparición*; a regional approach in Menjívar and Rodríguez, "State Terror in the US–Latin American Interstate Regime."

48. García, *El drama de la autonomía militar*, 500, 504.

49. Argentina's National Commission on Disappeared People, *Nunca Más (Never Again)* (London: Faber and Faber, 1986 [1984]), 285.

50. Stern, *Remembering Pinochet's Chile*, xiv; Guy, "Shifting Meanings of Childhood and N.N."

51. O'Donnell, "Democracia en la Argentina," 28. See Chapter 7 for youth in advertising.

52. Ad for Flecha in *Siete Días* No. 1975, 14 and in *Gente* No. 578, August 19, 1976, 18–19.

53. Mayor Horacio Gutiérrez, "Sobre la familia y las Fuerzas Armadas," *RECEM* No. 85, February 1976, 91–103.

54. "Carta abierta a los padres argentinos," *Gente* No. 595, December 16, 1976, 7–8; see also "Instrucciones para arruinar a su hijo," *Gente* No. 581, September 9, 1976, 67.

55. Filc, *Entre el parentesco y la política*.

56. Dirección de Enseñanza Media y Superior, Circular No. 27, March 23, 1977, JVGA.

57. Ministerio de Cultura y Educación, *Subversión en el ámbito educativo* (Buenos Aires, 1978).

58. Dirección de Enseñanza Media y Superior, Circular No. 187, October 27, 1977, JVGA.

59. Invernizzi and Gociol, *Un golpe a los libros*, 107–12.

60. Instituto Nacional de Estadísticas y Censos, *La juventud en la Argentina*

(Buenos Aires: Ministerio de Desarrollo Social, 1985), 62, 66, especially Chapter 2 for the 1950s and 1960s.

61. Novaro and Palermo, *La dictadura argentina*, 179–229; Pineau, "Impacto de un asueto," 74–79.

62. Ministerio de Educación y Cultura, *Cifras educativas, 1970–1982*, 191.

63. Dirección de Derechos Humanos, *Huellas*, 14; Godoy and Broda, "El poder de la palabra bajo vigilancia."

64. Interview with Mabel S.; see also Interview with Raquel Resta, Memoria Abierta Archive.

65. Centro de Estudios Legales y Sociales, *Adolescentes detenidos-desaparecidos*, 8.

66. "Las líneas de la política educativa," *La Nación*, April 17, 1976, 4.

67. Tedesco, "Elementos para una sociología del curriculum escolar en la Argentina," 27.

68. "Formación Cívica: Guías para la enseñanza," Anexo con *Boletín de Comunicaciones del Ministerio de Educación*, No. 5, August 1976, 6; Filc, *Entre el parentesco y la política*, 53.

69. Dirección de Enseñanza Media y Superior, Circular No. 53, April 22, 1977; Circular No. 154, September 20, 1977; No. 62, May 1979, JVGA.

70. Lvovich, "Marchemos a la frontera."

71. Vila, "Rock nacional: crónicas de la resistencia juvenil," and "Rock Nacional and Dictatorship"; see also Pujol, *Rock y dictadura*.

72. Secretaría de Inteligencia del Estado, "Antecedentes ideológicos de artistas nacionales y extranjeros que desarrollan actividades en la Argentina," Mesa "Referencia," Folder 17,470, DIPPBA.

73. "Luna Park, 11.000 personas, una fiesta," *Expreso Imaginario* No. 1, August 1976, n.p.; "El rock, esa fiebre progresiva," *Siete Días* No. 480, August 27, 1976, 43–45.

74. "No es Beethoven, pero ya es un clásico," *Gente* No. 580, September 2, 1976, 53–56.

75. "El Almirante Massera refirióse a la sociedad occidental," *La Nación*, November 26, 1977, 22.

76. Vila, "Rock nacional: crónicas de la resistencia juvenil," 87; Pujol, *Rock y dictadura*, 92–96.

77. Interview with Eduardo C. See also Alabarces, *Entre gatos y violadores*; and Masiello, "La Argentina durante el Proceso."

78. "Antecedentes 'Almendra,'" Mesa Ds. Factor "Varios," Folder 15321, DIPPBA.

79. Interview with Pedro Pujó.

80. For journalistic depictions, see Ramos and Lebjowicz, *Corazones en llamas*; and Guerrero, *Historia del palo*.

81. Benedetti and Graziano, *Estación imposible*; Vila, "Rock nacional: crónicas de la resistencia juvenil."

82. "Testimonios desde el Bolsón," *Expreso Imaginario* No. 12, July 1977, 18–19; Gloria Guerrero, "Revistas subterráneas," *Expreso Imaginario* No. 14, September 1977, 20–21; Roberto Pettinato, "Artesanos," *Expreso Imaginario* No. 21, April 1978, 16; "Viajando por América," *Expreso Imaginario* No. 31, February 1979, 12.

83. See, for example, "Correo de lectores," *Expreso Imaginario* No. 11, June 1977, 3; No. 14, September 1977, 3–4; No. 15, October 1977, 3; No. 16, November 1977, 3–4.

84. Pipo Lernoud, "Los afiebrados robots del sábado por la noche," *Expreso Imaginario* No. 26, September 1978, 6–7.

85. Interview with Marcela M.

86. Carolina Serrano, "Dos modelos de juventud," *Jotapé* No. 2, ca. May 1980, n.p.

87. Interview with Marcelo Schapces, Memoria Abierta Archive.

88. "Una respuesta del Ejército a las inquietudes juveniles," *Vamos* No. 10, September 24, 1976, 17–21. On this "embarrassing" experience, see I. Gilbert, *La Fede*, 621–25.

89. "Comisión Nacional Secundaria, Circular Nacional, August 9, 1976," and "Reunión General Secundarios, 1978," Patricio Etchegaray Collection, PCA.

90. See the testimony in Berguier, Hecker, and Schifrin, *Estudiantes secundarios*, 80–81.

91. Lorenz, *Las guerras por Malvinas*; Novaro and Palermo, *La dictadura militar*, 435–44.

92. Centro de Estudios Legales y Sociales, *Conscriptos detenidos-desaparecidos* (Buenos Aires, 1982); Lorenz, *Las guerras por Malvinas*.

93. Lorenz, *Las guerras por Malvinas*, 198. For a detailed chronicle of rock and the Malvinas see Pujol, *Rock y dictadura*, 208–22.

94. O'Donnell, "Democracia en la Argentina," 16–19.

Conclusion

1. Crenzel, "La víctima inocente," 65–83.

2. Raggio, "La construcción de un relato."

3. On the uses of the figure of the "young victim" in memory writings, see Vezzetti, *Pasado y presente*, 207–16; Sarlo, "Cuando la política era joven."

4. Zolov, "Expanding our Conceptual Horizons."

5. Suri, "The Rise and Fall of an International Counterculture."

6. Svampa, *La sociedad excluyente*, 23.

7. O'Donnell, "Democracia en la Argentina," 28.

Bibliography

Primary Sources

Archival Sites and Repositories
(all in Buenos Aires, unless otherwise noted)

Public and Private Archives

Archivo General de la Nación
Biblioteca Nacional
    Archivo Arturo Frondizi
Centro de Estudios Históricos de la Policía Federal Argentina
    Ordenes del Día Collection
Comisión Provincial de la Memoria, La Plata
    Dirección de Inteligencia de la Policía de la Provincia de
        Buenos Aires Archive
Consejo Nacional de la Niñez, Adolescencia y Familia
    Consejo Nacional de Protección de Menores Archive
Facultad de Filosofía y Letras, Universidad de Buenos Aires
Instituto Superior del Profesorado Joaquín V. González
    Dirección General de Educación Media, Circulares Collection
John W. Hartman Center for Sales, Advertising and Marketing History,
    Duke University, Durham, N.C.
    J. Walter Thompson Company Collection
Liga de Madres de Familia
Obra de Protección de la Joven
Magendra Publishing House
    Archivo Fotográfico *Pelo*
Partido Comunista Argentino
Universidad de San Andrés, Biblioteca Max von Buch
    José Enrique Miguens Collection
University of Chicago, Special Collections and Archives
    Robert Havighurst Papers

Documentation Centers and Oral Archives

Centro de Documentación Audiovisual, Universidad Nacional de Córdoba
   Canal 10 Archive
Centro de Documentación e Información Educativa—Ministerio de Educación
Centro de Documentación e Investigación de la Cultura de Izquierda
   (CEDINCI)
Sistema de Información y Bibliotecas—Universidad de Buenos Aires
   Biblioteca de publicaciones periódicas
   Archivo de Historia Oral de la Universidad de Buenos Aires
Memoria Abierta (Asociación Civil), Buenos Aires
Museo Municipal del Cine Pablo Ducrós Hicken

Libraries

Biblioteca de la Asociación Psicoanalítica Argentina
Biblioteca del Congreso de la Nación
Biblioteca del Gobierno de la Ciudad de Buenos Aires
Biblioteca del Instituto Di Tella—Universidad Torcuato Di Tella
Biblioteca del Ministerio de Economía
Biblioteca del Ministerio de Educación
Biblioteca del Ministerio de Educación de la Provincia de Buenos Aires—
   La Plata
Biblioteca Nacional

Government Publications

Boletín Municipal de la Ciudad de Buenos Aires, 1956–72
Diario de Sesiones de la Cámara de Diputados de la Nación, 1958–62, 1963–65,
   1973–75
Diario de Sesiones de la Cámara de Senadores de la Nación, 1958–62, 1963–65,
   1973–75
Ministerio de Educación y Justicia (then "y Cultura"), *Boletín de Comunicaciones*
Poder Ejecutivo Nacional, *Boletín Oficial*, 1956–76
Sala de Representantes de la Ciudad de Buenos Aires, *Sesiones, ordenanzas y
   resoluciones*, 1973–75.

Educational and Social Statistics

Censo Nacional de Población y Viviendas, 1960. Buenos Aires: Dirección General
   de Estadísticas, 1963.
Censo Nacional de Población, Familias, y Viviendas, 1970. Buenos Aires: Ministerio
   de Economía, Dirección de Estadísticas, 1974.
Consejo de Rectores de Universidades Nacionales. *Censo Universitario 1972.*
   Buenos Aires: CRUN, 1974.
Consejo Federal de Inversiones, *La educación secundaria en la Argentina.*
   Buenos Aires: Consejo Federal de Inversiones, 1968.

Consejo Nacional de Desarrollo. *Origen socio-económico y otros factores que inciden sobre el acceso y elección de las carreras de enseñanza media*. Buenos Aires: Secretaría de CONADE, 1968.

Instituto Nacional de Estadísticas y Censos. *Boletín Trimestral*. Buenos Aires: INDEC, 1970–76.

Ministerio de Educación y Cultura. *Cifras educativas, 1965–1974*. Buenos Aires: Departamento de Estadística, 1977.

———.*Cifras educativas, 1974*. Buenos Aires: Centro de Documentación e Información Educativa, 1975.

———. *Estadística Educativa*. Buenos Aires: Departamento de Estadística Educativa, 1970.

———. *La educación en cifras, 1958–1967*. Buenos Aires: Departamento de Estadística Educativa, 1968.

———. *La educación en cifras, 1961–1970*. Buenos Aires: Departamento de Estadística Educativa, 1972.

———. *La educación en cifras, 1963–1972*. Buenos Aires: Departamento de Estadística Educativa, 1974.

Ministerio de Educación y Justicia. *La enseñanza media (1914–1963)*, 2 vols. Buenos Aires: Departamento de Estadística Educativa, 1964.

———. *Reglamento general para los establecimientos de enseñanza secundaria, normal y especial*. Buenos Aires: Poder Ejecutivo Nacional, 1957.

Universidad de Buenos Aires. *Censo de Alumnos, 1964*. Buenos Aires: Universidad de Buenos Aires, 1965.

———. *Censo de Alumnos, 1968*. Buenos Aires: Universidad de Buenos Aires, 1969.

Periodicals

Newspapers

ARGENTINA

Clarín (1957–58, 1963, 1968–75)
La Nación (1958, 1963, 1965–67)
La Opinión (1971–75)

La Prensa (1958, 1963)
La Razón (1956–67)
Noticias

UNITED STATES

New York Times (1966, 1969)

Popular Magazines

ARGENTINA

Adán
Análisis
Antena
Así
Así Segunda
Atlántida
Claudia

Confirmado
Diálogo con la pareja y el hijo
Esto es
Extra
Gente
Idilio
Leoplán

Mayoría
Mercado
Nocturno
Nuestros Hijos
Panorama
Para Ti
Periscopio
Primera Plana

Pulso
Qué sucedió en siete días
Radiolandia
Satiricón
Siete Días
Tía Vicenta
Vosotras

UNITED STATES
Billboard
Variety

Youth and Counterculture Magazines

Contracultura
Cronopios
Eco Contemporáneo
Expreso Imaginario

Grito Joven
La Bella Gente
Opium
Pelo

Political-Cultural Journals and Magazines

Antropología 3er Mundo
Che
Contorno
Crisis
Cristianismo y Revolución
Cuestionario

Envido
Escarabajo de Oro
Los Libros
Redacción
Tiempos Modernos

Political Press

De Frente (con las bases peronistas)
El combatiente
El Descamisado
El Peronista
Evita Montonera
Estrella Roja
Jotape
Juventud—Federación Juvenil Comunista

La causa peronista
Liberacion
Lucha Armada en la Argentina
Militancia
Mundo Peronista
Nuevo Hombre
Semanario CGT

Security Forces Press

Boletín de Educación e Instrucción del Ejército
Mundo policial
Revista de la Escuela de Comando y Estado Mayor de la Fuerza Aérea Argentina
    (RECEM)
Revista del Suboficial
Revista Militar (Círculo Militar)
Soldado Argentino

Psychological and Pedagogical Journals

Acta Psiquiátrica y Psicológica Argentina (then "de América Latina")
Actualidad Psicológica
Psique en la Universidad
Revista Argentina de Psicología
Revista Argentina de Psiquiatría y Psicología de la Infancia y la Adolescencia
Revista de Educación del Ministerio de Educación de la Provincia de Buenos Aires
Revista de Psicoanálisis
Revista de Psicología de la Universidad de La Plata
Revista Latinoamericana de Psicología

University Publications

Boletín de la Universidad de Buenos Aires
Centro (Revista del Centro de Estudiantes de la Facultad de Filosofía y Letras)
Gaceta de Filosofía y Letras
Revista de la Universidad de Buenos Aires
Revista de la Universidad de La Plata
Universidad: Aportes para la Reconstrucción Nacional

Catholic Publications

Boletín de la Agencia Informativa Católica Argentina
Criterio
Revista Eclesiástica Argentina

International Serial Publications

UNESCO, *Statistic Yearbook*, 1960–70
American University Field Staff, *East Coast South America Series*, 1960–65

Books

Essays, Pamphlets, Published Conference Minutes

Aberastury, Arminda, and Mauricio Knobel. *Adolescencia*. Buenos Aires: Kargieman, 1971.
———. *La adolescencia normal: Un enfoque psicoanalítico*. Buenos Aires: Paidós, 1971.
Arancibia, Rubén. *Qué quiere, qué siente el adolescente*. Buenos Aires: Universidad de El Salvador, 1964.
Asociación Argentina de Agencias de Publicidad. *Primera Convención Argentina de Agencias de Publicidad*. Mar del Plata: N.p., 1963.
Bleger, José, ed. *La identidad en el adolescente*. Buenos Aires: Paidós, 1973.
Brailovsky, Antonio, et al. *México y Argentina visto por sus jóvenes*. México City: Siglo XXI, 1970.
Brignardello, Luisa. *El movimiento estudiantil argentino: corrientes ideológicas y opiniones de sus dirigentes*. Buenos Aires: Macchi, 1972.

Cámara Argentina de Anunciantes. *Estudio de inversión publicitaria y rentabilidad de empresas*. Buenos Aires: Cámara Argentina de Anunciantes, 1974.

Carbal Prieto, Julio. *Los hippies y las drogas*. Buenos Aires: Latinoamericana, 1973.

Casos de la Segunda Tiranía: La UES. Buenos Aires: Poder Ejecutivo Nacional, 1958.

Castro, José. *La edad del amor*. Buenos Aires: Fabril, 1967.

Casullo, Fernando. *Diccionario de voces lunfardas y vulgares*. Buenos Aires: Freeland, 1964.

Centro de Estudios Legales y Sociales. *Adolescentes detenidos-desaparecidos*. Buenos Aires: CELS, 1982.

Círculo de Profesores de Educación Democrática. *Primer Congreso Argentino de Profesores de Educación Democrática. Buenos Aires, 11 al 15 de septiembre 1958*. Buenos Aires, 1959.

———. *Segundo Congreso Argentino de Profesores de Educación Democrática. Rosario, 11 al 15 de septiembre de 1959*. Buenos Aires, 1960.

Cirigliano, Gustavo, and Ana Zabala Ameghino. *El poder joven*. Buenos Aires: Librería de las naciones, 1969.

Comisión Interuniversitaria Permanente Coordinadora de la Enseñanza Media. *Jornadas Interuniversitarias sobre Enseñanza Media, Bahía Blanca, 6 al 12 de noviembre de 1960. Recomendaciones y declaraciones*. Buenos Aires: Universidad de Buenos Aires, 1960.

De Raffo, Elvira. *Dejar crecer*. Buenos Aires, 1959.

Eichelbaum de Babini, Ana María. *Estatus socioeconómico y crianza de niños*. Buenos Aires: Instituto de Sociología, 1965.

Enciclopedia del Mundo Actual, vol. 2: Temas culturales. Buenos Aires: Centro Editor de América Latina, 1973.

Escardó, Florencio. *Anatomía de la familia*. Buenos Aires: El Ateneo, 1961.

———. *Nueva geografía de Buenos Aires*. Buenos Aires: Americalée, 1971.

———. *Sexología de la familia*. Buenos Aires: El Ateneo, 1961.

Etcheverry, Delia. *El adolescente y la escuela secundaria*. Buenos Aires: EUdeBA, 1961.

Frondizi, Arturo. *Mensajes presidenciales*, vol. 1. Buenos Aires: Centro de Estudios Nacionales, 1978.

Genta, Jordán Bruno. *Guerra contrarrevolucionaria: doctrina política*. Buenos Aires: Nuevo Orden, 1964.

Germani, Gino. *Política y sociedad en una época de transición*. Buenos Aires: Paidós, 1962.

———. *Sociología de la modernización: Estudios teóricos, metodológicos y aplicados a América Latina*. Buenos Aires: Paidós, 1971.

Germani, Gino, and Ruth Sautu. *Regularidad y origen social de los estudiantes universitarios*. Buenos Aires: EUdeBA, 1965.

Giberti, Eva. *Adolescencia y educación sexual*. Buenos Aires: Roberto Antonio, 1969.

———. *Amor en la Argentina*. Buenos Aires: Merlin, 1970.

———. *Escuela para padres*, 3 vols. Buenos Aires: Omeba, 1961.

Gobello, José. *Diccionario del lunfardo y de otros términos antiguos y modernos usuales en Buenos Aires*. Buenos Aires: Peña Lillo, 1971.

González Trejo, Horacio. *Formas de alienación en la cultura argentina*. Buenos Aires: Carlos Pérez, 1969.

Goti Aguilar, Juan Carlos. *La censura en el cine*. Buenos Aires: Líbera, 1966.

Inglese, Osvaldo. *Universidad y estudiantes, Universidad y Peronismo*. Buenos Aires: Líbera, 1966.

Ivanissevich de D'Angelo Rodríguez, Magda. *Descenso a los infiernos de la burocracia en la enseñanza secundaria: Memorias de un inspector de zona*. Buenos Aires: N.p., 1970.

Jauretche, Arturo. *El medio pelo en la sociedad argentina (Apuntes para una sociología nacional)*. Buenos Aires: Peña Lillo, 1966.

Kleiner, Bernardo. *20 años de movimiento estudiantil reformista, 1943–1963*. Buenos Aires: Platina, 1964.

Knobel, Mauricio. *Infancia, adolescencia y familia*. Buenos Aires: Granica, 1973.

Kreimer, Juan Carlos. *Agarráte!!! Testimonios de la música joven argentina*. Buenos Aires: Galerna, 1970.

Leguizamón, Carlos. *La disciplina en la escuela secundaria*. Buenos Aires: EUdeBA, 1965.

Libro Negro de la Segunda Tiranía. Buenos Aires: Poder Ejecutivo Nacional, 1958.

Lipset, Seymour, ed. *Student Politics*. New York: Basic Books, 1967.

Lopez Bolado, Jorge Daniel. *Drogas y otras sustancias estupefacientes*. Buenos Aires: Pannedille, 1971.

Mafud, Julio. *La revolución sexual argentina*. Buenos Aires: Américalee, 1966.

———. *Las rebeliones juveniles en la sociedad argentina*. Buenos Aires: Américalee, 1969.

Marcilese, Mario. *30 días en la UES . . . y la juventud caminaba calle abajo*. La Plata: Alfredo Domínguez e Hijo, 1957.

Margullis, Mario. *Migración y marginalidad en la sociedad argentina*. Buenos Aires: Paidós, 1968.

Mariguella, Carlos. *Mini-manual of the Urban Guerrilla*. Chapel Hill: Documentary Press, 1985. Originally published in 1969.

Millán, Alberto, and Carlos Fontán Ballestra. *Las reformas al Código Penal: Ley 15.567*. Buenos Aires: Abeledo Perrot, 1968.

Moffat, Alfredo. *Estrategias para sobrevivir en Buenos Aires*. Buenos Aires: Jorge Alvarez, 1967.

Moras Mom, Jorge. *Toxicomanía y delito*. Buenos Aires: Abeledo Perrot, 1975.

Nasatir, David. *Estudio sobre la juventud argentina*. Buenos Aires: Instituto de Sociología, 1965.

———. *Impacto de la experiencia universitaria sobre el pensamiento político*. Buenos Aires: Instituto de Sociología, 1965.

Perón y la juventud. Buenos Aires: Secretaría de Prensa y Difusión, 1954.

Perugorría, Jorge. *Cien respuestas para los que piden la prueba de amor*. Buenos Aires: Paulinas, 1972.

Pithod, Abelardo. *La revolución cultural en la Argentina*. Buenos Aires: Cruz y Fierro, 1974.

Rascovsky, Arnaldo. *El filicidio*. Buenos Aires: Orión, 1973.

———. *La matanza de los hijos y otros ensayos*. Buenos Aires: Kargieman, 1970.

Rascovsky, Arnaldo, and David Liberman, eds. *Psicoanálisis de la manía y la psicopatía*. Buenos Aires: Paidós, 1965.

Ratier, Hugo. *El cabecita negra*. Buenos Aires: Centro Editor de América Latina, 1971.

Reca, Telma, ed. *Temas de psiquiatría y psicología de la niñez y la adolescencia*. Buenos Aires: CEAM, 1969.

Rychlowski, Bruno. *Sexo y adolescencia*. Buenos Aires: Ediciones Paulinas, 1970.

Sastre de Cabot, Joefina. *La formación del profesor de enseñanza media*. Tucumán: Universidad Nacional de Tucumán, 1967.

Sebreli, Juan José. *Buenos Aires: Vida cotidiana y alienación*. Buenos Aires: Siglo Veinte, 1991. Originally published in 1964.

Silvert, Kalman, and Frank Bonilla. *Education and the Social Meaning of Development*. New York: N.p., 1961.

Spranger, Eduard. *Psicología de la edad juvenil*. Buenos Aires: Revista de Occidente, 1929.

Tedín Bravo, Miguel. *Historia del Barrio Clínicas*. Córdoba: N.p., 1970.

REPORTS BY U.S. AND INTERNATIONAL ORGANIZATIONS

Unión Panamericana. *Estado actual de la educación secundaria en la América Latina*. Washington: Unión Panamericana, 1957.

———. *Reunión técnica sobre el planeamiento de la educación media*. México City: Unión Panamericana and Secretaría de Educación Pública, 1965.

United States Senate. *The World Narcotics Problem: The Latin American Perspective*. Washington: Government Printing Office, 1973.

Published Documents

Barchetti, Roberto. *Documentos de la resistencia (1955–1970)*. La Plata: De la Campana, 1997.

———. *Documentos, 1970–73*. La Plata: De la Campana, 1995.

———. *Documentos, 1973–76*. La Plata: De la Campana, 1997)

de Santis, Daniel. *A vencer o morir: El PRT-ERP, Documentos*, 2 vols. Buenos Aires: EUdeBA, 1998.

Lafiandra, Félix, comp. *Los panfletos: Su aporte a la Revolución Libertadora*. Buenos Aires: Itinerarium, 1955.

Memoirs and Memory Writing

Actis, Munú, Cristina Aldini, Liliana Gardella, Miriam Lewin, and Elisa Tokar. *Ese infierno: conversaciones con cinco mujeres sobrevivientes de la ESMA*. Buenos Aires: Sudamericana, 2001.

Anguita, Eduardo, and Martín Caparrós. La *voluntad: Una historia de la militancia revolucionaria en la Argentina*, 3 vols. Buenos Aires: Norma, 1997.

Anzorena, Oscar, comp. *JP: Historia de la Juventud Peronista (1955–1988)*. Buenos Aires: Ediciones del Cordón, 1989.

Augier, Pola. *Los jardines del cielo: Experiencias de una guerrillera*. Buenos Aires: Sudestada, 2010.

Berguier, Rubén, Eduardo Hecker, and Ariel Schifrin. *Estudiantes secundarios: sociedad y política*. Buenos Aires: Centro Editor de América Latina, 1986.

Bonasso, Miguel. *Diario de un clandestino*. Buenos Aires: Planeta, 2001.

———. *El presidente que no fue*. Buenos Aires: Planeta, 1997.

Cantilo, Miguel. *Chau loco . . . los hippies en la Argentina de los setenta*. Buenos Aires: Galerna, 2000.

Diana, Marta. *Mujeres guerrilleras: La militancia revolucionaria de los setenta en el testimonio de sus protagonistas femeninas*. Buenos Aires: Planeta, 1997.

Diez, Rolo. *El mejor y el peor de los tiempos*. Buenos Aires: Nuestra América, 2010.

Dirección de Derechos Humanos. *Huellas: Semblanzas de vida de detenidos-desaparecidos y asesinados por el terrorismo de Estado*. La Plata: Universidad Nacional de La Plata, 2010.

Ferreyra Beltrán, Alejandro. *Memoria de los vientos*. Córdoba: Babel, 2007.

Garaño, Santiago, and Werner Pertot. *La otra Juvenilia: Militancia y represión en el Colegio Nacional de Buenos Aires, 1971–1986*. Buenos Aires: Biblos, 2002.

Gatica, Hugo. *Tiempos de liberación: Memorias de un militante de la JP, 1973–1976*. Santa Rosa: Pitangua, 2008.

Gómez, Hugo Alejandro. *Montoneros en Morón: Militantes y militancia, 1973–1976*. Morón: Macedonia, 2008.

Grinberg, Miguel. *La música progresiva en la Argentina (cómo vino la mano)*. Buenos Aires: Convergencia, 1977.

Guelar, Diana, Vera Jarach, and Beatriz Ruiz. *Los chicos del exilio: Argentina (1975–1984)*. Buenos Aires: El País del Nomeolvides, 2002.

Guerrero, Gloria. *La historia del palo: Crónicas del rock argentino*. Buenos Aires: De la Urraca, 1995.

Landrú, and Edgardo Russo. *¡Landrú por Landrú! apuntes para una autobiografía*. Buenos Aires: El Ateneo, 1993.

Mattini, Luis. *Cartas profanas: novela de la correspondencia entre Santucho y Gombrowicz*. Buenos Aires: Peña Lillo, 2008.

———. *Los perros*, vol. 2. Buenos Aires: Peña Lillo, 2006.

Narzole, Cacho. *Nada a cambio: Una historia militante*. Buenos Aires: Imago Mundi, 2009.

Nebbia, Litto. *Una mirada: Reflexiones y anécdotas de vida*. Buenos Aires: Catálogos, 2004.

Oliveri, Marcelo. *Éramos tan hippies . . . otra historia del rock en la Argentina*. Buenos Aires: Corregidor, 2007.

Pintos, Víctor. *Tanguito*. Buenos Aires: Planeta, 1992.

Ramos, Laura, and Cynthia Lebjowicz. *Corazones en llamas: Historias del rock argentino en los ochenta*. Buenos Aires: Aguilar, 1991.

Ramus, Susana. *Sueños sobrevivientes de una montonera: A pesar de la ESMA*. Buenos Aires: Colihue, 2000.

Robles, Adriana. *Perejiles: Los otros Montoneros*. Buenos Aires: Colihue, 2004.

Rotunno, Catalina, and Eduardo Díaz de Guijarro, eds. *La construcción de lo posible: la Universidad de Buenos Aires de 1955 a 1966*. Buenos Aires: del Zorzal, 2003.

Szulansky, Gustavo. *Franca: 18 años*. Buenos Aires: Juvenilia Ediciones, 2006.

Toer, Mario, ed. *El movimiento estudiantil de Perón a Alfonsín*, vol. 1. Buenos Aires: Centro Editor de América Latina, 1988.

Fiction

Bioy Casares, Adolfo. *Diario de la guerra del cerdo*. Buenos Aires: Emecé, 1969.

Caparrós, Martín. *No velas a tus muertos*. Buenos Aires: Corregidor, 1985.

Casullo, Nicolás. *Para hacer el amor en los parques*. Buenos Aires: Tiempo Contemporáneo, 1971.

Giralt, Santiago. *Nelly R., la amante del general: Novela (anti)histórica*. Buenos Aires: Emecé, 2008.

Gudiño Kieffer, Eduardo. *Carta abierta a Buenos Aires violento*. Buenos Aires: Emecé, 1970.

Kordon, Bernardo. *Reina del Plata*. Buenos Aires: Milton, 1983. Originally published in 1951.

Piglia, Ricardo. "La invasión" [1967]. In *La invasión*. Barcelona: Alfaguara, 2006.

Poggi, Jorge. *Perdón por la letra*. Buenos Aires: Catálogos, 2004.

Verbitsky, Bernardo. *La esquina*. Buenos Aires: Sudamericana, 1953.

———. *Una cita con la vida*. Buenos Aires: Platina, 1958.

Viñas, David. *Dar la cara*. Buenos Aires: Jamcana, 1962.

Interviews and Personal Communications

To protect my interviewees' privacy, I refer to them with their first name and last initial, unless they were public figures, in which case I use their full name.

With Former Students at the School of Philosophy and Literature, University of Buenos Aires (all conducted in the City of Buenos Aires)

Analía (b. in 1942 in the City of Buenos Aires), August 23, 2007

Elena A. (born in 1940 in the City of Buenos Aires), September 1, 2007.

Eduardo F. (b. in 1940 in the City of Buenos Aires), July 28, 2007

Hilda L. (b. in 1950 in the City of Buenos Aires), August 22, 2007.

Isidoro Cheresky (b. in 1940 in the City of Buenos Aires), August 21, 2007

Jorge Lafforgue, November 30, 2006.

Mabel G. (b. in 1947 in Entre Rios, moved to the City of Buenos Aires in 1958), July 31, 2007.

María Emilia (b. in 1945 in the City of Buenos Aires), March 16, 2007.

María Ester (b. in 1944 in the City of Buenos Aires), March 12, 2007.

Maria Rosa (b. in 1940 in the City of Buenos Aires), July 23, 2007.

Mirtha Lischetti, July 30, 2007

Rodolfo T. (b. 1942), August 21, 2007

Sara Z. (b. in 1953 in the City of Buenos Aires), August 13, 2007

With Former Young People from Valentín Alsina, Lanús

Alicia S. (b. 1944 in Valentín Alsina, Lanús), August 10, 2007.

Carlos U. (b. in 1944 in Valentín Alsina, Lanús), September 16, 2007.

Carlos R. (b. in 1951 in Valentín Alsina, Lanús), September 13, 2007

Eduardo C. (b. in Valentín Alsina, Lanús, in 1955), August 12, 2007

Ester M. (b. in 1954 in Valentín Alsina, Lanús), July 15, 2007

Gerardo D. (b. in 1951 in Valentín Alsina, Lanús), September 18, 2007.

José C. (b. in 1952 in Valentín Alsina), September 20, 2007.

Marta E. (b. in 1954 in Valentín Alsina), June 13, 2007

Mabel S. (b. in 1952 in Valentín Alsina, Lanús), September 12, 2007.

Mercedes B. (b. in 1947 in Valentín Alsina), July 25, 2007

Ricardo T. (b. in 1948 in Valentín Alsina, Lanús), September 2, 2007.

Tony (b. in 1950 in Valentín Alsina, Lanús), September 10, 2007.

With Selected Informants

Dr. Eva Giberti, former adolescent psychologist and creator of the School for Parents, August 1, 2008.

Miguel Grinberg, rock journalist and counterculture organizer, September 11, 2007.

Pedro Pujó, former producer for Mandioca label October 23, 2009.

Mario Rabey, former producer for Mandioca label, July 20, 2007.

Daniel Ripoll, former director of *Pelo*, rock concert organizer, June 27, 2007.

Héctor Zimmerman, former editor of the magazines *Cronopios* and *La Bella Gente*, July 13, 2008.

Argentine Movies Consulted

Breve cielo. Dir. and script by David Kohon. Released on June 5, 1969.

Dar la cara, Dir. and script by José Martínez Suárez (with David Viñas). Released on November 29, 1962.

Demasiado jóvenes. Dir. and script by Leopoldo Torres Ríos. Released on March 13, 1958.

Detrás de un largo muro. Dir. Lucas Demare. Script by Sixto Pondal Ríos. Released on July 3, 1958.

El Club del Clan. Dir. Enrique Carreras. Script by Alexis de Arancibia. Released on March 1, 1964.

El profesor hippie. Dir. Fernando Ayala. Script by Abel Santa Cruz. Released on July 31, 1969.

Fiebre de Primavera. Dir. and script by Enrique Carreras. Released on March 18, 1965.

Hasta que se ponga el sol. Dir. and script by Aníbal Uset (with Jorge Alvarez). Released on March 3, 1973.

La edad difícil. Dir. and script by Leopoldo Torres Ríos. Released on July 27, 1956.

La hora de los hornos. Dir. Fernando Solanas and Octavio Getino. Released in 1968.

La mano en la trampa. Dir. and script by Leopoldo Torre Nilsson (with Beatriz Guido and Ricardo Luna). Released on June 8, 1961.

La patota. Dir. Daniel Tinayre. Script by Eduardo Borrás. Released on August 11, 1960.

La Terraza. Dir. Leopoldo Torre Nilsson. Script by Beatriz Guido, Ricardo Luna, and Ricardo Becher. Released on October 17, 1963.

Los de la mesa diez. Dir. and script by Simón Feldman (with Osvaldo Dragún). Released on October 18, 1960.

Los jóvenes viejos. Dir. and script by Rodolfo Kuhn. Released on June 5, 1962.

Pajarito Gómez, una vida feliz. Dir. and script by Rodolfo Kuhn (with Carlos del Peral and Francisco Urondo). Released on August 9, 1965.

Prisioneros de una noche. Dir. David Kohon. Script by Carlos Latorre. Released on January 30, 1962.

Tiro de Gracia. Dir. and script by Ricardo Becher (with Sergio Mulet). Released on October 2, 1969.

Tres veces Ana. Dir. and script by David Kohon. Released on November 2, 1961.

Una cita con la vida. Dir. Hugo del Carril. Script by Eduardo Borrás. Released on April 24, 1958.

Venga a bailar el rock. Dir. Carlos Stevani. Script by Enrique Morello. Released on August 29, 1957.

Secondary Sources

Acha, Omar, and Pablo Ben. "Amorales, patoteros, chongos y pitucos: La homosexualidad masculina durante el primer peronismo." *Trabajos y comunicaciones* 30.1 (2006).

Adamovsky, Ezequiel. *Historia de la clase media argentina*. Buenos Aires: Planeta, 2009.

Adams, Mary Louise. *The Trouble with Normal: Postwar Youth and the Making of Heterosexuality in Canada*. Toronto: University of Toronto Press, 1999.

Aguilar, Gonzalo. "La generación del 60: La gran transformación del modelo." In *Cine Argentino: Modernidad y Vanguardias, 1957–1983*, ed. Claudio España, 2:82–98. Buenos Aires: Fondo Nacional de las Artes, 2004.

Aguirre, Patricia. *Estrategias de consumo: Qué comen los argentinos que comen*. Buenos Aires: Miño y Dávila, 2005.

Alabarces, Pablo. *Entre gatos y violadores: Una historia del rock nacional*. Buenos Aires: Colihue, 1993.

Alonso Piñeiro, Armando. *Breve historia de la publicidad argentina*. Buenos Aires: Alzamor, 1974.

Altamirano, Carlos. *Bajo el signo de las masas (1943–1973)*. Buenos Aires: Ariel, 2001.

———. "Memoria del 69." *Estudios* 4 (1994): 9–13.

———. *Peronismo y cultura de izquierda*. Buenos Aires: Temas, 2001.

Altschuler, Glenn. *All Shook Up: How Rock 'n' Roll Changed America*. New York: Oxford University Press, 2003.

Alvarado, Maite, and Renata Rocco-Cuzzi. "'Primera Plana': El nuevo discurso periodístico de la década del '60." *Punto de Vista* 22 (December 1984).

Archetti, Eduardo. *Masculinities: Football, Tango, and Polo in Argentina*. Oxford: Berg, 1999.

Avellaneda, Andrés. *Censura, autoritarismo y cultura en la Argentina, 1960–1983*. 2 vols. Buenos Aires: CEAL, 1986.

Austin, Joe, and Michael Willard, eds. *Generations of Youth: Youth Cultures and History in Twentieth-Century America*. New York: New York University Press, 1998.

Bailey, Beth. *From Front Porch to Back Seat: Courtship in Twentieth Century America*. Baltimore: Johns Hopkins University Press, 1989.

———. *Sex in the Heartland*. Cambridge, Mass.: Harvard University Press, 1999.

Ballent, Anahí. *Las huellas de la política: Vivienda, ciudad, peronismo en Buenos Aires, 1943–1955*. Buenos Aires: Prometeo/Universidad Nacional de Quilmes, 2006.

Balvé, Beba, and Beatriz Balvé. *El '69: Huelga política de masas*. Buenos Aires: Contrapunto, 1988.

Barbanti, Marco. "Cultura cattolica, lutta anticomunista e moralità pubblica (1948–1960)." *Rivista di storia contemporanea* 21.1 (January 1992): 173–90.

Barbosa, Francisco. "Insurgent Youth: Culture and Memory in the Sandinista Student Movement." PhD. diss., Indiana University, 2006.

Barcan, Ruth. *Nudity: A Cultural Anatomy*. New York: Berg, 2004.

Barletta, Ana. "Peronización de los universitarios (1966–1973): Elementos para rastrear la constitución de una política universitaria peronista." *Pensamiento Universitario* 9.9 (August 2001): 82–90.

———. "Una izquierda universitaria peronista (1966–1973): Entre la demanda académica y la demanda política." *Prismas* 6 (2002): 275–88.

Barrancos, Dora. *Mujeres en la sociedad argentina: Una historia de cinco siglos*. Buenos Aires: Sudamericana, 2007.

Barr-Melej, Patrick. "Siloísmo and the Left in Allende's Chile: Youth, 'Total Revolution,' and Humanism in the Road to Socialism." *Hispanic American Historical Review* 86.4 (2006): 747–84.

Bartoletti, Julieta. "Montoneros: De la movilización a la organización." Ph.D. diss., Universidad Nacional de San Martín, 2010.

Beebe, Roger, Denise Fulbrook, and Ben Saunders. *Rock over the Edge: Transformations in Popular Music*. Durham: Duke University Press, 2002.

Ben, Pablo. "Male Sexuality, the Popular Classes, and the State: Buenos Aires, 1880–1955." Ph.D. diss., University of Chicago, 2009.

Benedetti, Sebastián, and Martín Graziano. *Estación imposible: Contracultura y periodismo en los '70, la historia del* Expreso Imaginario. Buenos Aires: Oliveri Editor, 2007.

Berger, John. *Ways of Seeing*. London: Viking Press, 1973.

Biagini, Hugo. *La Reforma Universitaria: Antecedentes y consecuentes*. Buenos Aires: Leviatán, 2000.

Bianchi, Susana. *Catolicismo y Peronismo: Religión y política en la Argentina, 1943–55.* Tandil: Instituto de Estudios Históricos, 2001.

Biddle-Perry, Geraldine, and Sarah Cheang. *Hair: Styling, Culture, and Fashion.* London: Berg, 2008.

Blanco, Alejandro. *Razón y modernidad: Gino Germani y la sociología en la Argentina.* Buenos Aires: Siglo XXI, 2006.

Bliss, Katherine, and Ann Blum. "Dangerous Driving: Adolescence, Sex, and the Gendered Experience of the Public Space in Early-Twentieth Century Mexico." In *Gender, Sexuality, and Power in Latin American since the Independence,* edited by William French and Katherine Bliss, 163–84. Lanham, Md.: Rowman and Littlefield, 2007.

Bordo, Susan. *Unbearable Weight: Feminism, Western Culture, and the Body.* Berkeley: University of California Press, 1993.

Bourdieu, Pierre. *Distinction: A Social Critique of the Judgment of Taste.* Cambridge, Mass: Harvard University Press, 1984.

———. *Sociology in Question.* London: Sage, 1993.

Bourdieu, Pierre, and Jean-Claude Passeron. *The Inheritors: French Students and Their Relation to Culture.* Chicago: University of Chicago Press, 1979.

Braustein, Peter, and Michael William Doyle, eds. *Imagine Nation: The American Counterculture of the 1960s and 1970s.* New York: Routledge, 2002.

Breines, Windi. *Young, White, and Miserable: Growing Up Female in the 1950s.* Boston: Beacon Press, 1992.

Brennan, James. *The Labor Wars in Cordoba, 1955–1976: Ideology, Work, and Labor Politics in an Argentine Industrial City.* Cambridge, Mass.: Harvard University Press, 1994.

Brennan, James, and Mónica Gordillo. *Córdoba rebelde: El Cordobazo, el clasismo y la movilización social.* La Plata: De la Campana, 2008.

Buchbinder, Pablo. *Historia de la Facultad de Filosofía y Letras.* Buenos Aires: EUdeBA, 1997.

———. *Historia de las Universidades Argentinas.* Buenos Aires: Sudamericana, 2005.

Bucholtz, Mary. "Youth and Cultural Practice." *Annual Review of Anthropology* 31 (2002): 525–53.

Burgos, Raúl. *Los Gramscianos argentinos: Cultura y política en la experiencia de 'Pasado y Presente.'* Buenos Aires: Siglo XXI de Argentina, 2004.

Caimari, Lila. *Perón y la Iglesia Católica: Religión, Estado y sociedad en la Argentina (1943–1955).* Buenos Aires: Ariel, 1995.

Calveiro, Pilar. *Poder y desaparición: Los campos de concentración en la Argentina.* Buenos Aires: Colihue, 1998.

———. *Política y/o violencia: Una aproximación a la guerrilla de los años 70.* Buenos Aires: Norma, 2005.

Candelari, María, and Patricia Funes. "La Universidad de Buenos Aires, 1955–1966: Lecturas de un recuerdo." In *Cultura y política en los años '60,* edited by Enrique Oteiza, 18–37. Buenos Aires: CBC, 1997.

Cano, Daniel. *La educación superior en la Argentina.* Buenos Aires: GEL-FLACSO, 1985.

Capussotti, Enrica. *Gioventù perduta: Gli anni Cinquanta dei giovani e del cinema in Italia*. Florence: Giunti Editore, 2004.

Carassai, Sebastián. "Ni de izquierda ni peronistas, medioclasistas. Ideología y política de la clase media argentina a comienzos de los años setentas." *Desarrollo Económico* 52 (2012): 95–117.

Carey, Elaine. *Plaza of Sacrifices: Gender, Power, and Terror in 1968 Mexico*. Albuquerque: University of New Mexico Press, 2005.

Carli, Sandra. *Niñez, pedagogía y política: Transformaciones de los discursos de la infancia en la historia de la educación argentina entre 1880 y 1955*. Buenos Aires: Miño y Dávila, 2002.

Carnovale, Vera. "Moral y disciplinamiento interno en el PRT-ERP." *Nuevo Mundo Mundos Nuevos, Debates*, 2008, Released on July 12, 2008, http://nuevomundo .revues.org/index38782.html.

Caro Hollander, Nancy. "Women Workers and Class Struggle: The Case of Argentina." *Latin American Perspectives* 4.1-2 (Winter–Spring 1977): 180-93.

Carrillo-Rodríguez, Illa. "Latinoamericana de Tucumán: Mercedes Sosa y los itinerarios de la música popular argentina en la larga década del sesenta." In *Ese ardiente jardin de la república: Formación y desarticulación de un 'campo cultural' en Tucumán, 1880-1976*, edited by Fabiola Orquera, 239-65. Córdoba: Alción, 2010.

Castagna, Gustavo. "La generación del 60: Paradojas de un mito." In *Cine Argentino: La otra historia*, edited by Sergio Wolf, 89-119. Buenos Aires: Letra Buena, 1994.

Castrejón Díez, Jaime. *La educación superior en México*. Mexico City: Edicol, 1979.

Castrillón, Ernesto. "Hippies a la criolla: Historia de la Cofradía de la Flor Solar." *Todo es Historia* 370 (May 1998): 45-62.

Cattaruzza, Alejandro. "El mundo por hacer: Una propuesta para el análisis de la cultura juvenil en la Argentina de los años setenta." *Entrepasados* 13 (1997): 67-76.

Ceballos, Carlos. *Estudiantes universitarios y política, 1955-1970*. Buenos Aires: CEAL, 1985.

Chamosa, Oscar. *Argentina's Folklore Movement: Sugar Elites, Criollo Workers, and the Politics of Cultural Nationalism, 1900-1955*. Tucson: University of Arizona Press, 2010.

Ciria, Alberto, and Horacio Sanguinetti. *La Reforma Universitaria*. Buenos Aires: Centro Editor de América Latina, 1983.

Ciriza, Alejandra, and Eva Rodríguez Agüero. "Militancia, política y subjetividad: La moral del PRT-ERP." *Políticas de la memoria* 4-5 (Summer 2004-5): 85-92.

Cohen, Deborah, and Lessie Jo Frazier. "Defining the Space of Mexico '68: Heroic Masculinity in the Prisons and 'Women' in the Streets." *Hispanic American Historical Review* 83.4 (November 2003): 617-60.

Cohen, Stanley. *Folk Devils and Moral Panics: The Creation of the Mods and the Rockers*. Oxford: Martin Robertson, 1980.

Collins, Marcus. *Modern Love: An Intimate History of Men and Women in Twentieth-Century England*. London: Atlantic Books, 2003.

Connell, R. W. *Masculinities*. Cambridge: Polity Press, 2005.

Cosse, Isabella. "Argentine Mothers and Fathers and the New Psychological Paradigm of Child-Rearing (1958–1973)." *Journal of Family History* 35.2 (2010): 180–202.

———. *Pareja, sexualidad y familia en los años sesenta*. Buenos Aires: Siglo XXI, 2010.

———. "Probando la libertad: Cambios y continuidades en el cortejo y el noviazgo entre los jóvenes porteños (1950–1970)." *Entrepasados* 39 (2008): 31–47.

Cousinet, Graciela, ed. *Extramuros: Historia del rock mendocino*. Mendoza: Universidad Nacional de Cuyo, 2001.

Cowan, Ben. "Sex and the Security State: Gender, Sexuality, and 'Subversion' in Brazil's Escola Superior de Guerra, 1964–1985." *Journal of the History of Sexuality* 16.3 (2007): 459–61.

Crenzel, Emilio. "La víctima inocente: De la lucha antidictatorial al relato del *Nunca Más*." In *Los desaparecidos en la Argentina: Memorias, representaciones e ideas, 1983–2008*, edited by Emilio Crenzel, 65–83. Buenos Aires: Biblos, 2010.

Davis, Fred. *Fashion, Culture, and Identity*. Chicago: University of Chicago Press, 1992.

D'Emilio, John. "The Homosexual Menace: The Politics of Sexuality in Cold War America." In *Passion and Power: Sexuality in History*, edited by Christina Simmons and Kathy Peiss, 226–40. Philadelphia: Temple University Press, 1989.

D'Emilio, John, and Estelle Freedman. *Intimate Matters: A History of Sexuality in America*. Chicago: University of Chicago Press, 1990.

De Grazia, Victoria. *Irresistible Empire: America's Advance through Twentieth-Century Europe*. Cambridge, Mass.: Harvard University Press, 2005.

Delich, Francisco. *Crisis y protesta social: Córdoba, 1969–1973*. Buenos Aires: Siglo XXI, 1973.

De Riz, Liliana. *La política en suspenso 1966/1976*. Buenos Aires: Paidós, 2001.

Díaz, Claudio. *Libro de viajes y extravíos: Un recorrido por el rock argentino (1965–1985)*. Urquillo, Córdoba: Narvaja Editor, 2005.

Doherty, Thomas. *Teenagers and Teenpics: The Juvenilization of American Movies in the 1950s*. Boston: Hyman Books, 1988.

Donatello, Luis Miguel. "Aristocracismo de la salvación: El Catolicismo 'liberacionista' y los Montoneros." *Prismas* 9 (2005): 241–58.

Dreyfus-Armand, Genevieve, ed. *Les Annés 68: Les temps de la contestation*. Paris: Complexe, 2000.

Dummitt, Christopher. *The Manly Modern: Masculinity in Postwar Canada*. Vancouver: University of British Columbia Press, 2007.

Dunn, Christopher. *Brutality Garden: Tropicália and the Emergence of a Brazilian Counterculture*. Chapel Hill: University of North Carolina Press, 2000.

Dussel, Inés. *Currículum, humanismo y democracia en la enseñanza media (1863–1920)*. Buenos Aires: FLACSO, 1997.

Dussel, Inés, and Pablo Pineau. "De cuando la clase obrera entró al paraíso: La educación técnica estatal durante el primer peronismo." In *Discursos pedagógicos e imaginario social en el primer peronismo (1945–1955)*, edited by Sandra Carli, 107–43. Buenos Aires: Galerna, 1997.

Elena, Eduardo. "Point of Departure: Ernesto Guevara's Argentina." In *Che's Travels: The Making of a Revolutionary in 1950s Latin America*, edited by Paulo Drinot, 21–51. Durham: Duke University Press, 2010.

Elhrich, Laura. "Rebeldes, intransigentes y duros en el activismo peronista, 1955–1962." Master's thesis, Universidad Nacional de General Sarmiento, 2011.

Ehrenreich, Barbara, Elizabeth Hess, and Sonia Jacobs. *Re-Making Love: The Feminization of Sex*. New York: Garden City, 1987.

Entwistle, Joanne. *The Fashioned Body: Fashion, Dress, and Modern Social Theory*. Cambridge: Polity Press, 2000.

Fass, Paula. *The Damned and the Beautiful: American Youth in the 1920s*. New York: Oxford University Press, 1977.

———. *Kidnapped: Child Abduction in America*. New York: Oxford University Press, 1997.

Fassin, Didier, and Patrice Bourdelais. "Les frontières de l'espace moral." In *Les constructions de l'intolérable: Etudes d'anthropologie et d'histoire sur les frontières de l'espace moral*, 3–16. Paris: La Découverte, 2005.

Feijóo, María del Carmen, and Marcela Nari. "Women in Argentina during the 1960s." *Latin American Perspectives* 23.1 (Winter 1996).

Feldman, Simón. *La generación del sesenta*. Buenos Aires: Gedisa, 1990.

Felitti, Karina. "El debate médico sobre anticoncepción y aborto en Buenos Aires en los años sesenta del siglo XX." *Dynamis* 27 (2007): 333–57.

———. "El placer de elegir: anticoncepción y liberación sexual en la década del sesenta." In *Historia de las mujeres en la Argentina*, vol. 2, edited by Fernanda Gil Lozano, María Gabriela Ini, and Valeria Pita, 155–70. Buenos Aires: Taurus, 2000.

———. *La revolución de la píldora: Sexualidad y política en los sesenta*. Buenos Aires: Edhasa, 2012.

Fendrik, Silvia. *Psicoanalistas de niños: La verdadera historia*, vol. 3: *Arminda Aberastury y Telma Reca*. Buenos Aires: Letra Viva, 2006.

Fernández Bitar, Marcelo. *Historia del rock en la Argentina: Una investigación cronológica*. Buenos Aires: Distal, 1987.

Ferrero, Roberto. *Historia crítica del movimiento estudiantil en Córdoba*, vol. 3. Córdoba: Alción, 2006.

Filc, Judith. *Entre el parentesco y la política: Familia y dictadura, 1976–1983*. Buenos Aires: Editorial Biblos, 1997.

Foucault, Michel. *A History of Sexuality*, vol. 1: *An Introduction*. New York: Penguin, 1985.

Fowler, David. *Youth Culture in Modern Britain, c. 1920–1970*. London: Palgrave-Macmillan, 2008.

Franco, Marina. *Un enemigo para la nación: orden interno, violencia y "subversión," 1973–76*. Buenos Aires: Fondo de Cultura Económica, 2012.

Frank, Gillian. "Discophobia: Antigay Prejudice and the 1979 Backlash against Disco." *Journal of the History of Sexuality* 15.2 (May 2007): 276–303.

Frank, Robert. "Imaginaire politique et figures symboliques internationales: Castro, Ho, Mao et le Che." In *Les Annés 68: Les temps de la contestation*, edited by Genevieve Dreyfus Armand, 31–47. Paris: Complexe, 2000.

Frank, Thomas. *The Conquest of Cool: Business Culture, Counterculture, and the Rise of Hip Consumerism*. Chicago: University of Chicago Press, 1997.

Freedman, Estelle. "'Uncontrolled Desires': The Response to the Sexual Psychopath, 1920–1960." *Journal of American History* 74.1 (June 1987): 83–106.

Frith, Simon. *Sound Effects: Youth, Leisure, and the Politics of Rock 'n' Roll*. New York: Pantheon Books, 1981.

Gallart, María Antonia. "The Evolution of Secondary Education in Argentina, 1916–1970." Ph.D. diss., University of Chicago, 1983.

García, Prudencio. *El drama de la autonomía militar: Argentina bajo las juntas militares*. Madrid: Alianza, 1995.

Gayol, Sandra. *Sociabilidad en Buenos Aires: Hombres, honor y cafés, 1862–1910*. Buenos Aires: Ediciones del Signo, 2000.

Gerchunoff, Pablo, and Lucas Llach. *El ciclo de la ilusión y el desencanto: Un siglo de políticas económicas argentinas*. Buenos Aires: Ariel, 1998.

Giachetti, Diego. *Anni sessanta comincia la danza: Giovani, capelloni, studenti ed estrimisti negli anni della contestazione*. Pisa: BFS, 2002.

Gilbert, Isidoro. *La Fede: Alistándose para la revolución, 1921–2005*. Buenos Aires: Sudamericana, 2009.

Gilbert, James. *A Cycle of Outrage: America's Reactions to the Juvenile Delinquent in the 1950s*. New York: Oxford University Press, 1986.

———. *Men in the Middle: Searching for Masculinity in the Fifties*. Chicago: University of Chicago Press, 2005.

Gillespie, Richard. *Soldiers of Perón: Argentina's Montoneros*. Oxford: Clarendon Press, 1982.

Gillis, John. *Youth and History: Tradition and Change in European Age Relations, 1700–Present*. New York: Academic Press, 1974.

Gilman, Claudia. *Entre la pluma y el fusil: Debates y dilemas del escritor revolucionario en América Latina*. Buenos Aires: Siglo XXI, 2003.

Giunta, Andrea. *Vanguardia, internacionalismo y política: Arte argentino en los sesenta*. Buenos Aires: Paidós, 2001.

Godoy, Cristina, and Vanina Broda. "El poder de la palabra bajo vigilancia durante la última dictadura." In *Dictadura y educación*, vol. 2, edited by Carolina Kaufman, 27–64. Buenos Aires: Miño y Dávila, 2003.

Goldar, Ernesto. *Buenos Aires: Vida cotidiana en la década del '50*. Buenos Aires: Plus Ultra, 1980.

Gootenberg, Paul. *Andean Cocaine: The Making of a Global Drug*. Chapel Hill: University of North Carolina Press, 2008.

Gordillo, Mónica. *Córdoba en los '60: La experiencia del sindicalismo combativo*. Córdoba: Universidad Nacional de Córdoba, 1996.

Gordon, Beverley. "American Denim: Blue Jeans and Their Multiple Layers of Meaning." In *Dress and Popular Culture*, edited by Patricia Cunningham and Susan Voso Lab, 31–45. Bowling Green, Ohio: Popular Press, 1991.

Gosse, Van. *Where the Boys Are: Cuba, Cold War America and the Making of a New Left*. New York: Verso, 1993.

Gould, Jeff. "Solidarity under Siege: The Latin American Left, 1968." *American Historical Review* 112.2 (January 2009): 348–75.

Grammático, Karin. *Mujeres montoneras: Una historia de la Agrupación Evita, 1973–1974*. Buenos Aires: Luxemburg, 2011.

Grossberg, Lawrence. *We Gotta Get Out of This Place: Popular Conservatism and Postmodern Culture*. New York: Routledge, 1994.

Grosz, Elizabeth. "Feminism and the Crisis of Reason." In *Feminist Epistemologies*, edited by Linda Alcoff and Elizabeth Potter, 25–43. New York: Routledge, 1993.

———. *Volatile Bodies: Toward a Corporeal Feminism*. Bloomington: Indiana University Press, 1994.

Gutierrez, Leandro, and Juan Carlos Korol. "Historia de empresas y crecimiento industrial en la Argentina: El caso de Fábrica Argentina de Alpargatas," *Desarrollo Económico* 28.111 (October–December 1988): 401–24.

Gutman, Daniel. *Tacuara: La primera guerrilla urbana en la Argentina*. Buenos Aires: Vergara, 2004.

Guy, Donna. "Girls in Prison: The Role of the Buenos Aires Casa Correccional de Mujeres as an Institution of Child Rescue, 1895–1940." In *Crime and Punishment in Latin America: Law and Society since Late Colonial Times*, edited by Ricardo Salvatore, Carlos Aguirre, and Gilbert Joseph, 369–89. Durham: Duke University Press, 2001.

———. *Sex and Danger in Buenos Aires: Prostitution, Family, and Nation in Argentina*. Lincoln: University of Nebraska Press, 1991.

———. "The Shifting Meanings of Childhood and N.N." *Latin American Perspectives* 35.4 (July 2008): 15–29.

———. *Women Build the Welfare State: Performing Charity and Creating Rights in Argentina, 1880–1955*. Durham: Duke University Press, 2009.

Hall, Stanley. "Initiation into Adolescence." *Proceedings of the American Antiquarian Society* 12 (1897–98): 376–401.

Hebdige, Dick. *Hiding in the Light: On Images and Things*. New York: Routledge, 1988.

———. *Subculture: The Meanings of Style*. New York: Routledge, 1979.

Hershfield, Joanne. *Imagining la Chica Moderna: Women, Nation, and Visual Culture in Mexico, 1917–1936*. Durham: Duke University Press, 2008.

Herzog, Dagmar. *Sex after Fascism: Memory and Morality in Twentieth Century Germany*. Princeton: Princeton University Press, 2005.

Hilb, Claudia, and Daniel Lutzky. *La nueva izquierda argentina, 1960–1980*. Buenos Aires: CEAL, 1984.

Hodgdon, Tim. *Manhood in the Age of Aquarius: Masculinity in Two Countercultural Communities, 1965–1983*. New York: Columbia University Press, 2008.

Hollenbach, Margaret. *Lost and Found: My Life in a Group Marriage Commune*. Albuquerque: University of New Mexico Press, 2004.

Hunt, Lynn. *The Family Romance of the French Revolution*. Berkeley: University of California Press, 1992.

Huyssen, Andreas. *After the Great Divide: Modernism, Mass Culture, Postmodernism*. Bloomington: Indiana University Press, 1986.

Invernizzi, Hernán, and Judith Gociol. *Un golpe a los libros: Represión a la cultura durante la última dictadura militar*. Buenos Aires: EUdeBA, 2002.

Ivaska, Andrew. "Anti-Mini Militants Meet Modern Misses: Urban Style, Gender, and the Politics of National Culture in 1960s Dar es Salaam." *Gender and History* 14.3 (2002): 584–607.

James, Daniel. "The Peronist Left, 1955–1975." *Journal of Latin American Studies* 8.2 (November 1976): 273–96.

———. *Resistance and Integration: Peronism and the Argentine Working Class, 1946–76*. New York: Cambridge University Press, 1988.

Jarman-Ivens, Freya, ed. *Oh, Boy! Masculinities and Popular Music*. New York: Routledge, 2007.

Jáuregui, Carlos. *La homosexualidad en la Argentina*. Buenos Aires: Tarso, 1987.

Jeffreys, Sheila. *Anticlimax: A Feminist Perspective on the Sexual Revolution*. London: Women's Press, 1990.

Jensen, Joli. "Fandom as Pathology: The Consequences of a Characterization." In *The Adoring Audience: Fan Culture and Popular Media*, edited by Lisa Lewis, 9–28. New York: Routledge, 1992.

Jobs, Richard. *Riding the New Wave: Youth and the Rejuvenation of France after the Second World War*. Stanford: Stanford University Press, 2007.

Kampwirth, Karen. *Women and Guerilla Movements: Nicaragua, El Salvador, Chiapas, Cuba*. University Park: Pennsylvania State University, 2002.

King, John. *El Di Tella y el desarrollo cultural argentino en la década del '60*. Buenos Aires: Gaglianone, 1985.

Klubitschko, Doris. *El origen social de los estudiantes de la Universidad de Buenos Aires*. Buenos Aires: Programa de las Naciones Unidas para el Desarrollo, 1980.

Koon, Tracy. *Believe, Obey, Fight: Political Socialization of Youth in Fascist Italy, 1922–1945*. Chapel Hill: University of North Carolina Press, 1985.

Kreimer, Juan Carlos, and Carlos Polimeni, eds. *Ayer no más: 40 años de rock en la Argentina*. Buenos Aires: Musimundo, 2006.

Kriger, Clara. *Cine y peronismo: El Estado en escena*. Buenos Aires: Siglo XXI, 2009.

Kroes, Rob. "American Mass Culture and European Youth Culture." In *Between Marx and Coca-Cola: Youth Cultures in Changing European Societies, 1960–1980*, edited by Axel Schildt and Detlef Siegfried, 82–105. New York: Berghahn Books, 2006.

Lafforgue, Jorge. *Cartografía personal: Escritos y escritores de América Latina*. Buenos Aires: Taurus, 2005.

Langland, Victoria. "Birth Control Pills and Molotov Cocktails: Reading Sex and Revolution in 1968 Brazil." In *In from the Cold: Latin America's New Encounter with the Cold War*, edited by Gilbert Joseph and Daniela Spenser, 308–49. Durham: Duke University Press, 2008.

————. "Speaking of Flowers: Student Movements and Collective Memory in Authoritarian Brazil." Ph.D. diss., Yale University, 2004.

Lenci, María Laura. "La radicalización de los Católicos en la Argentina: Peronismo, Cristianismo y Revolución." *Cuadernos del Centro de Investigaciones Socio-Históricas* 4 (1998): 175–99.

Leonard, Virginia W. *Politicians, Pupils, and Priests: Argentine Education since 1943.* New York: Peter Lang, 1989.

Loaeza, Soledad. "Mexico in the Fifties: Women and Church in Holly Alliance." *Women's Studies Quarterly* 33.3–4 (2005): 138–60.

Lobato, Mirta. *Historia de las trabajadoras en la Argentina, 1869–1960.* Buenos Aires: Edhasa, 2007.

Longoni, Ana, and Mariano Mestman. *Del Di Tella a "Tucumán Arde": Vanguardia artística y política en el '68 argentino.* Buenos Aires: El cielo por asalto, 1998.

Lorenz, Federico. *Las guerras por Malvinas.* Buenos Aires: Edhasa, 2006.

Lvovich, Daniel. "Marchemos a las fronteras: Estrategias movilizadoras del régimen militar destinadas a sectores juveniles e infantiles." Paper presented at the *XII Jornadas Interescuelas/Departamentos de Historia,* Universidad Nacional del Comahue, 2009.

Mangone, Carlos, and Jorge Warley. *Universidad y peronismo (1946–1955).* Buenos Aires: Centro Editor de América Latina, 1984.

Mannheim, Karl. "The Problem of Generations." In *Essays on the Sociology of Knowledge,* 276–319. London: Routledge, 1952. Originally published in 1936.

Manzano, Valeria. "Argentina Tercer Mundo: Lugar, emociones y política revolucionaria, 1966–1976." *Desarrollo Económico* 54 (2014), forthcoming.

————. "The Blue Jean Generation: Youth, Gender, and Sexuality in Buenos Aires, 1958–1975." *Journal of Social History* 42.3 (2009).

————. "Las batallas de los laicos: Mobilización estudiantil en Buenos Aires, septiembre y octubre de 1958." *Boletín del Instituto de Historia Argentina y Americana Dr. Emilio Ravignani* 31 (2009).

————. "Sexualizing Youth: Morality Campaigns and Representations of Youth in Early-1960s Buenos Aires." *Journal of the History of Sexuality* 14.4 (October 2005).

Maristany, José J. "Entre Arlt y Puig, el *affaire* Correas: Acerca de 'La narración de la historia.'" *Orbis Tertius* 13.14 (2008): 1–14.

Martin, Linda, and Kerry Sagrave. *Anti-Rock: The Opposition to Rock 'n' Roll.* Hamden, Conn.: Archon, 1988.

Marwick, Arthur. *The Sixties: Cultural Revolution in Britain, France, Italy, and the United States, c. 1958–1974.* New York: Oxford University Press, 1998.

Marzullo, Osvaldo, and Pancho Muñoz. *Rock en la Argentina: La historia y sus protagonistas.* Buenos Aires: Galerna, 1985.

Masiello, Francine. "La Argentina durante el Proceso: las múltiples resistencias de la cultura." In *Ficción y política: la narrativa argentina durante el proceso militar,* edited by Daniel Balderston. Buenos Aires: Alianza, 1987.

Mazzei, Daniel. *Medios de comunicación y golpismo: El derrocamiento de Illia.* Buenos Aires: Grupo Editor Universitario, 1997.

McClary, Susan. "Same as It Ever Was: Youth Culture and Music." In *Microphone Friends: Youth Music and Youth Cultures*, edited by Andrew Ross and Tricia Rose, 29–40. New York: Routledge, 1994.

McCracken, Grant. *Big Hair: A Journey into the Transformation of Self*. New York: Overlook, 1995.

McGee Deutsch, Sandra. "Christians, Homemakers, and Transgressors: Extreme Right-Wing Women in Twentieth-Century Brazil." *Journal of Women's History* 16.3 (Fall 2004): 123–37.

McRobbie, Angela. *Feminism and Youth Culture*. New York: Routledge, 2000.

McRobbie, Angela, and Simon Frith. "Rock and Sexuality" [1978]. In *On Record: Rock, Pop, and the Written Word*, edited by Simon Frith and Andrew Goodwin, 371–89. New York: Routledge, 1990.

Mead, Margaret. *Coming of Age in Samoa: A Psychological Study of Primitive Youth for Western Civilization*. New York: Perennial Classics, 2001. Originally published in 1928.

Medovoi, Leerom. *Rebels: Youth and the Cold War Origins of Identity*. Durham: Duke University Press, 2005.

Menjívar, Cecilia, and Néstor Rodríguez. "State Terror in the US–Latin American Interstate Regime" In *When States Kill: Latin America, the U.S., and Technologies of Terror*. Austin: University of Texas Press, 2005.

Merkin, Marta, Juan José Panno, Gabriela Tijman, and Carlos Ulanovsky. *Días de radio: Historia de la radio en la Argentina*. Buenos Aires: Espasa Calpe, 1995.

Míguez, Eduardo. "Familias de clase media: La formación de un modelo." In *Historia de la vida privada en la Argentina*, vol. 2, edited by Fernando Devoto and Marta Madero, 21–45. Buenos Aires: Taurus, 1999.

Mintz, Steven. "Reflections on Age as a Category of Historical Analysis." *Journal of the History of Childhood and Youth* 1.1 (Winter 2008): 191–94.

Mitterauer, Michel. *A History of Youth*, Oxford: Blackwell, 1992.

Mochkofsky, Graciela. *Timerman: El periodista que quiso ser parte del poder (1923–1999)*. Buenos Aires: Sudamericana, 2003.

Modern Girl around the World Research Group. "The Modern Girl around the World: A Research Agenda and Preliminary Findings." *Gender and History* 17.2 (2005): 245–94.

Monsiváis, Carlos. "Del cinturón de castidad al condón: De usos amorosos y hábitos sexuales." In *Ciudado con el corazón: Los usos amorosos en el México moderno*, edited by Joaquín Blanco, 163–86. Mexico City: Instituto Nacional de Antropología e Historia, 1995.

Montanaro, Pablo. *Francisco Urondo: la palabra en acción. Biografía de un poeta militante*. Rosario: Homo Sapiens, 2003.

Moore, Robin. *Music and Revolution: Cultural Change in Socialist Cuba*. Berkeley: University of California Press, 2006.

Morero, Sergio, Ariel Eidelman, and Guido Lichtman. *La noche de los bastones largos*. Buenos Aires: GEL, 1999.

Morgade, Graciela. "State, Gender, and Class in the Social Construction of Argentine Women Teachers." In *Women and Teaching: Global Perspectives on the Feminization of a Profession*, edited by Regina Cortines and Sonsoles San Román, 81–103. New York: Palgrave, 2006.

Mossuz-Lavau, Janine. *Les lois de l'amour: Les politiques de la sexualité en France de 1950 à nos jours*. Paris: Éditions Payot, 1991.

Moyano, María José. *Argentina's Lost Patrol: Armed Struggle, 1969–1979*. New Haven: Yale University Press, 1995.

Muiño, Oscar. *La otra juventud: De la insignificancia al poder. Protagonistas y relato de la Junta Coordinadora Nacional de la Juventud Radical: 1968–83*. Buenos Aires: Corregidor, 2011.

Mulvey, Laura. "Visual Pleasure and Narrative Cinema." *Screen* 16.3 (1975): 6–18.

Nari, Marcela. "Abrir los ojos, abrir la cabeza: El feminismo en la Argentina de los años 70." *Feminaria* 9.18–19 (1996): 15–21.

———. *Políticas de maternidad y maternalismo politico: Buenos Aires, 1890–1940*. Buenos Aires: Biblos, 2004.

Neiburg, Federico. *Los intelectuales y la invención del peronismo: Estudios de antropología social y cultural*. Buenos Aires: Alianza, 1998.

Nielsen, Jorge. *Televisión argentina, 1951–1975: La información*. Buenos Aires: Ediciones del Jilguero, 2001.

Novaro, Marcos, and Vicente Palermo. *La dictadura militar (1976–1983): Del golpe de Estado a la restauración democrática*. Buenos Aires: Paidós, 2003.

Obregón, Martín. *Entre la cruz y la espada: La Iglesia Católica durante los primeros años del "Proceso."* Bernal: Universidad Nacional de Quilmes, 2005.

O'Donnell, Guillermo. *Bureaucratic Authoritarianism: Argentina, 1966–1973*. Berkeley: University of California Press, 1988.

———. "Democracia en la Argentina: Micro y macro." In *"Proceso," crisis y transición democrática*, vol. 1, edited by Oscar Oszlack, 13–30. Buenos Aires: Centro Editor de América Latina, 1984.

Ollier, María Matilde. *La creencia y la pasión: Público, privado y político en la izquierda revolucionaria*. Buenos Aires: Ariel, 1998.

Orlove, Benjamin, ed. *The Allure of Foreign: Imported Goods in Postcolonial Latin America*. Ann Arbor: University of Michigan Press, 1997.

Orquera, Yolanda Fabiola. "Marxismo, peronismo, indocriollismo: Atahualpa Yupanqui y el norte argentino." *Studies in Latin American Popular Culture* 27 (2008): 185–205.

Osgerby, Bill. *Playboys in Paradise: Masculinity, Youth, and Leisure-Style in Modern America*. London: Berg, 2001.

———. *Youth in Great Britain since 1945*. Oxford: Blackwell, 1998.

Palladino, Grace. *Teenagers: An American History*. New York: Basic Books, 1996.

Parsons, Talcott. "Age and Sex in the Social Structure of the United States." In *Essays in Sociological Theory*, 89–102. New York: Free Press, 1954. Originally published in 1942.

Passerini, Luisa. "Youth as a Metaphor for Social Change: Fascist Italy and America in the 1950s." In *A History of Young People in the West*, vol. 2, edited by Giovanni Levi and Jean-Claude Schmitt, 281–341. Cambridge, Mass.: Harvard University Press, 1997.

Pederiva, Ana Barbara. *Jovem Guarda: Cronistas Sentimentais da Juventude.* São Paulo: Compahia Editora Nacional, 2000.

Peña, Fernando, ed. *60/90 Generaciones: Cine argentino independiente.* Buenos Aires: Fundación Eduardo Constantini, 2003.

Perelli, Carina. "The Military's Perception of Threat in the Southern Cone of South America." In *The Military and Democracy: The Future of Civil-Military Relations in Latin America,* edited by Louis W. Goodman, Johanna S. R. Mendelson, and Juan Rial, 93–105. Lanham, Md.: Lexington Books, 1990.

Perniola, Mario. "Between Clothing and Nudity." In *Fragments for a History of the Human Body,* vol. 2, edited by Michel Feher, Ramona Nadaff, and Nadia Tazi, 237–65. Cambridge, Mass.: MIT Press, 1989.

Pesce, Víctor. "El discreto encanto de 'El club del clan.'" *Cuadernos de la Comuna* 23 (December 1989): 19–28.

Petty, Michael. "Political Socialization among Secondary School Boys." Ph.D. diss., University of Chicago, 1971.

Piccone-Stella, Simonetta. *La prima generazione: Regazze e regazzi nel miracolo economico italiano.* Milan: FrancoAngeli, 1993.

Pieper Mooney, Jadwiga. *The Politics of Motherhood: Maternity and Women's Rights in Twentieth-Century Chile.* Pittsburgh: University of Pittsburgh Press, 2008.

Pineau, Pablo, "Impactos de un asueto educacional: las políticas educativas de la dictadura (1976–1983)." In *El principio del fin: Políticas y memorias de la educación en la última dictadura militar (1976–1983),* edited by Pablo Pineau, 11–109. Buenos Aires: Colihue, 2006.

Pion-Berlin, David. "Latin American National Security Doctrines: Hard- and Soft-line Themes." *Armed Forces and Society* 15.3 (1989): 411–29.

Plotkin, Mariano. *Freud in the Pampas: Origins and Development of a Psychoanalytical Culture in Argentina.* Stanford: Stanford University Press, 2001.

———. *Mañana es San Perón: Propaganda, rituales políticos y educación en el régimen peronista (1946–55).* Buenos Aires: Ariel, 1993.

Podalsky, Laura. *Specular City: Transforming Culture, Consumption, and Space in Buenos Aires, 1955–1973.* Philadelphia: Temple University Press, 2004.

Poiger, Uta. *Jazz, Rock, and Rebels: Cold War Politics and American Culture in a Divided Germany.* Berkeley: University of California Press, 2000.

Portantiero, Juan Carlos. *Estudiantes y política en América Latina, 1918–1938: El proceso de la Reforma Universitaria.* Mexico City: Siglo XXI, 1978.

Pozzi, Pablo. *Por las sendas argentinas: El PRT-ERP, la guerrilla marxista.* Buenos Aires: EUdeBA, 2001.

Prasad, Devi, and Tony Smythe, eds. *Conscription: A World Survey.* London: War Resisters International, 1968.

Prochasson, Christophe. "Le socialisme des indigneés: Contribution à l'histoire des èmotions politiques." In *L'indignation: Histoire d'une emotion politique et morale, XIX–XXe siècles,* edited by Anne-Claude Ambroise-Rench and Christian Delporte, 173–90. Paris: Nouveau Monde, 2008.

Pucciarelli, Alfredo, ed. *La primacía de la política: Lanusse, Perón y la Nueva Izquierda en tiempos del GAN.* Buenos Aires: EUdeBA, 1999.

Pujol, Sergio. *Historia del baile: De la milonga a la disco*. Buenos Aires: Emecé, 1999.

———. *La década rebelde: Los sesenta en la Argentina*. Buenos Aires: Emecé, 2002.

———. *Rock y dictadura*. Buenos Aires: Emecé, 2004.

Raggio, Sandra. "La construcción de un relato emblemático de la represión: La 'noche de los lápices.'" In *Los desaparecidos en la Argentina: Memorias, representaciones e ideas, 1983-2008*, edited by Emilio Crenzel, 137-59. Buenos Aires: Biblos, 2010.

Rapisardi, Favio, and Alejandro Modarelli. *Fiestas, baños y exilios: Los gays porteños durante la última dictadura*. Buenos Aires: Sudamericana, 2001.

Recchini de Lattes, Zulma. *Dynamics of the Female Labour Force in Argentina*. Paris: UNESCO, 1983.

———. *La participación económica femenina en la Argentina desde la segunda posguerra hasta 1970*. Buenos Aires: Cuadernos del CENEP No. 11, 1977.

———. *Los aspectos demográficos de la urbanización en la Argentina, 1869-1960*. Buenos Aires: Ediciones del Instituto, 1973.

Rein, Mónica. *Politics and Education in Argentina, 1946-1962*. New York: Sharpe, 1998.

Reyes Matta, Fernando. "The 'New Song' and Its Confrontation in Latin America." In *Marxism and the Interpretation of Culture*, edited by Cary Nelson and Lawrence Grossberg, 447-61. Urbana: University of Illinois Press, 1988.

Ridenti, Marcelo. *O fantasma da revolução brasileira*. São Paulo: UNESP, 2005.

Ríos, José Arthur. *The University Student and Brazilian Society*. Detroit: Latin American Studies Center, Michigan State University, 1971.

Rivera, Jorge B. *La investigación en comunicación social en la Argentina*. Buenos Aires: Puntosur, 1987.

Rodríguez Molas, Ricardo. *El servicio militar obligatorio*. Buenos Aires: Centro Editor de América Latina, 1983.

Roseman, Mark, ed. *Generations in Conflict: Youth Revolt and Generation Formation in Germany, 1770-1968*. New York: Cambridge University Press, 1995.

Rot, Gabriel. *Los orígenes perdidos de la guerrilla en la Argentina: Jorge Ricardo Masetti y el Ejército Guerrillero del Pueblo*. Buenos Aires: El cielo por asalto, 2000.

Saldaña-Portillo, María Josefina. *The Revolutionary Imagination in the Americas in the Age of Development*. Durham: Duke University Press, 2003.

Salvatore, Ricardo D. "Yankee Advertising in Buenos Aires: Reflections on Americanization." *Interventions* 7.2 (2005): 216-35.

Sandvoss, Cornel. *Fandom: The Mirror of Consumption*. Cambridge: Polity Press, 2005.

Sarlo, Beatriz. "Cuando la política era joven." *Punto de Vista* 58 (December 1997): 15-19.

———. *La batalla de las ideas*. Buenos Aires: Ariel, 2001.

———. *La pasión y la excepción*. Buenos Aires: Siglo XXI, 2003.

———. *Tiempo pasado: cultura de la memoria y giro subjetivo: una discusión*. Buenos Aires: Siglo XXI, 2005.

———. *Tiempo presente*. Buenos Aires: Siglo XXI, 2005.

Scarzanella, Eugenia. "El ocio peronista: Vacaciones y 'turismo popular' en la Argentina (1943–1955)." *Entrepasados* 14 (1998): 65–86.

Schildt, Axel, and Detlef Siegfried, eds. *Between Marx and Coca-Cola: Youth Cultures in Changing European Societies, 1960–1980*. New York: Berghahn Books, 2006.

Sebreli, Juan José. *Escritos sobre escritos, ciudades bajo ciudades, 1950–1997*. Buenos Aires: Sudamericana, 1997.

Sedgwick, Eve Kosofsky. *Between Men: English Literature and Male Homosocial Desire*. New York: Columbia University Press, 1985.

Seigel, Micol. "Beyond Compare: Comparative Method after the Transnational Turn." *Radical History Review* 91 (Winter 2005): 62–90.

Serrano, Manuel Martín. *Historia de los cambios de las mentalidades de los jóvenes entre 1960 y 1990*. Madrid: Ministerio de Asuntos Sociales—Instituto de la Juventud, 1994.

Servetto, Alicia. *73/76: el gobierno peronista contra las "provincias montoneras."* Buenos Aires: Siglo XXI, 2010.

Siegfried, Detlef. "Understanding 1968: Youth Rebellion, Generational Change, and Postindustrial Society." In *Between Marx and Coca-Cola: Youth Cultures in Changing European Societies, 1960–1980*, edited by Axel Schildt and Detlef Siegfried, 59–81. New York: Berghahn Books, 2006.

Sigal, Silvia. *Intelectuales y poder en la década del sesenta*. Buenos Aires: Puntosur, 1991.

Sigal, Silvia, and Eliseo Verón. *Perón o muerte: Los fundamentos discursivos del fenómeno peronista*. Buenos Aires: Legasa, 1986.

Simmel, Georg. "The Secret and the Secret Society." In *Sociology: Inquiries in the Construction of Social Forms*. Leiden: Brill, 2009.

Sirinelli, Jean-François. "Éloge de la complexité." In *Pour une histoire culturelle*, edited by Jean-Pierre Rioux and Jean-François Sirinelli, 430–44. Paris: Pluriel, 1997.

———. *Les baby boomers: Une génération (1945–1969)*. Paris: Hachette, 2003.

———. *Mai 68: L'événement Janus*. Paris: Fayard, 2008.

Sohn, Anne-Marie. *Âge tendre et tête de bois: Histoire des jeunes des annés 1960*. Paris: Hachette, 2001.

Solomon-Godeau, Abigail. "The Other Side of Venus: The Visual Economy of Feminine Display." In *The Sex of Things: Gender and Consumption in Historical Perspective*, edited by Victoria de Grazia and Ellen Furlongh, 113–48. Berkeley: University of California Press, 1996.

Sorcinelli, Paolo, and Angelo Varni, eds. *Il secolo dei giovani: Le nuove generazioni e la storia del Novecento*. Bologna: Donzelli Editore, 2005.

Sorensen, Diana. *A Turbulent Decade Remembered: Scenes from the Latin American Sixties*. Stanford: Stanford University Press, 2007.

Staller, Karen. *Runaways: How the Sixties Counterculture Shaped Today's Practices and Policies*. New York: Columbia University Press, 2006.

Stark, Steven. *Meet the Beatles: A Cultural History of the Band That Shook Youth, Gender, and the World*. New York: Harper, 2005.

Stern, Steve. *Remembering Pinochet's Chile: On the Eve of London, 1998*. Durham: Duke University Press, 2004.

Suasnábar, Claudio. *Universidad e intelectuales: Educación y política en la Argentina (1955–1976)*. Buenos Aires: Manantial, 2004.

Sullivan, James. *Jeans: A Cultural History of an American Icon*. New York: Gotham Books, 2006.

Suri, Jeremy. "The Rise and Fall of an International Counterculture, 1960–1975." *American Historical Review* 114.1 (February 2009): 45–68.

Svampa, Maristella. *La sociedad excluyente: La Argentina bajo el signo del neoliberalismo*. Buenos Aires: Taurus, 2005.

Szusterman, Celia. *Frondizi and the Politics of Developmentalism, 1958–1962*. London: Macmillan, 1993.

Taibo, Paco Ignacio. *68*. Mexico City: Joaquín Mortiz, 1991.

Tamagne, Florence. "'C'mon everybody': Rock 'n' roll et identités juvénils en France (1956–1966)." In *Jeunesse oblige: Histoire des jeunes en France XIXe-XXIe siècle*, edited by Ludivine Bantigny and Ivan Jablonka, 183–97. Paris: Presses Universitaries de France, 2009.

Tarcus, Horacio. "El Mayo argentino." *Observatorio Social de América Latina* 24 (October 2008): 161–80.

Tcach, César. "Los Nores Martínez: Policía y sacristía en una ciudad de enclave (Córdoba 1962–63)." In *Córdoba Bicentenaria: Claves de su historia contemporánea*, 273–95. Córdoba: Universidad Nacional de Córdoba, 2010.

Tedesco, Juan Carlos. "Elementos para una sociología del curriculum escolar en la Argentina." In *El proyecto educativo autoritario: Argentina (1976–1982)*, edited by Cecilia Braslavsky, Raúl Carciofi, and Juan Carlos Tedesco, 17–73. Buenos Aires: FLACSO, 1982.

———. "Modernización y democratización en la universidad argentina, un panorama histórico." In *La Universidad latinoamericana: Visión de una década*, edited by Patricio Dooner and Iván Lavados, 143–87. Santiago de Chile: Corporación de Promoción Universitaria, 1979

Terán, Oscar. *En busca de la ideología argentina*. Buenos Aires: Catálogos, 1988.

———. *Nuestros años sesenta: La formación de una izquierda intelectual en la Argentina*. Buenos Aires: Puntosur, 1991.

Thornton, Sarah. *Club Cultures: Music, Media, and Subcultural Capital*. Hanover: University Press of New England, 1996.

Torrado, Susana. *Estructura social de la Argentina*. Buenos Aires: de la Flor, 1995.

———. *Historia de la familia en la Argentina moderna, 1870–2000*. Buenos Aires: de la Flor, 2003.

———. "Transición de la nupcialidad: dinámica del mercado matrimonial." In *Población y bienestar en la Argentina del primero al segundo Centenario: una historia social del siglo XX*, vol. 1, edited by Susana Torrado, 409–27. Buenos Aires: Edhasa, 2007.

Torre, Juan Carlos. "A partir del Cordobazo." *Estudios* 4 (July–December 1994): 17–24.

———, ed. *Nueva Historia Argentina*, vol. 8: *Los años peronistas (1943–1955)*. Buenos Aires: Sudamericana, 2002.

Torre, Juan Carlos, and Elisa Pastoriza. "La democratización del bienestar." In *Nueva Historia Argentina*, vol. 8: *Los años peronistas (1943–1955)*, edited by Juan Carlos Torre, 237–312. Buenos Aires: Sudamericana, 2002.

Tortti, María Cristina. *El "viejo" Partido Socialista y los orígenes de la "Nueva Izquierda."* Buenos Aires: Prometeo, 2010.

Tossounian, Cecilia. "The Argentine Modern Girl and National Identity, Buenos Aires, 1920–40." In *Comsuming Modernity: Gendered Behaviour and Consumerism before the Baby Boom*, edited by Cheryl Krasnick Wash and Dan Malleck, 220–36. Vancouver: University of British Columbia Press, 2013.

Touris, Claudia. "Neo-integralismo, denuncia profética y Revolución en la trayectoria del Movimiento de Sacerdotes para el Tercer Mundo." *Prismas* 9 (2005): 229–39.

Trigo, Abril. "The Politics and Anti-Politics of Uruguayan Rock." In *Rockin' Las Americas: The Global Politics of Rock in Latina/o America*, edited by Héctor Fernández L'Hoeste, Debora Paccini Hernandez, and Eric Zolov, 115–41. Pittsburgh: University of Pittsburgh Press, 2004.

Troncoso, Oscar. "Las formas del ocio." In *Buenos Aires: Historia de cuatro siglos*, vol. 2, edited by José Luis Romero and Luis Alberto Romero, 143–87. Buenos Aires: Altamira, 2000.

Varela, Mirta. *La televisión criolla: De sus inicios a la llegada del hombre a la luna (1951–1969)*. Buenos Aires: Edhasa, 2005.

Vasallo, Alejandra. "Movilización, política y orígenes del feminismo argentino en los 70." In *Historia, género y política en los años '70*, edited by Andrea Andújar, 61–88. Buenos Aires: Feminaria, 2005.

Verbitsky, Horacio. *Ezeiza*. Buenos Aires: Planeta, 1995.

Vezzetti, Hugo. *Pasado y presente: Guerra, dictadura y sociedad en la Argentina*. Buenos Aires: Siglo XXI, 2002.

———. *Sobre la violencia revolucionaria: Memorias y olvidos*. Buenos Aires: Siglo XXI, 2009.

Vila, Pablo. "Peronismo y folklore: ¿Un réquiem para el tango?" *Punto de Vista* 26 (April 1986).

———. "Rock Nacional and Dictatorship in Argentina." *Popular Music* 6.2 (May 1987): 129–48.

———. "Rock nacional: crónicas de la resistencia juvenil." In *Los nuevos movimientos sociales*, vol. 1, edited by Elizabeth Jelin, 95–102. Buenos Aires: Centro Editor de América Latina, 1985.

———. "Rock Nacional: The Struggle for Meaning." *Latin American Music Review* 10.1 (Spring–Summer 1989): 1–28.

Waksman, Steve. *Instruments of Desire: The Electric Guitar and the Shaping of Musical Experience*. Cambridge, Mass.: Harvard University Press, 2001.

Walter, Richard. *Student Politics in Argentina: The University Reform Movement and Its Effects*. New York: Basic Books, 1968.

Weeks, Jeffrey. *Sex, Politics, and Society: The Regulation of Sexuality since 1800*. London: Longman, 1989.

Weissman, Patricia. *Toxicomanías: Historia de las ideas psicopatológicas sobre el consumo de drogas en la Argentina*. Mar del Plata: Universidad Nacional de Mar del Plata, 2002.

Whiteley, Sheila. *Women and Popular Music: Sexuality, Identity, and Subjectivity*. London: Routledge, 2000.

———, ed. *Sexing the Groove: Popular Music and Gender*. New York: Routledge, 1997.

Wollman, Elizabeth. *The Theater Will Rock: A History of the Rock Musical from Hair to Hedwig*. Ann Arbor: University of Michigan Press, 2007.

Zanca, José. *Los intelectuales católicos y el fin de la cristiandad (1955–1966)*. Buenos Aires: Fondo de Cultura Económica—Universidad de San Andrés, 2006.

Zarrabeitia, César. *Militancia estudiantil: Desde los orígenes de la UNNE hasta finales de la década del sesenta*. Corrientes: N.p., 2007.

Zolov, Eric. "'¡Cuba sí, yanquis no!' The Sacking of the Instituto Cultural México-Americano in Morelia, Michocán, in 1961." In *In from the Cold: Latin America's New Encounter with the Cold War*, edited by Gilbert Joseph and Daniela Spenser, 214–50. Durham: Duke University Press, 2008.

———. "Expanding Our Conceptual Horizons: The Shift from an Old to a New Left in Latin America." *A Contracorriente* 5.2 (Winter 2008): 47–72.

———. *Refried Elvis: The Rise of a Mexican Counterculture*. Berkeley: University of California Press, 1999.

Index

Cantilo, Miguel, 129–30, 148. *See also* Pedro y Pablo

Careta, 242–44

Catholics: conservative groups, 8, 16, 18, 223–24, 235–36; and education, 46–47, 68–69; and family, 35–38, 223–24; and Peronism, 25–29; and radicalization, 169, 172–73, 183; and sexuality, 115–18; and student movement, 45, 50, 58–60, 62–63, 161–64; and young women, 98, 100, 111–12; and youth leisure, 70–71. *See also* Acción Católica Argentina; League of Mothers; Moledo, Manuel

Censorship, 9, 21, 58, 194; and advertising, 198–99; and the authority-reconstitution project, 223–24, 239–42; and media, 34–35, 43

Centro Nacional de Reeducación Social (CENRESO, National Center of Social Reeducation), 227–28

Cold War, 43, 63, 113, 221

Columbia Broadcasting System (CBS), 73, 76, 123, 142

Communist Party, 2, 27, 59, 64, 174, 177, 244

Confederación General del Trabajo (CGT, Workers General Confederation), 62, 64–65, 110, 112, 163

Confederación General del Trabajo de los Argentinos (CGTA, Workers General Confederation of Argentines), 162–64, 169–71

Confederación General Universitaria (CGU, University General Confederation), 24

Conscription, 125, 127–29; during last military dictatorship, 245–46

Consejo Nacional de Protección de Menores (CNPM, National Council of Minors' Protection), 33–34

Cordobazo, 164, 166–68, 191

Correas, Carlos, 58–59, 67

Counterculture, 11, 14, 145–49, 252. *See also* Hippies; Rock culture

Cristianismo y Revolución, 162–63, 173

Cuban Revolution, 11; and New Left, 169, 174; and student movement, 60–61

Curone, Marta, 28

Desapariciones. See Runaways

Detrás de un largo muro, 100

Disappeared, 6, 233, 237–38, 245–46; and human rights, 248–49

Dolce Vita: Federico Fellini movie and, 75, 97; and Penjerek case, 109–14

Drugs: fears of, 111–13, 136–37, 222–24; legislation, 227–28; and New Left, 150, 228–29; as public problem, 224–27; youth consumption, 147–48

Education: and modernization, 44, 52–54, 67–68, 236–37; and youth, 7–8. *See also* Secondary school; University

Ejército Guerrillero del Pueblo (EGP, Guerrilla Army of the People), 40–41, 59

Ejército Revolucionario del Pueblo. *See* Partido Revolucionario de los Trabajadores-Ejército Revolucionario del Pueblo

El Club del Clan, 78–81; and fandom, 82–83; responses to, 83–85; and taste, 84–87, 95. See also *Nueva ola*; Ortega, Palito

"Enemy within": and repression, 221–23, 254; and sexuality, 112–13

Eros, 204–5. *See also* Homosexuality

Escala Musical, 73, 76, 87

Escardó, Florencio, 31, 35, 115–16, 197

Expreso Imaginario, 241–43

Family: and "adolescent crisis," 31–33; and intergenerational conflict, 104–6; marriage, 105–6, 118–19; and modernization, 30–31, 41–43, 111–12; New Left and, 205, 215–16; Peronist family romance, 185–92; protection of, 34–36, 223–24; and youth leisure, 74–75, 79–82, 94–95. *See also* Authority: patriarchal; League of Mothers

Fandom, 83–85

Fashion, 69–70, 88–93; and eroticism, 195–97; and masculinity, 142–43; and politics, 199–201; unisex, 196–97

Federación Argentina de Entidades Anticomunistas (FAEDA, Argentine Federation of Anticommunist Groups), 137

Federación de Estudiantes Nacionales (FEN, Federation of National Students), 161–63, 166

Federación Juvenil Comunista (FJC, Communist Youth Federation): and dictatorship, 244; and youth leisure, 39, 75–76, 78, 83. *See also* Federación Metropolitana de Estudiantes Secundarios

Federación Metropolitana de Estudiantes Secundarios (FEMES, Metropolitan Federation of Secondary School Students), 50–52

Federación Universitaria Argentina (FUA, Argentine University Federation), 45, 62

Federación Universitaria de Buenos Aires (FUBA, University Federation of Buenos Aires), 45, 61

Feminism, 202–3

Firmenich, Mario, 188, 228

Folklore, 77–79; and politics, 153–54, 174, 239

Fraternity of long-haired boys: characteristics, 132–41 passim, 145; definition, 125–26. *See also* Hippies; *Náufragos*; Rock culture

Frente de Liberación Homosexual (FLH, Homosexual Liberation Front), 204–6, 223

Frondizi, Arturo: developmentalist politics, 4, 7, 21, 33, 38, 76; educational policies, 35, 45

Frondizi, Risieri, 60–61

Fuerzas Armadas Peronistas (FAP, Peronist Armed Forces), 173, 175, 218

Fuerzas Armadas Revolucionarias (FAR, Revolutionary Armed Forces), 151, 175, 205

Fugas. See Runaways

García, Charly, 127. *See also* Sui Géneris

Gender, 3, 7; metaphors, 85–86, 144; and New Left, 209–10, 213–16; and Right, 223–24, 231; and rock culture, 138–41, 156; secondary school students, 25–26, 46; and sociocultural modernization, 13, 17, 97–99, 113–15, 250–52; and university students, 102–3; and youth consumption, 80–83. *See also* Masculinity; Sexuality; Young men; Young women

Generation: first-generation students and, 53–55, 103; frustrated, 38–39, 43; intergenerational relations, 30–31, 41, 71, 107–8, 130–31, 138; intragenerational differences, 86–91, 242–43; military ideas on, 237–38, 245–46; "mufado," 133–34; of 1960, 37–38, 75; Peronism and, 23–27, 159–60, 177–79, 187–92; and radicalization, 164, 176–77; and youth, 7–8

Germani, Gino: and "crisis of our time," 30–31; and modern family, 41; and modernizing narratives, 168–69, 174; in School of Humanities and Social Sciences, 55–56, 59

Giberti, Eva, 3, 31, 33, 35–36; on long pants, 89; on moral panics, 112; on sexual education, 115–16, 119; on unisex fashion, 137

Grinberg, Miguel, 133, 148–49; on premarital sex, 117

Guerrillas, 5, 11–12, 18, 124, 149, 167, 228, 233; and young men, 128–29; and young women, 201–2, 214–15, 231; and youth, 40–41, 59, 151, 159, 175–78, 221–22

of the People): and conscription, 128–29; and gender, 213–15; and militancy, 210–11; and rock culture, 150–53; and sexuality, 205, 216–17; and Tendencia Revolucionaria, 186–87; and youth, 177, 192

Pavone, Rita, 81, 93

Pedro y Pablo, 130, 140, 152, 240. *See also* Cantilo, Miguel

Pelo, 141, 143–45; and Buenos Aires Rock Festival, 145–46; on politics, 254–55

Penjerek, Norma, 97, 110–11; case of, 97–98, 110–14, 121–22; and sociocultural modernization, 250

Pequenino, Eddie, 73–74

Perón, Juan Domingo, 3–5, 15–16, 20–22, 64, 93, 173; return in 1973, 185–87; third presidency, 123, 128, 149, 153, 183–84, 198, 223–24, 228–29; and UES, 23–28, 42; on youth, 23–24, 160, 176–78, 188–91; youth on, 38, 156, 179

Peronism, 1, 4–5, 8, 11, 15, 18; anti-Peronism and, 21–22, 24–25, 28–29; and education, 22, 26–28, 46–47, 54–56; first governments, 20–21; re-evaluations of, 68, 169; right-wing, 6, 178, 183–86, 190–91, 224, 228, 230, 246; and youth, 38, 40, 45, 158–60, 176–78, 185, 187–89, 192. *See also* Montoneros; Revolutionary Tendency; Unión de Estudiantes Secundarios

Piba de barrio (neighborhood girl), 207–8, 250

Pill, 6, 13, 19, 118–19, 222–23. *See also* Sexuality: contraception

Police: and drugs, 225–28; and morals, 113–14, 223–24; and rock culture, 136–37, 139, 154, 240–41; and runaways, 108–9, 111; and student movements, 50–51, 64–65, 165–66, 183–84; and youth sociability, 71–72

Political culture, 14, 214, 219–20; definition of, 158–59, 168–69, 190–94. *See also* New Left; Third World.

Psychological experts, 20–21, 249; and "adolescent crisis," 30–32; and modernization, 35–36, 42–43; and runaways, 107; and sexual education, 115–16

Radicalization, 3, 11; and May of 1969, 167–68, 199; and *Revolución Argentina*, 66, 124–25

Radio Corporation of America (RCA), 73, 76–77; on El Club del Clan, 78–79, 81; on rock music, 138–39, 147

Reca, Telma, 20, 30–32, 35, 59

Reformism, 3; and Peronism, 24, 45, 55–56; transformations of, 60–62, 65–66, 68. *See also* University Reform Movement

Revolución Argentina: definition, 64; demise of, 124, 167–68; opposition to, 162–64; and university politics, 65–66. *See also* Onganía, Juan Carlos

Revolución Libertadora, 4, 21; and education, 47, 56; and youth, 27–28

Revolutionary Tendency (Peronism), 178–92 passim

Ripoll, Daniel, 143. See also *Pelo*

Rivas, Violeta, 79–80, 86–87

Rock culture: Argentine, 123–25; arrival in Argentina, 70–73; commercial aspects, 73–74, 76–77, 141–42; and counterculture, 145–49; and dictatorship, 239–43; and masculinity, 129–38, 140–42, 251–52; playing of, 73–74, 133–34, 138–39, 145; and politics, 151–55; *progresivos* and *complacientes*, 143–44; and youth sociability, 74–76, 104, 134–35

Romero, José Luis, 59

Runaways, 107–9; discussions about, 112–13. *See also* Penjerek, Norma

Sandro, 82

Sanmartino, Ernesto, 112–13

Santaolalla, Gustavo, 147, 292 (n. 92). *See also* Arco Iris

School of Humanities and Social Sciences (Facultad de Filosofía y Letras, Universidad de Buenos Aires), 15–16; and political radicalization, 173–74, 181; and university renovation, 55–61, 67. *See also* Students—university; University

Secondary school: and authoritarianism, 47–49, 235–38; coeducation, 25, 35–36, 47, 52; debates over, 46–47; Democratic Education Program, 28–29, 182; discipline, 49–50; enrollments, 22, 46–47, 236–37; pedagogies, 48–49; policies, 33, 181–82, 236–37; teaching-training branch, 46, 101–2; technical branch, 46–47, 126, 182–83, 236. *See also* Students—secondary school

Second Vatican Council, 33, 62, 65, 159, 161

Secretaria ejecutiva (executive secretary), 102–3. *See also* Young women: and labor market

Sexuality, 1–9, 13–17, 250–51; adultery, 32, 216, 235; and authoritarianism, 223–24, 231, 246; contraception, 115, 118–19, 223–24; double standard of, 122, 203, 207–8; fears of, 109–10, 112–14; pre-marital sex, 39–40, 98–99, 115–22, 206–8; masturbation, 115–16; menstruation, 116–17; and New Left, 155, 161, 193–94, 200–202, 205–6, 216–18; pre-nuptial medical certificate and, 120–21; representations of, 26–27, 37–40, 58–59, 75, 89–90, 196–99; sexual awakening and, 31–32; sexual revolution and, 114–15, 202–6; and rock music, 70–72, 80, 82, 127, 140–41, 147–48; virginity, 69, 75, 99–100, 117–18, 122, 206–8. *See also* Gender; Homosexuality

Social clubs, 2, 71, 73, 75–76; and new wave, 78, 82, 134

Socialist Party, 2, 27, 61, 210

Spinetta, Luis Alberto, 138, 140–41,

240–41; and "liberation," 153–56. *See also* Almendra

Students: in relation to youth, 3–4, 12–13, 16–17, 44, 67–68

—secondary school: discipline and, 49–50, 126–27; political activism, 28, 44–45, 50–51, 154, 158–59, 175–76, 181–85, 211–12, 215, 243–44; repression, 229–31, 235–38; school life, 47–49; sexuality, 117–18, 207; sociability, 24–25, 52–53, 77, 92. *See also* Federación Juvenil Comunista; Laica o Libre conflict; Secondary school; Unión de Estudiantes Secundarios; Unión Nacionalista de Estudiantes Secundarios

—university: political activism, 2, 5, 10, 24, 44–45, 55–56, 60–62, 103, 158–59, 161–68, 179–81; representations of, 41, 58–59, 63–64; repression, 64–66, 229–31, 235–37; sexuality, 115, 117–19, 207–8; sociability, 56–58. *See also* *Cordobazo*; Federación de Estudiantes Nacionales; Federación Universitaria Argentina; Federación Universitaria de Buenos Aires; Intregralistas; Juventud Universitaria Peronsita; May of 1969; Movimiento Ateneísta; Reformism; Tendencia Anti-Imperialista Universitaria; University Reform Movement

Sui Géneris, 127–28, 140, 153

Tacuara, 50, 110

Tanguito, 87, 132–34, 140

Tedesco, Johny, 79, 81, 83. *See also* El Club del Clan

Teenager, 9–10, 107

Teenpics, 71–72, 88, 93

Tendencia Anti-Imperialista Universitaria (TAU, Anti-Imperialist University Trend), 62, 66

Third World, 3, 10–12, 18, 157–58, 252–54; and culture, 173–75; definition, 168–69; and emotions, 170–71,

191–92; and Peronism, 176–77; and travel, 172–73, 183–84. *See also* New Left; Political culture

Trasvasamiento generacional (generational transference), 160, 177–78, 187. *See also* Juventud Peronista; Perón, Juan Domingo: on youth

Travel, 25, 146–48, 171–73, 183–84, 253

Triple A, 178, 188, 227, 230–31

Tucumán Arde, 170–72

Unión de Estudiantes Secundarios (UES, Secondary School Students Union), 15–16; in 1950s, 22–29; in 1970s, 175, 179, 181–86, 189, 211–12, 215, 231, 243. *See also* Juventud Peronista; Perón, Juan Domingo: and UES; Students—secondary school

Unión Feminista Argentina (Argentine Feminist Union), 202–3

Unión Nacional de Estudiantes (UNE, National Student Union), 161–63, 166

Unión Nacionalista de Estudiantes Secundarios (Nationalist Secondary School Students Union), 50–51

United States, 8–10; and counterculture, 148–49; counterinsurgency training, 231; drug policies, 226–27; invasion of Bay of Pigs, 61; invasion of Santo Domingo, 63; postwar youth, 23, 32; and rock, 70, 72, 74; and sexuality, 113, 116, 119–20

University: and authoritarianism, 228–30, 237; enrollments, 44–45, 180, 236; and military intervention, 64–65, 164; and modernization 12–13, 16, 44–45, 56–57, 61–62, 67–68, 170; and Peronism, 173–74, 179–80. *See also* Students—university

University of Buenos Aires (UBA), 8, 14, 16, 31, 35, 54–55, 61, 64, 115, 173, 179–81, 195, 226, 237

University of Córdoba, 50, 65–66, 181

University of the Northeast, 62, 164

University Reform Movement, 2–3,

44–45; left-wing criticism, 161–62; right-wing criticism, 63–64, 236. *See also* Radicalization; Reformism

Urondo, Francisco, 84, 205, 212–13

Vaquero. See Jeans

Viola, Roberto, 236, 243

Viñas, David, 7; on Cuba, 60–61; on frustrated generation, 38–39; on jeans, 90

Walsh, Rodolfo, 170

Young men, 3, 7, 17, 251–52; and conscription, 128–29; and education, 126–27; and fashion, 88–91, 95, 142–43, 197; and labor market, 129–30; during last dictatorship, 238–39, 244–45; and leisure, 87; and politics, 151–52, 175–76, 182–83, 188–90, 214–15, 217–19, 230–32; and rock culture, 123–25; supervision of, 112, 114; and travel, 171–73. *See also* Fraternity of long-haired boys; Masculinity; Rock culture; Sexuality

Young women, 1, 2, 5, 9, 11, 13, 17, 250–51; in counterculture, 146–48; and education, 100–103, 238; and fashion, 92–94, 194–98; and labor market, 102–3; and leisure, 69, 74–75, 88, 103–5; and migration, 99–100; and modernization, 97–99; and politics, 200–203, 213–16, 231; and rock culture, 134–35, 139–40, 145, 241–42; and sexuality, 114–21, 206–8, 224–25. *See also* Moral panic; Penjerek, Norma; Runaways

Youth: as category, 1–3, 7–9, 15–16, 18–19, 20–22, 31–33, 36, 39–41, 167–68, 233–35; and class, 1, 2, 10–11, 15, 17, 22, 40–41, 53, 85–93, 155; and generation, 7–8; and transnationality, 6–7, 10–11

Youth culture, 9–10, 69–70, 91
—of contestation: definition, 124–25, 252; rock as part of, 153, 155

www.ingramcontent.com/pod-product-compliance
Lightning Source LLC
Chambersburg PA
CBHW020332150125
20402CB00001B/37